P9-DHC-871

DIRECTORY OF EUROPEAN UNION POLITICAL PARTIES

Related titles from John Harper Publishing

The European Parliament (4th edition, 2000), by Richard Corbett, Francis Jacobs and Michael Shackleton

Political Parties of the World (4th edition, 1996), by Alan J. Day, Richard German and John Campbell

DIRECTORY OF EUROPEAN UNION POLITICAL PARTIES

Compiled and edited by

ALAN J. DAY

JOHN HARPER
PUBLISHING

DIRECTORY OF EUROPEAN UNION POLITICAL PARTIES

Published by John Harper Publishing, 27 Palace Gates Road, London N22 7BW, UK
Telephone. + 44 (0) 20 8881-4774. *Email*. jhpublish@aol.com

©John Harper Publishing 2000

ISBN 0-9536278-6-1 (Cased edition)

ISBN 0-9536278-5-3 (Paperback edition)

Page makeup by Midlands Book Typesetting Company, Loughborough, UK

Printed and bound in Great Britain by Bookcraft (Bath) Ltd.

Contents

Introduction

The 15 member states of the European Union (EU), being for the most part well-established parliamentary democracies, have the world's most mature party system as well as one of the most variegated. At the beginning of the year 2000, over 140 political parties held seats in the 15 national parliaments, while several hundred more were active at various levels, many of them represented in regional or provincial legislatures or in local councils. The present volume sets out factual reference information on these formations current to end-1999, encompassing contact data (including email and website addresses), leadership details, policy orientation, history, current political/electoral status and affiliations to international and European party organizations. Parties are presented in the alphabetical order of the their names in English, accompanied by own-language titles where appropriate. Those represented in national legislatures and/or the European Parliament are covered in main entries, which are followed by country sections dealing with regional and minor parties.

Each country/dependency section begins with an introduction describing the prevailing constitutional situation, focusing on parliamentary structures and electoral procedures. A comparative table showing the results of the two most recent general elections is included. Also presented in the country introductions are details of the availability of state financial assistance to political parties and of the sums disbursed under such arrangements.

Parties in dependencies of EU countries are covered in the cases of Denmark (the Faroe Islands and Greenland), France (the French overseas departments and territories) and Spain (the North African enclaves of Ceuta and Melilla), on the grounds that these dependencies elect representatives to the metropolitan parliaments, and in the cases of the French and Spanish dependencies also participate in European Parliament elections. For similar reasons a separate section is included for the UK province of Northern Ireland. Overseas dependencies of the UK and the Netherlands with no role in either national or European elections are not covered.

The country sections are followed by an appendix giving full listings of the composition of the party groups in the European Parliament resulting from the elections held throughout the EU in June 1999, when a total of some 120 parties obtained representation (in some cases on joint lists with other formations). Acknowledgement is made as the main source for this appendix to *The European Parliament* (4th edition, 2000) by Richard Corbett, Francis Jacobs and Michael Shackleton, also published by John Harper Publishing.

The most important source of information for party entries has been the parties themselves, via email, fax and telephone contact and also through the websites which most EU parties maintain these days. Also beneficial has been input from international party organizations, notably the Socialist International, the Liberal International, the Christian Democrat International, the European Democrat International, the European Federation of Green Parties and the European Free Alliance. Thanks are finally due to numerous functionaries in national parliaments, government ministries and London embassies for providing information.

AJD, Bath, January 2000

About the author

Alan J. Day has edited or contributed to many political reference titles, including *Political Parties of the World* (4th edition, 1996), *Think Tanks: An International Directory* (1993) and *Border and Territorial Disputes* (3rd edition, 1992). He has been editor of *The Annual Register* since 1988 and was co-editor of the *Political Handbook of the World* in 1993-97.

Austria

Capital: Vienna   **Population:** 8,050,000

First founded in 1919 following the demise of the Austro-Hungarian Empire in World War I, the Republic of Austria was re-established after World War II and obtained international recognition as a "sovereign, independent and democratic state" under the Austrian State Treaty signed on 15 May 1955 by Austria, France, the UK, the USA and the USSR. The Austrian constitution provides for a parliamentary system of government based on elections by secret ballot and by "free, equal and universal suffrage"; as amended in 1945, it proscribes any attempt to revive the pre-war Nazi Party. There is a bicameral parliament consisting of a 183–member lower house called the National Council (*Nationalrat*) and a 63–member upper house called the Federal Council (*Bundesrat*), both together forming the Federal Assembly (*Bundesversammlung*). The *Nationalrat* is elected for a four-year term under an exact proportional representation system (subject to a minimum requirement of 4% of the national vote) by all citizens over 19 years of age. Members of the *Bundesrat* are elected for from four to six years by the legislatures of the nine Austrian provinces (*Länder*), each of which has an elected assembly (*Landtag*). The President of the Republic (*Bundespräsident*) is elected for a six-year term (to a maximum of two terms) by universal suffrage, the functions of the post being mainly ceremonial but including the appointment of the Federal Chancellor (*Bundeskanzler*) as head of government, who recommends ministerial appointments for confirmation by the President. Each member of the government must enjoy the confidence of a majority of members of the *Nationalrat*. Austria joined what became the European Union on Jan. 1, 1995, and elects 21 members to the European Parliament.

Under the Parties Financing Act of 1975, parties represented in the *Nationalrat* are granted federal budget support (for publicity and campaigning) in the form of a basic sum and additional amounts in proportion to the number of votes received in the previous election, subject to at least 1% of the valid votes being obtained. Parties also receive state contributions to their national and European Parliament election expenses. The total amount of such financial support paid in 1998 was 201,718,700 schillings (about $15 million), rising to 475,689,591 schillings (about $35.6 million)

Elections to the *Nationalrat* on Oct. 3, 1999, resulted as follows:		
	Seats *1999 (1995)*	Percentage *1999 (1995)*
Social Democratic Party of Austria　…　…	65　(71)	33.2 (38.1)
Freedom Movement　…　…　…　…　…　…　…	52　(40)	26.9 (21.9)
Austrian People's Party　…　…　…　…　…　…	52　(53)	26.9 (28.3)
The Greens–Green Alternative…　…　…　…	14　(9)	7.4　(4.8)
Liberal Forum　…　…　…　…　…　…　…　…　…	0　(10)	3.7　(5.5)

1

in 1999, in which both national and European elections were held. Of this funding, the total amount available to the Social Democratic Party of Austria (SPÖ) in 1999 was 261,501,373 schillings (about $19.6 million). Separate state assistance is available to research foundations linked to the parties, totalling 123,768,389 schillings (about $9.3 million) in 1999, of which, for example, the SPÖ-linked Karl Renner Institute received 38,715,936 schillings (about $2.9 million).

Austrian People's Party
Österreichische Volkspartei (ÖVP)
Address. Lichtenfelsgasse 7, A-1010 Vienna
Telephone. (+43–1) 401-260
Fax. (+43–1) 4012-6000
Email. email@oevp.at
Website. http://www.oevp.or.at
Leadership. Wolfgang Schüssel (chair); Maria Rauch-Kallat (secretary-general)
Founded in 1945 from pre-war Christian Democratic groups, the ÖVP was the leading government party in 1945–66, in coalition with what later became the →Social Democratic Party of Austria (SPÖ). In sole power from 1966, the ÖVP was narrowly defeated by the SPÖ in the 1970 election, after which it was in opposition for 16 years. Although it lost ground in the 1986 election, simultaneous SPÖ losses dictated the formation of a "grand coalition" of the two major parties, which survived through the 1990 election and beyond, with the ÖVP as junior partner. Meanwhile, the party had become enmeshed in public controversy over the wartime record of Kurt Waldheim, whose election as President in 1986 with ÖVP backing was accompanied by claims that as a Germany Army officer he had participated in Nazi atrocities in the Balkans during World War II.

Waldheim's successor as President, Thomas Klestil, was elected in 1992 as the ÖVP-backed nominee. But provincial elections in the early 1990s showed falling support for the ÖVP, mainly to the benefit of the right-wing Freedom Party of Austria (FPÖ, which became the →Freedom Movement in 1995). This trend was confirmed in the October 1994 federal election, in which the ÖVP's representation fell from 60 to 52 seats and its share of the vote to a low of 27.7%. The party nevertheless continued its coalition with the SPÖ, this being the only viable option if the FPÖ was to be excluded from the government. But Vice-Chancellor Erhard Busek later paid the price of the ÖVP's election setback, being replaced as party chair in April 1995 by Wolfgang Schüssel, who therefore also became Vice-Chancellor.

The ÖVP/SPÖ coalition unexpectedly collapsed in October 1995 over budget policy differences, precipitating a new federal election on Dec. 17. To general surprise, the ÖVP emerged with slightly higher representation of 53 seats, on a vote share of 28.3%, and in March 1996 entered a further coalition headed by the SPÖ. In Austria's first direct elections to the European Parliament in October 1996 the ÖVP headed the poll with 29.6% and seven seats, following which Klestil was re-elected as President in April 1997 with ÖVP backing. Strains arose in the coalition in March 1998 when the SPÖ insisted on maintaining Austria's neutrality, whereas the ÖVP favoured a commitment to NATO membership. In the June 1999 Euro-elections the ÖVP slipped to second place behind the SPÖ in percentage terms, although it improved to 30.6% of the vote and again won seven seats.

The governmental dominance of the SPÖ, combined with the rise of the FPÖ at provincial level, culminated in the ÖVP being reduced, very narrowly in terms of the popular vote, to third-party status in the October 1999 national elections, in which its vote share was a post-war low of 26.9%, although it retained 52 seats. Protracted negotiations resulted in Schüssel becoming Chancellor in a controversial new coalition with the Freedom Movement in early February 2000. At provincial level, the ÖVP then held the governorships of Lower Austria, Upper Austria and Styria in coalition with the SPÖ and FPÖ, of Salzburg and Tyrol in coalition with the SPÖ and of Vorarlberg in coalition with the FPÖ, while also participating in the coalition governments of Burgenland, Carinthia and Vienna.

Claiming a membership of c.300,000, the ÖVP is affiliated to the International Democrat Union and the Christian Democrat International. The party's seven representatives in the European Parliament sit in the European People's Party/European Democrats group.

Freedom Movement
Die Freiheitlichen (DF)
Address. Kärntner Strasse 28, A-1010 Vienna
Telephone. (+43–1) 512–3535
Fax. (+43–1) 512–3277
Email. joerg.haider@fpoe.at
Website. http://www.fpoe.at
Leadership. Jörg Haider (chair); Edith Haller (deputy chair); Herbert Scheibner (parliamentary group chair); Peter Westenthaler (secretary-general)
This party took its present name in January 1995, when the Freedom Party of Austria (FPÖ) decided that, such was public antipathy to traditional party politics, the word "party" should be dropped from its official title. Usually described by the international media as a far-right or even "neo-Nazi" formation because of its opposition to immigration, the party has rejected such descriptions, pointing out that it is fully democratic and that its aim is to preserve the country's cultural identity and the employment prospects of the Austrian people.

The FPÖ had been formed in 1956 as a merger of three right-wing formations, notably the League of Independents, which had won 14 lower house seats in 1953 on a platform of opposition to the post-war party system. FPÖ representation languished in the 1960s and 1970s, although some of its policies, including more precise proportional representation in elections, were enacted. In 1983 it won 12 seats and joined a coalition government with what later became the →Social Democratic Party of Austria (SPÖ). Subsequently, the moderate federal leadership of Norbert Steiger came into increasing ideological conflict with the right-wing provincial Carinthian FPÖ, which contested the 1984 provincial election on a platform of opposition to the provision of bilingual education for the Slovene minority. This argument culminated in Steiger being replaced by youthful populist Jörg Haider in September 1986.

The SPÖ responded by terminating the ruling coalition, but in the resultant federal elections in November 1986 the FPÖ almost doubled its vote share to 9.7%, on a populist platform which included opposition to foreign immigration. In 1989 Haider became governor of the southern province of Carinthia in a coalition between the FPÖ and the →Austrian People's Party (ÖVP), but was obliged to resign two years later after asserting in a *Landtag* debate that "an orderly employment policy was carried out in the Third Reich, which the government in Vienna cannot manage". Developing its populist policies in the 1990 federal election, the opposition FPÖ increased its vote to 16.6%, thereafter also making a series of major gains in provincial elections. The party failed in 1993 to bring about a national referendum on the immigration issue, and Haider's opposition to the government's aim of European Union membership failed to prevent the Austrian electorate voting decisively in favour in June 1994. Nevertheless, after registering a further advance in the Vorarlberg provincial election in September 1994, the FPÖ's share of the vote rose to 22.6% (and 42 seats) in the October federal elections, although the party remained in opposition.

3

Following the collapse of the federal coalition of the SPÖ and the ÖVP in October 1995, general elections in December resulted in an unexpected failure to progress by what was now the Freedom Movement, which slipped to 40 seats and 21.9%. The party nevertheless quickly recovered forward momentum against a new SPÖ/ÖVP federal coalition, winning 27.5% of the vote and six seats in Austria's first direct elections to the European Parliament in October 1996. Its subsequent advances at provincial level featured a 42% vote share in Carinthia in March 1999, as a result of which Haider again became provincial governor (in coalition with the SPÖ and the ÖVP).

In the June 1999 Euro-elections the party fell back to 23.5% and five seats. But Haider achieved a major advance in the October 1999 federal election, his party's 26.9% vote share giving it 52 *Nationalrat* seats and its number of votes making it Austria's second-strongest party ahead of the ÖVP. The eventual outcome in early February 2000 was that the Freedom Movement entered a controversial new coalition headed by the ÖVP. At provincial level, apart from heading the Carinthia government, the FPÖ also participated in the administrations of Lower Austria, Upper Austria, Burgenland and Styria in coalition with the ÖVP and the SPÖ and of Vorarlberg in coalition with the ÖVP.

Claiming 50,000 members, the FPÖ was an affiliate of the Liberal International until being replaced in that organization by the breakaway →Liberal Forum. The movement's five representatives in the European Parliament are part of the "unattached" contingent.

The Greens–Green Alternative
Die Grünen–Die Grüne Alternativen (GA)
Address. Lindengasse 40, A-1070 Vienna
Telephone. (+43–1) 5212-5200
Fax. (+43–1) 526–9110
Email. bundesbuero@gruene.at
Website. http://www.gruene.at
Leadership. Alexander Van der Bellen (spokesperson); Madeleine Petrovic (parliamentary group chair); Michaela Sburny (secretary-general)
The GA was formed in 1987 as a union of three alternative groupings which had won a total of eight seats in the 1986 election, although the conservative →United Greens of Austria subsequently opted to retain their organizational independence. Its component groups had already become influential campaigning on environmentalist issues, their biggest success being the referendum decision in 1978 not to proceed with the country's first nuclear power station at Zwentendorf. As a parliamentary party, the GA has not only sought to bring environmental concerns to the forefront of economic and industrial decision-making but has also pressed for the dismantling of the *Proporz* system whereby the two main post-war parties have shared out the top posts in government bodies and nationalized industries.

The GA increased its representation to 10 seats in the 1990 federal election and thereafter unsuccessfully opposed the government's policy of joining the European Union. In the October 1994 federal elections the formation advanced to 7% of the national vote, giving it 13 seats, but it fell back to 4.8% and nine seats in the December 1995 elections. In Austria's first direct elections to the European Parliament in October 1996, the GA improved to 6.8%, which gave it one seat. It doubled this tally to two seats in the June 1999 Euro-elections (with 9.2% of the vote) and then advanced to 14 *Nationalrat* seats in the October 1999 federal elections (with 7.4% of the vote). At provincial level the GA was in late 1999 represented in the parliaments of seven of the nine Austria provinces (the exceptions being Burgenland and Carinthia), in opposition in each case.

Claiming an individual membership of 3,000 as well as many affiliated groups, the GA is a member of the European Federation of Green Parties. Its two representatives in the European Parliament sit in the Greens/European Free Alliance group.

Liberal Forum
Liberales Forum (LIF)
Address. Reichsratstrasse 7/10, A-1010 Vienna
Telephone. (+43–1) 402-7881
Fax. (+43–1) 402-7889
Email. lif@lif.at
Website. http://www.lif.or.at
Leadership. Heide Schmidt (leader); Gerhard Kratky (secretary-general)
The LIF was launched in February 1993 by five lower house deputies of the Freedom Party of Austria (FPÖ), which later became the →Freedom Movement. The dissidents disagreed with the strident right-wing and anti-foreigner stance of the FPÖ's post-1986 leadership headed by Jörg Haider. The chief defector, Heide Schmidt, had been the FPÖ presidential candidate in 1992, winning 16.4% of the first-round vote. The Forum backed the successful government line in favour of EU membership in the June 1994 referendum. In the October 1994 federal elections it prevented an even bigger advance for its parent party by itself winning 11 seats on the strength of 5.7% of the popular vote. In the December 1995 contest, however, it fell back to 10 seats and 5.5%.

In Austria's first direct elections to the European Parliament in October 1996 the LIF won 4.3% of the vote and one seat. Heide Schmidt was again the party's candidate in the 1998 presidential election, winning 11.1% of the vote. But in the June 1999 Euro-elections the LIF failed to surmount the 4% barrier and so lost its single seat. It also failed in the October 1999 parliamentary elections, winning only 3.7% of the vote and so ceasing to be represented in the *Nationalrat*. At provincial level, the LIF was in late 1999 represented in the provincial parliaments of Styria and Vienna, in opposition in each case.

In 1993 the LIF was designated to replace the FPÖ as the Austrian affiliate of the Liberal International. The party has a membership of 2,000.

Social Democratic Party of Austria
Sozialdemokratische Partei Österreichs (SPÖ)
Address. Löwelstrasse 18, A-1014 Vienna
Telephone. (+43–1) 534-270
Fax. (+43–1) 535–9683
Email. international@spoe.or.at
Website. http://www.spoe.at
Leadership. Viktor Klima (chair); Peter Kostelka (parliamentary group chair); Andreas Rudas (general secretary)
The SPÖ is descended from the Social Democratic Workers' Party dating from 1874, which advocated social revolution and the transformation of the Austro-Hungarian Empire into a federal state of coexisting nations. It had no direct political influence before World War I, although it became the largest parliamentary party on the strength of universal male franchise. On the establishment of the Austrian Republic in 1919 it was briefly in government under Karl Renner, but went into opposition in 1920, remaining committed to "Austro-Marxism" and prepared to resort to armed struggle if the bourgeoisie sought to resist social revolution. The party came under increasing pressure in the early 1930s, as the pro-fascist Dollfus government adopted authoritarian methods, dissolving the *Nationalrat* in March 1933 and introducing rule by decree. The party's paramilitary

Republican Defence League, itself already banned, responded by mounting an uprising in Vienna in February 1934 but was quickly defeated. Following the proclamation of a quasi-fascist constitution three months later, the party went underground and participated with other democratic forces in anti-fascist resistance until German forces occupied Austria in 1938.

On the re-establishment of the Republic in 1945, the SPÖ adopted a pro-Western stance and participated in a broad-based coalition government including the →Communist Party of Austria. From November 1947, however, it became the junior partner in a two-party coalition with the →Austrian People's Party (ÖVP) that endured until 1966, when the SPÖ went into opposition. In 1970 it returned to power as the sole governing party under the leadership of Bruno Kreisky, forming a minority government until 1971, when it gained an absolute majority in the lower house which it retained in the 1975 and 1979 elections. A party congress in 1978 renounced public ownership as a necessary requirement of democratic socialism.

Losing its overall majority in the 1983 election, the SPÖ formed a coalition with the Freedom Party of Austria (FPÖ)—later the →Freedom Movement—and Kreisky handed over the government and party leadership to Fred Sinowatz. The latter resigned in June 1986 as a result of the controversial election of Kurt Waldheim as President and was replaced as Chancellor by Franz Vranitzky. In September 1986, because of the FPÖ's move to the right, the SPÖ terminated the coalition but lost ground sharply in November elections. It therefore formed a "grand coalition" with the ÖVP in January 1987, under Vranitzky's chancellorship, thereby provoking the resignation of Kreisky as SPÖ honorary chair. Later that year an SPÖ congress gave qualified support to the government's privatization programme.

The SPÖ/ÖVP coalition was maintained after the October 1990 elections, in which the SPÖ remained substantially the largest party. In 1991 the party renamed itself "Social Democratic" rather than "Socialist", retaining the SPÖ abbreviation. The government's key external policy of EC/EU membership was endorsed by the electorate in June 1994 by a 2:1 majority. In the October 1994 federal elections, however, the SPÖ vote slipped to a new post-war low of 35.2% and the party opted to continue its coalition with the ÖVP. In October 1995, however, the coalition collapsed over budget policy differences, with the result that new lower house elections were held in December. Against most predictions, Vranitzky led the SPÖ to a significant electoral recovery, yielding 71 seats and 38.1% of the vote. In March 1996 he was appointed to a fifth term as Chancellor, heading a further coalition between the SPÖ and the ÖVP.

Austria's first direct elections to the European Parliament in October 1996 produced a slump in SPÖ support, to 29.2% and six seats. In January 1997 Vranitzky resigned as Chancellor, a week after the SPÖ had pushed through the controversial privatization of the Creditanstalt, the country's second-largest bank. The architect of the privatization, Finance Minister Viktor Klima, succeeded him as Chancellor and, in April 1997, as SPÖ chair. Subsequent regional elections showed an erosion of SPÖ support, which recovered only to 31.7% in the June 1999 European Parliament elections, in which the party increased from six to seven seats.

The October 1999 parliamentary elections produced a setback for both federal coalition parties, the SPÖ falling to 33.2% and 65 seats. Klima failed in a lengthy attempt to form a new government, so that the SPÖ went into opposition in February 2000. At provincial level in late-1999 the SPÖ held the governorships of Burgenland (in coalition with the ÖVP and FPÖ) and of Vienna (in coalition with the ÖVP), as well as participating in the governments of the other seven provinces.

The SPÖ has an official membership of 700,000 and is a founder member of the Socialist International. Its seven representatives in the European Parliament are members of the Party of European Socialists group.

Other Parties

Austrian Natural Law Party (*Österreichische Naturgesetz-Partei*, ÖNP), led by Lothar Krenner, won 0.05% of the vote in 1994 parliamentary elections. *Address.* Biberstrasse 22/2, A-1010 Vienna; *Telephone.* (+43-1) 512-6612; *Fax.* (+43-1) 513-9660; *Email.* lothar.krenner@telecom.at; *Website.* http://www.oenp.or.at

Christian Electors' Union (*Christliche Wählergemeinschaft*, CWG), won 0.2% of the national vote in 1994 parliamentary elections and 0.1% in 1999.

Citizens' Initiative against the Abandonment of Austria (*Bürgerinitiave gegen den Ausverkauf Österreichs*), contested the 1994 parliamentary elections under the electoral designation "No" (*Nein*) in opposition to EU and NATO membership and in favour of Austrian neutrality, winning 0.9% of the vote; in the 1999 elections it took 0.4% of the popular vote.

Communist Party of Austria (*Kommunistische Partei Österreiches*, KPÖ), led by Walter Baier, founded by pro-Soviet Social Democrats in 1919, in government in 1945–47 and represented in the lower house until 1959; reputedly one of the richest Austrian parties on the strength of industrial holdings acquired under the post-war Soviet occupation; took only 0.3% of the vote in 1994 parliamentary elections, improving to 0.5% in 1999. *Address.* Weyringergasse 33/5, A-1040 Vienna; *Telephone.* (+43-1) 503-6580; *Fax.* (+43-1) 503-411/499; *Email.* kpoe@magnet.at; *Website.* http://www.kpoenet.at

The Independents (*Die Unabhängigen*, DU), led by Richard Lugner, opposed to the post-war party system; Lugner won an impressive 9.9% of the vote in the 1998 presidential election, but the DU managed only 1% in the 1999 parliamentary elections. *Address.* Gablenzgase 11, Vienna 15; *Telephone.* (+43-1) 98140; *Fax.* (+43-1) 98140; *Email.* service@ldu.at; *Website.* http://www.ldu.at

League of Democratic Socialists (*Bund Demokratischer Sozialisten*, BDS), a Marxist grouping with links with the ⇒Socialist Party of Great Britain. *Address.* Gussriegelstrasse 50, A-1000 Vienna

People's True Extra-Parliamentary Opposition Party (*Volkstreue Ausserparlamentarische Opposition*, VAPO), extreme right-wing group, founded by Gottfried Küssel, identified with attacks on immigrants in the early 1990s; arrested in January 1992, Küssel was sentenced to 11 years' imprisonment in October 1994 for founding VAPO.

Revolutionary Marxist League (*Revolutionär Kommunistische Liga*, GRM), a small Trotskyist formation dating from 1972, affiliated to the Fourth International, United Secretariat. *Address.* Postfach 325, A-1060 Vienna; *Telephone/Fax.* (+43-1) 504-0010; *Email.* rkl@magnet.at

United Greens of Austria (*Vereinte Grüne Österreichs*, VGÖ), led by Adi Pinter, founded in 1982 by conservative ecologists and briefly part of the coalition which became the →Green Alternative, winner of one lower house seat in 1986 but none in 1990 or 1994 (taking only 0.1% of the vote on the latter occasion).

Belgium

Capital: Brussels   **Population:** 10,250,000

The Kingdom of Belgium is a constitutional monarchy with a parliamentary democracy in which most political parties are based in the country's linguistic communities, principally the majority Flemish-speaking population in the north and the French-speaking Walloon community in the south. The constitutional monarch, as head of state, has limited powers, with central executive authority residing in the Prime Minister and the Council of Ministers being responsible to a federal bicameral legislature. The lower house is the Chamber of Representatives (Chambre des Représentants or Kamer van Volksvertegenwoordigers), reduced from 212 to 150 members from 1995 and elected for a maximum four-year term by universal compulsory suffrage of those aged 18 and over according to a complex system of proportional representation. The Chamber has virtually equal powers with the upper house, which is the 71-member Senate (Sénat/Senaat), 40 of whose members are elected directly and the remainder indirectly, also for a four-year term. Belgium was a founder member of what is now the European Union and elects 25 members to the European Parliament.

A lengthy process of constitutional reform, inaugurated in 1970 and involving the phased devolution of substantial powers to the linguistic regions, culminated with the final parliamentary approval on July 14, 1993, of legislation transforming Belgium into a federal state. Under the changes, the country is divided into three regions (Flanders, Wallonia and bilingual Brussels), each with a government and directly-elected legislature (of 118, 75 and 75 members respectively) endowed with broad economic and social powers, and into three communities(Flemish, French and German) for cultural purposes. The Flemish community council is identical with the

Elections to the Chamber on June 13, 1999, resulted as follows:				
	Seats		Percentage	
	1999 (1995)		1999 (1995)	
Flemish Liberals and Democrats	23	(21)	14.3	(13.1)
Christian People's Party (Flemish)	22	(29)	14.1	(17.2)
Socialist Party (Walloon)	19	(21)	10.1	(11.9)
Liberal Reformistist Party and Democratic Front of French-Speakers (Walloon) ...	18	(18)	10.1	(10.3)
Flemish Bloc	15	(11)	9.9	(7.8)
Socialist Party (Flemish)	14	(20)	9.6	(12.6)
Ecologist Party (Walloon)	11	(6)	7.3	(4.0)
Christian Social Party (Walloon)	10	(12)	6.1	(7.7)
Live Differently (Flemish)	9	(5)	7.0	(4.4)
People's Union (Flemish)	8	(5)	5.6	(4.7)
National Front (Walloon)	1	(2)	1.5	(2.3)

Flanders regional council; the French community council is indirectly constituted by the 75 Wallonia regional council members and 19 from the Brussels council; and the 25-member German community council is directly elected.

Although there is no direct public funding of parties in Belgium, those already represented in the federal legislature benefit from certain facilities during election campaigns, amounting to indirect state subsidy sufficient to cover the maximum authorized expenditure of BF40 million (about $1.2 million) on such campaigns.

Christian People's Party
Christelijke Volkspartij (CVP)
Address. Wetstraat 89, B-1040 Brussels
Telephone. (+32–2) 238–3814
Fax. (+32–2) 230-4360
Email. inform@cvp.be
Website. http://www.cvp.be
Leadership. Stefaan de Clercq (president); M. Van Peel (chair in federal Chamber); Chris Taes (secretary-general)

Historically descended from the *Katholieke Vlaamse Volkspartij*, which was the Flemish wing of the pre-war Belgian Catholic Party, the CVP was created in 1945 as the Flemish counterpart of the French-speaking →Christian Social Party (PSC), initially within a single party structure. From 1947 the CVP/PSC participated in successive coalition governments, except for the period 1954–58. By the mid-1960s the CVP and the PSC had effectively become separate parties, the former considerably larger than the latter in terms of electoral support. Consistently the strongest single parliamentary party, the CVP provided the Prime Minister in coalitions, with the Socialists and the →Democratic Front of French-Speakers of Brussels in 1979–80; with the Socialists and Liberals briefly in 1980; with the Socialists in 1980–81; with the Liberals in 1981–88; with the Socialists and the →People's Union in 1988–91; and with the Socialists in 1992-99.

In the November 1991 Chamber elections the CVP's representation fell from 43 to 39 seats out of 212 and its share of the vote from 19.5% to 16.7%. After 13 years of almost continuous incumbency as CVP Prime Minister, Wilfried Martens gave way to Jean-Luc Dehaene in the government formed in March 1992. In the June 1994 European Parliament elections the party took 17% of the vote (compared with 21.1% in 1989) and four of the 25 Belgian seats. In further Chamber elections in May 1995 the CVP unexpectedly increased its vote share to 17.2%, winning 29 out of 150 seats, so that Dehaene remained head of a federal coalition with the Socialists. In simultaneous elections for the 118-member Flemish regional council the CVP won a plurality of 35 seats (with 26.8% of the vote), providing the minister-president of Flanders in the person of Luc van den Brande, who headed a coalition with the Flemish Socialists.

From 1996 the CVP shared in the Dehaene coalition's deep unpopularity over official mishandling of a gruesome paedophile case, amidst widespread protest against expenditure cuts introduced to enable Belgium to qualify for the single European currency. On the eve of the June 1999 general, regional and European elections, moreover, two major food safety scares proved to be the death-knell for the government. Support for the CVP fell to 14.1% in the Chamber elections, its resultant 22 seats relegating it to second place behind the →Flemish Liberals and Democrats (VLD), with the result that the party went into opposition for the first time since 1958. The CVP also lost ground in the Flemish regional council elections (taking 22.1% of the vote and 28 seats) and was obliged to surrender the post of minister-president to the VLD. In the Euro-elections the CVP declined to 13.5% of the vote and its representation from four to three seats.

The CVP is a member of the Christian Democrat International and the European Union of Christian Democrats. Its three representatives in the European Parliament sit in the European People's Party/European Democrats group.

Christian Social Party
Parti Social Chrétien (PSC)
Address. Rue des Deux Églises 41/45, B-1040 Brussels
Telephone. (+32–2) 238–0111
Fax. (+32–2) 238–0129
Email. info@psc.be
Website. http://www.psc.be
Leadership. Philippe Maystadt (president); Joëlle Milquet (vice-president); J.-P. Poncelet (chair in federal Chamber); Jean-François Brouillard (secretary-general)
The PSC has its historical origins in the Catholic Union, one of several such organizations set up in Belgium in the 19th century. It is directly descended from the Belgian Catholic Party (PCB) created in 1936 and more specifically from the *Parti Catholique Social* (PCS), the PCB's French-speaking section. As the country's strongest party, the PCB took part in coalition governments before and during World War II, the PCS providing Belgium's wartime Prime Minister. At Christmas 1945 the PCB was reconstituted, the PCS becoming the PSC and the Flemish wing becoming the →Christian People's Party (CVP), at that stage within one overall party structure. Having confirmed its dominant position in the 1946 elections, the joint party entered a coalition with the Socialists in 1947. Thereafter the PSC/CVP tandem participated continuously in the central government until 1999, except for the period 1954–58.

From the mid-1960s the PSC and CVP effectively became two separate parties, the former becoming substantially the smaller of the two. The PSC has therefore been a junior partner in recent coalitions headed by the CVP, with the Socialists and the →Democratic Front of French-Speakers of Brussels in 1979–80; with the Socialists and Liberals briefly in 1980; with the Socialists in 1980–81; with the Liberals in 1981–88; with the Socialists and the →People's Union in 1988–91; and with the Socialists since 1992. In the November 1991 Chamber elections PSC representation slipped from 19 to 18 seats out of 212 and its vote share from 8% to 7.8%. In the June 1994 European Parliament elections the PSC retained two of the 25 Belgian seats but its vote share fell to 6.9% from 8.1% in 1989. This setback coincided with disclosures of financial corruption in the Brussels section of the party. Nevertheless, in the May 1995 Chamber elections the PSC retained a 7.7% vote share, winning 12 of the 150 seats, and took third place in the simultaneous elections to the Walloon regional council, with 16 of the 75 seats and 21.6% of the vote. Thereafter, in addition to remaining in the federal coalition, the PSC also maintained its coalition with the Walloon Socialists in the regional government of Wallonia.

In simultaneous federal, regional and European elections held in June 1999, support for the PSC fell to 6.1% in the Chamber elections and its representation to 10 seats, with the result that the party went into opposition for the first time since 1958. In the Walloon regional elections the PSC fell to 17.1% of the vote and 14 seats and likewise vacated the regional government. In the Euro-elections the CVP declined to 4.9% of the vote and its representation from two seats to one.

The PSC is a member of the Christian Democrat International and the European Union of Christian Democrats. Its single representative in the European Parliament sits in the European People's Party/European Democrats group.

Democratic Front of French-Speakers
Front Démocratique des Francophones (FDF)
Address. Chaussée de Charleroi 127, B-1060 Brussels
Telephone. (+32-2) 538-8320
Fax. (+32-2) 539-3650
Email. fdf@fdf.be
Website. http://www.fdf.be
Leadership. Olivier Maingain (president); Claude Desmedt (chair in federal Chamber); Didier van Eyll (chair in French community council); François Roelants du Vivier (chair in Brussels council); Serge de Patoul (secretary-general)
Founded in May 1964 with the aim of preserving the French character of the Belgian capital, the FDF incorporated various militant francophone groupings of Brussels. Its three Chamber seats in the 1965 elections were increased to 10 by 1977, after which it joined a coalition government with the Christian Socials and Socialists and assisted with the enactment of the 1978 Egmont Pact on regional devolution. Under the plan, Brussels was to become a separate (bilingual) region, i.e. not included in surrounding Flanders as some Flemish nationalists had demanded. Having risen to 11 seats in 1978, the FDF went into opposition again from 1980 and slipped to six seats in 1981. Two of these deputies defected to the Walloon →Socialist Party in March 1985 and the FDF was reduced to three seats in the October 1985 elections, retaining them in 1987 and 1991.

The FDF retained representation in the May 1995 Chamber elections by virtue of an alliance with the →Liberal Reformist Party (PRL). In simultaneous elections, the PRL/FDF alliance became the largest bloc in the Brussels regional council, winning 28 of the 75 seats (with 35% of the vote), and the second largest in the Walloon regional council, with 19 of the 75 seats and a 23.7% vote share. The FDF was allocated one portfolio in the six-party Brussels regional government.

The PRL-FDF alliance was maintained in the June 1999 elections, retaining 18 federal Chamber seats on a slightly reduced vote of 10.1%, improving to 21 seats (24.7% of the vote) in the Walloon regional council and slipping to 27 seats (34.4%) in the Brussels regional council. In the simultaneous European Parliament elections the FDF was allied with both the PRL and the →Citizens' Movement for Change (MCC), the joint list winning three seats on a 10% vote share. The FDF received no portfolios in the new federal government which included the PRL, but was represented in the new regional administrations of Wallonia and Brussels. The party has an official membership of 13,485.

Ecologist Party
Ecologistes Confédérés pour l'Organisation de Luttes Originales (ECOLO)
Address. Rue du Séminaire 8, B-5000 Namur
Telephone. (+32-81) 227-871
Fax. (+32-81) 230-603
Email. info@ecolo.be
Website. http://www.ecolo.be
Leadership. Jacky Morael and Jean-Luc Roland (federal secretaries)
Originally founded in 1978 by Walloon environmentalists, ECOLO was reorganized for the 1981 elections, in which it co-operated with the Flemish →Live Differently (AGALEV) grouping and won two Chamber seats. Having established a significant local government presence, ECOLO increased its Chamber tally to five seats in 1985 (standing independently), but slipped back to three seats in 1987. The November 1991 elections brought a major advance, to 10 seats out of 212, with 5.1% of the vote, double the party's 1987 share. In the June 1994 European Parliament elections ECOLO won 4.8% of the national vote and one

seat, compared with 6.3% and two seats in 1989. Its share in the May 1995 Chamber elections fell back to 4.0%, giving it six of the 150 seats, while in simultaneous regional polling it won eight and seven seats respectively on the 75-member Walloon and Brussels regional councils (with 10.4% and 9.0% of the vote respectively).

ECOLO resumed its electoral advance in the June 1999 federal, regional and European elections. Its representation in the federal Chamber almost doubled to 11 seats (from a vote share of 7.3%); it won 14 seats in both the Walloon and Brussels councils (with 18.2% and 18.3% respectively); it again took three seats on the 25-member council of the German-speaking community (with 12.7% of the vote); and it increased its European Parliament representation to three seats (with 8.4% of the vote). It alsoIn July 1999 ECOLO joined a new federal coalition headed by the →Flemish Liberals and Democrats, Isabelle Durant being appointed Deputy Prime Minister and Minister for Mobility and Transport. The ECOLO and AGALEV members in the federal Chamber form a single group under the chairmanship of Jef Tavernier.

ECOLO is a member of the European Federation of Green Parties. Its three representatives in the European Parliament sit in the Greens/European Free Alliance group.

Flemish Bloc
Vlaams Blok (VB)
Address. Madouplein 8 bus 9, B-1210 Brussels
Telephone. (+32–2) 219-6009
Fax. (+32-2) 217-1958
Email. vlblok@vlaams-blok.be
Website. http://www.vlaams-blok.be
Leadership. Frank Vanhecke (pesident); Karel Dillen (founder and honorary president);
Roeland Raes (deputy president); Gerolf Annemans (chair in federal Chamber); Filip Dewinter (chair in Flemish council)

The ultra-nationalist Flemish Bloc first came into being for the December 1978 elections as an alliance between the Flemish People's Party, established in 1977 by Lode Claes following a split in the →People's Union (VU), and the Flemish National Party, led by Karel Dillen and also founded in 1977. Having won one seat in that contest, the two parties formally merged under Dillen's leadership in May 1979 on a platform of opposition to the 1978 Egmont Pact on devolution on the grounds that it demanded too many concessions of Flemings. Having increased its Chamber tally to two seats in 1987, the Bloc experienced a surge of support in the 1990s on a platform which now emphasized opposition to immigration. In the November 1991 elections the Bloc's representation in the Chamber increased to 12 seats and its vote share to 6.6%, ahead of the VU, for long the main vehicle of Flemish nationalism. During the campaign brown-shirted VB militants were involved in numerous violent incidents involving foreigners.

In the June 1994 European Parliament elections the Bloc won two seats and increased its vote to 7.8% (from 4.1% in 1989) on a platform which combined anti-immigration policies with opposition to the Maastricht process of European union. It made further advances in local elections in October 1994, winning representation in 82 of the 308 municipal councils and a total of 202 seats nationally. The Bloc headed the poll in Antwerp, winning 29% of the vote and 18 of the 55 seats, but its leader in the city, Filip Dewinter, was excluded from the mayorship by a combination of the other parties represented. The VB again registered 7.8% of the national vote in the May 1995 Chamber elections, giving it 11 out of 150 seats, while in simultaneous polling for the 118-member Flemish regional council it won 15 seats with a 12.3% vote share.

The VB made a further advance in the June 1999 federal, regional and European elections, winning 15 seats in the federal Chamber (with 9.9% of the vote) and 20 seats on the

Flemish regional council (with 15.5% of the vote), also also retaining two European Parliament seats (on an increased vote share of 9.4%).

The VB's two representatives in the European Parliament are among the "unattached" contingent. The party claims a membership of about 25,000.

Flemish Liberals and Democrats–Citizens' Party
Vlaamse Liberalen en Demokraten (VLD)–Partij van de Burger

Address. Melsensstraat 34, B-1000 Brussels

Telephone. (+32–2) 549-0020

Fax. (+32–2) 512–6025

Email. vld@vld.be

Website. http://www.vld.be

Leadership. Karel de Gucht (president); H. Coveliers (chair in federal Chamber); Clair Ysebaert (secretary-general)

The VLD is descended from the historic Belgian Liberal Party, which was founded in 1846 as the country's earliest political formation. It was in power in 1857–70 and 1878–84 but was then overtaken on the left by the new Belgian Labour Party, becoming the country's third political force behind the Catholics and Socialists. Having participated in a succession of coalitions after World War II, notably the 1954–58 Socialist-Liberal government, the Liberal Party was reconstituted in 1961 as the Party of Liberty and Progress (PLP). In 1970 the Flemish wing (*Partij voor Vrijheid en Vooruitgang*, PVV) became an autonomous formation, leaving the PLP as a Walloon party. Having participated in various coalitions in the 1970s, both the PVV and its Walloon counterpart, by now called the →Liberal Reformist Party (PRL), were in government with the →Christian People's and →Christian Social parties in 1981–88, being regarded as the right-wing component of the coalition. In the November 1991 general elections the opposition PVV increased its Chamber representation from 25 to 26 seats out of 212 and its vote share from 11.5% to 11.9%.

In November 1992, in a move to broaden its support base, the PVV switched to its current VLD designation, also using the sub-title Party of Citizens (*Partij van de Burger*). In the June 1994 European Parliament elections the VLD took 11.4% of the vote and three of the 25 Belgian seats, against 10.6% and two seats for the PVV in 1989. In municipal and provincial elections in October 1994 the VLD replaced the Flemish Socialists as the second-largest party in Flanders. It made a further advance in the May 1995 Chamber elections, winning 21 of the 150 seats with 13.1% of the vote, but not enough to oust the incumbent coalition. In simultaneous regional polling the VLD consolidated its position as second party in Flanders, winning 26 of the 118 seats in the Flemish regional council. In light of the party's relatively disappointing performance, Guy Verhofstadt resigned as leader and was succeeded in September 1995 by Herman de Croo.

Verhofstadt resumed the VLD presidency in 1997 and led the party to a significant advance in the June 1999 federal, regional and European, assisted by the deep unpopularity of the incumbent government. The party's representation in the federal Chamber increased to 23 seats (from a vote share of 14.3%); its seat tally in the Flemish regional council improved to 27 (with 22% of the vote); and it again won three European Parliament seats (with an increased vote share of 13.6%). In July 1999 Verhofstadt became Prime Minister of a new federal coalition which also included the PRL, the two Socialist parties, the →Ecologist Party and →Live Differently.

Claiming a membership of 80,000, the VLD is a member party of the Liberal International. Its representatives in the European Parliament sit in the European Liberal, Democratic and Reformist group.

Liberal Reformist Party
Parti Réformateur Libéral (PRL)
Address. Rue de Naples 41, B-1050 Brussels
Telephone. (+32–2) 500–3511
Fax. (+32–2) 500–3500
Email. prl@prl.be
Website. http://www.prl.be
Leadership. Daniel Ducarme (president); D. Bacquelaine (chair in federal Chamber); Jacques Simonet (secretary-general)

Descended from the historic Belgian Liberal Party and its successors (see previous entry), the French-speaking PRL came into being in June 1979 as a merger of the Party of Reforms and Liberty of Wallonia (PRLW) and the Brussels Liberal Party. Of these, the PRLW had been formed in November 1976 as successor to the Party of Liberty and Progress (*Parti de la Liberté et du Progrès*, PLP), which had continued as the main Walloon Liberal party after the Flemish wing had become a separate formation in 1970, later becoming the →Flemish Liberals and Democrats (VLD). The Brussels Liberals had adopted the party's historic name in June 1974 as successor to the distinct Liberal Democrat and Pluralist Party (PLDP) founded in January 1973. The PLP and the successor PRL (with the Flemish Liberals, who were consistently the stronger) participated in various coalitions, most recently with the →Christian People's Party and the →Christian Social Party in 1981–88, being regarded as the coalition's right-wing component.

In the November 1991 general elections, the opposition PRL's representation in the Chamber fell from 23 to 20 seats out of 212 and its vote share from 9.4% to 8.2%. In the June 1994 European Parliament elections the PRL won 9.0% of the vote and three seats compared with 8.7% and two seats in 1989. For the May 1995 Chamber elections the PRL presented a joint list with the →Democratic Front of French-Speakers (FDF) of Brussels, winning 18 out of 150 seats on a 10.3% vote share. In simultaneous elections, the PRL/FDF alliance became the largest bloc in the Brussels regional council, winning 28 of the 75 seats (with 35% of the vote), and the second largest in the Walloon regional council, with 19 of the 75 seats and a 23.7% vote share. The PRL was allocated two portfolios in the six-party Brussels regional government.

The PRL-FDF alliance was maintained in the June 1999 elections, retaining 18 federal Chamber seats on a slightly reduced vote of 10.1%, improving to 21 seats (24.7% of the vote) in the Walloon regional council and slipping to 27 seats (34.4%) in the Brussels regional council. In the simultaneous European Parliament elections the PRL was allied with both the FDF and the →Citizens' Movement for Change (MCC), the joint list winning three seats on a 10% vote share. In July 1999 the PRL joined a new federal coalition headed by the VLD, while the party also provided the minister-presidents of the new Brussels regional and French-speaking community governments, respectively Jacques Simonet and Hervé Hasquin.

Claiming a membership of 40,000, the PRL is a member party of the Liberal International. The PRL members of the European Parliament sit in the European Liberal, Democratic and Reformist group.

Live Differently
Anders Gaan Leven (AGALEV)
Address. Brialmonstraat 23, B-1210 Brussels
Telephone. (+32-2) 219-1919
Fax. (+32-2) 223-1090
Email. postmaster@agalev.be
Website. http://www.agalev.be

Leadership. Jos Geysels (political secretary); Luc Lemiengre (secretary)

This Flemish environmentalist formation won two Chamber seats in the 1981 elections standing jointly with the Walloon →Ecologist Party (ECOLO). Established as an independent party in 1982, AGALEV increased its representation to four seats in 1985, six in 1987 and seven in November 1991, when its share of the poll was 4.9%. In the June 1994 European Parliament elections, it retained one seat with 6.7% of the vote (as against 7.6% in 1989), while in the May 1995 Chamber elections it slipped to 4.4% of the national vote, winning five out of 150 seats. In simultaneous regional balloting, AGALEV took 7.1% of the vote in Flanders, winning seven of the 118 regional council seats.

AGALEV resumed its electoral advance in the June 1999 federal, regional and European elections. Its representation in the federal Chamber almost doubled to nine seats (with a vote share of 7.0%); it won 12 seats in the Flemish regional council (with 11.6% of the vote); and a joint list of AGALEV and the Flemish →Socialist Party (SP) won two seats on the Brussels regional council (with 3.1% of the vote). In the simultaneous European Parliament elections AGALEV improved from one to two seats (with 7.5% of the vote). In July 1999 AGALEV joined a new federal coalition headed by the →Flemish Liberals and Democrats, Magda Aelvoet being appointed Minister of Consumer Protection, Public Health and Environment. The AGALEV and ECOLO members in the federal Chamber form a single group under the chairmanship of Jef Tavernier.

AGALEV is a member of the European Federation of Green Parties. Its two representatives in the European Parliament sit in the Greens/European Free Alliance group.

National Front
Front National (FN)
Address. Clos du Parnasse 12/8, B-1050 Brussels
Telephone/Fax. (+32-2) 511-7577
Email. fn@frontnational.be
Website. http://www.frontnational.be
Leadership. Daniel Féret (president); Guy Hance, Alain Sadaune (vice-presidents); Jacqueline Merveille (secretary-general)

The extreme right-wing FN, modelled on the ⇒National Front of France, was founded in 1983 on a platform of opposition to non-white immigration. Based mainly in the French-speaking community, it achieved a breakthrough in the November 1991 elections, winning one Chamber seat with 1.1% of the vote. A further advance came in the June 1994 European Parliament elections, when it took 2.9% of the vote and one of the 25 Belgian seats. In October 1994 the FN leadership announced the expulsion of a member who had been shown on television desecrating a Jewish grave. In local elections the same month the party doubled its share of the vote in Wallonia compared with the previous contest in 1988. In the May 1995 Chamber elections the NF advanced to 2.3% of the national vote, winning two seats, while in simultaneous regional balloting it won six seats on the 75-member Brussels regional council (with 7.5% of the vote) and two seats in Wallonia (with 5.2% of the vote).

The FN lost ground in the June 1999 elections, winning only one Chamber seat (with 1.5% of the vote), two on the Brussels regional council (with 2.6%) and one in Wallonia (with 4.0%). It also lost its single European Parliament seat, taking only 1.5% of the vote in that contest. The party claims a membership of 1,000.

People's Union
Volksunie (VU)
Address. Barrikadenplein 12, B-1000 Brussels
Telephone. (+32-2) 219-4930

Fax. (+32-2) 217-3510
Email. secretariat@volksunie.be
Website. http://www.volksunie.be
Leadership. Patrik Vankrunkelsven (president); Geert Bourgeois (chair of Chamber group);
Paul Van Grembergen (chair of Flemish council group); Laurens Appeltans (secretary-general)
The VU was founded in December 1954 as a nationalist party seeking autonomy for Flanders
on a "socially progressive, tolerant, modern and forward-looking" platform. It made a
breakthrough in the 1965 Chamber elections, winning 12 seats, which it increased to 20 in
1969 and to 22 in 1974. It fell back to 20 seats in 1977, in which year it entered government
for the first time, in coalition with the Christian Socials, Socialists and →Democratic Front of
French-Speakers (FDF) of Brussels, with the task of enacting regional devolution plans.
Enshrined in the 1978 Egmont Pact, these were opposed by many VU militants as being
inimical to Flemish interests, the result being the secession of a VU faction which later
became part of the →Flemish Bloc (VB). The VU retained only 14 seats in the December
1978 elections and reverted to opposition status. Rebuilding its strength, it won 20 seats in
1981 but slipped again in 1985 to 16. Having again won 16 seats in the December 1987
elections, it accepted participation in a coalition with the Christian Socials and Socialists
formed in March 1988 but withdrew in September 1991 over an arms export controversy.

In the November 1991 elections the VU retained only 10 seats (and 5.9% of the vote),
being overtaken by the VB. In the June 1994 European Parliament elections it slipped to 4.4%
of the vote, from 5.4% in 1989, while retaining one seat. The May 1995 Chamber elections
yielded a further setback for the VU, which fell to 4.7% of the national vote and five seats
(out of 150). In simultaneous regional elections it won 9% of the vote in Flanders and nine of
the 118 regional council seats, while in Brussels it won one seat and was allocated one
portfolio in the six-party Brussels regional government.

The VU gained ground in the June 1999 national, regional and European elections,
winning eight federal Chamber seats (with 5.6% of the vote) and 11 on the Flemish regional
council in an alliance with the →Complete Democracy for the 21st Century (ID21) grouping
(with 9.3%), although it lost its single seat on the Brussels regional council. In the
simultaneous European elections the VU-ID21 advanced to two seats on the strength of a
7.6% vote share.

The two VU-ID21 members of the European Parliament sit in the Greens/European Free
Alliance group.

Socialist Party
Parti Socialiste (PS)
Address. Blvd de l'Empereur 13, B-1000 Brussels
Telephone. (+32–2) 511-6966
Fax. (+32–2) 512-4632
Email. international@ps.be
Website. http://www.ps.be
Leadership. Elio Di Rupo (president); Maurice Bayenet and Philippe Moureaux
(vice-presidents); Cl. Eerdekens (chair in federal Chamber); Jean-Pol Baras (secretary-general)
Dating as a separate French-speaking party from October 1978, the PS is descended from the
Belgian Labour Party (POB) founded in April 1885 with its base in industrial Wallonia and its
support in organized labour. After obtaining universal male suffrage through a general strike,
the POB was well-represented in the Chamber from 1894 and was admitted to the
government-in-exile formed at Le Havre (France) in 1915 during World War I. In 1938
Paul-Henri Spaak became Belgium's first POB Prime Minister, but the German occupation of
Belgium in 1940 forced the party underground under the leadership of Achille van Acker.

Reconstituted in 1944 as the Belgian Socialist Party, with direct membership rather than group affiliation, it took part in post-war coalition governments until 1949 and again (with the Liberals) in 1954–58. Thereafter it was in coalition with the Christian Socials in 1961–66 and 1968–72; with the Christian Socials and Liberals in 1973–74; and with the Christian Socials, the →Democratic Front of French-Speakers (FDF) and the →People's Union (VU) in 1977–78. In October 1978 the Socialists emulated the other main Belgian political formations by formalizing the separation of their Flemish and French-speaking wings into autonomous parties, respectively the PS and the SP (see next entry).

Both the PS and the SP participated in coalitions with the Christian Socials and the FDF in 1979–80; with the Christian Socials and Liberals briefly in 1980; and with the Christian Socials in 1980–81. Both parties were then in opposition until, having become the largest lower house force in the December 1987 elections (for the first time since 1936), they joined a coalition with the Christian Socials and the VU in March 1988. Following the VU's withdrawal in September 1991, both Socialist parties lost ground in Chamber elections the following month (the PS falling from 40 to 35 seats out of 212 on a vote share of 15.6%) and joined a new coalition with the two Christian Social parties in March 1992. Concurrently, the PS also headed the regional governments of Wallonia and Brussels, championing the channelling of redevelopment resources to French-speaking areas and the maintenance of a large nationalized sector.

The murder in Liège in July 1991 of André Cools (a former PS Deputy Prime Minister) led eventually to the uncovering of the Agusta scandal, involving allegations of financial corruption in the party leadership in connection with a 1988 government contract for military helicopters awarded to an Italian firm. In January 1994 the disclosures resulted in the resignations of Guy Coëme (as federal Deputy Prime Minister), Guy Spitaels (as minister-president of Wallonia) and Guy Mathot (as interior minister of Wallonia), although all three denied any impropriety and the main focus of investigations was on the SP rather than the PS. In European Parliament elections in June 1994, the PS vote share slipped to 11.3% (from 14.5% in 1989 and 13.6% in the 1991 national balloting), so that it won only three of the 25 Belgian seats.

The May 1995 elections demonstrated the party's resilience, the PS winning 21 out of 150 seats on an 11.9% vote share and remaining a member of the federal centre-left coalition headed by the →Christian People's Party. In simultaneous regional elections the PS remained by far the strongest party in Wallonia, taking 30 of the 75 regional council seats with a 35.2% vote share, so that the party retained the leadership of the regional government. In the Brussels region the PS won 21.4% and 17 seats out of 75, enabling Charles Picqué of the PS to remain head of government in charge of a six-party administration.

Corruption allegations continued to dog the PS in the late 1990s, the party's headquarters being raided by the police in January 1997 after new evidence had emerged about financial contributions in return for government contracts. Having resigned as president of the Walloon regional assembly in February, Spitaels was indicted the following month on charges arising from the affair (which he denied). His trial and that of other PS and SP figures opened in September 1998 and resulted in December 1998 in all being found guilty and given suspended prison sentences.

The PS shared in the ruling coalition's general unpopularity in the June 1999 elections, being reduced to 19 seats in the federal Chamber (with 10.1% of the vote), to 25 seats in the Walloon regional council (with 29.5%) and to 13 seats on the Brussels regional council (with 16.0%). In simultaneous European Parliament elections the PS retained three seats but its vote share slipped to 9.6%. In July 1999 the PS entered a new federal coalition, this time headed by the →Flemish Liberals and Democrats and also including the two Green parties. The party also retained the leadership of the Walloon regional government, with Elio Di Rupo as minister-president.

The PS is a full member party of the Socialist International. Its three European Parliament representatives sit in the Party of European Socialists group.

Socialist Party
Socialistische Partij (SP)

Address. Keizerslaan 13, B-1000 Brussels
Telephone. (+32–2) 552-0293
Fax. (+32–2) 552-0255
Email. info@sp.be
Website. http://www.sp.be
Leadership. Patrick Janssens (chair); Dirk Van Der Maelen (chair in federal Chamber); Linda Blomme (national secretary)

As the Flemish section of the post-war Belgian Socialist Party, the SP had its origins in the *Belgische Werklieden Partij* founded in October 1885 as the Flemish wing of the Belgian Labour Party; it became an autonomous party on the formal separation of the two Socialist wings in October 1978. Before and subsequently it participated in all the central coalition governments of which the Walloon PS was a member (see previous entry). Having formally renounced Marxism and class struggle in 1980, the SP became more "social democratic" in orientation than its Walloon counterpart, distancing itself in particular from the pro-nationalization line of the latter. For long the weaker of the two parties electorally, the SP maintained its Chamber representation at 32 seats out of 212 in December 1987 but fell back to 28 seats in November 1991. In the June 1994 European Parliament elections the SP retained three Belgian seats but its vote share slipped to 10.8%, from 12.4% in the 1989 Euro-elections and 12.0% in the 1991 national poll. Following the appointment of Willy Claes (then SP Deputy Premier and Foreign Minister) to the post of NATO secretary-general in October 1994, Frank Vandenbroucke replaced him in the government and was succeeded as SP chair by Louis Tobback, hitherto Interior Minister. In March 1995 Vandenbroucke became the most senior casualty to date of the Agusta bribery scandal, resigning from the government after admitting that in 1991 he knew that the party held a large sum of undeclared money in a bank safe deposit. Also implicated was Claes, who as Economic Affairs Minister in 1988 had been closely involved in the helicopter contract at the centre of the bribery allegations. Despite these difficulties, the SP advanced to 12.6% in the May 1995 general elections (ahead of the Walloon Socialists), winning 20 of the 150 Chamber seats. In the simultaneous regional polling, it took 25 of the 118 Flemish council seats (with a 19.4% vote share) and continued to participate in the Flanders government, while winning two seats on the Brussels regional council (with 2.4%)

In October 1995 Claes was obliged to resign his NATO post when the Belgian parliament voted in favour of his being brought to trial. Court proceedings opened in September 1998 and resulted in December in Claes and 12 other defendants being found guilty of corruption and given suspended prison sentences. Claes said that he would appeal to the European Court of Human Rights.

The SP shared in the ruling coalition's general unpopularity in the June 1999 elections, being reduced to 14 seats in the federal Chamber (with 9.6% of the vote) and to 19 seats in the Flemish regional council (with 15.0%), which retaining two seats on the Brussels regional council on a joint list with →Live Differently (AGALEV) which took 3.1% of the vote. In simultaneous European Parliament elections the SP lost one of its three seats on a reduced vote share of 8.8%. In July 1999 the SP entered a new federal coalition, this time headed by the →Flemish Liberals and Democrats and also including the two Green parties. The party also provided the new minister-president of the German-speaking community (Karl-Heinz Lambertz), having won four of the 25 council seats with a 15.0% vote share.

Claiming a membership of 76,000, the PS is a full member party of the Socialist International. Its two European Parliament representatives sit in the Party of European Socialists group.

Other Parties

Many minor parties contested the June 1999 elections at federal, regional or European level, most of them failing to achieve 0.1% of the respective vote totals. The following list focuses on the better-supported groupings in this category but is not exhaustive.

Alive (*Vivant*), led by Dirk Vangossum, French-speaking formation urging abolition of taxes and social charges on the workplace and a big increase in VAT to compensate; won 130,703 votes (2.1%) in 1999 federal Chamber elections (but no seats) and one seat on Brussels regional council (with 1.5%). *Address.* Blvd du Midi 25-27, 4ème étage, B-1000 Brussels; *Telephone.* (+32-2) 513-0888; *Fax.* (+32-2) 502-0107; *Email.* cadministratie@vivant.be; *Website.* http://www.vivant.be

Christian Liberal Party (*Parti Libéral Chrétien/Partij der Liberale Christenen*, PLC), also called the Party of the Liberty of the Citizen, led by Luc Eykerman and Paul Moors. *Address.* Ave de Scheut 46, B-1070 Brussels; *Telephone.* (+32-2) 524-3966; *Fax.* (+32-2) 521-6071

Christian Social Party (*Christlisch Soziale Partei*, CSP), led by Mathieu Grosch, the Christian Social party of Belgium's small German-speaking minority, secured one seat in the 1994 and 1999 European Parliament elections (with only 0.2% of the overall vote), on the ticket of the (Flemish) →Christian People's Party; the CSP MEP sits in the European People's Party/European Democrats group.

Citizens' Movement for Change (*Mouvement des Citoyens pour le Changement*, MCC), led by Nathalie de T'serclaes, founded in 1998 by Gérard Deprez on the strength of public outrage at official mishandling of the Dutroux paedophile controversy; allied with →Liberal Reformist Party and →Democratic Front of French-Speakers in the 1999 national, regional and European elections, it secured four representatives in the various assemblies, Deprez being elected to the European Parliament and chosing to join the European People's Party/European Democrats group. *Address.* Ave Générale de Gaulle 40, B-1050 Brussels; *Telephone.* (+32-2) 640-4047; *Fax.* (+32-2) 640-0241; *Email.* info@lemcc.be; *Website.* http://www.lemcc.be/mcc

Communist Party (*Parti Communiste,* PC), led by Pierre Beauvois, French-speaking formation (autonomous since 1992) descended from the historic Belgian Communist Party (PCB/KPB) founded in 1921, powerful after World War II on a pro-Soviet tack but in decline since the mid-1950s, unrepresented in the Chamber since 1985, has renounced Marxism-Leninism in favour of socialist democracy. *Address.* Rue Rouppe 4, B-1000 Brussels; *Telephone.* (+32-2) 548-0290; *Fax.* (+32-2) 548-0295

Communist Party (*Parti Kommunistische*, KP), Flemish formation (autonomous since 1992) descended from the historic Belgian Communist Party (PCB/KPB) founded in 1921 (see previous entry). *Address.* Galgenberg 29, B-9000 Ghent; *Telephone.* (+32-9) 225-4584; *Fax.* (+32-9) 233-5678; *Email.* kp@democratisch-links.be; *Website.* http://www.democratisch-links.be

Complete Democracy for the 21st Century (*Integrale Democratie voor de 21ste Eeuw*, ID21), right-wing Flemish grouping, contested June 1999 Flemish council and European elections on joint list with →People's Union (*Volksunie*). *Address.* Noordstraat 80, B-1000 Brussels, *Telephone.* (+32-2) 223-3933; *Fax.* (+32-2) 223-3934; *Email.* info@id21.be; *Website.* http://www.id21.be

Democratic Right (*Droite Démocratique*, DD), radical right-wing formation led by Christian Galloy. *Address.* Ave des Bécassines 29, B-1160 Brussels; *Telephone/Fax.* (+32-2) 675-8274; *Website.* http://users.skynet.be/dd

Humanist Feminist Party (*Humanistische Feministische Partij/Parti Féministe Humaniste*, HFP/PFH), originally founded in 1972, adopted its present name in 1990, seeking to promote women's rights and female representation in elected bodies. *Address.* Ave des Phalènes 35, B-1050 Brussels

Natural Law Party (*Natuurwetpartij*, NWP), led by Bart Sarazijn and Leopold Fransen, Belgian branch of the well-funded worldwide network of such parties advocating the teachings of Indian guru Maharishi. *Address.* Meeuwerkiesel 51, B-3960 Bree; *Telephone & Fax.* (+32-89) 461-919; *Email.* nwp@skynet.be; *Website*: http://users.skynet.be/nwp

New Front of Belgium (*Front Nouveau de Belgique/Front Nieuw België*, FNB), a "democratic nationalist party" led by Marguerite Bastien, founded in 1997; won one seat on Brussels regional council in June 1999 with 1.3% of the vote, but only 0.4% in federal Chamber elections and 0.6% in Walloon regional council elections (and no seats). *Address.* Rue de la Cambre 336, B-1200 Brussels; *Telephone/Fax.* (+32-2) 770-8866; *Website.* http://www.fnb.to

Party of Belgian German-Speakers (*Partei der Deutschsprachigen Belgier*, PDB), led by Guido Breuer, founded in 1971 to campaign for equal rights for the German-speaking minority; won three seats in 1999 elections for German-speaking community council. *Address.* Kaperberg 6, B-4700 Eupen; *Telephone.* (+32-87) 555-987; *Fax.* (+32-87) 555-984; *Email.* guido.breuer@skynet.be; *Website.* http://users.skynet.be/pdb

Radical Reformist Fighters in the Struggle for an Honest Society (*Radikale Omvormers Strijders en Strubbelaars voor een Eerlijke Maatschappij*, ROSSEM**),** formed prior to the 1991 Chamber elections by Jean-Pierre van Rossem, this populist/alternative formation compiled its full title so that its acronym would be the same as the last name of its founder and leader, a wealthy anarchist. Despite the arrest of the latter on fraud charges shortly before polling, the so-called ROSSEM List took three Chamber seats, with 3.2% of the vote. A five-year prison sentence passed on van Rossem in February 1995 could not be carried out because he was covered by parliamentary immunity. The party did not contest the 1995 or 1999 Chamber elections. *Address.* Petunialaan 2, B-8301 Knokke-Heist

Social-Liberal Democrats (*Sociaal-Liberale Democraten*, SoLiDe), led by Anouk Sinjan, Flemish-based centre-left party, won 0.1% of the vote in 1999 federal Chamber elections. *Address.* Th. Donnéstraat 59, B-3540 Herk-de-Stad; *Telephone.* (+32-13) 441-483; *Fax.* (+32-13) 461-902; *Email.* solide@ping.be; *Website.* http://www.ping/be/solide

Walloon Party (*Parti Wallon*, PW), left-wing nationalist party advocating a socialist Wallonia, founded in 1985 as a merger of the *Rassemblement Wallon* (RW) and other radical

Walloon groups under the leadership of Jean-Claude Piccin. Founded in 1968, the RW had participated in a coalition government with the Christian Socials and Liberals in 1974–77, helping to secure the passage of the Egmont Pact on devolution; but it had been weakened by defections of moderates to what became the →Liberal Reformist Party. Whereas the RW won two Chamber seats in the 1981 elections on a joint list with the →Democratic Front of French-Speakers, in 1985 the PW failed to gain representation and was no more successful in subsequent electoral contests, winning only 0.2% in the 1999 federal Chamber elections. *Address.* Rue du Faubourg 14, B-1430 Quenast; *Telephone.* (+32-67) 670-019

Workers' Party of Belgium (*Partij van de Arbeid van België/Parti du Travail de Belgique*, PvdA/PTB), led by Nadine Rosa-Rosso, founded in 1979 in opposition to the reformism of the →Communist Party, part of the All Power to the Workers (*Alle Macht Aan de Arbeiders*, AMADA) movement in the 1979 Euro-elections, unsuccessful then and subsequently in securing representation; won 0.5% of the vote in the 1995 and 1999 federal Chamber elections. *Address.* Lemonnierlaan 171/2, B-1000 Brussels; *Telephone.* (+32-2) 513-7760; *Fax.* (+32-2) 513-9831; *Email.* ptb@ptb.be; *Website.* http://www.wpb.be

Denmark

Capital: Copenhagen   **Population:** 5,250,000

Under its 1953 constitution the Kingdom of Denmark is a democratic, multi-party constitutional monarchy in which legislative power is vested in the unicameral *Folketing*, whose members are elected under a highly complex proportional system for a four-year term (subject to dissolution) by universal suffrage of those aged 18 years and above. Of the 179 *Folketing* members, 135 are elected by proportional

Elections for the 175 metropolitan *Folketing* seats on March 11, 1998, resulted as follows:

	Seats 1998 (1994)	Percentage 1998 (1994)
Social Democratic Party	63 (62)	35.9 (34.6)
Liberal Party (*Venstre*)	42 (42)	24.0 (23.3)
Conservative People's Party	16 (27)	8.9 (15.0)
Socialist People's Party	13 (13)	7.6 (7.3)
Danish People's Party	13 (–)	7.4 (–)
Centre Democrats	8 (5)	4.3 (2.8)
Radical Liberal Party	7 (8)	3.9 (4.6)
Red–Green Unity List	5 (6)	2.7 (3.1)
Christian People's Party	4 (0)	2.5 (1.9)
Progress Party	4 (11)	2.4 (6.4)
Others	0 (1)	0.1 (1.0)

One of the two deputies elected from the Faroes joined the Conservative People's group and the other was a Faroese Social Democrat who remained independent; of the two Greenland deputies, one joined the Social Democratic group and the other the Liberal (*Venstre*) group.

21

representation in 17 metropolitan districts, with 40 additional seats being divided to achieve overall proportionality among parties that have secured at least 2 percent of the vote nationally. In addition, the Faroe Islands and Greenland are allotted two representatives each (see separate sections below). Denmark joined what became the European Union on Jan. 1, 1973, and elects 16 representatives to the European Parliament.

Under legislation enacted in December 1986, state funding is available (a) to parties represented in the *Folketing* in approximate proportion to their number of members, and (b) to party organizations and independent candidates contesting national, regional or local elections on the basis of the number of votes received in the previous election (subject to a minimum requirement of 1,000 votes). Parties must not use income from one category of subsidy for expenditure in the other. The total amount available in 1998 was DKr165.9 million (about $26 million), of which DKr94.2 million was for parliamentary groups and DKr71.7 million for party organizations. As the largest formation, the Social Democratic Party received a total of DKr47.5 million (about $7.5 million), DKr23.9 million for its parliamentary group and DKr23.6 million for its party organization.

Centre Democrats
Centrum-Demokraterne (CD)
Address. **Ny** Vestergade 7, DK-1471 Copenhagen K
Telephone. (#45-33) 127-115
Fax. (#45-33) 120-115
Email. cd@online.pol.dk
Website. http://www.centrumdemokraterne.dk
Leadership. Mimi Stilling Jakobsen (chair); Peter Duetoft (parliamentary group chair); Yvonne Herløv Andersen (secretary-general)

The CD was established in November 1973 by right-wing dissidents of the →Social Democratic Party (SD) led by Erhard Jakobsen, who objected to the "increasingly leftist course" of the then SD government, particularly its plans for increased taxation. Favouring a mixed economy and rejecting "socialist experiments", the new party won 13 seats and 7.8% of the vote in the December 1973 elections, but fell back to three seats and 2.2% in 1975. Recovery in 1977 to 10 seats and 6.4% was followed by a further setback in the 1979 elections, in which the CD tally was six seats and 3.2%. The 1981 contest yielded the CD's best result to date (15 seats and 8.3%), with the result that in September 1982 the party entered a four-party non-socialist coalition headed by the 13Conservative People's Party (KFP). Cut back to eight seats and 4.6% in 1984, the CD was the only coalition party to gain in the 1987 elections (to nine seats and 4.8%); it almost held its ground in the 1988 contest (nine seats and 4.7% vote) but went into opposition to a three-party coalition headed by the KFP. Under the new leadership of Mimi Jakobsen (a former Social Affairs Minister), the CD retained nine seats in the 1990 elections (with 5.1% of the vote).

Following the resignation of the centre-right coalition in January 1993, the CD joined a four-party centre-left administration headed by the SD. Strongly pro-European, the CD was a party to the "national compromise" which secured referendum approval of the Maastricht Treaty at the second attempt in May 1993. In the June 1994 European Parliament elections, the CD slumped to 0.9% and lost its two existing seats. It partially recovered to 2.8% and five seats in the September 1994 national elections, joining a three-party centre-left coalition again headed by the SD.

The CD withdrew from the ruling coalition in December 1996 in protest against a deal reached by the SD with the →Socialist People's Party and the →Red–Green Unity List in order to secure passage of the 1997 budget. Although it continued to give general external support to the government, in the March 1998 general election it lined up with the centre-right opposition and advanced to eight seats and a 4.3% vote share. It remained in opposition, while giving strong backing to the government's successful advocacy of a "yes" vote in the May 1998 referendum on the EU's Amsterdam Treaty. The CD again failed to win representation in the June 1999 elections to the European Parliament.

Christian People's Party
Kristeligt Folkeparti (KrFP)
Address. Allegade 24A/1, DK-2000 Frederiksberg
Telephone. (#45-33) 277-810
Fax. (#45-33) 213-116
Email. krf@krf.dk
Website. http://www.krf.dk
Leadership. Jann Sjursen (leader and parliamentary group chair); Ib Algot Nielsen (secretary-general)
The KrFP was founded in April 1970 as an inter-denominational formation of Christian groups opposed to abortion on demand, pornography and the permissive society in general. The party achieved representation in the *Folketing* for the first time in 1973, winning seven seats and 4.0% of the vote. It advanced to nine seats and 5.3% in 1975 but lost ground in subsequent elections, taking only four seats and 2.3% in 1981. In September 1982 it was allocated two portfolios in a centre-right coalition headed by the →Conservative People's Party (KFP), but left the government after the 1988 elections, in which it just attained the 2% minimum required for representation and retained four seats. It again won four seats in the 1990 contest (on a 2.3% vote share) and in January 1993 was allocated two portfolios in a centre-left coalition headed by the →Social Democratic Party.

The KrFP slipped to 1.1% in the June 1994 European Parliament elections (insufficient for representation) and took only 1.8% in the September 1994 national elections, thus exiting from both the *Folketing* and the government. The party recovered to 2.5% in the March 1998 general election, enough to re-enter the *Folketing* with four seats.

Claiming a membership of 6,500, the KrFP is affiliated to the Christian Democrat International and the European People's Party.

Conservative People's Party
Konservative Folkeparti (KFP)
Address. Nyhavn 4, Postboks 1515, DK-1020 Copenhagen K
Telephone. (#45-33) 134-140
Fax. (#45-33) 933-773
Email. konservative@konservative.dk
Website. http://www.konservative.dk
Leadership. Bendt Bendtsen (leader and parliamentary group chair); Poul Andreassen (chair); Jan Høgskilde (secretary-general)
The KFP was founded in February 1916 by progressive elements of the old *Hoejre* (Right) grouping that had been represented in the *Folketing* since 1849 but had lost its traditional dominance with the rise of the →Liberal Party (*Venstre*) and the →Social Democratic Party (SD). The new party abandoned the reactionary stance of the old *Hoejre*, adopting a programme featuring support for proportional representation and social reform. It provided parliamentary support for three *Venstre* governments in the 1920s but was in opposition from

1929 until joining a national unity coalition during World War II. After the war it maintained its pre-war electoral strength of 16-20% in most elections up to 1971 before falling to under 10% in the 1970s (and to a low of 5.5% and only 10 seats in 1975). It was in opposition to centre-left coalitions or minority SD governments for most of the period to 1982, the exceptional years being 1950-53, when it governed with the *Venstre*, and 1968-71, when it was in coalition with the →Radical Liberal Party (RV) and the *Venstre*. The KFP strongly backed Denmark's entry into the European Community in 1973 and also remained a staunch supporter of Danish membership of NATO.

Under the leadership of Poul Schlüter, the KFP recovered to 12.5% and 22 seats at the 1979 elections and to 14.5% and 26 seats in 1981, with the result that in September 1982 Schlüter became the first Conservative Prime Minister since 1901, heading a four-party centre-right coalition with the *Venstre*, the →Centre Democrats (CD) and the →Christian People's Party. Committed to reducing the role of the state, the Schlüter government was to remain in office for more than a decade, albeit with changes in its party composition in 1988 and 1990. A further KFP advance to a high of 23.4% and 42 seats in 1984 was followed by a decline to 20.8% and 38 seats in 1987 and to 19.3% and 35 seats in the 1988 snap elections, called by Schlüter after the government had been defeated on an opposition motion that visiting warships should be informed of Denmark's nuclear weapons ban. He was nevertheless able to form a new minority government, this time consisting of the KFP, the *Venstre* and the RV. The KFP fell back to 16.0% and 30 in the December 1990 elections, after which Schlüter was obliged to form a minority two-party coalition with the *Venstre* because the other centre-right parties declined to participate. In June 1992 the government was severely embarrassed when Danish voters disregarded its advice by narrowly rejecting the Maastricht Treaty on European Union.

The KFP participated in the seven-party "national compromise" of October 1992 establishing the terms of joint support for the Maastricht Treaty in a further referendum. Before it could be held, the "Tamilgate" scandal, relating to the exclusion of relatives of Tamil refugees in the late 1980s, unexpectedly brought about the downfall of the Schlüter government in January 1993 and the installation of a majority coalition (the first since 1971) headed by the SD. In opposition, the KFP in September 1993 elected Hans Engell, a former Defence and Justice Minister, to succeed Schlüter as party chair. The party won 17.7% of the vote in the June 1994 European balloting, increasing its representation from two to three seats. It slipped to 15.0% percent and 27 seats in the September 1994 national elections, remaining in opposition.

Engell was obliged to resign as KFP chair in February 1997 after being involved in a car accident and being found to be over the legal alcohol limit; he was replaced by Per Stig Møller (a former Environment Minister). The March 1998 general election resulted in a major setback for the party, which declined to 8.9% of the vote and 16 seats, losing votes to the new →Danish People's Party in particular. Møller was subsequently succeeded as party leader by Bendt Bendtsen. In the June 1999 European Parliament elections the KFP lost two of its three seats, winning only 8.6% of the vote.

Claiming a membership of 25,000, the KFP is a member of the International Democrat Union and the European Democrat Union. Its European Parliament representative sits in the European People's Party/European Democrats group.

Danish People's Party
Dansk Folkeparti (DF)
Address. Christiansborg, DK-1240 Copenhagen K
Telephone. (+45-33) 375-199
Fax. (+45-33) 375-191

Email. df@df.dk

Website. http://www.danskfolkeparti.dk

Leadership. Pia Kjærsgaard (chair); Kristian Thulesen Dahl (parliamentary group chair); Steen Thomsen (secretary-general)

The DF was launched in October 1995 by four disaffected deputies of the right-wing →Progress Party (FP), including Pia Kjærsgaard, who had been ousted as FP leader earlier in the year. The DF espoused the same policies as the FP but was regarded as being to the right of the parent party. Its overall objective is "to re-establish Denmark's independence and freedom to ensure the survival of the Danish nation and the Danish monarchy"; it opposes in particular the development of Denmark into a multi-ethnic society through immigration. It is also opposed to membership of the European Union (EU), arguing that European cooperation should be limited to free trade and protection of common natural assets.

After winning 6.8% of the vote in the November 1997 local elections, in its first general election in March 1998 the DF easily outpolled the rump FP, winning 13 seats with a 7.4% vote share. It unsuccessfully opposed approval of the EU's Amsterdam Treaty in the May 1998 referendum, taking some comfort from the size (44.9%) of the "no" vote. In the June 1999 European Parliament elections the DF won 5.8% of the vote and one of Denmark's 16 seats.

The party's official membership is 3,664. Its representative in the European Parliament sits in the Union for a Europe of Nations group.

Liberal Party
Venstre (V)

Address. Søllerødvej 30, DK-2840 Holte

Telephone. (#45-45) 802-233

Fax. (#45-45) 803-830

Email. venstre@venstre.dk

Website. http://www.venstre.dk

Leadership. Anders Fogh Rasmussen (leader and parliamentary group chair); Claus Hjort Frederiksen (secretary-general)

The *Venstre* (literally "Left", although the party has long opted for the rubric "Liberal") was founded in June 1870 as Denmark's first organized party, derived from the Friends of the Peasants (*Bondevennerne*) and drawing its main support from small independent farmers (and later from sections of the urban middle class) opposed to the conservatism and political hegemony of the old *Hoejre* (Right), forerunner of the present-day →Conservative People's Party (KFP). It became dominant in the then lower house by the 1880s but remained in opposition due to *Hoejre* control of the upper house. In 1901, however, what was then called the *Venstre* Reform Party formed a majority government under Johan Henrik Deuntzer, who was succeeded as Prime Minister by Jens Christian Christensen in 1905. The party was weakened in the latter year by the formation of the breakaway →Radical Liberal Party (RV) but recovered partially in 1910 when it reunited with the small Moderate *Venstre* faction under the simple title *Venstre*. The party remained dominant until the 1924 elections, when it was replaced as Denmark's leading political formation by the →Social Democratic Party (SD), although it was again in power in 1926-29.

In opposition through the 1930s, *Venstre* experienced electoral decline, to 17.8% of the vote in 1935 compared with a high of 47.9% in 1903. After participating in the World War II national unity government, it rose to 23.4% in 1945 and formed a minority government under Knut Kristensen. Despite improving to 28.0% in 1947, *Venstre* went into opposition until 1950, when it formed a coalition with the KFP under the premiership of Erik Eriksen, who oversaw the introduction of the 1953 constitution. It then remained in opposition for 15 years, during which it support declined from 25.1% in 1957 to 18.5% in 1968, when it entered a centre-right coalition with the RV and KFP. This coalition lasted until 1971, but the watershed December 1973 elections, yielding fragmentation of the party structure (and only 22 seats for the *Venstre* on a 12.3% vote share), resulted in a highly minority *Venstre* government under Poul Hartling. Despite almost doubling its support to 23.3% and 42 seats in 1975, the *Venstre* went into opposition and slumped to 12.0% and 21 seats at the 1977 elections.

In August 1978 the *Venstre* entered its first-ever formal peace-time coalition with the SD, but this collapsed a year later, precipitating elections in which the *Venstre* obtained 12.5% and 22 seats. Having slipped to 11.3% and 21 seats in the 1981 elections, in September 1982 it joined a four-party centre-right government headed by Poul Schlüter of the KFP and also including the →Centre Democrats (CD) and the →Christian People's Party (KrFP). The KFP/*Venstre* tandem was to survive for over a decade, creating an all-time longevity record for a non-socialist government, although the CD and KrFP were replaced by the RV in 1998-90, after which the KFP and the *Venstre* formed a two-party coalition that lasted until January 1993. During this period *Venstre* electoral support improved to 12.1% and 22 seats in 1984, slipped to 10.5% and 19 seats in 1987, rose to 11.8% and 22 seats in 1988 and rose again to 15.8% and 29 seats in 1990.

As a pro-European party, the *Venstre* shared in the Schlüter government's embarrassment over the electorate's rejection of the EU's Maastricht Treaty in June 1992. In October 1992 it participated in the seven-party "national compromise" establishing the terms of joint support for the treaty in a second referendum. Before it was held, the Schlüter government resigned in January 1993 over the "Tamilgate" affair, so that the *Venstre* returned to opposition. Under the new leadership of Uffe Ellemann-Jensen (former Foreign Minister), the party headed the poll in the June 1994 European Parliament elections, winning 19.0% and four of Denmark's 16 seats. In September 1994 it was the principal victor in general elections, receiving its highest vote share (23.3%) for two decades and 42 seats. During the campaign Ellemann-Jensen controversially proposed the formation of a centre-right coalition that would for the first time include the populist →Progress Party. In the event, the party continued in opposition to another SD-led government.

Venstre repeated its 1994 success in the March 1998 national elections, again winning 42 seats with a slightly higher vote share of 24.0%. It remained in opposition, while giving strong backing to the SD-led government's successful advocacy of a "yes" vote in the May 1998 referendum on the EU's Amsterdam Treaty. In the June 1999 European Parliament elections *Venstre* headed the poll with 23.3%, increasing its representation from four to five seats.

Claiming a membership of some 84,000, the *Venstre* is a member party of the Liberal International. Its representatives in the European Parliament sit in the European Liberal, Democratic and Reformist group.

Progress Party
Fremskridtspartiet (FP)
Address. Christiansborg, DK-1240 Copenhagen K
Telephone. (#45-33) 374-699
Fax. (#45-33) 151-399
Email. fp@ft.dk
Website. http://www.frp.dk
Leadership. Per Larsen (chair); Martin Ipsen (secretary-general)
The FP was launched in August 1972 by Mogens Glistrup, a tax lawyer, who advocated the abolition of income tax, the dismissal of most civil servants and a major reduction of the state's role in the economy. The resultant increase in consumer demand would, he envisaged, yield more revenue from value-added tax (VAT), sufficient to cover drastically reduced

government expenditure. More idiosyncratically, he also urged the abolition of Denmark's defence forces and the replacement of the Defence Ministry by a telephone answering machine giving the message "we surrender" in Russian. The party caught a populist tide in the watershed 1973 general elections, contributing to the fragmentation of the party system by winning 28 seats and 15.9% of the vote, so that it became the second strongest party in the *Folketing*. It fell back to 24 seats and 13.6% in 1975, recovered to 26 seats and 14.6% in 1977 and then declined progressively to 20 seats (11.0%) in 1979, 16 seats (8.9%) in 1981 and six seats (3.6%) in 1984.

Meanwhile, Glistrup's parliamentary immunity was regularly suspended so that he could face charges of tax fraud in what turned out to be the longest trial in Danish history. Finally convicted in 1983 and sentenced to three years' imprisonment, he was expelled from the *Folketing*, re-elected in the 1984 elections (on temporary release from prison) and again expelled soon afterwards and returned to prison (from which was released in March 1985). Meanwhile, the FP's slump in the 1984 elections had exacerbated internal party dissension over his leadership style, resulting in the election of a new leadership under Pia Kjærsgaard and the moderation of the FP's more controversial policies. In particular, it now endorsed Denmark's continued membership of NATO and the preservation of the welfare state. On the other hand, it took a strong anti-immigration stance, seeking to articulate growing public concern on the issue.

The FP advanced slightly in the 1987 elections (to nine seats and 4.8%), before becoming the main victor in the 1988 poll (rising to 16 seats and 9.0%). It fell back to 12 seats and 6.4% in the 1990 contest, prior to which Glistrup was expelled from the FP *Folketing* group for indiscipline and subsequently suspended from party membership. The FP was the only parliamentary party that opposed Danish ratification of EU's Maastricht Treaty in both the 1992 and the 1993 referendums, its lack of Euro-enthusiasm producing a slump in its vote to 2.9% in the June 1994 European Parliament elections. It recovered its 1990 share of 6.4% in the September 1994 national elections, although its representation slipped to 11 seats. During the campaign the →Liberal Party leader caused controversy by publicly envisaging the formal inclusion of the FP in a future centre-right coalition.

Internal divisions in the FP in 1995 resulted in the ousting of Pia Kjærsgaard as leader and her replacement by Kirsten Jacobsen, following which a dissident faction including four FP deputies broke away to form the →Danish People's Party (DF). The result was that the FP's vote slumped to 2.4% in the March 1998 general elections and its representation to four seats. In October 1999, however, the four FP deputies, including Jacobsen, resigned from the party after an FP congress had voted for the readmission of Glistrup. The four deputies formed the "Liberty 2000" grouping in the *Folketing*, so that the FP was left without parliamentary representation and was therefore required to re-register with the Interior Ministry if it wished to contest the next general elections.

Radical Liberal Party
Det Radikale Venstre (RV)
Address. Christiansborg, DK-1240 Copenhagen K
Telephone. (#45-33) 374-747
Fax. (#45-33) 137-251
Email. radikale@radikale.dk
Website. http://www.radikale.dk
Leadership. Johannes Lebech (chair); Jørgen Estrup (parliamentary group chair); Anders Kloppenborg (secretary-general)
Preferring to be known in English by the inaccurate title "Social Liberal Party", the RV dates from 1905 as a left-wing splinter group of the historic →Liberal Party (*Venstre*) inspired by

the example of the ⇒Radical Party of France. Its original Odense Programme called for Danish neutrality in war, constitutional reform (including universal adult suffrage), a secret ballot, democratic local elections, provision for referendums on major issues, progressive taxation and land reform. Progress towards these aims was achieved by all-RV governments that held office in 1909-10 and 1913-20 (under the premiership of Carl Theodor Zahle, and more especially by the 1929-40 coalition between the RV and the now dominant →Social Democratic Party (SD). Having participated in the World War II national unity government and the post-war all-party administration, the RV returned to coalition with the SD in 1957-64 (with the →Single-Tax Party participating in 1957-60). During this period the party share of the vote rose from 8.1% in 1945 to 8.6% in 1953 but slipped to 5.3% by 1964, in which year it won only 10 *Folketing* seats out of 175.

Having recovered to 7.3% and 13 seats in 1967, the RV made a major advance in January 1968, to 15.0% and 27 seats, under the leadership of Hilmar Baunsgaard, who became Prime Minister of a non-socialist coalition that also included the *Venstre* and the →Conservative People's Party (KFP). This lasted until 1971, when the RV slipped to a vote share of 14.3% (retaining 27 seats) and went into opposition; the next three elections also yielded major setbacks, to 11.2% and 20 seats in 1973, 7.1% and 13 seats in 1975, and 3.6% and six seats in 1977. Recovering to 5.4% and 10 seats in 1979, the RV slipped to 5.1% and nine seats in 1981 and remained outside the KFP-led centre-right coalition formed in September 1982. It improved to 5.5% and 10 seats in 1984 and to 6.2% and 11 seats in 1987, after which contest RV leader Niels Helveg Petersen rebuffed the SD's attempt to form a centre-left coalition and thereafter gave external support to a further centre-right government.

Having slipped to 5.6% and 10 seats in the 1988 elections, the RV accepted five cabinet posts in a new KFP-led coalition, but withdrew from participation in 1990 over its opposition to the latest austerity budget. In the December 1990 elections it slumped to a post-war low of 3.5% and seven seats, but nevertheless entered the SD-led centre-left coalition formed in January 1993, receiving three portfolios. In the June 1994 European Parliament balloting, the RV was the only government party to increase its vote share, to 8.5% (yielding one of the 16 seats). In the September 1994 national elections it scored 4.6% and increased its seat total to eight, thereafter joining another SD-led coalition that also included the →Centre Democrats (CD).

Following the exit of the CD in December 1996, the RV became the SD's only formal coalition partner. In the March 1998 national elections the RV lost some ground, winning seven seats on a 3.9% vote share. It nevertheless continued as the junior coalition party, receiving four portfolios out of 20 in the new SD-led minority government. In the June 1999 European Parliament elections the RV improved to 9.1% of the vote while again winning one seat.

Claiming a membership of 6,000, the RV is a member party of the Liberal International. Its representative in the European Parliament sits in the European Liberal, Democratic and Reformist group.

Red-Green Unity List
Enhedslisten-de Roed-Groenne (ELRG)
Address. Studiestræde 24, DK-1455 Copenhagen K
Telephone. (#45-33) 933-324
Fax. (#45-33) 320-372
Email. elmepe@ft.dk
Website. http://www.ehhedslisten.dk
Leadership. 21-member collective; Søren Kolstrup (parliamentary group chair); Keld Albrechtsen (secretary)

DENMARK

The ELRG was established in 1989 as an alliance of three parties of leftist and/or environmentalist orientation. Strongly opposed to Danish membership of NATO and the European Community (later Union), it was part of the campaign against Danish ratification of the Maastricht Treaty (successful in Denmark's first referendum in June 1992, but unsuccessful in the second in May 1993). It achieved a breakthrough in the September 1994 general elections, winning 3.1% of the vote and six seats. Thereafter, its external support was important for the survival of the centre-left coalition government headed by the →Social Democratic Party (SD), notably in the passage of the 1997 budget.

The ELRG lost ground in the March 1998 national elections, slipping to 2.7% of the vote and five seats. It continued thereafter to give qualified external support to a new SD-led minority government.

Social Democratic Party
Socialdemokratiet (SD)
Address. Thorvaldsenvej 2, DK-1998 Frederiksberg C
Telephone. (#45-35) 391-522
Fax. (#45-35) 394-030
Email. socialdemokratiet@net.dialog.dk
Website. http://www.socialdemokratiet.dk
Leadership. Poul Nyrup Rasmussen (chair); Ole Stavad, Lene Jensen (deputy chairs); Ole Løvig Simonsen (parliamentary group chair); Willy Stig Andersen (general secretary)
Founded in 1871 to represent the emerging industrial working class, the SD first won seats in the *Folketing* in 1884 and in 1913-20 supported a minority government of the →Radical Liberal Party (RV). It became the strongest parliamentary party (with 55 out of 148 seats) in 1924, in which year it formed its first government under the premiership of Thorvald Stauning. In opposition from 1926, the party returned to government in 1929 under Stauning, who headed a coalition with the RV until the German occupation in May 1940 and thereafter, until his death in May 1942, a national unity government. Having achieved its its highest voting support to date in the 1931 elections (46.1%), the SD was instrumental in the 1930s in introducing advanced welfare state legislation and other social reforms on the Scandinavian model.

The SD continued to be the dominant party after World War II, although it has never won an overall majority and has averaged about a third of the vote in recent elections. Stauning's successor as Prime Minister and SD leader, Vilhelm Buhl, headed the immediate post-war all-party coalition formed in May 1945, but the party lost support in the October 1945 elections and went into opposition. Talks with the Danish Communists on the creation of a broad Labour Party came to nothing. The SD returned to power in November 1947 as a minority government under Hans Hedtoft until his death in January 1955 and then under Hans Christian Hansen. In May 1957 the SD formed a majority coalition with the RV and the →Single-Tax Party, under the premiership of Hansen until his death in February 1960 and then under Viggo Kampmann. After improving to 42.1% and 76 seats in the November 1960 elections (its best post-war result), the party formed a two-party coalition with the RV, under Kampmann until he was succeeded as party leader and Prime Minister by Jens Otto Krag in September 1962.

Krag reverted to a minority SD government after the September 1964 elections (in which the party slipped to 41.9% but retained 76 seats); however, after losing ground in the next two elections, the party was in opposition from January 1968 until, following SD gains in the September 1971 elections (to 37.3% and 70 seats), Krag was able to form a new minority government the following month. Immediately after the October 1972 referendum decision in favour of European Community membership, Krag unexpectedly resigned in January 1973

29

and was succeeded by trade union leader Anker Jørgensen. Later that year the SD was weakened by the formation of the →Centre Democrats by a right-wing splinter group which claimed that the party was moving too far to the left. Heavy SD losses in the December 1973 elections (to 25.6% and 46 seats, its worst result in half a century) sent the party into opposition; but a partial recovery in the January 1975 contest (to 30.0% and 53 seats) resulted in an SD minority government under Jørgensen. Following a further SD recovery in the February 1977 elections (to 37.0% and 65 seats), Jørgensen in August 1978 negotiated the SD's first-ever formal coalition with the *Venstre* Liberals in peace-time. However, after another SD advance in the September 1979 elections (to 38.3% and 68 seats), Jørgensen formed an SD minority government.

The SD suffered a setback in the 1981 elections, falling to 59 seats and 32.9% of the vote. It nevertheless remained in office until September 1982, when Jørgensen resigned and was replaced by Denmark's first Prime Minister from the →Conservative People's Party since 1901. The SD lost further ground at the January 1984 and September 1987 elections (to 56 seats and 31.6%, then to 54 seats and 29.3%), by which time the party had experienced its longest period of opposition since the 1920s. After unsuccessfully seeking to form a coalition with the RV and the →Socialist People's Party (SFPP), Jørgensen resigned as SD chair after the 1987 elections and was succeeded (in November 1987) by Svend Auken. But a lacklustre SD performance in further elections in May 1988 (in which it slipped to 55 seats and 29.9%) kept the party in opposition. It improved sharply at the next contest in December 1990 (to 69 seats and 37.4%), but remained in opposition, with the eventual result that in April 1992 Auken was replaced as party chair by Poul Nyrup Rasmussen. Two months later the SD shared in the general embarrassment of the pro-European government parties when Danish voters narrowly rejected the Maastricht Treaty of the European Union (EU).

The SD participated in the seven-party "national compromise" of October 1992 establishing the terms of joint support for the Maastricht Treaty in a further referendum. Before it could be held, the "Tamilgate" scandal unexpectedly brought about the downfall of the centre-right coalition in January 1993 and the installation of a majority coalition (the first since 1971) headed by the SD and including the RV, the →Centre Democrats (CD) and the →Christian People's Party. The Maastricht Treaty was duly approved at the second time of asking in May 1993, but a significant minority of SD activists and voters remained in the "no" camp. The party's continuing difficulties over the EU were apparent in the June 1994 European Parliament elections, when the SD managed only 15.8% of the vote and three of the 16 Danish seats. In the September 1994 national elections, however, the party recovered to 34.6%, yielding 62 seats and enabling Rasmussen to form a three-party minority coalition with the RV and the CD.

The CD's resignation from the government in December 1996, in protest against an agreement between Rasmussen and the →Socialist People's Party and the →Red–Green Unity List ensuring passage of the 1997 budget, reduced the ruling coalition to two parties. Although it lost ground in the November 1997 local elections, in the March 1998 national elections the SD unexpectedly increased its vote share to 35.9% and its representation to 63 seats. Rasmussen accordingly formed another minority government in coalition with the RV. In the June 1999 European Parliament elections the SD posted its customary poor performance in such contests, again winning only three seats (with a 16.5% vote share). The 1999 annual SD congress in September 1999 called for a debate on whether Denmark should enter the single European currency, Rasmussen responding that the issue would be decided at the 2000 congress.

Claiming a membership of 100,000, the SD is a member party of the Socialist International. Its representatives in the European Parliament sit in the Party of European Socialists group.

Socialist People's Party
Socialistisk Folkeparti (SFP)
Address. Christiansborg, DK-1240 Copenhagen K
Telephone. (#45-33) 374-491
Fax. (#45-33) 147-010
Email. sf@sf.dk
Website. http://www.sf.dk
Leadership. Holger K. Nielsen (chair), Jes Lunde (parliamentary group chair), Ole Hvas Kristiansen (secretary-general)

The SFP was founded in November 1958 by a dissident faction of the →Communist Party of Denmark (DKP) led by former DKP chair Aksel Larsen, following the latter's expulsion from the party for praising Titoism in Yugoslavia and criticizing the Soviet Union's suppression of the 1956 Hungarian Uprising. The new party advocated left-wing socialism independent of the Soviet Union, unilateral disarmament, Nordic co-operation, and opposition to NATO and to Danish accession to the European Community (EC).

The SFP won 11 seats and 6.1% of the vote at its first elections in 1960, fell back slightly in 1964 but advanced to 20 seats and 10.9% in 1966. Apart from the 1971 contest, the next five elections brought a gradual decline for the SFP, to a low of six seats and 3.9% in 1977, in part because of competition from the new →Left Socialists party, founded by SFP dissidents in 1967. In 1972 the SFP took a leading role in the unsuccessful "no" campaign in the Danish referendum on EC entry, acting in this as on other issues as an unofficial left wing of the →Social Democratic Party (SD). During the 1970s the SFP usually gave external support to the SD-led minority governments characteristic of the decade.

The four elections from 1979 yielded an SFP resurgence, to an all-time high of 27 seats and 14.6% in 1987, when it was the only party to make significant gains and became the third-strongest parliamentary party. It remained in opposition to the Schlüter centre-right government and lost ground in the 1988 contest, falling to 24 seats and 13.0% of the vote. SD gains in the 1990 elections further reduced the SFP tally, to 15 seats and 8.3%. The party campaigned on the "no" side in the June 1992 referendum in which Danish voters narrowly rejected the Maastricht Treaty of what became the European Union (EU), although it no longer advocated Denmark's withdrawal. In October 1992, after some agonizing, the KFP joined the seven-party "national compromise" setting new terms for approval of the treaty, which was given by voters at the second time of asking in May 1993.

In June 1994 the SFP won 8.6% of the vote in European Parliament elections, thus retaining the one seat it won in 1989. It declined to 13 seats and 7.3% in the September 1994 general elections, partly because of a rise in support for the new →Red-Green Unity List (ELRG), thereafter pledging conditional support for the reconstituted SD-led coalition. This support proved crucial in 1996 over the passage of the disputed 1997 budget, on the basis of a deal between the SD, the SFP and the ELGR which gave the two non-governmental parties a promise of increased social spending. The SFP again won 13 seats in the March 1998 national elections, with a slightly increased vote share of 7.6%. In the June 1999 European Parliament elections it retained its single seat with 7.1% of the vote.

With an official membership of 8,000, the SFP is a member of the New European Left Forum (NELF). Its European Parliament representative sits in the European United Left/Nordic Green Left group.

Other Parties and Movements

Common Course (*Fælles Kurs*, FK), led by Preben Moeller Hansen (a trade union leader and former Communist), founded in 1986 as a left-wing populist party opposed to immigration,

NATO and the European Community (later Union); won four *Folketing* seats in 1987 but lost them in 1988 and has not been represented since. *Address.* Thoravej 25, DK-2400 Copenhagen NV; *Telephone.* (+45-38) 888-803; *Fax.* (+45-38) 881-465

Communist Party of Denmark (*Danmarks Kommunistiske Parti*, DKP), led by Mogens Høver, founded in 1919 and represented in the *Folketing* from 1932, participated in the immediate post-war coalition government, winning 18 seats in 1945 but declining steadily thereafter to nil in 1960, having been weakened by the formation of the →Socialist People's Party; re-entered the *Folketing* in 1973 with six seats, rising to seven in 1975 and 1977, but unrepresented since 1979. *Address.* Studiesstræde 24/1, DK-1455 Copenhagen K; *Telephone.* (+45-33) 916-644; *Fax.* (+45-33) 320-372

Communist Party of Denmark–Marxist-Leninist (*Danmarks Kommunistiske Parti–Marxister-Leninister*, DKP-ML), Trotskyist formation led by Jørgen Petersen. *Address.* Griffenfeldsgade 26, DK-2200 Copenhagen N; *Telephone.* (+45-31) 356-069; *Fax.* (+45-35) 372-039; *Email.* dkp-ml@dkp-ml.dk; *Website.* http://www.dkp-ml.dk

Danish Centre Party (*Dansk Center Parti*, DCP), led by Per W. Johansson, deceptively named anti-immigration formation established in 1992, advocating a complete embargo on immigration and admittance of refugees. *Address.* PB 150, DK-2880 Bagsværd; *Telephone/Fax.* (+45-44) 972-738; *Email.* dcp@post7.tele.dk; *Website.* http://home7.inet.tele.dk/dcp

Democratic Renewal (*Demokratisk Fornyelse*, DF), electoral alliance of various left-wing and centrist groups opposed to membership of the European Union; won only 0.3% of the vote in 1998 general elections. *Address.* Askevej 16, DK-3630 Jægerspris; *Telephone/Fax.* (+45-47) 500-692; *Email.* dem-forny@image.dk; *Website.* http://www.image.dk/~dem_for

Green Party (*Partiet de Grønne*), sub-titled **Realistic-Ecological Alternative** (*Oekoloisk-Realistik Alternativ*), led by Anders Wamsler and Jean Thierry, founded in 1983, has remained small because of the strong environmentalist current in several mainstream parties and also because of the recent success of the →Red-Green Unity List; affiliated to the European Federation of Green Parties. *Address.* Westend 15 st.th, DK-1661, Copenhagen V; *Telephone.* (+45-33) 253-339; *Email.* groenne@mail.danbbs.dk; *Website.* http://www.groenne.dk

Humanistic Party (*Det Humanistiske Parti*), led by Christian Adamsen, founded in 1984, espousing non-violence. *Address.* Skt Jorgens Allé 7, DK-1615 Copenhagen V; *Telephone.* (+45-31) 247-060

International Socialists (*Internationale Socialister*, IS), Trotskyist formation linked to the International Socialist Tendency. *Address.* PB 5113, DK-8100 Århus; *Telephone.* (+45-86) 193-024; *Email.* soc.revy@vip.cybercity.dk; *Website.* http://soc.revy.homepage.dk

June Movement (*Junibevægelsen*, JB), anti-EU formation led by Jens-Peter Bonde and named after the month of the initial Danish referendum rejection of the Maastricht Treaty; won 15.2% and two seats in the 1994 elections to the European Parliament, improving to 16.1% and three seats in the 1999 contest on a platform of vigorous opposition to any attempt to take Denmark into the single European currency; its MEPs sit in the Europe of Democracies and Diversities group at Strasbourg. *Address.* Skindergade 29/1, DK-1159 Copenhagen K; *Telephone.* (+45-33) 930-046; *Fax.* (+45-33) 930-067; *Email.* juninet@inform-bbs.dk; *Website.* http://www.eusceptic.org/juninet

Left Socialist Party (*Venstresocialisterne*, VS), founded in December 1967 by left-wing dissidents of the →Socialist People's Party (SFP), won four *Folketing* seats in 1968, lost them in 1971, regained them in 1975, reached high point of six seats in 1979, falling to five in 1981 and 1984, but weakened thereafter by factionalism and retro-defections to the SFP; unrepresented in the national parliament since 1987, much of its natural support having switched to the →Red-Green Unity List or other radical groupings. *Address*. Griffenfeldsgade 41, DK-2200 Copenhagen N; *Telephone/Fax*. (+45-31) 350-608; *Email*. vs@venstresocialisterne.dk; *Website*. http://www.venstresocialisterne.dk

Natural Law Party (*Naturlovspartiet*, NLP), Danish component of international network of such parties. *Address*. Vesterbrogade 41D, DK-1620 Copenhagen V; *Telephone*. (+45-70) 251-008; *Fax*. (+45-59) 937-614; *Website*. http://www.naturlovspartiet.dk

Party of the Consciously Workshy, a highly "alternative" party led by the comedian Jacob Haugaard, who in September 1994 was elected to the *Folketing* with a large vote in Jutland on a platform that included support for "a following wind on all cycle paths"; he was not re-elected in 1999.

People's Movement against the European Union (*Folkesbevægelsen mod EF-Unionen*), led by Lis Jensen and Ole Krarup, founded to articulate rank-and-file anti-European feeling in officially pro-European parties, won 18.9% and four seats in the 1989 European Parliament elections, falling to 10.3% and two seats in 1994 (when it faced competition from the →June Movement) and to 7.3% and one seat in 1999; its MEP sits in the Europe of Democracies and Diversities group at Strasbourg. *Address*. Sigurdsgade 39A, DK-2200 Copenhagen N; *Telephone*. (+45-35) 821-800; *Fax*. (+45-35) 821-806; *Email*. katte-ud@post1.tele.dk; *Website*. http://www.inform.dk/sturm/folkenet

Schleswig Party (*Schleswigsche Partei*), led by Peter Bieling, founded in August 1920 following the incorporation of former German northern Schleswig into Denmark; representing the German minority, it had one *Folketing* seat until 1964 and again in 1973-79, latterly in alliance with the →Centre Democrats. *Address*. Vestergade 30, DK-6200 Åbenrå; *Telephone* (+45-74) 623-833; *Fax*. (+45-74) 627-939; *Email*. sp@post6.tele.dk; *Website*. http://www.bdn.dk/sp

Single-Tax Party, also known as the **Justice Party of Denmark** (*Danmarks Retsforbund*), led by Mette Langdal Kristiansen, founded in 1919 to propagate the theories of US economist Henry George, won between two and four *Folketing* seats in 1930s and 1940s, rising to 12 in 1950 but falling unevenly to nil in 1960, following participation in a coalition government headed by the 13Social Democratic Party from 1957; re-entered *Folketing* in 1973 with five seats, lost them all in 1975, won six seats in 1977 and five in 1979, but has been unrepresented since 1981. *Address*. Lyngbyvej 42, DK-2100 Copenhagen Ø; *Telephone*. (+45-39) 204-488; *Fax*. (+45-39) 204-450; *Email*. ref@post5.tele.dk; *Website*. http://www.retsforbundet.dk

Socialist Workers' Party (*Socialistisk Arbejderparti*, SAP), far-left grouping which had made little electoral impact. *Address*. Nørre Allé 11A, PB 547, DK-2200 Copenhagen N; *Telephone*. (+45-31) 397-948; *Fax*. (+45-35) 373-217; *Email*. sap@sap-fi.dk; *Website*. http://www.sap-fi.dk

Danish Dependencies

Faroe Islands

Capital: Tórshavn   **Population:** 46,000

Under the 1993 Danish constitution the Faroe Islands are an internally self-governing part of the Kingdom of Denmark, whose government retains responsibility for their foreign affairs, defence, judiciary and monetary affairs. Executive power is formally vested in the Danish monarch, who is represented in Tórshavn by a High Commissioner, but actual authority for Faroese affairs (including fisheries) is exercised by a government (*Landsstyret* or *Landsstyrid*) headed by a chief minister (*Løgmadur* or *Lagmand*). Legislative authority is vested in a Faroes parliament (*Lagting* or *Løgting*), 27 of whose seats are filled by direct proportional election under universal adult suffrage and up to five more by distribution to party lists under an equalization system. Two representatives from the Faroes are elected to the *Folketing* in Copenhagen in Danish national elections. The Faroe Islands remained outside the European Community (later Union) when Denmark joined in 1973 but later signed a special trade agreement with the grouping.

The March 1998 elections to the Danish *Folketing* in the Faroes resulted in the return of candidates of the People's and Social Democratic parties.

Elections to the *Løgting* on April 30, 1998, resulted as follows:				
	Seats		Percentage	
	1998	*(1994)*	*1998*	*(1994)*
Republican Party	8	(4)	23.8	(13.7)
People's Party	8	(6)	21.3	(16.0)
Social Democratic Party...	7	(5)	21.9	(15.4)
Union Party	6	(8)	18.0	(23.4)
Self-Government Party	2	(2)	7.7	(5.6)
Centre Party	1	(2)	4.1	(5.8)

Centre Party
Midflokkurin (Mfl)
Address. PO Box 3237, 110 Tórshavn
Email. jal@kambsdal.olivant.fo
Leadership. Tordur Niclasen (chair)
The Mfl was founded in 1991 in opposition to the then coalition government of the →Social Democratic and →People's parties. It won two seats out of 32 in the July 1994 election (and continued in opposition) but failed to retain representation in the 1998 polling.

Christian People's Party/Faroes Progressive and Fishing Industry Party
Kristiligi Fólkaflokkurin/Framburds– og Fiskivinnuflokkurin (KF/FFF)
Address. Brekku 5, 700 Klaksvík
Telephone. (+298) 457-580
Fax. (+298) 457-581
Leadership. Rev. Niels Pauli Danielsen (chair)
The KF/FFF was formed prior to the 1978 elections as an alliance of the centrist Progressive Party (which had been in coalition government in 1963-66) and centre-oriented fishing industry elements. Favouring increased self-government for the Faroes, it won two seats in 1978, 1980 and 1984, subsequently entering a centre-left coalition headed by the →Social Democratic Party. It again won two seats in 1988, switching to the resultant centre-right coalition headed by the →People's Party, but withdrawing in June 1989. It retained two seats in the 1990 and 1994 elections, but failed to win representation in 1998, when it took only 2.5% of the vote.

People's Party
Fólkaflokkurin (Fkfl)
Address. Árvegur, PO Box 208, Tórshavn
Email. jal@kambsdal.olivant.fo
Leadership. Óli Breckmann (chair); Anfinn Kallsberg (parliamentary leader)
The moderate conservative and pro-autonomy Fkfl was founded in 1940 as a merger of a right-wing faction of the →Self-Government Party (Sjfl) and the small Commerce Party (*Vinnuflokkur*). It first entered a coalition government in 1950, with the →Union Party (Sbfl) until 1954 and thereafter with the Sjfl until 1958. In 1963–66 its then leader, Jógvan Sundstein, headed a coalition with the →Republican Party (Tjfl), the →Christian People's Party/Progressive and Fishing Industry Party (KF/FFF) and the Sjfl. The party was again in opposition from 1966 to 1974, when it joined a centre-left coalition with the →Social Democratic Party (Jvfl) and the Tjfl, this alliance being continued after the 1978 election. In 1981 it entered a centre-right coalition with Sbfl and the Sjfl, becoming the second strongest parliamentary party in the 1984 elections with seven seats, but nevertheless going into opposition.

The Fkfl became the strongest party, with eight seats, in the 1988 election, after which Sundstein formed a centre-right coalition with the Tjfl, the Sjfl and the KF/FFF. This gave way to a Fkfl/Tjfl/Sbfl governing alliance in mid-1989, but the Fkfl's two new partners withdrew support in October 1990, precipitating an early election the following month in which the Fkfl slipped to seven seats. In January 1991 the party became the junior partner in a coalition with the Jvfl but withdrew in April 1993 over a fisheries policy disagreement. It declined to six seats in the July 1994 election, after which it remained in opposition.

In the April 1998 elections the Fkfl advanced to eight seats with 21.3% of the vote. Accordingly, Anfinn Kallsberg of the Fkfl became prime minister of a coalition which also included the Tjfl and the Sjfl.

The Fkfl again won one of the two Faroes seats in the Danish elections of March 1998, its deputy (Óli Breckmann) joining the metropolitan ⇒Liberal Party (*Venstre*) parliamentary group. The Fkfl is affiliated to the International Democrat Union.

Republican Party
Tjódveldisflokkurin (Tjfl)
Address. Villingadalsvegi, 100 Tórshavn
Telephone. (+298) 314-412
Email. hoh@fl.fo

Leadership. Finnbogi Ísakson (chair)

Its title meaning literally "Party for People's Government", the Tjfl was founded in 1948 as a left-wing party advocating secession from Denmark, citing as justification a 1946 plebiscite in which 48.7% had voted for independence and 47.2% for home rule under Danish sovereignty. Having won two seats in 1950, it improved sharply to six in 1954 and subsequently participated in centre-left coalitions in 1963-66, 1974-80 and 1985-88. It again won six seats in the 1988 election and joined a coalition headed by the →People's Party (Fkfl), but this finally collapsed in October 1990.

The Tjfl fell back to four seats in the November 1990 election and was in opposition until joining a coalition headed by the →Social Democratic Party in April 1993. It again won four seats in the July 1994 election, after which it went into opposition. It returned to government after advancing to eight seats (with 23.8% of the vote) in the April 1998 elections, joining a coalition headed by the Fkfl and also including the →Self-Government Party.

Self-Government Party
Sjálvstýrisflokkurin (Sjfl)

Address. Årvegur, PO Box 208, 110 Tórshavn

Email. spg@post.olivant.fo

Leadership. Helena Dam A. Neystabø (chair)

Also known in English as the Home-Rule Party, the Sjfl was founded in 1906 by the poet Joannes Patursson to campaign for real powers for the Faroes parliament (which then had a consultative role) and the preservation of the Faroese language. Opposing the pro-Danish line of the →Union Party (Sbfl), it won 51.7% of the popular vote in 1916 (but not a parliamentary majority) and 49.8% in 1918, when it obtained an absolute majority of seats for the first (and so far only) time. Following the defection of its left wing to the →Social Democratic Party (Jvfl) in 1928, a right-wing faction broke away in 1940 to join the →People's Party (Fkfl), leaving the rump Sjfl as a centrist party. Having fallen to 16.7% and four seats in 1940, the Sjfl was unrepresented from 1943 to 1946, when it regained two seats in an electoral alliance with the Jvfl.

From the granting of home rule to the Faroes in 1948, the party was a partner in coalition governments in 1948-50 and 1954-75 and was then opposition until until January 1981, when it joined a centre-right coalition with the →Union Party (Sbfl) and the Fkfl. Having slipped to one seat in 1966, the Sjfl recovered to two in 1974 and went up to three in 1980. After losing one seat in the 1984 election (on a slightly higher vote share), it entered a centre-left coalition headed by the Jvfl. After retaining two seats in the November 1988 election, it joined a centre-right coalition headed by the Fkfl but withdrew in June 1989. In early elections in November 1990 it moved back to three seats but remained in opposition until April 1993, when it joined another centre-left coalition.

The Sjfl slipped back to two seats in July 1994 (with 5.6% of the vote) but nevertheless joined a four-party coalition headed by the Sbfl. It continued in government after the April 1998 elections, in which it again won two seats (with 7.7% of the vote), joining a three-party coalition headed by the Fkfl and also including the Tjfl.

Social Democratic Party
Javnadarflokkurin (Jvfl)

Address. Marinargø 3, 188 Hoyvëk

Telephone. (+298) 319-397

Fax. (+298) 319-397

Email. hps@hagstova.fo

Website. http://www.javnadarflokkurin.fo

Leadership. Jóannes Eidesgaard (chair); Eydolvur Dimon (secretary-general)

Its Faroese title meaning "Equality Party", the Jvfl dates from 1925 and first gained representation in 1928, when it was strengthened by the adhesion of a splinter group of the →Self-Government Party (Sjfl). After making a breakthrough to six seats in 1936, it was a member of the first home rule government in 1948-50 and in 1958 became the strongest parliamentary party, winning eight seats out of 30 and forming a coalition with the Sjfl and the Union Party (Sbfl) under the premiership of Peter Mohr Dam. It was to retain a narrow plurality until 1978, although 27.6% was its highest vote share. In opposition from 1962, the Jvfl returned to government in 1966 and was continuously in office until 1980, providing the Prime Minister in 1966-68 and in 1970-80, latterly in the person of Atli Dam. After four years in opposition, the Jvfl again became the largest party in 1984, with eight seats out of 32, enabling Atli Dam to form a centre-left coalition with the Sjfl, the →Republican Party (Tjfl) and the →Christian People's Party/Progressive and Fishing Industry Party (KF/FFF).

A shift to the right in the 1988 election reduced the Jvfl to seven seats and consigned it to opposition. An early election in November 1990 restored the Jvfl to plurality status, with 10 seats, so that in January 1991 Atli Dam formed a two-party coalition with the →People's Party (Fkfl). In April 1993 Atli Dam was succeeded as Jvfl leader and Prime Minister by Marita Petersen, but in October 1993 the Fkfl withdrew from the government and was replaced by the Tjfl and the Sjfl. In the July 1994 election the Jvfl went down to a heavy defeat, winning only five seats (and 15.4% of the vote), partly because of competition from the new →Workers' Front (Vf). It nevertheless joined a new coalition headed by the Sbfl and including the Sjfl and the Vf.

The Jvfl went into opposition after the April 1998 elections, despite increasing its representation to seven seats on a 21.9% vote share. In the previous month's Danish elections, the Jvfl had won one of the two Faroes seats in the metropolitan legislature, although its representative (Jóannes Eidesgaard) did not formally join the Danish ⇒Social Democratic Party group. The party has a membership of 1,800.

Union Party
Sambandsflokkurin (Sbfl)

Address. Aarvegur, PO Box 208, Tórshavn

Email. edmund-j@post.olivant.fo

Leadership. Edmund Jønsen (chair)

The conservative Sbfl was founded in 1906 in support of the maintenance of close relations between the islands and the Danish Crown and therefore in opposition in particular to the →Self-Government Party (Sjfl). It won 62.4% of the vote in its first election in 1906 and 73.3% in 1910, remaining the majority parliamentary party until 1918, when it was overtaken by the Sjfl. It recovered its dominance in the 1920s, but the advent of the →Social Democratic Party (Jvfl) in 1925 heralded increasing fragmentation of the party structure. In 1936 the Sbfl vote dropped sharply to 33.6% and since 1943 the party has never exceeded a 30% share. Following the introduction of home rule in 1948, the Sbfl provided the Faroes' Prime Minister until 1958: Andreas Samuelsen headed a coalition of the Jvfl and the Sjfl in 1948-50, while Kristian Djurhuus led one with the People's Party (Fkfl) in 1950-54 and another with the Fkfl and the Sjfl in 1954-58. It continued in government in 1958-62, but went into opposition after the 1962 election, in which it won only six seats and 20.5% of the vote.

Although it remained at six seats in the 1966 election, it entered a coalition with the Jvfl and the Sjfl that lasted until 1974, with then party leader Pauli Ellefsen holding the premiership in 1968-70. Having slipped to five seats and 19.1% in the 1974 election, the Sbfl won a narrow plurality in 1978 (eight seats and 26.3% of the vote) but remained in opposition.

It retained eight seats on a 23.9% vote share in the 1980 contest, following which Ellefsen formed a coalition with the Fkfl and the Sjfl that lasted until 1984. In the latter year it slipped to seven seats (and 21.2%) and reverted to opposition status, subsequently registering an identical electoral result in 1988. In June 1989 the Sbfl joined a coalition headed by the Fkfl and including the →Republican Party (Tjfl), but this collapsed in October 1990, causing an early election the following month in which the Sbfl won six seats.

After four years in opposition, the Sbfl became the largest party in the July 1994 election, with eight seats, and subsequently formed a coalition with the Jvfl, the Sjfl and the new →Workers' Front under the premiership of Sbfl leader Edmund Jønsen. In the April 1998 polling, the Sbfl fell back to six seats (with 18.0% of the vote) and returned to opposition status.

The Sbfl again won one of the two Faroes seats in the March 1998 Danish elections, its deputy opting to join the ⇒Conservative People's Party parliamentary group in Copenhagen.

Workers' Front
Verkmannafylkingin (Vf)
Address. Årvegur, PO Box 208, 110 Tórshavn
Leadership. Óli Jacobsen (chair)
The Vf was founded in 1994 by left-wing dissidents of the →Social Democratic Party (Jvfl) in alliance with some trade union leaders unhappy with the recent performance of the Jvfl in government. In its first election in July 1994 the Vf won three seats (from 9.5% of the vote) and obtained one portfolio in a coalition government headed by the right-wing →Union Party and also including the Jvfl and the →Self-Government Party. Its government role ended at the April 1998 election, in which it slumped to 0.8% of the vote and no seats.

Greenland

Capital: Nuuk (Godthaab)   **Population:** 56,000

The Arctic island of Greenland is a part of the Kingdom of Denmark but has had internal self-government since May 1979, as approved by referendum in January 1979 by 70.1% of participating voters. Greenland accordingly has its own 31-member parliament (*Landsting*), which is popularly elected by proportional representation, and a government (*Landsstyre*) with responsibility for internal economic and social affairs, while the Danish government retains responsibility for foreign affairs, defence and monetary policy. Greenland entered the European Community (later Union) in 1973 as part of Denmark, but withdrew with effect from Feb. 1, 1985, on the strength of a local referendum decision against membership in February 1982.

Elections to the *Landsting* on Feb. 16, 1999, resulted as follows:				
	Seats		Percentage	
	1999	*(1995)*	*1999*	*(1995)*
Forward (*Siumut*)	11	(12)	35.3	(38.5)
Community Party (*Atassut*)	8	(10)	25.3	(29.7)
Eskimo Brotherhood	7	(6)	22.1	(20.3)
Alliance of Candidates	4	(–)	12.3	(–)
Others	1	(3)	5.0	(11.5)

The March 1998 elections to the Danish *Folketing* in Greenland again resulted in the return of candidates of the *Siumut* and *Atassut* parties.

Alliance of Candidates
Kattusseqatigiit
Kandidatforbundet
Address. c/o Landsting, 3900 Nuuk
Leadership. Anthon Frederiksen (chair)
This pro-business and anti-independence grouping of independents won 12.3% of the vote and four seats (out of 31) in the February 1999 *Landsting* election, following which it formed part of the parliamentary opposition.

Centre Party
Akulliit Partiiat (AP)
Address. PO Box 456, 3900 Nuuk
Leadership. Bjarne Kreutzmann (chair)
The liberal pro-market AP was formed prior to the 1991 Greenland election, in which it won two seats in the *Landsting*. It retained two seats in the March 1995 election and remained in opposition. It failed to gain representation in the February 1999 election.

Community Party
Atassut
Address. PO Box 399, 3900 Nuuk
Telephone. (+299) 323-366
Fax. (+299) 325-840
Email. rudo@greennet.gl
Website. http://www.atassut.gl
Leadership. Daniel Skifte (chair); Otto Steenholdt (political vice-chair); Erik H.K. Heilmann (organization vice-chair); Godmann Filemonsen (secretary)
Describing itself as "Greenland's liberal party", the centrist *Atassut* was founded in 1978 and achieved official status as a political party in 1981 under the leadership of Lars Chemnitz, who was chair of the pre-autonomy Greenland council. In the April 1979 election preceding the move to autonomy it was defeated by the →Forward (*Siumut*) party and went into opposition, from where it campaigned in favour of Greenland remaining in the European Community in the 1982 referendum—unsuccessfully as it turned out. *Atassut* retained opposition status after the 1983 election despite winning a larger popular vote than Forward, which got the same number of seats. Chemnitz resigned the party leadership in March 1984 and *Atassut* lost ground in the June 1984 election, therefore remaining in opposition.

In the May 1987 election *Atassut* again overtook *Siumut* in popular vote terms but won the same number of seats (11) and therefore continued in opposition. Its status was not changed by the 1991 contest, in which it fell back to eight seats, but in March 1995 *Atassut* won 25.3% of the vote and 10 seats (out of 31) and accepted participation in a coalition headed by *Siumut*. However, *Atassut* slipped back to eight seats (and 25.3% of the vote) in the February 1999 *Landsting* elections, going into opposition to a coalition of *Siumut* and the →Eskimo Brotherhood.

Atassut has consistently returned one of Greenland's two members of the *Folketing* in Copenhagen, where its deputy usually sits in the parliamentary group of the Danish ⇒Liberal Party (*Venstre*).

Eskimo Brotherhood
Inuit Ataqatigiit (IA)
Address. PO Box 321, 3900 Nuuk
Telephone. (+299) 23702
Email. inuit.ataqatigiit@greennet.gl
Leadership. Josef Motzfeldt (chair)

The IA was founded in 1978 by a group of Marxist-Leninists who had been active in the Young Greenland Council in Copenhagen and who opposed the home rule arrangements then being negotiated, advocating instead Greenland's "total independence from the capitalist colonial power". The new party also urged that Greenland citizenship should be restricted to those with at least one Eskimo parent and that the US military base at Thule should be closed. Having failed to persuade Greenlanders to vote against home rule in the January 1979 referendum, the IA failed to obtain representation in the April 1979 election, but was on the winning side in the 1982 referendum in which Greenlanders voted to leave the European Community. Having effectively absorbed the small Wage-Earners' Party (*Sulissartut*), the IA won two seats in the 1983 Greenland election. It increased to three seats in the next contest in 1984, when it joined a coalition government headed by the →Forward (*Siumut*) party. The coalition collapsed in March 1987 after the then IA leader, Aqqaluk Lynge, had accused the *Siumut* prime minister of being "totally passive" in the face of the US government's enhancement of the Thule base. Having improved to four seats in the resultant May 1987 election, the IA joined another coalition with *Siumut* with increased ministerial responsibilities, but again withdrew in 1988. The IA moved up to five seats in the March 1991 election and again formed a coalition with *Siumut*, under a new prime minister. In the March 1995 election the IA made further progress, to six seats (out of 31) and 20.3% of the vote, but went into opposition after failing to persuade *Siumut* to take up its revived demand for complete independence for Greenland.

The IA gained further ground in the February 1999 *Landsting* election, winning seven seats and a vote share of 20.3%. Having moderated its pro-independence line, it joined a coalitoon government with *Siumut*, receiving two portfolios out of seven as well as the presidency of the *Landsting*.

Forward
Siumut
Address. PO Box 399, 3900 Nuuk
Telephone. (+299) 323-366
Fax. (+299) 325-840
Email. siumut@greennet.gl
Leadership. Lars Emil Johansen (chair)

The socialist *Siumut* party was founded in July 1977, derived from earlier pro-autonomy groups and the political review *Siumut*. Having supported the autonomy arrangements approved by referendum in January 1979, *Siumut* won an absolute majority of 13 seats (out of 21) in the April 1979 election and formed Greenland's first home rule government under the premiership of Jonathan Motzfeldt. Opposed to Greenland's membership of the European Community, *Siumut* campaigned successfully for a vote in favour of withdrawal in the 1982 referendum. In the April 1983 election the party slipped to 11 seats (out of 24) but continued as a minority government until another election in June 1984, when it again won 11 seats (out of 25) and formed a majority coalition with the small 13Eskimo Brotherhood (IA). The coalition collapsed in March 1987, amid dissension over the status of the US military base at Thule, and *Siumut* retained 11 seats (out of 27) in the resultant May 1987 election, whereupon Motzfeldt sought to negotiate a "grand coalition" with the →Community (*Atassut*) party. This provoked opposition from within *Siumut*, the eventual outcome being a further left-wing coalition with the IA.

Triggered by allegations of corruption among government ministers, an early election in May 1991 resulted in *Siumut* again winning 11 seats (out of 27) and forming a new coalition with the IA, although Motzfeldt was obliged, in view of the scandal, to vacate the premiership and *Siumut* leadership in favour of Lars Emil Johansen. In the next election in March 1995 *Siumut* won 38.5% of the vote and 12 seats (out of 31), but attempts to reconstitute the *Siumut*/IA combination foundered on the IA's revived demand for complete independence for Greenland. The outcome was the formation of a "grand coalition" between *Siumut* and *Atassut* committed to maintaining Greenland's autonomous status.

Motzfeldt regained the *Siumut* leadership and the premiership in September 1997 when Johansen accepted appointment as deputy director of the state fisheries company. In the February 1999 *Landsting* election *Siumut* slipped to 11 seats and 35.3% of the vote. It nevertheless formed a coalition government with the IA (the latter having moderated its pro-independence aim) under the continued premiership of Motzfeldt.

An affiliate of the Socialist International, *Siumut* has consistently returned one of Greenland's two members of the *Folketing* in Copenhagen, where its deputy usually sits in the parliamentary group of the Danish ⇒Social Democratic Party.

Finland

Capital: Helsinki   **Population:** 5,200,000

Under its 1919 constitution as amended, the Republic of Finland is a democratic parliamentary state with a President elected for a six-year term by universal adult suffrage in two rounds of voting if no candidate obtains an absolute majority in the first. The President has considerable executive powers (particularly in the foreign policy sphere) and appoints a Council of Minister under a Prime Minister which must enjoy the confidence of the 200-member unicameral Diet (*Eduskunta*) elected for a four-year term by universal adult suffrage. Parliamentary elections are held under a system of proportional representation in 15 electoral districts, with the number of seats being allocated according to the most recent population census figures. One of the electoral

Parliamentary elections on March 21, 1999, resulted as follows:				
	Seats		Percentage	
	1999	*(1995)*	*1999*	*(1995)*
Finnish Social Democratic Party	51	(63)	22.9	(28.3)
Centre Party of Finland...	48	(44)	22.4	(19.9)
National Coalition	46	(39)	21.0	(17.9)
Left Alliance	20	(22)	10.9	(11.2)
Swedish People's Party...	12	(12)	5.1	(5.1)
Green Union	11	(9)	7.5	(6.5)
Finnish Christian Union	10	(7)	4.2	(3.0)
Reform Group	1	(–)	1.1	(–)
True Finns Party	1	(1)	1.0	(1.3)
Others	0	(3)	3.9	(6.8)

districts is formed by the autonomous Åland Islands (inhabited mainly by ethnic Swedes), which return one deputy to the Finnish Diet. Finland joined what became the European Union on Jan. 1, 1995, and elects 16 members of the European Parliament.

The state contributes to the financing of the national and international activities of political parties represented in the Diet in proportion to their number of seats. In 1999 the total amount available was FMk70.2 million (about $12.3 million), of which, for example, the Finnish Social Democratic Party was allocated just under FMk19 million (about $3.3 million).

Presidential elections held on Jan. 16 and Feb. 6, 2000, resulted in the candidate of the Finnish Social Democratic Party, Tarja Halonen, becoming Finland's first female President with 51.6% of the second-round vote.

Centre Party of Finland
Suomen Keskusta (KESK)
Address. Pursimiehenkatu 15, 00150 Helsinki
Telephone. (#358-9) 172-721
Fax. (#358-9) 653-589
Email. keskusta@keskusta.fi
Website. http://www.keskusta.fi
Leadership. Esko Aho (chair); Mauri Pekkarinen (parliamentary group chair); Paavo Väyrynen (1994 presidential candidate); Eero Lankia (secretary-general)

The Centre Party was founded in 1906 as the Agrarian Union, committed to improving the lot of Finland's large rural population and also to national independence, social justice and democracy. Its chief ideologue was Santeri Alkio (1862-1930), who wrote the first detailed Agrarian programme. Following Finland's declaration of independence in 1917, the Agrarians were part of the successful opposition to right-wing attempts to install a monarchy, while welcoming the victory of the anti-Bolshevik Whites in the 1918 civil war. On the declaration of a republic in 1919, the party increased its electoral support to 19.7% and began its long career in government. Of the 63 governments formed since independence, 48 have included the Agrarian/Centre Party, which has provided the Prime Minister on 20 occasions, as well as three Presidents, namely Lauri Kristian Relander (1925-32), Kyösti Kallio (1937-40) and Urho Kekkonen (1956-81).

The Agrarians reached an inter-war electoral peak of 27.3% in 1930, but were usually the second party after the →Finnish Social Democratic Party (SSDP), with which they formed a "red-green" coalition from 1937. The Agrarians subsequently shared government responsibility for Finland's hostilities with the USSR in 1939-40 and 1941-44, resulting in the loss of a tenth of Finnish territory. Under the leadership of V.J. Sukselainen, the party took 21.4% of the vote in the 1945 elections and became the third largest party in the Diet. Rising to 24.2% in 1948, it became the largest parliamentary party and retained this status in the 1951 and 1954 elections. Kekkonen held the premiership in five out of the seven governments formed between 1950 and 1956. Elected President in 1956, he was to complete four consecutive terms before resigning during his fifth (in October 1981) because of ill-health. His main contribution in the foreign policy sphere was to refine the so-called "Paasikivi-Kekkonen line", involving preferential relations with the USSR in the context of neutrality and non-alignment. By this strategy, he hoped to secure the return of the Finnish territories ceded during World War II, but faced a firm Soviet refusal to consider territorial change.

42

The Agrarians fell back to third position in the 1958 elections and were weakened by the formation in 1959 of the Finnish Rural Party (SMP) by right-wing Agrarian dissidents (→True Finns Party). They nevertheless continued to play a pivotal role in successive coalitions and in 1962 recovered a Diet plurality, winning 53 seats and 23.0% of the vote. In November 1963 Ahti Karjalainen (Agrarian) formed the first non-socialist government since World War II, the other participants being the conservative →National Coalition (KOK), together with what became the →Liberal People's Party (LKP) and the →Swedish People's Party (RKP/SFP). It resigned the following month and was eventually succeeded in September 1964 by one of the same party composition but headed by the Agrarian leader, Johannes Virolainen. In 1965 the Agrarians followed the Scandinavian trend by changing their name to Centre Party, aiming to broaden their support beyond the declining rural population. In the 1996 elections, however, the party slipped to 49 seats and 21.2% and joined a centre-left coalition headed by the SSDP. Because of competition from the SMP, KESK lost further ground in the next two elections, falling to 37 seats and 17.1% in 1970 and to 35 seats and 16.4% in 1972. Karjalainen was nevertheless again Prime Minister in 1970-71 and the party participated in subsequent centre-left combinations.

Having recovered to 39 seats and 17.6% in 1975, KESK provided the Prime Minister (Martti Miettunen) of centre-left coalitions in office until 1977, when it switched to a subordinate ministerial role. It slipped back to 36 seats and 17.3% in the 1979 elections (which it fought in alliance with the LKP), thereafter participating in SSDP-led coalitions until 1987. In 1980 Paavo Väyrynen was elected KESK chair at the age of 34. In 1982 the LKP became a constituent organization of KESK, which inched up to 38 seats and 17.6% in the 1983 elections. In 1986 the LKP reverted to independent status; but its support remained with KESK, which improved to 40 seats and 17.6% (again) in the 1987 elections, after which the party had the unusual experience of being in opposition for a whole parliamentary term. Its reward in the 1991 elections was a surge to a plurality of 55 seats and 24.8%, enabling it to form a centre-right coalition with KOK, the RKP/SFP and the →Finnish Christian Union (SKL), with KESK leader Esko Aho (37) becoming the youngest Prime Minister in Finnish history.

Contending with deepening economic recession, the Aho government also faced dissent within the coalition parties on its aim of accession to the European Union (EU), not least within KESK itself. An additional farm support package served to defuse opposition to the entry terms in KESK rural ranks, and accession was duly approved in the October 1994 referendum, although not before the anti-EU SKL had withdrawn from the coalition. Meanwhile, former KESK leader Väyrynen had been placed third in the first round of presidential elections in January 1994, winning only 19.5 of the vote. In the March 1995 legislative elections, moreover, KESK was the main loser, falling to 44 seats and 19.9%, and went into opposition to a five-party coalition headed by the SSDP.

KESK made a comeback in the October 1996 European Parliament elections, heading the poll with 24.4% (which gave it four of Finland's 16 seats) on a platform of opposition to further European integration. In the March 1999 national elections KESK advanced to 48 seats (on a 22.4% vote share) but remained in opposition to another SSDP-led coalition. In the June 1999 European Parliament elections KESK slipped to 21.3% of the vote but again won four seats.

With an official membership of 270,000, KESK is an affiliate of the Liberal International. Its European Parliament representatives sit in the European Liberal, Democratic and Reformist group.

Finnish Christian Union
Suomen Kristillinen Liitto (SKL)
Address. Mannerheimintie 40D, 00100 Helsinki
Telephone. (#358-9) 3488-2200

Fax. (#358-9) 3488-2228
Email. skl@skl.fi
Website. http://www.skl.fi
Leadership. C.P. Bjarne Kallis (chair); Jouko Jääskeläinen (parliamentary group chair); Milla Kalliomaa (secretary)
The SKL is an evangelical party founded in 1958 to propagate Christian values in public life and to resist secularization. It won its first Diet seat in 1970 on a 1.1% vote share, advancing to four seats and 2.5% in 1972 and to nine seats and 3.3% in 1975, when it benefited from the electoral slump of the Finnish Rural Party (SMP) (→True Finns Party). After SKL candidate Raino Westerholm had won a respectable 9% of the vote in the 1978 presidential elections, the party retained nine seats on a 4.8% vote share in the 1979 Diet elections. It slipped back to three seats and 3.0% in 1983, while in 1987 its reduced share of 2.6% gave it five seats on the strength of local electoral alliances with the →Centre Party of Finland (KESK) and the →Liberal People's Party (LKP). It advanced again in 1991, to eight seats and 3.1%, and opted for its first taste of government, joining a non-socialist coalition headed by KESK and including the conservative →National Coalition and the →Swedish People's Party.

Opposed to Finnish accession to the European Union (as supported by its coalition partners), the SKL withdrew from the government in June 1994. In the March 1995 Diet elections the SKL slipped to seven seats and 3.0% of the vote, remaining in opposition and subsequently losing one deputy to KESK. It revived to 10 seats and 4.2% in the March 1999 elections, but again continued in opposition. A vote share of 2.4% in the June 1999 European Parliament elections gave the SKL one seat.

With an official membership of 16,500, the SKL is affiliated to the Christian Democrat International. Its representative in the European Parliament sits in the European People's Party/European Democrats group.

Finnish Social Democratic Party
Suomen Sosiaalidemokraattinen Puolue (SSDP)
Address. Saariniemenkatu 6, 00530 Helsinki
Telephone. (#358-9) 478-988
Fax. (#358-9) 712-752
Email. palaute@sdp.fi
Website. http://www.sdp.fi
Leadership. Paavo Lipponen (chair); Antero Kekkonen, Liisa Jaakonsaari (deputy chairs); Antti Kalliomäki (parliamentary group chair); Kari Laitinen (general secretary)
The party was founded in 1899 as the Finnish Workers' Party to represent the growing ranks of organized labour as well as landless labourers, adopting its present name in 1903, when Finland was still part of the Russian Empire. The advent of universal suffrage in 1906 enabled the SSDP to become the largest parliamentary party (with 37% of the vote in that year), but its reforms were blocked by the Tsar. Following Finland's declaration of independence in 1917, radical Social Democrats fought on the losing Red side in the 1918 civil war (and later founded the →Finnish Communist Party), whereas the non-revolutionary majority led by Vainö Tanner made its peace with the victorious Whites and embarked on a reformist path in the independent Finnish Republic declared in 1919. Despite electoral competition from Communist-front formations and the powerful Agrarians, the Social Democrats were usually the strongest party in the inter-war period, but managed only one period of minority government (in 1926-27) before entering a "red-green" coalition with the Agrarians in 1937. The SSDP vote rose to 39.8% in 1939, whereupon Tanner not only backed Finland's losing popular cause in the 1939-40 Winter War with the USSR but also supported Finnish participation in Nazi Germany's invasion of the USSR in 1941 with the aim of recovering lost

territory. The SSDP leadership rejected adhesion to the Communist-led Finnish People's Democratic League (SKDL) formed in 1944, but many pro-Soviet party sections defected to the new organization. Finland's defeat in 1944, combined with post-war Soviet regional ascendancy, resulted in Tanner being imprisoned in 1946-48 for wartime pro-German activities.

Having won only 25.1% of the vote in the 1945 elections, the SSDP remained in a coalition government with the SKDL and the Agrarians (later called the →Centre Party, KESK), but internal strife between pro-Soviet left and anti-communist right was to fester for more than two decades. With its vote share remaining stable at around 26% in successive elections, the party participated in coalition governments in 1951 and 1954-57, the latter a centre-left combination with the Agrarians. In the 1956 presidential elections Karl-August Fagerholm of the SSDP was narrowly defeated by Urho Kekkonen (Agrarian). In 1957 Fagerholm was also defeated (by one vote) for the SSDP chair, the victor being a rehabilitated Tanner, whose return provoked a new phase of internal party strife. In the 1958 elections the SSDP lost its customary status as the biggest parliamentary party (and declined further in 1962). In 1959 left-wing dissidents broke away to form what became the Social Democratic League of Workers and Smallholders (TPSL), which won seven seats in the 1966 election in alliance with the SKDL. But the same contest yielded a major recovery for the SSDP to 27.2% of the vote, well ahead of its rivals. Moreover, the TPSL failed to win seats in the 1970 and 1972 contests, while successive SSDP-led centre-left coalitions—under Rafael Paasio (who had succeeded the 82-year-old Tanner as party leader in 1963), Mauno Koivisto and Kalevi Sorsa—confirmed the ascendancy of the SSDP's moderate wing. The party headed the poll in all four elections of the 1970s, but had fallen to 23.9% of the vote by 1979.

In January 1982 Koivisto was elected President of Finland as the SSDP candidate and a new centre-left coalition was formed under Sorsa's premiership. A strong SSDP advance in the 1983 elections, to 26.7%, enabled Sorsa to form another government embracing KESK, the Finnish Rural Party (SMP) (→True Finns Party) and the →Swedish People's Party (RKP/SFP). The March 1987 elections produced a setback for the SSDP, to 24.1% and 56 seats, only just ahead of the conservative →National Coalition (KOK), which became the lead party in a new coalition surprisingly including the SSDP. At the 34th SSDP congress in June 1987 Sorsa was succeeded as party chair by Pertti Paasio (son of Rafael). The same congress adopted a new programme which defined the party's six central aims as being a world of cooperation, peace and freedom; coexistence with nature; the transfer of power from capital owners to working people; a shift from representative democracy to "an active civil state"; a culturally equal society; and a vigorous process of social reform. In February 1988 President Koivisto was elected to a second six-year term as candidate of the SSDP.

The March 1991 elections ended a quarter-century of continuous SSDP government office, the party slipping to 22.1% and 48 seats and going into opposition to a centre-right coalition. Having replaced Paasio as SSDP chair in November 1991, Ulf Sundqvist (an ethnic Swede) himself resigned the leadership in February 1993 over allegations of financial impropriety in his previous post as executive director of the STS-Bank. He was succeeded by Paavo Lipponen, who steered the party into supporting Finnish accession to the European Union in the October 1994 referendum, although rank-and-file SSDP opposition was considerable. In March 1995 Lipponen led the party to a major victory in legislative elections, its vote share rising to a post-1945 high of 28.3%, which yielded 63 seats out of 200. In April 1995 Lipponen formed a five-party "rainbow" coalition that included KOK, the RKP/SFP, the →Left Alliance and the →Green Union. Meanwhile, in Finland's first direct presidential elections in January-February 1994, SSDP candidate Martti Ahtisaari had won a second-round victory with 53.9% of the vote, having headed the first-round voting with 25.9%.

In the first direct Finnish elections to the European Parliament in October 1996, the SSDP fell back to 21.5% of the vote and four of the 16 seats, appearing to be damaged by the government's decision to take Finland into the EU's exchange rate mechanism. Further buffeted by events, the party recovered only slightly in the March 1999 national elections, to a 22.9% vote share and 51 seats, 12 less than in 1995. It nevertheless remained the largest party, forming a new coalition government of the same parties with Lipponen continuing as Prime Minister. In the June 1999 Euro-elections the SDDP was relegated to third place, with only 17.8% of the vote and three seats.

With an official membership of 72,000, the SSDP is a member of the Socialist International. Its representatives in the European Parliament sit in the Party of European Socialists group.

Green Union
Vihreä Liitto (VL or VIHR)
Address. Eerikinkatu 24/A7, 00100 Helsinki
Telephone. (#358-9) 693-3877
Fax. (#358-9) 693-3799
Email. vihreat@vihrealiitto.fi
Website. http://www.vihrealiitto.fi
Leadership. Satu Hassi (chair); Ulla Anttila (parliamentary group chair); Ari Heikkinen (secretary)
The VL was formed in February 1987 as a cooperative body for various existing local and national environmentalist organizations, the latter including the Green Parliamentary Group (*Vihreä Eduskuntaryhmä*), which had won two seats in 1983. Presenting a mainstream environmentalist platform, the Greens increased to four seats in the March 1987 elections and to 10 in March 1991. They fell back to nine seats on a 6.5% vote share in March 1995 but nevertheless took ministerial office for the first time the following month, when Pekka Haavisto became Environment Minister in a five-party "rainbow" coalition headed by the →Finnish Social Democratic Party (SSDP).

Bolstered by its government status and despite being fundamentally "Eurosceptic", the VL advanced to 7.6% in the October 1996 direct elections to the European Parliament, taking one of the 16 seats. In the March 1999 national elections it won 7.5% of the vote and 11 seats, subsequently joining a new SSDP-led coalition in which it took two portfolios. In the June 1999 European Parliament elections the VL made a major advance to 13.4% of the vote and two seats.

The VL is affiliated to the European Federation of Green Parties. Its two members of the European Parliament sit in the Greens/European Free Alliance group.

Left Alliance
Vasemmistoliitto (VAS)
Vänsterförbundet
Address. Siltasaarenkatu 6, 00530 Helsinki
Telephone. (#358-9) 774-741
Fax. (#358-9) 7747-4200
Email. vas@vasemmistoliitto.fi
Website. http://www.vasemmistoliitto.fi
Leadership. Suvi-Anne Siimes (chair); Outi Ojala (parliamentary group chair); Ralf Sund (secretary)
VAS was launched in April 1990 at a Helsinki congress of representatives of the leading Communist and left-socialist groups, who took cognizance of the collapse of East European

communism then in progress. Following the congress, the →Finnish Communist Party (SKP) and its electoral front organization, the Finnish People's Democratic League (*Suomen Kansan Demokraattinen Liitto*, SKDL), voted to disband in favour of the new party, which adopted a left-socialist programme and declared its opposition to Finnish membership of the European Community, later Union (EC/EU), as favoured by most other parties.

The SKP had been founded in 1918 by the pro-Bolshevik wing of the →Finnish Social Democratic Party (SSDP) and had remained banned until 1944, when Finland accepted its second military defeat in five years by the USSR. Reflecting Moscow's new influence in internal Finnish affairs, the SKDL front was created in 1944 and established a sizeable electoral constituency, winning 23.5% of the vote in 1945, becoming the largest parliamentary party in 1958-62 and participating in various centre-left coalitions until 1982. Meanwhile, the SKP had in 1969 split into majority "revisionist" and minority "Stalinist" wings, the latter being formally ousted from the party in 1984 and two years later launching its own Democratic Alternative (*Demokraattinen Vaihtoehtoe*, DEVA) electoral front, which achieved little more than to weaken the SKDL, whose electoral support slumped to 9.4% in 1987 against 4.2% for DEVA.

In its first general elections in March 1991, VAS won 10.2% of the vote and 19 seats, thereafter forming part of the opposition to the 1991-95 centre-right government. It was prominent in the unsuccessful "no" campaign in the October 1994 referendum on EU accession, acting as a focus for considerable anti-EU sentiment among SSDP activists. In a substantial swing to the left in the March 1995 parliamentary elections, VAS advanced to 11.2% and 22 seats, subsequently being allocated two portfolios in a five-party "rainbow" coalition headed by the SSDP and also including the conservative →National Coalition, the →Swedish People's Party and the →Green Union.

The VAS won 10.5% and two seats in the European Parliament elections in October 1996. In the March 1999 national elections it took 10.9% of the vote, slipping to 20 seats. It nevertheless continued in a new SSDP-led coalition of the same composition. In the June 1999 Euro-elections the VAS slipped to 9.1% and was reduced to one seat.

The VAS has an official membership of 14,000 and is a member of the New European Left Forum (NELF). Its representative in the European Parliament sits in the European United Left/Nordic Green Left group.

Liberal People's Party
Liberaalinen Kansanpuolue (LKP)
Address. Frederikinkatu 58A/6, 00100 Helsinki
Telephone. (#358-0) 440227
Fax. (#358-0) 440771
Email. liberal@liberaalit.fi
Website. http://www.liberaalit.fi
Leadership. Altti Majava (chair); Kaarina Talola (general secretary)
The LKP was launched in 1965 as a merger of the Finnish People's Party (*Suomen Kansanpuolue*, SKP) and the Liberal Union (*Vapaamielisten Liitto*, VL), both descended from the pre-independence liberal movement by way of the National Progressive Party (*Kansallinen Edistyspuolue*), which had a significant following in the inter-war years (and provided two Finnish Presidents). Post-war divisions and electoral weakness led in 1950 to the formation of the SKP, which recovered some support and participated in various coalition governments in the 1950s and early 1960s. The more conservative VL, dating from 1951, obtained negligible electoral support prior to the 1965 merger creating the LKP.

The LKP won nine seats and 6.5% of the vote in 1966, but its support gradually declined in subsequent elections, to four seats and 3.7% in 1979. During this period it participated in many coalition governments of the centre-left parties. At a national congress in June 1982, the LKP voted to become a constituent group of the much larger →Centre Party of Finland (KESK), while retaining its own identity. However, an unhappy experience in the 1983 elections impelled the LKP to resume independent status in June 1986, whereafter it won only 1.0% of the vote in 1987 and failed to gain representation. It was no more successful in 1991 and 1995 (when its share of the vote was 0.6%). For the 1999 elections it was allied with the →Young Finns Party, which had won two seats in 1995; but the alliance failed to win representation.

With an official membership of 3,000, the LKP is a member party of the Liberal International.

National Coalition
Kansallinen Kokoomus (KK/KOK)
Address. Kansakoulukuja 3, 00100 Helsinki
Telephone. (#358-9) 69381
Fax. (#358-9) 694-3736
Email. kokoomus@kokoomus.fi
Website. http://www.kokoomus.fi
Leadership. Sauli Ninistö (chair); Ben Zyskowicz (parliamentary group chair); Maija Perho (secretary-general)

The moderate conservative KOK was founded in December 1918 following the victory of the anti-Bolshevik Whites in the civil war that ensued after the end of Russian rule. Although monarchist in sympathy, the new party reconciled itself with the republic declared in 1919 and participated in several inter-war coalitions, averaging around 15% of the vote. In the early 1930s it gravitated towards the semi-fascist Lapua rural movement, but KOK leader J.K. Paasikivi later broke with the far right. KOK participated in all five governments in office from 1939 to 1944 (providing the Prime Minister on two occasions) and thus shared responsibility for the conduct of the 1939-40 Winter War against the USSR and for Finland's participation in Nazi Germany's invasion of the USSR in 1941.

KOK was in opposition to successive centre-left coalitions from 1944 to 1958, its vote share fluctuating from a high of 17.3% in 1948 to a low of 12.8% in 1954. On the other hand, Paasikivi served in the powerful post of President from 1946 to 1956 and was instrumental in establishing a consensus on Finland's post-war policy of good relations with the USSR, as continued by his successor, Urho Kekkonen of what became the →Centre Party (KESK), and therefore known as the "Paasikivi-Kekkonen line". Between 1958 and 1966 KOK participated in several coalition governments, including the first completely non-socialist administration since the war, formed in 1963 and headed by KESK. Having slipped to 13.8% in the 1966 elections, KOK reverted to opposition status and was to remain out of office for over two decades. Under the successive chairmanships of Juhta Rihtniemi (1965-71) and Harri Holkeri (1971-79), the party moved to a more centrist position, notably by endorsing the "Paasikivi-Kekkonen line". One consequence was the departure of traditionalist elements in 1973 to join the →Constitutional Party of the Right. But KOK compensated by attracting additional support in the centre, rising steadily to 22.1% of the vote in 1983 and establishing itself as the second strongest party after the →Finnish Social Democratic Party (SSDP).

KOK made another advance in the 1987 elections (to 23.1% and 53 seats) and proceeded to form a four-party coalition with the SSDP, the →Swedish People's Party (RKP/SFP) and the Finnish Rural Party (SMP) (→True Finns Party), with Holkeri becoming Finland's first KOK Prime Minister since 1944. The coalition was weakened by the withdrawal of the SMP in August 1990 and also faced sharply deteriorating economic conditions. In the March 1991 elections KOK slipped to 19.3% and 40 seats (the third largest contingent) and was obliged to accept a subordinate role in a four-party non-socialist coalition headed by KESK and also including the RKP/SFP and the →Finnish Christian Union (SKL). In presidential elections in January 1994 the KOK candidate, Raimo Ilaskivi, came in fourth place in the first round with 15.2% of the vote. KOK strongly backed Finland's accession to the European Union, although internal strains were apparent when Deputy Prime Minister Pertti Salolainen resigned as KOK chair in June 1994 after some party members had criticized his role in the accession negotiations.

The general elections of March 1995 brought a further setback to KOK, which fell to 17.9% and 39 seats. It nevertheless opted to join a "rainbow" coalition headed by the SSDP and also including the RKP/SFP, the →Left Alliance and the →Green Union. The party advanced to 20.2% of the vote and four seats in the October 1996 European Parliament elections and to 21.0% and 46 seats in the March 1999 national elections, after which it joined another SSDP-led coalition government. In the June 1999 European Parliament elections KOK won 25.3% of the vote, retaining its four seats.

With an official membership of 50,000, KOK is affiliated to the Christian Democrat International and the International Democrat Union. Its representatives in the European Parliament are members of the European People's Party/European Democrats group.

Reform Group
Remonttiryhma (REM)
Address. Mannerheimintie 40A, 00100 Helsinki
Telephone. (+358-9) 414-3352
Fax. (+358-9) 645-379
Email. risto.kuisma@eduskunta.fi
Leadership. Risto Kuisma (chair); Seija Lahti (secretary)

The REM was launched in 1997 by veteran trade union activist and member of parliament Risto Kuisma, who defected from the →Finnish Social Democratic Party and initially joined the →Young Finns but soon accused the latter of elitism and founded his own party. Describing itself as "the movement of people who want change", the REM stands for full employment and a radical reduction in income tax. In the March 1999 parliamentary elections it won 1.1% of the vote and one seat.

Swedish People's Party
Svenska Folkpartiet (SFP)
Ruotsalainen Kansanpuolue (RKP)
Address. Gräsviksgatan 14, PO Box 282, 00181 Helsinki
Telephone. (#358-0) 694-2322
Fax. (#358-0) 693-1968
Email. sfp@sfp.fi
Website. http://www.sfp.fi
Leadership. Jan-Erik Enestam (chair); Elisabeth Rehn (1994 presidential candidate); Ulla-Maj Wideroos (parliamentary group chair); Peter Heinström (secretary)

The RKP/SFP was founded in 1906, when Finland was still a duchy of the Russian Empire, to represent the political and social interests of the ethnic Swedish population, which was then economically dominant. Being ethnically based, the party has traditionally encompassed a wide spectrum of ideological preferences, although it is usually characterized as centrist with progressive leanings. Its share of the overall vote has shown a gradual decline over recent decades (from 8.4% in 1945 to 5.1% in 1995), in line with the falling proportion of ethnic Swedes in the population; but its post-war representation in the Diet has remained rather more constant (the 1995 tally being 12 seats, compared with a high of 15 in 1951 and a low of 10 in the elections of the

1970s). The RKP/SFP's parliamentary contingent customarily includes the single deputy returned by the ethnic Swedish inhabitants of the autonomous Åland Islands, where the main local parties, modelled on those of Sweden, form the Ålands Coalition for Finnish national elections.

The RKP/SFP has been in government more often than it has been in opposition, having participated in about two-thirds of all Finnish coalitions formed since 1906, including centre-left, centre-right and ideologically-mixed combinations. The pattern after 1945 was RKP/SFP participation in successive centre-left coalitions headed by the →Finnish Social Democratic Party (SSDP) or the →Centre Party (KESK), although in 1963-66 it was a member of the first entirely non-socialist governments since the war. Subsequent centre-left combinations also included the RKP/SFP as a pivotal member, while in 1987 it joined a four-party coalition headed by the conservative →National Coalition (KOK) and also including the SSDP and the Finnish Rural Party (SMP) (→True Finns Party). Having slipped from 13 to 12 seats in the 1991 elections, the RKP/SFP joined another non-socialist coalition, this time headed by KESK and including KOK and the →Finnish Christian Union.

For the January-February 1994 presidential elections the RKP/SFP candidate was Defence Minister Elisabeth Rehn, who surprised many (given her Swedish ethnicity and gender) by taking second place in the first round, with 22% of the vote, and thus going forward to the second round, in which she was defeated by the SSDP candidate but won a creditable 46.1% of the vote. The RKP/SFP supported Finland's accession to the European Union (as approved in the October 1994 referendum) and was allocated one of Finland's 16 seats in the European Parliament. Having retained 12 seats in the March 1995 parliamentary elections, it accepted two portfolios in a five-party "rainbow" coalition headed by the SSDP and also including KOK, the →Left Alliance and the →Green Union.

In the October 1996 direct elections to the European Parliament the RKP/SFP retained its single seat with 5.8% of the vote. In the March 1999 national elections it again won 12 seats (with 5.1% of the vote) and opted to join another five-party coalition headed by the SSDP. In the June 1999 European Parliament elections it advanced to 6.8%, retaining its single seat.

With an official membership of 40,000, the RKP/SFP is affiliated to both the International Democrat Union and the Liberal International. Its representative in the European Parliament sits in the European Liberal, Democratic and Reformist group.

True Finns Party
Perussuomlaiset (PS)
Address. Mannerheimintie 40B, 00100 Helsinki
Telephone. (#358-9) 454-0411
Fax. (#358-9) 454-0466
Email. timo.soini@eduskunta.fi
Leadership. Timo Soini (chair); Rolf (Fred) Sormo (secretary)

The PS was founded prior to the 1999 elections as successor to the Finnish Rural Party (SMP), following serious internal disputes in the latter. The SMP had been derived from the Finnish Smallholders' Party, which was launched in 1959 by a dissident faction of what later became the →Centre Party of Finland (KESK). Led by the charismatic Veikko Vannamo, the breakaway party took an anti-establishment, "Poujadist" line, defending the rights of "forgotten Finland" and claiming that the parent party had neglected the interests of small farmers and small businessmen. Renamed the SMP after obtaining negligible support in the 1962 and 1966 elections, the party came to prominence in 1968 when Vennamo won over 11% in challenging incumbent Urho Kekkonen (KESK) for the presidency. It achieved a breakthrough in the 1970 parliamentary elections, winning 10.5% and 18 seats (mainly as the expense of KESK), and retained 18 seats in 1972, although it support slipped to 9.2%.

The SMP was then weakened by splits arising from criticism of Vennamo's authoritarian leadership style and right-wing opposition to his willingness to co-operate with parties of the left. In the 1975 elections the rump SMP slumped to two seats and 3.6%, recovering only partially to seven seats and 4.5 % in 1979, in which year Vennamo stood down as leader and was succeeded by his son Pekka. The 1983 elections yielded another breakthrough for the SMP, which won 17 seats and 9.7% of the vote and thereafter entered government for the first time as part of a coalition headed by the →Finnish Social Democratic Party (SSDP) and including KESK and the →Swedish People's Party (RKP/SFP). In the 1984 municipal elections the SMP obtained over 600 council seats.

The SMP fell back to nine seats and 6.3% in the 1987 elections but nevertheless joined a four-party coalition headed by the conservative →National Coalition and including the SSDP and the RKP/SFP. It withdrew from the coalition in August 1990 in protest against new pensions proposals, but lost further support to a resurgent KESK in the 1991 elections, falling to seven seats and 4.8% and remaining outside the resultant non-socialist coalition headed by KESK. Having been part of the unsuccessful opposition to Finnish accession to the European Union, the SMP almost disappeared from the Diet in the March 1995 elections, winning only one seat on a 1.3% vote share.

A period of internal division followed, culminating in the creation of PS as the successor party. In the March 1999 elections the PS just managed to retain one seat, winning only 1% of the vote.

Other Parties

Communist Workers' Party (*Kommunistinen Työväenpuolue*, KTP), led by Timo Lahdenmäki and Heikki Männikö, founded in 1988 by a Stalinist faction of the Democratic Alternative (later part of the →Left Alliance), contested the 1991, 1995 and 1999 elections under the slogan "For Peace and Socialism", winning 0.2% and 0.1% of the vote respectively; contested 1996 Euro-elections on joint list with →Finnish Communist Party and other leftist groups.. *Address.* PL 93, Vantaa: *Telephone.* (+358-9) 857-1022; *Fax.* (+358-9) 857-3097; *Email.* ktp@kaapeli.fi; *Website.* http://www.kaapeli.fi

Ecological Party (*Ekologinen Puolue*, EP), led by Pertti (Veltto) Virtanen (chair) and Jukka Wallenius, founded in 1990 as a populist formation aiming to provide a "non-ideological" alternative to the left-leaning →Green Union; failed to win representation in the 1991 Diet elections, but secured one seat on a 0.3% vote share in March 1995, losing it in 1999 with only 0.4%. *Address.* Mannerheimintie 40A, 00100 Helsinki; *Telephone.* (+358-9) 432-3566; *Fax.* (+358-9) 432-2717

Finnish Communist Party (*Suomen Kommunistinen Puolue*, SKP), led by Yrjö Hakanen (chair), Riitta Tynjä (vice-chair) and Arto Viitaniemi (general secretary), relaunched in 1997 as self-declared successor to the historic SKP, in opposition to the participation of the →Left Alliance in a "neo-liberal" government; won 0.8% of the vote in both the 1995 and 1999 elections; contested 1996 Euro-elections on joint list with →Communist Workers' Party and other leftist groups. *Address.* Petter Wetterintie 1A, 6 krs, 00810 Helsinki; *Telephone.* (+358-9) 5840-0350; *Fax.* (+358-9) 5840-0355; *Email.* skp@skp.fi; *Website.* http://www.skp.fi

Finnish Pensioners' Party (*Suomen Eläkeläisten Puolue*, SEP), led by Erkki Pulli and Saara Mölsä, launched in 1986 but has had minimal electoral impact, winning 0.1% of the vote in 1995 and 0.2% in 1999.

League for a Free Finland (*Vapaan Suomen Liitto*, VSL), right-wing nationalist formation which won 1% of the vote in 1995 and 0.4% in 1999.

Natural Law Party (*Luonnonlain Puolue*, LLP), the Finnish branch of the world-wide natural law political movement, took 0.3% in the 1995 elections and 0.1% in 1999. *Address.* Hatanpään valtatie 7, 33100 Tampere; *Telephone.* (+358-3) 222-7000; *Fax.* (+358-3) 222-7001; *Email.* info@llp.fi; *Website.* http://www.llp.fi

Patriotic National Alliance (*Isänmaallinen Kansallis-Litto*, IKL), led by Ajan Suunta, right-wing formation seeking to stimulate Finnish patriotism. *Address.* PL 22, 61801 Kauhajoki; *Fax.* (+358-6) 231-1747; *Email.* ikl@kauhajoki.fi. *Website.* http://kauhajoki.fi/~ikl

Pensioners for the People (*Elakeläiset Kansan Asialla*, EKA), senior citizens' grouping, won only 0.2% in 1999 elections.

Socialist League (*Sosialistiliitto*, SL), led by Juhani Lohikoski, Trotskyist formation, contested 1999 elections as part of "Change 99" (*Muutos 99*) alliance in order to agitate against parliamentary politics. *Address.* PO Box 288, 00171 Helsinki; *Telephone.* (+358-9) 278-2244; *Email.* sl.org@saunalahti.fi; *Website.* http://www.dlc.fi/~sosliitto

Young Finns Party (*Nuorsuomalainen Puolue*, NSP), led by Risto E.J. Penttilä, also known as the "Progessive Finnish Party", founded in 1994 as a radical pro-market party arguing that Finland needed a deregulated economy to compete in the European Union following accession at the beginning of 1995; won two seats and 2.8% in the 1995 parliamentary elections, but failed to retain representation in 1999 on a joint list with the →Liberal People's Party. *Address.* Lönnrotinkatu 32A, 00180 Helsinki; *Telephone.* (+358-9) 685-6211; *Fax.* (+358-9) 685-6233; *Email.* nuorsuom@nuorsuom.fi; *Website.* http://www.nuorsuom.fi

France

Capital: Paris　　　　　　　　　　　　　　　**Population:** 58,500,000

The French Republic has one of the world's most developed multi-party systems that is perpetually fluid but essentially unchanging in its broad ideological structure. Under the 1982 constitution of the Fifth Republic as amended, an executive President, who appoints the Prime Minister, is elected for a seven-year term by universal suffrage of citizens above the age of 18 years, the requirement being an absolute majority of the votes cast either in the first round of voting or, if necessary, in a second. Legislative authority is vested in a bicameral Parliament (*Parlement*) consisting of (i) a 321-seat Senate (*Sénat*) whose members are indirectly elected for a nine-year term (a third being renewed every three years), 309 by electoral colleges of national and local elected representatives in the metropolitan and overseas departments/territories and 12 by the *Conseil Supérieur des Français de l'Étranger* to represent French citizens living abroad; and (ii) a 577-member National Assembly (*Assemblée Nationale*) directly elected for a maximum five-year term by universal adult suffrage. For the March 1986 Assembly elections the then Socialist-led government introduced a system of department-based proportional representation for the first time under the Fifth Republic; however, the incoming centre-right administration enacted legislation providing for a return to the previous system of majority voting in two rounds in single-member constituencies. France was a founder member of what is now the European Union and elects 87 members to the European Parliament.

Under laws enacted in March 1988 and January 1990, state funding is payable to (i) political parties with parliamentary representation, in proportion to the size of their respective groups; (ii) all accredited presidential candidates (with the two reaching the second round receiving additional sums), according to a complex formula for the reimbursement of varying proportions of the ceilings set for campaign expenses; and (iii) Assembly election candidates who receive at least 5% of the first-round vote, at a rate equivalent to 10% of the applicable expenses ceilings. The total amount disbursed in 1990 under category (i) was FF260,267,857 (about $51 million), of which, for example, the Socialist Party, then substantially the largest Assembly party, received FF95,530,134 (about $18.8 million).

Presidential elections on April 23 and May 7, 1995, resulted in Jacques Chirac of the Rally for the Republic being elected in the second round with 52.6% of the votes cast, against 47.4% for the Socialist Party candidate.

National Assembly elections held on May 25 and June 1, 1997, resulted as follows

	Seats 1997 (1993)		Percentage* 1997 (1993)	
Socialist Party	241	(54)	23.5	(17.6)
Rally for the Republic	134	(247)	15.7	(20.4)
Union for French Democracy	108	(213)	14.2	(19.1)
French Communist Party	38	(23)	9.9	(9.2)
Left Radical Party	12	(6)	1.5	(0.9)
Various Greens	7	(0)	6.8	(5.0)
National Front	1	(0)	14.9	(12.4)
Various left	21	(10)	2.8	(3.6)
Various right	14	(24)	6.6	(4.9)
Independents and others	1	(0)	4.0	(6.9)

*First-round vote

Citizens' Movement
Mouvement des Citoyens (MDC)
Address. 9 rue du Faubourg-Poissonnière, 75009 Paris
Telephone. (+33-1) 4483-8300
Fax. (+33-1) 4483-8320
Email. info@mdc-france.org
Website. http://www.mdc-france.org
Leadership. Jean-Pierre Chevènement (president); George Sarre (delegate president); Paul Loridant (secretary-general); Nicole Morichaud (national secretary)
The MDC was launched in 1993 by former →Socialist Party (PS) minister Jean-Pierre Chevènement on a platform of opposition to the Maastricht Treaty and further European

integration. In the 1994 European Parliament elections Chevènement headed the "Alternative Politics" (*L'Autre Politique*) list, winning 2.5% of the vote and no seats. Having won a National Assembly by-election in December 1995, the MDC contested the mid-1997 Assembly elections in alliance with the PS, winning seven seats in its own right and subsequently joining the new PS-led coalition government, in which Chevènement became Interior Minister. The MDC deputies in the Assembly joined the Radical, Citizen and Green group headed by the →Left Radical Party (PRG), while in the Senate the MDC secretary-general, Paul Loridant, sits in the Communist, Republican and Citizen group headed by the →French Communist Party. The MDC was part of the PS-headed list for the June 1999 Euro-elections (with the PRG), taking two of the 22 seats won by the list.

Together with the PS and PRG members, the MDC representatives in the European Parliament sit in the Party of European Socialists group. The party is a member of the New European Left Forum (NELF).

French Communist Party
Parti Communiste Français (PCF)
Address. 2 place du Colonel Fabien, 75019 Paris
Telephone. (+33-1) 4040-1212
Fax. (+33-1) 4040-1356
Email. pcf@pcf.fr
Website. http://www.pcft.fr
Leadership. Robert Hue (national secretary); Alain Bocquet (Assembly group (chair); Hélène Luc (Senate group chair)
The PCF came into being in December 1920 when a majority of delegates at the Tours congress of the →Socialist Party (then the SFIO) voted to join the Soviet-run Communist International (Comintern), whereas the anti-Bolshevik minority opted to maintain the SFIO. From 1921 to 1933 the PCF pursued a hardline policy of class war and opposition to all "bourgeois" parties, including the SFIO. From 1934, however, it gave priority to the struggle against fascism and supported (without joining) the 1936-38 Popular Front government headed by the Socialists. The PCF approved the August 1939 non-aggression pact between Nazi Germany and the USSR, but reverted to anti-fascist mode following the German invasion of the USSR in June 1941, its activists subsequently playing a prominent role in the French Resistance. The party joined the post-liberation government formed by Gen. de Gaulle in 1944, although it was denied any powerful portfolios. With the onset of the Cold War, it was excluded from the 1947 government headed by Paul Ramadier (SFIO) and was to remain in opposition for 34 years.

Strongly based in the General Confederation of Labour (the largest trade union body), the PCF outvoted the SFIO in most elections under the Fourth Republic, winning 25-29% of the vote. Having opposed the creation of the Fifth Republic in 1958, the PCF saw its vote fall to 18.9% in Assembly elections later that year but recovered to 20-22% in the contests of the 1960s and 1970s. In December 1966 the then PCF leader, Waldeck Rochet, signed an agreement with the Socialist-led Federation of the Democratic and Socialist Left (FGDS) providing for reciprocal voting support in the March 1967 Assembly elections. The arrangement resulted in PCF representation almost doubling, to 73 seats, although this tally was reduced to 34 in elections held in June 1968 in the aftermath of the "May events" that nearly toppled President de Gaulle. The PCF repudiated the Soviet-led military intervention that suppressed the 1968 "Prague Spring" in Czechoslovakia, although it remained in most respects an orthodox Marxist-Leninist party aligned to Moscow and opposed to French membership of NATO and the European Community. In 1969 the Communist presidential candidate, Jacques Duclos, came a creditable third in the first round, with 21.3% of the vote.

Following the election of François Mitterrand as leader of the new Socialist Party (PS) in 1971, the following year the PCF signed a common programme with the PS and the Left Radical Movement (MRG), now the →Left Radical Party. The union yielded major left-wing gains in the March 1973 Assembly elections, which restored Communist representation to 73 seats. From 1974, however, serious strains developed within the alliance, not least because the steady growth of PS strength was viewed by the PCF as imperilling the union's equilibrium and as encouraging the Socialists to revert to a centre-left strategy. At its 22nd congress in February 1976 the PCF repudiated the thesis of the dictatorship of the proletariat and came out in favour of a specifically French model of socialism. The party nevertheless kept its distance from the revisionist "Eurocommunist" line then being advanced by the Italian Communists. Mainly because of PS and MRG resistance to further PCF nationalization proposals, no agreement was reached on a revised common programme for the March 1978 Assembly elections, in which the PCF presented its own manifesto. Second-round reciprocal support nevertheless applied, with the result that the PCF rose to 86 seats amid a left-wing advance that fell short of an overall majority.

The PCF candidate in the watershed May 1981 presidential elections was the then party leader, Georges Marchais, who obtained 15.4% of the first-round vote, whereafter the PCF swung behind Mitterrand in the second round and contributed to the PS leader's victory. In the resultant Assembly elections of June 1981, second-round support arrangements among the left-wing parties yielded most benefit to the Socialists, who won an absolute majority, while the PCF fell to 44 seats. The French Communists nevertheless entered government for the first time since 1947, obtaining four portfolios in the new PS-led administration. But strains quickly developed between the PS and PCF in government, notably over the latter's refusal to condemn the imposition of martial law in Poland and its opposition to the deployment of new US nuclear missiles in Europe. In the European Parliament elections of June 1984 the PCF took only 11.2% of the vote, less than in any national election since 1932. When Laurent Fabius of the PS formed a new government in July 1984, the Communists refused to participate, on the grounds that he was equivocal on giving priority to economic expansion and job-creation. In September 1984 the PCF deputies broke with the PS-led Assembly majority and voted against the government for the first time in the budget debate of December 1984.

At the PCF congress of February 1985 the party leadership under Marchais firmly resisted the demand of a "renovator" group for changes in policy and for greater internal party democracy. The Assembly elections of March 1986 produced a further setback for the PCF, which slipped to 35 seats and 9.8% of the vote, in part because some of its working-class support in city suburbs with a high immigrant population switched to the far-right →National Front (FN). Further internal strains and defections served to harden the Marchais line, which prevailed at the PCF conference in Nanterre in June 1987, when hardliner André Lajoinie was adopted as PCF presidential candidate. Prior to its 26th congress in December 1987, the PCF central committee expelled Pierre Juquin for having announced his presidential candidacy as a Communist "renovator". In the first round of the April-May 1988 presidential contest that saw the re-election of Mitterrand, Lajoinie recorded the PCF's lowest-ever national vote share (6.8%), while Juquin got 2.1%. In the June 1988 Assembly elections the PCF recovered somewhat to 11.3% in the first round, but slipped to representation of 27 seats.

Still resisting pressure for change in the PCF, Marchais responded to the collapse of East European communism in 1989-90 and of the USSR in 1991 by claiming that he had been "duped" by his erstwhile comrades in that part of the world. The party suffered a further setback, to 9.2% of the first-round vote, in the March 1993 Assembly elections which brought the right back to governmental power, but displayed resilience in its strongholds by retaining 23 seats. Avowedly because of ill-health, Marchais formally vacated the PCF leadership at the party's 28th congress in January 1994 and was succeeded by Robert Hue, who was assigned the title "national secretary" as part of a decision to abandon "democratic centralism" in party decision-making. The Communist list won only 6.9% of the vote in the June 1994 European Parliament elections (and seven of the 87 French seats). In the April-May 1995 presidential elections, Hue took fifth place in the first round with 8.6% of the vote, whereupon the PCF backed the unsuccessful candidacy of Lionel Jospin (PS) in the second round.

In a high-profile Assembly by-election for a Marseilles constituency in October 1996, the PCF candidate defeated an FN challenge on the strength of second-round backing from centre-left parties. For the mid-1997 Assembly elections the PCF issued a joint declaration of policy objectives with the PS, but the two parties confined their electoral cooperation to mutual second-round support. The PCF shared in the victory of the left, winning 38 seats and a first-round vote share of 9.9%, and subsequently accepting portfolios in a Socialist-led coalition government. In the June 1999 European Parliament elections the PCF list slipped to six seats on a vote share of 6.8%, two of the elected candidates being "independents".

The PCF members of the European Parliament sit in the European United Left/Nordic Green Left group. The party is a member of the New European Left Forum (NELF).

The Greens
Les Verts
Address. 107 ave Parmentier, 75011 Paris
Telephone. (+33-1) 4355-1001
Fax. (+33-1) 4355-1615
Email. verts@verts.imaginet.fr
Website. http://www.verts.imaginet.fr
Leadership. Jean-Luc Bennahmias (national secretary); Dominique Voynet (1995 presidential candidate); Marie-Anne Isler Béguin, Martine Billard, Denis Baupin, Stéphane Pocrain (spokespersons)
The Greens were organized as a unified mainstream environmentalist party in January 1984, officially embracing the suffix Ecologist Confederation–Ecologist Party (*Confédération Écologiste–Parti Écologiste*). This cumbersome nomenclature reflected the complexities of the movement's evolution since it fielded René Dumont for the presidency in 1974 and received 1.3% of the first-round vote. In the 1978 Assembly elections the earlier movement presented 200 candidates under the banner *Écologie 78*, winning 2.1% of the vote, while the *Écologie Europe* list took 4.4% in the 1979 European Parliament elections. Encouraged by that relative success, the movement in February 1980 joined with other groups to create the *Mouvement d'Écologie Politique* (MEP), which in 1981 backed the presidential candidacy of Brice Lalonde, then leader of Friends of the Earth and later founder of →Ecology Generation (GE). As Ecology Today (*Aujourd'hui l'Ecologie*), the MEP presented 82 candidates in the 1981 Assembly elections, winning 1.2% of the first-round vote (and no seats). In November 1982 the MEP became a political party called *Les Verts-Parti Écologiste* (VPE), which won some 6% of the overall vote in the 1983 municipal elections and elected several dozen councillors. The adoption of the longer title referred to above occurred at a Clichy congress (in January 1984) which achieved a merger of the VPE with various other environmentalist group.

Standing as *Les Verts-Europe Écologie*, the formation again failed to win representation in the 1984 European Parliament elections, when its vote fell to 3.4%, and was no more successful in the 1986 Assembly elections, when it managed only 1.1% of the first-round vote. Subsequent internal divisions were reflected in the rejection by a Paris general assembly in September 1986 of a policy paper presented by the movement's four spokesmen urging rapprochement with like-minded groups. Four new spokesmen were elected from among the "fundamentalist" wing, one of whom, Antoine Waechter, stood in the 1988 presidential elections, winning 3.8% of the first-round vote. The Greens declined to present official candidates for the June 1988 Assembly elections in protest against the return to constituency-based polling as opposed to the proportional system used in 1986. Returning to the electoral fray, they polled strongly in the 1989 European Parliament elections on a joint list with other groups, winning 10.6% of the vote and nine seats.

The 1993 Assembly elections yielded a 4% first-round vote for the Greens but no seats, despite an agreement with the GE not to run competing candidates. At their annual conference in November 1993 the Greens moved sharply to the left, electing Dominique Voynet as 1995 presidential candidate, while the disaffected Waechter later broke away to form the →Independent Ecological Movement. Standing separately in the 1994 European Parliament elections, neither the Greens nor the GE gained sufficient support to win seats. Standing as the sole Green candidate in the 1995 presidential contest, Voynet was placed eighth of nine candidates, taking 3.3% of the first-round vote.

For the mid-1997 Assembly elections the Greens presented 455 candidates, 29 of whom were backed by the →Socialist Party (PS) while the Greens agreed to support PS candidates in 70 constituencies. The outcome was a breakthrough for the Greens, to seven Assembly seats on the strength of a first-round vote of 6.8% achieved in alliance with other groups. The Greens thereupon joined the new PS-led coalition government, in which Voynet became Minister of Town and Country Planning and the Environment. Its Assembly deputies joined the Radical, Citizen and Green group headed by the →Left Radical Party. In the June 1999 European Parliament elections the Greens advanced strongly to 9.7% of the vote, taking nine of the 87 French seats, the leader of the list being the celebrated 1968-vintage revolutionary Daniel Cohn-Bendit.

The French Greens are affiliated to the European Federation of Green Parties. Their representatives in the European Parliament sit in the Greens/European Free Alliance group.

Hunting, Fishing, Nature, Traditions
Chasse, Pêche, Nature, Traditions (CPNT)
Address. 245 blvd de la Paix, 64000 Pau
Telephone. (+33-5) 5914-7171
Fax. (+34-5) 5914-7172
Email. info@cpnt.asso.fr
Website. http://www.cpnt.asso.fr
Leadership. Jean Saint Josse (president); Michel Raymond (secretary-general)
The CPNT movement advocates the protection and furtherance of traditional countryside pursuits and maintenance of the rural way of life and values. Opposed to further European integration, it contested the 1994 European Parliament elections without success (taking 3.9% of the vote), but made a breakthrough in the 1999 contest, winning 6.8% and six seats.

The CPNT members of the European Parliament sit in the Europe of Democracies and Diversities group.

Left Radical Party
Parti Radical de Gauche (PRG)
Address. 13 rue Duroc Paris
Telephone. (+33-1) 4566-6768
Fax. (+33-1) 4566-4793
Email. prg-nat@club-internet.fr
Website. http://www.radical-gauche.org

Leadership. Jean-Michel Baylet (president); Roger-Gérard Schwartzenberg (Assembly group chair)

The PRG is the current rubric of what was the Left Radical Movement (MRG) until 1996, following a succession of name changes that were disputed in the courts. The MRG had originated in July 1972 as a left-wing faction of the historic →Radical Party which endorsed the common programme issued the previous month by the →Socialist Party (PS) and the →French Communist Party (PCF), whereas the Radical majority then led by Jean-Jacques Servan-Schreiber declined to join the new Union of the Left. Initially organized as the Radical-Socialist Study and Action Group, the left-wing faction was expelled in October 1972 and contested the March 1973 Assembly elections on a joint list with the PS called the *Union de la Gauche Socialiste et Démocrate*, taking 11 of the 100 seats won by the alliance. The faction formally constituted itself as the MRG in December 1973 under the presidency of Robert Fabre, taking as its watchword the famous Radical slogan *"Pas d'ennemi à gauche"* ("No enemy to the left").

In contentious negotiations on revision of the common programme for the March 1978 Assembly elections, the MRG caused the first formal breakdown of talks in September 1977, when Fabre rejected the extensive nationalization programme demanded by the PCF. In the 1988 elections the MRG presented its own policy platform which differed from those of the PS and PCF in important respects; but the electoral alliance with the PS was maintained, and reciprocal support arrangements between the PS/MRG and the PCF again came into play in the second round. The result was that the MRG took 10 of the 113 seats won by the PS/MRG alliance. Immediately after the polling, Fabre repudiated the original common programme of the left and resigned the MRG presidency. He was succeeded by Michel Crépeau, who favoured the continuation of left-wing union, whereas the MRG right advocated reversion to a centre-left orientation and eventually, for the most part, rejoined the parent Radical Party or other centre-left groupings.

Crépeau stood as the MRG candidate in the first round of the 1981 presidential elections, winning only 2.2% of the vote. In the second round the MRG backed François Mitterrand of the PS, whose victory resulted in the appointment of a left-wing government in which Crépeau obtained a ministerial portfolio. In the June 1981 Assembly elections the MRG increased its seat tally to 14 by virtue of a further alliance with the victorious PS. Thereafter, the MRG participated in the PS-led government throughout its five-year tenure, while regularly seeking to assert its distinct political identity. In the 1984 European Parliament elections, for example, it was the principal component of a centre-left/ecological list called *Entente Radicale Écologiste pour les États-Unis d'Europe*, which secured 3.3% of the vote and no seats. The MRG also contested the 1986 Assembly elections in its own right (the move to proportional representation obviating the need for a joint list with the PS), but mustered only 0.4% of the total vote and two seats. The party nevertheless maintained a significant presence in local and regional government.

In opposition in 1986-88, the MRG experienced much internal agonizing about whether to maintain its leftward orientation or to turn to the centre. In the event, it was again allied with the PS in the 1988 Assembly elections held after the re-election of Mitterrand to the presidency. With majority voting by constituency having been reinstated, the MRG obtained nine seats and was allocated three ministerial posts in the resultant PS-led coalition. It remained in government for the next five years, but had little success in its attempts to build a "second force" within the then "presidential majority". In the March 1993 Assembly elections the MRG shared in the heavy defeat of its Socialist allies, although left-wing voting discipline and the MRG's resilience in its remaining strongholds enabled the party to retain six seats with a first-round vote share of 0.9%.

Again in opposition, the MRG was temporarily strengthened by the adhesion of controversial businessman Bernard Tapie, who had served two brief spells as a minister in 1992-93 and had been elected as a "presidential majority" candidate in the 1993 Assembly elections. In the June 1994 European Parliament elections Tapie headed the MRG's *Énergie Radical* list, which won 13 seats on an impressive vote share of 12.1%, while the PS under the new leadership of Michel Rocard performed so badly that Rocard had to resign. Having backed Rocard's efforts to build a broader social democratic party, the MRG was much less enthusiastic about his left-wing successor, Henri Emmanuelli, and initially announced that its leader, Jean-François Hory, would contest the 1995 presidential elections with the aim of rallying the centre-left opposition. In the event, the selection of Lionel Jospin as the PS candidate served to restore the PS/MRG axis, in that Hory withdrew his candidacy and the MRG contributed to Jospin's powerful, albeit losing, performance in the presidential contest. Shortly after the second-round polling (in May 1995), the MRG's "Tapie era" finally ended when the former tycoon (by now bankrupt) was sentenced to a prison term after being convicted of attempted match-fixing when he owned Marseilles football club.

Hory resigned as MRG president in October 1995 and was succeeded by Jean-Michel Baylet in January 1996, when a party congress also elected six vice-presidents. These included the former Socialist minister, Bernard Kouchner, whose Reunite (*Réunir*) grouping, founded in November 1994, was merged into the MRG. With a view to sharpening its public image, the party decided to adopt the one-word title "Radical" for campaigning purposes, thereby creating much scope for confusion as between it and the historic Radical Party. In March 1996 a Paris court ordered it to revert to the MRG name within four months. It then opted for the title "Radical Socialist Party" (PRS), under which name it won 12 seats in the mid-1997 Assembly elections in alliance in many constituencies with the PS. In then joined the new PS-led coalition government, receiving one portfolio.

The party was subsequently told by a court that its PRS title was also unlawful because of potential confusion, so that in January 1998 it almost reverted to its original name by becoming the "Left Radical Party" (PRG). In the June 1999 European Parliament elections the party was part of a joint list with the PS and the →Citizens' Movement, the list heading the poll with 22% of the vote and 22 seats, of which the PRG took two.

Liberal Democracy
Démocratie Libérale (LD)
Address. 105 rue de l'Université 75007 Paris
Telephone. (+33-1) 4062-3030
Fax. (+33-1) 4062-3040
Email. info@democratie-liberale.asso.fr
Website. http://www.democratie-liberale.asso.fr
Leadership. Alain Madelin (president); José Rossi (Assembly group chair); Laurent Dominati (secretary-general)

The liberal conservative LD was launched following the mid-1997 Assembly elections as successor to the Republican Party (*Parti Républicain*, PR), adopting the suffix "Independent Republicans and Republicans". The PR had been formed in May 1977 as a merger of the National Federation of Independent Republicans (*Fédération Nationale des Républicains Indépendants*, FNRI), the Social and Liberal Generation (*Génération Sociale et Libérale*, GSL), Act for the Future (*Agir pour l'Avenir*) and various support committees which had backed Valéry Giscard d'Estaing in his successful bid for the presidency in 1974. The PR's social liberal and strongly pro-European orientation was closely based on the theses advanced by Giscard d'Estaing his 1977 book *Démocratie Française*.

The FNRI had been established in June 1966 by Giscard d'Estaing as leader of a modernizing faction that had broken away from the →National Centre of Independents and Peasants (CNIP) in 1962 in order to be able to criticize government policy while remaining part of the ruling "majority". On founding the FNRI Giscard d'Estaing himself left the government of Georges Pompidou (although other FNRI representatives continued to participate) and led the new party to significant advances in the 1967 and 1968 Assembly elections (to 42 and 61 seats respectively) on the basis of his celebrated "oui, mais" ("yes, but") line of qualified support for the Gaullist-led government. In April 1969 Giscard d'Estaing effectively supported the winning "no" side in the constitutional referendum which yielded the resignation of President de Gaulle, whereupon the FNRI backed the victorious Pompidou in the June 1969 presidential elections. The FNRI leader then resumed his former post as Economy and Finance Minister, retaining it in successive Gaullist-led governments under the Pompidou presidency, while the FNRI slipped to 55 seats in the 1973 Assembly elections.

Following Pompidou's death in office in April 1974, Giscard d'Estaing was elected President in May as candidate of the FNRI and other centrist formations, taking second place in the first round (with 32.9% of the vote) and winning a narrow 50.7% victory in the run-off against François Mitterrand of the →Socialist Party (PS). He proceeded to appoint Jacques Chirac (Gaullist) to head a government with strong centrist representation, including his principal FNRI lieutenant, Michel Poniatowski, at the powerful Interior Ministry. Growing strains between the Giscardian and Gaullist wings of the "majority" from 1975 resulted in Chirac's resignation in August 1976 and his replacement by a non-Gaullist (Raymond Barre), whereafter Chirac relaunched the Gaullist party as the →Rally for the Republic (RPR). The superior organization of the new RPR over the FNRI and other centrist parties (and the challenge to presidential authority which the RPR represented) was highlighted in March 1977 when Chirac defeated a candidate backed by the President in elections for the important post of mayor of Paris.

Seeking to build an effective counterweight to the RPR for the 1978 Assembly elections, the new PR participated in the formation of the broader Union for French Democracy (UDF), winning 71 of the 124 UDF seats. PR representatives took prominent portfolios in the reconstituted Barre government, but suffered from association with scandals such as the De Broglie affair. In 1981 the PR and the rest of the UDF endorsed Giscard d'Estaing's re-election bid, although the President chose to stand as a "citizen-candidate" without specific party attribution. Following his narrow defeat by Mitterrand in the second round, the PR shared in the decimation of the UDF in the June 1981 Assembly elections, retaining only 32 seats. After five years in opposition, however, the PR shared in the centre-right's victory in the March 1986 Assembly elections, winning 59 seats in its own right and accordingly taking a prominent role in the resultant centre-right "cohabitation" government headed by Chirac of the RPR.

In mid-1987 the then PR president and government minister, François Léotard, disappointed Chirac by announcing that the PR would not support the RPR leader in the first round of the 1988 presidential elections, but rather would put up its own candidate. After speculation that Léotard would run himself, in September 1987 the PR gave its backing to Barre (not a PR member). However, the former Prime Minister managed only third place in the first round of voting in April 1988 (with 16.5%) and was eliminated, whereafter the PR backed Chirac in his losing contest with Mitterrand in the second round. In the June 1988 Assembly elections the PR shared in the defeat of the centre-right alliance, although its individual seat tally of 58 out of 129 for the UDF showed electoral resilience. The PR was then in opposition for five years, during which it established itself as the organizational core of UDF, although the traditional reluctance of the centrist parties to develop party structures outside parliament continued to be apparent.

In the landslide victory of the RPR/UDF alliance in the March 1993 Assembly elections, the PR took 104 of the 213 seats won by the UDF and was accordingly allocated important portfolios in the new centre-right "cohabitation" government headed by Edouard Balladur of the RPR. The PR was subsequently tainted by a series of corruption scandals that necessitated the resignations of several of its ministers, including in October 1994 the then PR president Gérard Longuet, amid allegations of irregular party financing activities. The February 1994 murder of PR deputy Yann Piat (once a member of the far-right →National Front) added to the party's poor public image. The decision of Giscard d'Estaing (by now heading the UDF) not to contest the 1995 presidential elections deprived the PR of its obvious candidate, with the result that the party opted for Balladur as the more centrist of the two RPR contenders. After Balladur had been eliminated in the first round, the PR supported the victorious candidacy of Chirac in the second, being rewarded with a strong ministerial presence in the resultant centre-right government. In June 1995 François Léotard was elected to resume the PR presidency in succession to Longuet.

The PR shared in the defeat of the centre-right in the mid-1997 Assembly elections, whereupon the party converted itself into the DL under the leadership of former Finance Minister Alain Madelin, embracing a more free-market economic policy. In the new Assembly the 44-strong Liberal Democracy and Independents group was separate from the UDF. In May 1998 a DL convention decided that the party should formally withdraw from the UDF and instead become an autonomous component of the "Alliance" umbrella organization which the RPR and UDF had created that month (→New Union for French Democracy). In the June 1999 European Parliament elections the DL opted to stand on a joint list with the RPR and other groups, but the result was a disappointing third place yielding 12.8% of the vote and 12 seats, of which the DL took four.

The RPR-DL members of the European Parliament sit in the European People's Party/European Democrats group.

National Centre of Independents and Peasants
Centre National des Indépendants et Paysans (CNIP)
Address. 146 rue de l'Université, 75007 Paris
Telephone. (+33-1) 4062-6364
Fax. (+33-1) 4556-0263
Leadership. Jean Perrin (president); Annick du Roscoat (secretary-general)

The CNIP is derived from the *Centre National des Indépendants* (CNI), which was formed in July 1948 on the initiative of Roger Duchet and René Coty and quickly succeeded in federating most independent parliamentarians of the moderate right. The CNI became the CNIP in January 1949 when it absorbed the small peasant-based *Parti Républicaine de la Liberté*. Between 1951 and 1962 the CNIP took part in various coalition governments, with party members Antoine Pinay being Prime Minister in 1952 and Coty serving as President in 1952-59. In July 1954 the CNIP was joined by Gaullist dissidents of the *Action Républicaine et Sociale* who had supported the Pinay government. In 1958 the CNIP supported the return to power of Gen. de Gaulle and the creation of the Fifth Republic, reaching its electoral peak in the November 1958 Assembly elections, in which it won 22% of the vote and 132 seats. One of these was filled by Jean-Marie Le Pen, who was later to become leader of the far-right →National Front (FN).

The CNIP's influence declined in the 1960s. Deeply divided over de Gaulle's policy of withdrawal from Algeria, it finally broke with him in October 1962. In Assembly elections the following month it lost almost all its representation, as its outgoing deputies either were defeated or transferred to the "majority" camp as Independent Republicans (later the nucleus of the Republican Party, now →Liberal Democracy). In 1967-68 the CNIP was in alliance with Jean Lecanuet's *Centre Démocrate*, but proposals for a formal merger came to nothing. Although nominally an opposition leader during this period, CNIP honorary president Pinay declined invitations to stand against de Gaulle and Georges Pompidou in the presidential elections of 1965 and 1969 respectively. In 1974 the CNIP supported the successful presidential candidacy of Valéry Giscard d'Estaing (Independent Republican) and thereafter became one of the four main parties of the "presidential majority", being represented from 1976 in successive governments headed by Raymond Barre.

The CNIP contested the March 1978 Assembly elections in alliance with other non-Gaullist "majority" parties (winning nine seats), although it did not join the →Union for French Democracy formed on the eve of the poll. Having backed Giscard d'Estaing's unsuccessful re-election bid in 1981, the CNIP was reduced to five seats by the Socialist landslide in the June 1981 Assembly elections, despite an electoral pact with the other centre-right parties. Another pact for the 1986 Assembly elections brought the CNIP a similar level of representation as a component of the victorious centre-right front, although its influence was further eroded by the Socialist victory in the 1988 presidential and Assembly elections. Through this period the CNIP maintained a significance presence in the Senate, where its representatives sat in broader centre-right groups. Continuance of the relationship in the 1993 Assembly elections was impaired by the CNIP's public support for the anti-immigration policies of the FN. However, both in that contest and in the 1997 Assembly elections successful "various right" candidates included a number of CNIP adherents.

National Front
Front National (FN)
Address. 4 rue Vauguyon, 92210 Saint Cloud
Telephone. (+33-1) 4112-1018
Fax. (+33-1) 4112-1086
Email. contact@front-nat.fr
Website. http://www.front-nat.fr
Leadership. Jean-Marie Le Pen (president); Jean-Claude Martínez (vice-president); Bruno Gollnisch (secretary-general)

The right-wing populist FN was founded in October 1972 on an anti-immigration, law and order, and strongly pro-market platform, bringing together various groups and personalities of the far right. The party has consistently denied that it is racist, pointing to the presence of French Afro-Caribbeans in its ranks and claiming that it welcomes non-whites provided they fully embrace French culture and civilization. Its founder and leader, Le Pen, had served in the elite Parachute Regiment and had been a National Assembly deputy in 1956-62, initially as a member of the *Union de Défense des Commerçants et Artisans* (UDCA) led by Pierre Poujade and later under the auspices of the →National Centre of Independents and Peasants (CNIP), and had been closely identified with the *Algérie Française* movement. The FN made little impact in the 1970s, winning only 2.5% of the vote in the 1973 Assembly elections and 3% in 1978, while Le Pen took only 0.7% in the first round of the 1974 presidential contest and was unable to stand in 1981 because he could not obtain the required sponsorship of at least 500 national or local elected representatives.

The return to national power of the left in 1981 and increasing public concern about immigration yielded a surge of support for the FN, which successfully repackaged itself as a legitimate force on the right of the centre-right opposition. This approach brought the first far-right electoral success in 25 years when, in the March 1983 municipal elections, an FN candidate was returned to one of the new district councils in the Paris region, while later in the year the then FN secretary-general, Jean-Pierre Stirbois, won 16.7% of the first-round vote in a local by-election in Dreux, thus bringing about a second-round alliance between the FN and the Gaullist →Rally for the Republic (RPR). The FN's major breakthrough came in the European Parliament elections of June 1984, when to the surprise of many observers it won 10.9% of the French vote and 10 seats. In the March 1985 regional elections it slipped to 8.7% of the first-round vote, and was weakend in late 1985 by a split which produced the rival *Front d'Opposition Nationale*. However, in the March 1986 Assembly elections (held under proportional representation), it secured 35 of the 577 seats, winning some 2.7 million votes (9.7%), many of them in working-class areas of high immigrant population where previously the →French Communist Party (PCF) had held sway. As a result of simultaneous regional elections, several RPR regional presidents were elected or re-elected with FN support.

Although the FN initially decided to support Jacques Chirac (then RPR Prime Minister) in the 1988 presidential elections, in May 1986 it withdrew its backing because of Chirac's insistence on abandoning proportional representation for Assembly elections. In January 1987 Le Pen announced his own presidential candidacy, thereby generating dissension within the RPR between those who rejected any co-operation with the far right and those who recognized that the centre-right candidate might need FN backing in the second round. In September 1987 Le Pen caused a major controversy when he publicly referred to Nazi extermination camps as a "detail" of the history of World War II, although he later expressed regret for the remark. The episode did him little damage in the 1988 presidential elections, in which he took fourth place in the first round with 14.4% of the vote (and declined to give endorsement to Chirac in the second). However, in Assembly elections in June 1988 (for which constituency-based majority voting again applied), the FN lost all but one of its seats despite achieving a first-round vote share of 9.7%. The successful FN candidate was Yann Piat (in the Var), but she was expelled from the FN in October 1988, whereafter she joined the Republican Party (and was assassinated in 1994) (→Liberal Democracy).

The FN regained an Assembly seat in a by-election for Dreux in December 1989, when Marie-France Stirbois (widow of Jean-Pierre, who had died in a car crash in November 1988) won 61.3% of the second-round vote. Le Pen acclaimed the result as demonstrating public support for the FN's opposition to immigration and to "French decadence", and called for the repatriation of all foreigners who had come to France since 1974. While not opposing French membership of the European Union (EU), the FN strongly endorsed the old Gaullist concept of a "Europe of nation states" and therefore was part of the opposition to the EU's Maastricht Treaty on closer union, which obtained wafer-thin referendum endorsement by French voters in September 1992. In the March 1993 Assembly elections, the FN failed to win representation, despite a national first-round vote share of 12.4% and an election campaign in which the "respectable" centre-right parties took up many of the FN's concerns about immigration and the rule of law.

In the June 1994 European Parliament elections the FN slipped back to 10.5% (winning 11 of the 87 French seats). In the 1995 presidential elections, however, Le Pen took fourth place in the first round with an all-time FN electoral high of 15.0% (4,573,202 votes). He again declined to give endorsement to Chirac of the RPR in the second round, announcing that he would cast a blank ballot in protest against "a detestable choice between two left-wing candidates". The FN continued its advance in municipal elections in June 1995, trebling its complement of councillors to 1,075 and winning control of three substantial southern towns (Toulon, Orange and Marignane). According to a post-election statement by Le Pen, the FN would apply "national preference" in the municipalities under its control, so that immigrants and foreigners would no longer get equal treatment in the allocation of subsidized housing, welfare benefits and public-sector jobs.

In February 1997 the FN narrowly won a high-profile mayoral by-election in Vitrolles, near Marseilles, and the following month gained more publicity when its 10th congress in Strasbourg attracted a major protest demonstration backed by the →Socialist Party (PS) and the PCF. In the mid-1997 National Assembly elections the NF advanced to 14.9% of the first-round vote, but returned only one deputy (from Toulon). It lost even this seat in a May 1998 by-election (called because the NF deputy had infringed party finance rules in the 1997 contest) and failed to regain it in a further by-election in September 1998 (called because of ballot irregularities in the first). There was evidence in these and other electoral contests that moderate conservative voters were prepared to combine with the left in unofficial "republican fronts" to defeat the FN. In November 1998 a Versailles appeal court disqualified Le Pen from elective office for a year and confirmed a suspended three-month sentence imposed on the FN leader for assaulting a PS candidate in the 1997 Assembly elections.

Simmering internal divisions in the FN came to a head in January 1999 when deputy leader and chief ideologue Bruno Mégret was elected leader of the "National Front–National Movement" (FN-*Mouvement National*, FN-MN) at a conference held in Marignane after some 17,000 of the 40,000 FN members had signed a petition in favour of a leadership election conference. Le Pen boycotted the conference and also dismissed Mégret's claim that he now led the authentic FN. The dispute between the two was about political strategy rather than ideology, in that Le Pen opposed any alliances with other parties, whereas Mégret favoured pragmatic electoral pacts with centre-right formations. Le Pen appeared to be losing the struggle when in March 1999 the influential FN mayor of Toulon declared his support for Mégret. However, in May a Paris court banned the Mégret faction from "usurping" the FN name and logo, with the result that it assumed the title →National Republican Movement (MNR).

Headed by Le Pen, the FN list in the June 1999 European Parliament elections easily outpolled the MNR, although it took only 5.7% of the vote and five seats. The FN's MEPs are part of the "unattached" contingent.

National Republican Movement
Mouvement National Républicain (MNR)
Address. 15 rue de Cronstadt, 75015 Paris
Telephone. (+33-1) 5656-6434
Fax. (+33-1) 5656-5247
Email. m-n-r@m-n-r.com
Website. http://www.m-n-r.com
Leadership. Bruno Mégret (president); Serge Martínez (secretary-general)
The MNR was founded in 1999 by a dissident faction of the radical right-wing →National Front (FN) led by Bruno Mégret, the FN deputy leader and chief ideologue, who had come into serious conflict with FN leader Jean-Marie Le Pen over political strategy. Whereas Le Pen opposed any alliances between the FN and other parties, Mégret favoured pragmatic electoral pacts with centre-right formations. After some 17,000 of the 40,000 FN members had signed a petition in favour of a leadership election conference, and Le Pen had opted to ignore the petition, a conference of the dissident faction in Marignane in January 1999 elected Mégret as leader of the "National Front–National Movement". Having boycotted the conference, Le Pen dismissed Mégret's claim that he now led the authentic FN.

The breakaway party was strengthened when in March 1999 the influential FN mayor of Toulon declared his support for it. However, in May a Paris court banned the Mégret faction from "usurping" the FN name and logo, with the result that it assumed the title National Republican Movement (MNR). In the June 1999 European Parliament elections the Mégret list was easily outpolled by the rump FN, winning only 3.3% of the vote and no seats.

New Union for French Democracy
Nouvelle Union pour la Démocratie Française (NUDF)
Address. 133bis rue de l'Université, 75014 Paris
Telephone. (+33-1) 5359-2000
Fax. (+33-1) 5359-2059
Email. internet@udf.org
Website. http://www.nouvelle-udf.org
Leadership. François Bayrou (president); Hervé de Charette (president delegate); Philippe Douste-Blazy (Assembly group chair); Pierre-André Wiltzer (secretary-general)

The "New" UDF was launched in 1999 following a UDF congress decision in November 1998 that the UDF constituent parties would formally combine into a unified organization and therefore cease to exist independently. The centre-right UDF had been created in February 1978 as an electoral alliance of the non-Gaullist "majority" (i.e. then ruling) parties, namely (i) what was then called the Republican Party (PR), which in 1997 became →Liberal Democracy and in May 1998 left the UDF; (ii) the Radical Party; (iii) what was then called the Centre of Social Democrats (CDS) and in 1995 become the Democratic Force (FD); (iv) what later became the Social Democratic Party (PSD); and (v) the *Clubs Perspectives et Réalités*, which in 1995 became the Popular Party for French Democracy (PPDF).

Of the original UDF components, the **Radical Party** was by far the oldest, having been founded in 1901 from pre-existing Radical groups sharing a commitment to anti-clericalism and the separation of Church and State. Its full title, rarely used under the Fifth Republic, was Radical Republican and Radical-Socialist Party (*Parti Républicain Radical et Radical-Socialiste*, PRRRS), reflecting the Radicals' history as the mainstay of the Third Republic (1871–1940) and their frequent cooperation with the left-wing parties under both the Third and Fourth Republics. The party was also often referred to as the *Parti Valoisien* after its headquarters address in Paris, from where it provided many Prime Ministers up to and after World War I, including Georges Clemenceau in 1906-09 and 1917-19. Its celebrated slogan was *"Pas d'ennemi à gauche"* ("No enemy to the left"), on which basis it participated in the anti-fascist Popular Front government formed in 1936 under the leadership of what was then the SFIO and much later became the →Socialist Party (PS). Despite a post-war electoral decline, the Radicals remained a focal point in the frequent coalition building of the Fourth Republic until its demise in 1958, providing the Prime Ministers of no less than 12 governments.

Traditionally eschewing rigid structures, the Radical Party suffered a series of splits in 1954-56, when Pierre Mendès-France moved the party to the left and tried to impose more internal discipline. By late 1958 Mendès-France and his left-wing followers had become the minority and subsequently broke away to participate in the formation of the Unified Socialist Party (PSU), part of which later joined the PS. During the first decade of the Fifth Republic (1958-68) the rump Radicals under the leadership of René Billères participated in moves towards union of the non-Communist left, joining the Federation of the Democratic and Socialist Left (FGDS) in 1965 and participating in the FGDS advance in the 1967 Assembly elections. After the May 1968 political and social crisis, however, Maurice Faure moved the party back to a centrist posture, which was consolidated following the election of Jean-Jacques Servan-Schreiber to the party presidency in 1971. The Radical majority's refusal to subscribe to a new union of the left involving the Socialists and the →French Communist Party (PCF) caused the exit of the left-wing minority in 1972 to form what became the Left Radical Movement (MRG), now called the →Left Radical Party (PRG).

In the 1974 presidential elections the Radicals backed the successful candidacy of Valéry Giscard d'Estaing (Independent Republican), but only after the first round and in return for specific policy commitments. Under the Giscard d'Estaing presidency the Radicals were included in successive centre-right coalitions, although their initial return to government was controversial: appointed Minister of Reforms, Servan-Schreiber was dismissed within a fortnight for criticizing the proposed resumption of French nuclear tests in the Pacific. Pursuing attempts to forge greater unity among the smaller centrist and centre-left parties, the Radicals in July 1977 absorbed the Movement of Social Liberals (*Mouvement des Sociaux Libéraux*, MSL), which had been formed earlier in the year by Gaullist dissidents led by Olivier Stirn.

The forerunner of the **Democratic Force** (*Force Démocrate*, FD) was the centrist, Christian democratic and pro-European Centre of Social Democrats (*Centre des Sociaux Démocrates*, CSD) founded in May 1976, although its constituent elements had their roots in a 19th-century movement aimed at reconciling Catholics with the Third Republic (1871–1940). After World War II these forces were represented by the Popular Republican Movement (*Mouvement Républicain Populaire*, MRP) led by Georges Bidault and other wartime resistance leaders, which was the strongest parliamentary party until the 1951 elections and took part in most Fourth Republic governments until its demise in 1958. Bidault was himself Prime Minister in 1946 and 1949–50; other MRP premiers were Robert Schuman (1947–48) and Pierre Pflimlin (1958). The immediate antecedents of the CDS were the Democratic Centre (*Centre Démocrate*, CD) and the Democracy and Progress Centre (*Centre Démocratie et Progrès*, CDP), both of which emerged under the Fifth Republic.

The CD had been launched in March 1966 by Jean Lecanuet, who had scored 15.9% in the 1965 presidential elections. In the 1969 contest most CD elements had backed Alain Poher (who received 23.3% in the first round and 41.8% in the second), although some had supported the successful Gaullist candidate, Georges Pompidou, thus abandoning the previous centrist policy of acting as a balancing force between the right-wing "majority" parties and the left-wing opposition. The CDP had been founded after the 1969 elections by centrist supporters of President Pompidou, notably Jacques Duhamel, Joseph Fontanet and René Pleven. In the 1973 Assembly elections the CD and the CDP had returned 24 and 34 deputies respectively, the former as part of the Reformers' Movement (created in 1971 by various centrist groups then outside the government "majority") and the latter in alliance with the ruling Gaullists and Independent Republicans. In the first round of the 1974 presidential elections the CDP had supported Jacques Chaban-Delmas (Gaullist) and the CD Giscard d'Estaing, but both parties had contributed to the victory of the latter in the second round. Both parties had joined the resultant centre-right government headed by Jacques Chirac and had been prominent in further moves towards greater cohesion of the centre, notably the six-party Federation of Reformers created in June 1975, prior to the launching of the CDS in May 1976 under the presidency of Lecanuet.

The forerunner of the **Popular Party for French Democracy** (*Parti Populaire pour la Démocratie Française*, PPDF) was the Perspectives and Realities Clubs (*Clubs Perspectives et Réalités*, CPR) grouping founded in 1965 by Jean-Pierre Fourcade, which had acted as a think tank for the UDF as a whole, providing a political home for centrist intellectuals reluctant to join a traditional political party. Many of its leading members were associated with the Republican Party component of the UDF (→Liberal Democracy), notably its chair from 1982 to 1984, Jean-François Deniau, who had been a minister and European commissioner under the Giscard d'Estaing presidency (1974–81). Having lost the French presidency in 1981, Giscard d'Estaing himself took the chairmanship of the CPR until 1989.

The **Social Democratic Party** (*Parti Social-Démocrate*, PSD) had been established in December 1973 as the Movement of Democratic Socialists of France (*Mouvement des Démocrates Socialistes de France*, MDSF) by a faction of the PS opposed to the common programme issued by the PS and PCF in 1972. Claiming to enshrine the authentic socialist tradition of Jean Jaurès and Léon Blum, the MDSF advocated centrist unity and joined both the Reformers' Movement·and the Federation of Reformers in the mid-1970s. The first MDSF vice-president, Émile Muller, won 0.7% of the vote in the first round of the 1974 presidential elections, whereafter the MDSF backed the successful candidacy of Giscard d'Estaing in the second. The MDSF transformed itself into the PSD in October 1982, at the same time absorbing some other social democratic elements.

The decision of the above parties to create the **Union for French Democracy** (*Union pour la Démocratie Française*, UDF) a month before the March 1978 Assembly elections was inspired in part by the decision of the (Gaullist) RPR to withdraw from first-round electoral pacts with the PR and CDS on the grounds that negotiation by these two parties of separate first-round agreements with the Radicals (the most left-wing of the "majority" parties) had violated the terms of the RPR/PR/CDS agreement. The UDF was backed from the outset by President Giscard d'Estaing (after whose 1977 book *Démocratie Française* the alliance was named) and by his Prime Minister, Raymond Barre. Its creation therefore heightened tensions between the Giscardian and Gaullist wings of the "majority", the former viewing it as an attempt to engineer electoral superiority. In the 1978 elections the UDF parties won increased aggregate representation of 124 seats (compared with 154 for the RPR), assisted by the operation of reciprocal voting support arrangements with the RPR in the second round. The elected UDF deputies included 71 from the PR, 35 from the CDS, seven Radicals and four from the MDSF. Immediately after polling the UDF council formally elevated the alliance to the status of a federation of its constituent parties, under the presidency of Jean Lecanuet (leader of the CDS). In the June 1979 elections to the European Parliament the strongly pro-European UDF list (*Union pour la France en Europe*) came top of the poll with 27.6%.

The UDF was the mainstay of Giscard d'Estaing's bid for a second presidential term in 1981 as a "citizen-candidate" rather than as the nominee of any party. Following his narrow second-round defeat by François Mitterrand (PS), the UDF formed an electoral alliance with the RPR for the June 1981 Assembly elections, called the *Union pour la Majorité Nouvelle* (UMN) and providing for single first-round candidates in 385 of the 474 metropolitan constituencies as well as reciprocal voting support for the best-placed second-round candidate in the others. The UDF nevertheless shared in the rout of the centre-right by the PS, winning 19.2% of the first-round vote and retaining only 63 Assembly seats, of which the PR took 32, the CDS 25 and the Radicals two. It therefore went into opposition for the next five years, the UMN alliance lapsing in 1983.

In April 1985 the UDF signed a new cooperation agreement with the RPR, with which it drew up a joint manifesto for the March 1986 Assembly elections (in which proportional representation applied). Presenting some candidates jointly with the RPR and others in its own right, the UDF played its part in the defeat of the PS-led government, increasing its representation to 131 seats out 577, the PR remaining the strongest UDF component with 59 seats. In the succeeding centre-right coalition headed by the RPR, the UDF parties received 17 ministerial posts out of 41. But the fragility of the ruling coalition became apparent in 1987 when the PR leader, François Léotard, announced that he would not support the RPR leader (and Prime Minister), Jacques Chirac, in the first round of the 1988 presidential elections. When it was announced in September 1987 that Barre (a centrist without formal party affiliation) would be a candidate, the PR and other UDF components declared their support for him. In the event, Barre came in third place in the first round in April 1988 with 16.5% of the vote, whereupon the UDF gave second-round support to Chirac in his unsuccessful attempt to deny Mitterrand a second term.

New Assembly elections held in June 1988 (by constituency-based majority voting) were contested by the UDF in an alliance with the RPR called the *Union du Rassemblement et du Centre* (URC). The centre-right parties lost their majority but the UDF showed resilience, for the first time returning more deputies (129) than the RPR (127), the UDF contingent including 58 PR, 49 CDS, three Radical and three PSD deputies. Immediately after the elections Giscard d'Estaing replaced Lecanuet as president of the UDF. In opposition over the next five years, most of the UDF contested the 1989 European elections on a joint list with the RPR (winning 28.9% of the vote and 26 seats), whilst the CDS presented an independent list which took 8.4% and seven seats. In June 1990 the UDF and RPR announced the creation of the *Union pour la France* (UPF), amid much talk about the need for a unified party. In reality, the UDF and the RPR continued their long struggle for supremacy on the centre-right, with the added ingredient of resumed rivalry between Giscard d'Estaing and Chirac. Also divisive was the Maastricht Treaty on European union, which was fully supported by the UDF, whereas important sections of the RPR campaigned for a "no" vote in the September 1992 referendum that yielded a narrow majority for French ratification.

As widely anticipated, the Assembly elections of March 1993 produced a landslide victory for the UDF/RPR alliance, which won 80% of the seats on a 40% first-round vote share. Crucially, the RPR emerged with 247 of the 577 seats, against 213 for the UDF parties, thus effectively dashing Giscard d'Estaing's further presidential ambitions. The PR remained dominant in the UDF elected contingent, taking 104 seats compared with 57 for the CDS (which had declined to give automatic support to better-placed centre-right candidates in the second round). The UDF parties were allocated important portfolios in the new "cohabitation" government headed by Edouard Balladur of the RPR, and in the European Parliament elections of June 1994 Giscard d'Estaing headed another joint UDF/RPR list (this time including the CDS), which slipped to 25.6%, giving it 28 seats.

The UDF was weakened by a series of corruption scandals that yielded the resignations of several ministers in 1994, with the result that both Giscard d'Estaing and Barre announced that they would not stand in the 1995 presidential elections. In the absence of a candidate from their own ranks, most UDF components initially supported Balladur as the more centrist of the two RPR contenders. After Balladur had been eliminated in the first round, however, the UDF officially swung behind the victorious candidacy of Chirac in the second, being rewarded with a strong ministerial presence in the resultant centre-right government headed by Alain Juppé of the RPR. In an apparent reconciliation of their longstanding personal rivalry, Giscard d'Estaing was invited to give "elder statesman" advice to the newly-installed President Chirac.

In July 1995 the CPR grouping converted itself into the PPDF under the leadership of Hervé de Charette and Jean-Pierre Raffarin, while in November 1995 the CDS became the FD under the leadership of François Bayrou. Both new creations remained under the UDF umbrella.

Giscard d'Estaing stood down as UDF leader in March 1996 (to devote himself to founding a centrist think tank) and indicated his preference that the succession should go to Alain Madelin (then of the PPDF, formerly a vice-president of the PR and subsequently leader of Liberal Democracy), who had the previous August been dismissed as Economy and Finance Minister after failing to persuade Prime Minister Juppé of the need for drastic measures to curb the budget deficit. However, UDF constituents preferred the PR leader, François Léotard, who secured 57.4% of delegates' vote at a national council meeting in Lyon. Thereafter, the growing influence of the far-right →National Front (FN) became an increasingly divisive issue, with some UDF elements being prepared to support left-wing candidates to defeat the FN, while the UDF leadership declined to give specific endorsement to anti-FN "republican fronts".

The UDF shared in the defeat of the centre-right in the mid-1997 Assembly elections, its aggregate representation falling to 108 seats following a first-round vote share of only 14.2%. Consigned to opposition, the UDF also lost ground in the March 1998 regional elections, following which five UDF politicians were elected as regional assembly presidents on the strength of FN support. Two of these subsequently stood down under pressure, but the other three were expelled from the UDF, with the result that one of them, Charles Millon, launched what later became the →Liberal Christian Right. In May 1998 the UDF and the RPR set up the "Alliance" as a joint umbrella organization, whereupon Liberal Democracy (successor to the PR) formally withdrew from the UDF and opted instead to become an autonomous component of the Alliance.

Mired in a party financing scandal, Léotard was in September 1998 succeeded as president of the UDF by François Bayrou, leader of Democratic Force (now the largest UDF component). At a congress in Lille in November 1998 the remaining UDF formations decided that they would cease to have separate existence and would instead combine into a unitary party. Bayrou resisted RPR pressure for another joint list for the June 1999 Euro-elections, opting for a separate UDF slate, which took 9.3% of the vote and only nine seats. The UDF then resorted to the time-honoured marketing stratagem of adding "New" to its title, so that it became "*La Nouvelle* UDF".

The NUDF is a member of the International Democrat Union and the European Democrat Union; through the FD it is also affiliated to the Christian Democrat International. The NUDF members of the European Parliament sit in the European People's Party/European Democrats group.

Rally for France and the Independence of Europe
Rassemblement pour la France et l'Indépendance de l'Europe (RPF-IE)
Address. 159 ave Charles de Gaulle, 92521 Neuilly-sur-Seine
Telephone. (+33-1) 5562-2424
Fax. (+33-1) 5562-2435
Email. rpf@rpf-ie.org
Website. http://www.rpf-ie.org
Leadership. Charles Pasqua (president): Philippe de Villiers (vice-president); Jean-Jacques Guillet (secretary-general)
Opposed to further European integration, the RPF-IE was formally established as a political party in November 1999, following the success of the RPF-IE list in the June 1999 European Parliament elections. It united the Rally for France (RPF), launched by former Gaullist Interior Minister Charles Pasqua in June 1998 as a breakaway from the →Rally for the Republic (RPR), and the Movement for France (*Mouvement pour la France*, MPF) led by Philippe de Villiers.

The MPF had been formed in November 1994 as the successor to The Other Europe (*L'Autre Europe*), which had been created to contest the June 1994 European Parliament elections, principally on the initiative of the French-British financier, Sir James Goldsmith. Opposed to the Maastricht process of European economic and monetary union, it also condemned the 1993 GATT world trade liberalization agreement, arguing that Western Europe needed to protect its industry and employment levels from Asian competition based on cheap labour. In the 1994 European poll The Other Europe list obtained 12.4% of the vote and 13 of the 87 French seats. In the 1995 presidential elections, MPF leader de Villiers (a former member of the →Union for French Democracy) was placed seventh out of nine first-round candidates, winning 4.7% of the vote.

In the June 1999 Euro-elections the RPF-IE list took second place, ahead of the RPR, winning 13.1% of the vote and 13 seats on a platform of opposition to further European integration and enlargement. In late 1999 the new formation numbered five Assembly members and six senators among its adherents.

The 13 RPF-IE members of the European Parliament sit in the Union for a Europe of Nations group.

Rally for the Republic
Rassemblement pour la République (RPR)
Address. 123 rue de Lille, 75007 Paris
Telephone. (+33-1) 4955-6300
Fax. (+33-1) 4551-4479
Email. webmaster@rpr.org
Website. http://www.rpr.asso.fr
Leadership. Michèle Alliot-Marie (president); Jean-Louis Debré (Assembly group chair)
Although established under its present name in December 1976, the broadly conservative RPR is directly descended from the *Rassemblement du Peuple Français* (RPF) established in April 1947 by Gen. Charles de Gaulle, who had been head of the London-based Free French forces during World War II and then Prime Minister of the first post-liberation government (1944-46). Formed with the central objective of returning de Gaulle to power, the RPF became the strongest Assembly party in 1951 (with 118 seats), but was weakened in 1952 by the creation of the dissident *Action Républicaine et Sociale* (ARS). When members of the rump RPF accepted ministerial posts in 1953, de Gaulle severed his links with the party, which was dissolved as a parliamentary group. Gaullist deputies then created the *Union des Républicains d'Action Sociale* (URAS), which became the *Centre National des Républicains Sociaux* (CNRS) in February 1954. Following de Gaulle's return to power in mid-1958 amid the collapse of the Fourth Republic, the movement was reconstituted for the November 1958 Assembly elections as the *Union pour la Nouvelle République* (UNR), which won a plurality of 188 seats. Inducted as President of the Fifth Republic in January 1959, de Gaulle appointed Michel Debré (UNR) as his Prime Minister.

Under the right-oriented Debré premiership a left-wing Gaullist faction formed the *Union Démocratique du Travail* (UDT), which was reunited with the UNR following the replacement of Debré by the technocratic Georges Pompidou in April 1962. In the November 1962 Assembly elections the UNR-UDT increased its dominance by winning 219 seats. In December 1965 de Gaulle won popular election for a second presidential term, comfortably defeating left-wing candidate François Mitterrand in the second round with 55.2% of the vote. For the March 1976 Assembly elections the UNR-UDT adopted the title *Union des Démocrates pour la Cinquième République* (UDCR), which slipped to 200 seats and henceforth relied on Valéry Giscard d'Estaing's Independent Republicans for a parliamentary majority. In November 1967 the UDCR title was formally adopted by the party, which at the same time absorbed a faction of the (Christian democratic) *Mouvement Républicain Populaire* (MRP) and other groups further to the left. In the wake of the May 1968 national crisis, the Gaullists registered a landslide victory in Assembly elections in June, winning 292 seats under the designation *Union pour la Défense de la République* and continuing in office under the reformist premiership of Maurice Couve de Murville. The new parliamentary group preferred the slightly different title *Union des Démocrates pour la République* (UDR), which was subsequently applied to the party as a whole.

De Gaulle resigned in April 1969 after unexpectedly being denied referendum approval of constitutional and regional reform proposals. He was succeeded in June elections by Pompidou, who won a comfortable 57.6% victory over a centrist candidate in the second round. The new Gaullist Prime Minister was Jacques Chaban-Delmas, seen as representative of the UDR's modernist wing, but corruption charges and other difficulties resulted in his replacement by the orthodox Pierre Messmer in July 1972. In the Assembly elections of March 1973 the UDR slumped to 183 seats, but Messmer continued as Prime Minister at the head of a coalition with centrist parties. Pompidou's death in office in April 1974 precipitated presidential elections in May, when Chaban-Delmas as the UDR candidate was eliminated in the first round (with only 14.6% of the vote). Many Gaullist voters preferred the more dynamic Giscard d'Estaing (Independent Republican), who won a narrow second-round victory over Mitterrand and proceeded to appoint Jacques Chirac (UDR) to head a government with strong centrist representation. Increasing strains between President and Prime Minister yielded Chirac's resignation in August 1976, whereupon the Gaullists ceased to hold the premiership but continued as part of the ruling coalition. In December 1976 Chirac engineered the conversion of the UDR into the RPR, which became his power base in increasingly acrimonious competition between the Gaullist and Giscardian wings of the "majority". In March 1977 Chirac was elected mayor of Paris, defeating the centrist candidate backed by the President.

After Chirac had failed to create a "majority" alliance for the March 1978 Assembly elections, the RPR slipped to 154 seats, against 124 for the new Union for French Democracy (UDF), grouping the Giscardian centrist parties (→New Union for French Democracy). In the June 1979 European Parliament elections the RPR list (called *Défense des Intérêts de la France*, reflecting traditional Gaullist doubts about the European idea) managed only 16.3% (and fourth place) as against the UDF's 27.6%. In the 1981 presidential elections, moreover, Chirac took a poor third place in the first round (with 18% of the vote) and was eliminated; although he said that he would personally vote for Giscard d'Estaing in the second round in May, his failure to urge RPR supporters to do likewise was seen as contributing to the incumbent's narrow defeat by Mitterrand. In the resultant Assembly elections in June the RPR shared in the centre-right's decimation by the →Socialist Party, slumping to 88 seats notwithstanding the presentation of single centre-right candidates in over three-quarters of the metropolitan constituencies under the banner of the *Union pour la Majorité Nouvelle* (UMN).

In opposition from 1981 to 1986, the RPR launched an internal modernization and rejuvenation programme, with Chirac bringing forward a new generation of leaders more favourable to European integration and more in tune with the changing social composition of France. On the basis of a declaration signed in April 1985, the RPR and the UDF presented a joint manifesto in the March 1986 Assembly elections as well as single candidates for many seats. In the resultant centre-right victory, the RPR emerged with 155 deputies in the new 577-seat Assembly elected by proportional representation, ahead of the UDF, so that Chirac was again appointed Prime Minister of a coalition government in which the RPR held 21 posts and the UDF parties 17. During the ensuing two years of "cohabitation" between a Socialist President and a Gaullist Prime Minister, the RPR experienced internal divisions about how to respond to the growing strength of the far-right →National Front (FN) led by Jean-Marie Le Pen, with some Gaullists rejecting any links with the FN and others arguing that the party could not be ignored, especially since the FN was making inroads into RPR support. The debate intensified in January 1987 when Le Pen announced his own candidacy in the 1988 presidential elections, having previously indicated that the FN would support Chirac. After some equivocation, the RPR leader announced in May 1987 that there would be no national alliance between the RPR and the FN, while not prohibiting the informal RPR/FN voting co-operation that was already a factor in some localities and regions.

In his second tilt at the presidency in April-May 1988, Chirac took second place in the first round (with 19.9% of the vote) and thus went forward to the second against Mitterrand, losing to the incumbent by 45.98% to 54.02%. The relatively wide margin of the RPR candidate's defeat was attributed in part to the refusal of Le Pen to instruct his four million first-round supporters to vote for Chirac in the second. Assembly elections in June 1988 (held by constituency-based majority voting) were contested by the RPR in an alliance with the UDF called the *Union du Rassemblement et du Centre* (URC), but not only did the centre-right parties lose their majority but also the RPR for the first time returned fewer deputies (127) than the UDF (129). In opposition over the next five years, the RPR and UDF contested the 1989 European Parliament on a joint list (winning 28.9% of the vote) and in

June 1990 announced the creation of yet another alliance, called the *Union pour la France* (UPF), amid much talk about the need for a unified party in the next legislative elections and a single presidential candidate. In reality, the RPR and the UDF continued their long struggle for supremacy on the centre-right, with the added spice of resumed personal rivalry between Chirac and Giscard d'Estaing. Also divisive in this period was the Maastricht Treaty on European union, which was supported wholeheartedly by the UDF, whereas important sections of the RPR (although not Chirac himself) campaigned for a "no" vote in the September 1992 referendum that yielded a very narrow majority for French ratification.

As widely forecast, the Assembly elections of March 1993 produced a landslide victory for the RPR/UDF alliance, which won 80% of the seats on a 39.5% first-round vote share. Crucially, the RPR emerged with 247 of the 577 seats (and 20.4% of the first-round vote), against 213 (and 19.1%) for the UDF parties, so that Chirac was able to nominate the new Prime Minister. His choice fell on Edouard Balladur, a former RPR Finance Minister and supposedly a Chirac loyalist, who was charged with running the government while the RPR leader concentrated on mounting a third attempt on the presidency. A leading RPR campaigner against the Maastricht Treaty, Philippe Séguin, was elected president of the National Assembly in April 1993. In the event, Balladur became so popular as Prime Minister that he was persuaded to renege on a pledge not to enter the presidential race. The upshot was that both Chirac and Balladur contested the 1995 elections, with the latter securing backing from within the UDF (which did not put up a candidate). Meanwhile, the RPR/UDF alliance was maintained for the June 1994 European Parliament elections, in which their combined vote slipped to 25.6%, yielding 28 of the 87 French seats.

After a slow start, Chirac's campaigning skills and command of the powerful RPR party machine, plus a late-breaking phone-tapping scandal in which Balladur was implicated, took the RPR leader to second place in the first round of the presidential balloting in April 1995 (with 20.8% of the vote), behind the Socialist candidate but ahead of Balladur (18.6%). Chirac therefore went into the second round in May and was at last victorious with 52.6% of the vote, despite again being denied second-round endorsement by the FN. Pledging himself to restoring "social cohesion", Chirac named Foreign Minister Alain Juppé (who had been the new President's campaign manager in his role as RPR secretary-general) to head a new coalition government maintaining approximate balance between the RPR and the UDF. At a party congress in October 1995 Juppé was formally elected to the RPR presidency in succession to Chirac, receiving 93% of the ballots in an uncontested election.

Damaged by corruption allegations in 1996, the RPR also experienced internal divisions on how the party should respond to the growing strength of the FN. Although the RPR leadership opposed any political cooperation with the FN, it declined to give formal backing to anti-FN "republican fronts" with the centre and left, despite narrowly defeating the FN in a mayoral by-election in Dreux in November 1996 on the strength of left-wing support. In an Assembly by-election in Vitrolles, near Marseilles, in February 1997 Juppé urged first-round RPR voters "to face up to their responsibilities" in the second, but the contest was won by the FN candidate. Meanwhile, an RPR national council meeting had approved an age-limit of 75 years for candidates in the next Assembly elections and of 70 thereafter; it had also declared its opposition to French-style "multiple mandates" often held by politicians and decided that in future party list elections at least one-third of RPR candidates with a chance of being elected would be women.

Despite the Juppé government's unpopularity, Chirac unexpectedly called early Assembly elections for May-June 1997. A general rout for the centre-right, in which the RPR slumped to 134 seats and a first-round vote share of 15.7%, resulted in Chirac having to accept "cohabitation" with a Socialist-led government. It also resulted in Juppé's immediate resignation as RPR president, in which post he was succeeded by Séguin at a special party congress in July. Séguin declared that the RPR should neither demonize the FN nor form tactical alliances with it, but should rather seek to appeal to most FN voters who were "neither fascists nor opposed to democracy". In regional elections in March 1998 the RPR/UDF were again outpolled by the left, though only narrowly. An injunction from both the RPR and UDF leaderships that their regional parties should not make deals with the FN to secure regional presidencies was observed by RPR federations (but not by the UDF).

Having failed to persuade a party conference that the RPR should shorten its name to "*Le Rassemblement*", Séguin was buffeted in early 1998 by further corruption cases involving RPR politicians in Paris and elsewhere. In April 1998 dissident RPR members of the Paris city council launched the →PARIS formation, in protest against the alleged corruption of the RPR administration. In the same month RPR members of the Assembly staged a surprise walk-out before a vote to approve French participation in the single European currency (euro), contending that their action did not indicate disapproval of the euro but opposition to the government's economic policies. In May 1998 RPR and UDF agreed to form a loose umbrella organization called the "Alliance". However, the RPR was weakened in June 1998 by the launching of a new movement by former Gaullist Interior Minister Charles Pasqua opposed to further European integration and enlargement. In February 1999 efforts by Séguin to persuade the UDF as a whole to present a joint list under his leadership in the forthcoming Euro-elections came to nought, amid much acrimony on both sides. In April 1999 Séguin unexpectedly resigned as RPR president, claiming that his authority had been undermined by Chirac. RPR secretary-general Nicolas Sarkozy became acting president and led the party in the June 1999 Euro-elections, in which the RPR presented a joint list with former UDF component →Liberal Democracy (DL) which also included →Civil Society and →Ecology Generation. The list was relegated to third place with 12.8% of the vote and 12 of the 87 seats (of which the RPR took six), being outpolled by Pasqua's new →Rally for France and the Independence of Europe (RPF-IE).

Sarkozy immediately resigned as RPR acting president and in September 1999 also vacated the post of secretary-general, asserting that he would not seek the party presidency. A divisive leadership contest resulted in the election in early December of former Sports Minister Michèle Alliot-Marie as RPR president. A pro-European, Alliot-Marie easily defeated Chirac-backed Jean-Paul Delevoye in the runoff balloting, to become the first woman leader of a major French party.

Claiming a membership of some 400,000, the RPR is a member of the International Democrat Union and of the European Democrat Union. Its representatives in the European Parliament sit in the European People's Party/European Democrats group.

Socialist Party
Parti Socialiste (PS)
Address. 10 rue de Solférino, 75333 Paris 07
Telephone. (+33-1) 4556-7700
Fax. (+33-1) 4556-7953
Email. infops@parti-socialiste.fr
Website. http://www.parti-socialiste.fr
Leadership. Lionel Jospin (political leader); François Hollande (first secretary)

The party was founded in April 1905 as the French Section of the Workers' International (*Section Française de l'Internationale Ouvrière*, SFIO), being a merger of the Socialist Party of France (inspired by Jules Guesde) and the French Socialist Party (led by Jean Jaurès). The SFIO sought to rally pre-1914 labour opposition to war within the Second International, but a majority of the party regarded World War I as one of French national defence (one notable exception being Jaurès, who was assassinated in July 1914 by a nationalist fanatic). At its

December 1920 congress in Tours the SFIO was split when a majority of delegates voted for membership of the Communist International (Comintern) and thus founded the →French Communist Party (PCF), while the minority maintained the SFIO as a non-revolutionary party. Having supported →Radical Party administrations from 1924, the SFIO became the largest party in the 1936 elections under the leadership of Léon Blum, who formed a Popular Front government with the Radicals, supported externally by the PCF. In opposition from 1938, the "reconstituted" SFIO went underground following the French surrender to Nazi Germany in 1940; it played an active part in the resistamce and also participated in the Algiers Committee set up by Gen. de Gaulle as leader of the Free French.

Following the liberation of France in 1944, the SFIO joined a provisional government headed by de Gaulle, becoming the third largest Assembly party in the 1945 elections with 139 seats, behind the PCF and the (Christian democratic) Popular Republican Movement, and retaining this ranking in both 1946 elections, although its representation fell to 93 seats. Eschewing alliance with the PCF in favour of centre-left cooperation, the SFIO headed the first two Fourth Republic governments (under Blum in 1946-47 and Paul Ramadier in 1947), instituting an extensive nationalization programme. In 1947 Vincent Auriol of the SFIO was elected President of France, and in the 1951 Assembly elections the SFIO recovered to 104 seats. Although it fell back to 95 seats in the 1956 elections, in 1956–57 the then SFIO leader, Guy Mollet, was Prime Minister of the Fourth Republic's longest-lasting government, playing a major role in the creation of the European Economic Community. However, internal dissension and defections over the role of the Mollet government in the 1956 Suez crisis and over the SFIO's support for the retention of French sovereignty in Algeria were intensified by the participation of Mollet and other SFIO ministers in the national unity government formed by de Gaulle on the collapse of the Fourth Republic in mid-1958. In Assembly elections in November 1958 the SFIO slumped to 40 seats, following which the party leadership supported the installation of de Gaulle as President of the Fifth Republic. The SFIO nevertheless refused to participate in the Gaullist-led government formed in January 1959 and was to remain in opposition for over two decades.

Having recovered somewhat to 66 seats in the 1962 Assembly elections, the SFIO in September 1965 joined with the Radicals and the small Convention of Republican Institutions (CIR) to form the Federation of the Democratic and Socialist Left (*Fédération de la Gauche Démocratique et Socialiste*, FGDS). Elected president of the FGDS was the CIR leader, François Mitterrand, who as leader of the former Democratic and Social Union of the Resistance (*Union Démocratique et Sociale de la Résistance*, UDSR) had participated in successive Fourth Republic governments and had opposed Gen. de Gaulle's return to power in 1958. As candidate of the FGDS, and supported by the PCF and other left-wing formations, Mitterrand took de Gaulle to the second round in the 1965 presidential elections (held by direct suffrage), winning 44.8% of the vote. In the 1967 Assembly elections the FGDS benefited from a second-round support pact with the PCF, winning a total of 121 seats. However, in further elections held in June 1968 in the wake of the May "events" the FGDS retained only 57 seats, amid a landslide to the Gaullists. This defeat heightened disagreements among the FGDS constituent groupings, in light of which Mitterrand resigned from the presidency in November 1968, shortly before the Radicals decided against joining a unified party based on the FGDS.

Notwithstanding the effective collapse of the FGDS, the SFIO pursued the goal of a broader "new" socialist party on the basis of a merger with Mitterrand's CIR and the Union of Clubs for the Renewal of the Left (*Union des Clubs pour le Renouveau de la Gauche*, UCRG). On the eve of the May 1969 presidential elections an intended founding congress of the new party was held at Alfortville, but the CIR refused to back the presidential candidacy of SFIO right-winger Gaston Defferre (mayor of Marseilles), who went on to score an ignominious 5% of the vote in the first round. Subsequently, the CIR did not participate when a new Socialist Party was proclaimed at the Issy-les-Moulineaux congress of July 1969, as a merger of the SFIO and the UCRG, whose leader, Alain Savary, was elected PS first secretary (and Mollet bowed out after 23 years as SFIO leader). However, renewed efforts to bring the CIR into the new party reached a successful conclusion in June 1971 with the holding of a "congress of socialist unity" at Epinay, with Mitterrand being elected first secretary of the enlarged PS.

Under Mitterrand's leadership, the PS adopted a strategy of "union of the left", in June 1972 signing a common programme with the PCF and the Left Radical Movement (MRG) (→Left Radical Party) that featured wide-ranging nationalization plans. On the basis of the programme, the left made major gains in the Assembly elections of March 1973, when the PS and the MRG (standing as the Union of the Socialist and Democratic Left) jointly returned 102 deputies, including 89 Socialists. The following year Mitterrand contested presidential elections as the agreed candidate of virtually the entire left in both rounds of voting, but was narrowly defeated by Valéry Giscard d'Estaing (Independent Republican) in the second round, receiving 49.2% of the vote. In 1975 the PS was further enlarged when it was joined by the minority wing of the Unified Socialist Party (*Parti Socialiste Unifié*, PSU) led by Michel Rocard and also by a "third component" consisting mainly of affiliated members of the Socialist-led CFDT trade union federation. However, the steady growth of PS strength engendered serious strains in the party's alliance with the PCF, culminating in the failure of the left to agree on a revised common programme for the March 1978 Assembly elections. In that contest reciprocal support arrangements were operated by the left-wing parties in the second round, but the PS tally of 103 seats (plus 10 for the MRG) was disappointing, even though the PS could claim to have become the strongest single party with around 23% of the first-round vote.

Standing as the PS candidate in the May 1981 presidential elections, Mitterrand obtained 25.9% in the first round, which was also contested by PCF and MRG candidates; backed by the entire left in the second round, he defeated incumbent Giscard d'Estaing by 51.8% to 48.2%, thus becoming President at his third attempt. Assembly elections in June 1981 gave the Socialists their first-ever absolute majority, of 285 seats out of 491. The new PS-led government, which included MRG and PCF ministers, was headed by Pierre Mauroy, while Lionel Jospin succeeded Mitterrand as PS first secretary. The Mauroy government proceeded to implement extensive nationalization measures, but was quickly obliged to abandon plans for state-led economic expansion in the interests of containing inflation and preventing currency depreciation. The PCF withdrew from the government in July 1984 when Mauroy was replaced as Prime Minister by Laurent Fabius, who faced considerable unrest in the party and country over the government's switch to orthodox economic policies. In the Assembly elections of March 1986 (held under proportional representation) the PS lost its absolute majority, although it remained the largest party with 206 seats and 31.6% of the vote. It accordingly went into opposition to a centre-right coalition headed by Jacques Chirac of the (Gaullist) →Rally for the Republic (RPR), with whom President Mitterrand was obliged to govern in uneasy political "cohabitation".

In opposition, the PS undertook a reassessment of its economic policies, including its traditional commitment to state ownership, and advocated a broad alliance of "progressive" forces against the centre-right. But the party's relations with the PCF remained badly strained, not least because of the growing influence of the "moderate" PS faction led by Rocard, who favoured realignment towards the centre. In the 1988 presidential elections Mitterrand was opposed in the first round by two Communist candidates (one official) as well as by Chirac for the RPR and Raymond Barre for the centrist →Union for French Democracy (UDF). He headed the poll with 34.1% of the vote, whereupon all the left-wing parties backed him in the second round, in which he easily defeated Chirac by 54.01% to 45.98%. In new Assembly elections in June 1988 (for which constituency-based majority voting was reinstated), the PS increased its representation to 260 seats out of 577, short of an overall majority but sufficient to underpin a PS-led government headed by Rocard that included the MRG and independent centrists. Immediately after the presidential contest, former Prime Minister Mauroy succeeded Jospin as PS first secretary.

Legislative setbacks and disagreements with Mitterrand provoked Rocard's resignation in May 1991 and his replacement by Édith Cresson (PS), who became France's first woman Prime Minister. She failed to stem plummeting support for the government and was replaced in April 1992 by Pierre Bérégovoy, a Mitterrand loyalist and hitherto Finance Minister. In January 1992, moreover, former Prime Minister Fabius, also a Mitterrand loyalist, was elected to succeed Mauroy as PS first secretary, following an extraordinary party congress in December 1991 at which delegates had accepted that only free-market policies could achieve economic growth. The Bérégovoy government had some success in restoring stability, and in September 1992 secured referendum approval of the controversial Maastricht Treaty on European union, albeit by a very narrow majority. But public disquiet at continuing economic recession was aggravated by a series of corruption and other scandals involving prominent PS politicians.

The PS went down to a widely-predicted heavy defeat in the March 1993 Assembly elections, retaining only 54 seats on a 17.6% first-round vote share and going into opposition to another "cohabitation" government of the centre-right. In the immediate aftermath, Rocard took over the PS leadership from Fabius and embarked upon an attempt to convert the party into a broader-based social democratic formation oriented towards the centre. However, unresolved internal party divisions contributed to a poor performance in the June 1994 European Parliament elections, in which the PS list managed only 14.5% (and 15 of the 87 French seats), compared with 23.6% in the 1989 contest. Rocard immediately resigned as party leader and was succeeded by Henri Emmanuelli, a former National Assembly president identified with the traditional PS left. Straitened financial circumstances were highlighted by the sale of the PS headquarters building in Paris, while the implication of PS officials in further corruption cases added to the party's problems in the run-up to the 1995 presidential elections.

An attempt to draft the outgoing president of the European Commission, Jacques Delors, as the PS presidential candidate was rebuffed by Delors himself in December 1994. In February 1995 a special PS congress in Paris endorsed former party leader Jospin as presidential candidate, on the basis of a primary election among party members in which the former Education Minister had easily defeated Emmanuelli, winning 66% of the votes. Closely supported by Delors, Jospin confounded the pundits by mounting an impressive presidential campaign and heading the first-round voting in April 1995, with 23.3% of the vote. He was defeated by Chirac of the RPR in the second round, but his tally of 47.4% as the candidate of the left served to restore Socialist morale after two years of turmoil. In June 1995 Jospin replaced Emmanuelli as PS first secretary and declared his intention to carry out a complete reform of party structures and policies before the next Assembly elections. The previous month Emmanuelli had received a suspended one-year prison sentence for receiving illicit campaign contributions as PS treasurer in the 1980s. Seven months after leaving office, Mitterrand died in January 1996 at the age of 79.

In late 1996 the PS national council decided that women candidates would be presented in at least 30% of constituencies in the next Assembly elections. In April 1997 the PS issued a joint declaration with PCF setting a 35-hour week (with no loss of wages) and a halt to major privatizations as central objectives of a left-wing government, although the two parties made no formal electoral pact. In contrast, the PS entered into agreements with both the Left

Radicals and the →Greens not to oppose a number of their candidates in the first round of voting. The outcome of the polling in May-June 1997 gave the PS a large relative majority of 241 seats (on a first-round vote share of 23.5%) and the left as a whole an overall majority. Jospin accordingly formed a coalition government dominated by the PS and also including the PCF, the Greens, the Left Radicals and the →Citizens' Movement (MDC) led by former PS minister Jean-Pierre Chevènement, facing a period of "cohabitation" with the Chirac presidency.

From January 1998 the Elf-Aquitaine affair, centring on financial corruption allegations against former PS Foreign Minister Roland Dumas (now the president of the Constitutional Court), caused some embarrassment for the party. The PS-led government, and Jospin in particular, nevertheless retained a high popularity rating, despite continuing high unemployment, as it implemented key policies such as the 35-hour week. The PS and its allies outpolled the centre-right in regional elections in March 1998, and the following month the government secured parliamentary approval for French entry into the single European currency, relying on centre-right votes to counter PCF and MDC opposition. In May 1998 PS candidate Odette Casanova narrowly prevented the far-right →National Front (FN) from regaining its single Assembly seat in Toulon, on the strength of second-round support from the centre-right parties. She repeated the feat in September 1998 when the by-election had to be re-run.

The PS contested the June 1999 European Parliament elections in alliance with the Left Radicals and the MDC, the joint list heading the poll with 22% of the vote and 22 of the 87 French seats, of which the PS took 18. For the elections the PS had subscribed to a joint manifesto of EU Socialist parties which had sought to bridge the gap between the pro-market "third way" line of the British ⇒Labour Party and the continental preference for the social market economy. In a speech to EU Socialists in October 1999, however, Jospin distanced the PS from the Anglo-Saxon model, asserting that "the market economy does not find harmony of its own accord" and that "it needs rules".

The PS is a member party of the Socialist International. Its representatives in the European Parliament sit in the Party of European Socialists group.

Workers' Struggle
Lutte Ouvrière (LO)
Address. BP 233, 75865 Paris 18
Leadership. Arlette Laguiller, François Duborg (spokespersons)
Descended from a Trotskyist group which in 1940 rejected membership of the French Committees for the Fourth International, the LO was founded in June 1968 as the direct successor to *Voix Ouvrière* following the banning of the latter and other student-based Trotskyist organizations in the wake of the May 1968 "events". It contested the 1973 Assembly elections jointly with the Communist League (itself later succeeded by the →Revolutionary Communist League, LCR), but the two groups put up separate candidates in the 1974 presidential elections, in which Arlette Laguiller of the LO won 2.3% in the first round. Having failed to return any of its 470 candidates in the 1978 Assembly elections on a platform that featured robust condemnation of the common programme of the mainstream left, the LO reverted to alliance with the LCR for the 1979 European Parliament elections, their joint list (*Pour les États-Unis Socialistes d'Europe*) winning 3.1% of the vote but no seats.

Laguiller again won 2.3% in the first round of the 1981 presidential contest and all 158 LO candidates were again unsuccessful in the ensuing Assembly elections. Standing on its own, the LO slipped to 2.1% in the 1984 Euro-elections, while Laguiller managed only 1.99% in the first round of the 1988 presidential contest and her party failed to win representation in either the 1988 or the 1993 Assembly elections. In her fourth presidential bid in 1995, however, Laguiller had her best result to date, winning 1,616,566 votes (5.3%) in the first round. The LO again won no seats in the mid-1997 Assembly elections, its candidates being credited with about 2% of the first-round vote.

For the June 1999 European Parliament elections the LO entered into a new alliance with the LCR on a platform of opposition to a "capitalist Europe" and in favour of a "Europe for workers". Headed by Laguiller, the joint list achieved an electoral breakthrough, winning 5.2% of the vote and five seats, three of which were taken by the LO.

The LO/LCR representatives in the European Parliament are members of the European United Left/Nordic Green Left group.

Other National Parties and Alliances

Anarchist Federation (*Fédération Anarchiste*), umbrella organization of local anarchist cells, rejects electoral politics, has occasionally been linked with acts of violence by extremist groups.

Bonapartist Party (*Parti Bonapartiste*, PB), led by Emmanuel Johans, founded in 1993 to promote the ideas and achievements of Emperor Napoleon Bonaparte.

Civil Society (*Société Civile*, SC), led by Christine de Veyrac, centre-right formation allied with →Rally for the Republic in June 1999 European Parliament elections, returning one representative (de Veyrac), who joined the European People's Party/European Democrats group.

Convention for a Progressive Alternative (*Convention pour une Alternative Progressiste*, CAP), led by Gilbert Wasserman, left-wing ecologist movement. *Address.* 17-19 rue des Envierges, 75020 Paris; *Telephone.* (+33-1) 4462-9791; *Fax.* (+34-1) 4462-9792; *Website.* http://www.perso.hol.fr/~cap

Ecology Generation (*Génération Écologie*, GE), established in 1990 by Brice Lalonde, a presidential candidate for Friends of the Earth (*Amis de la Terre*) and other groups in 1981 (when he received 3.9% of the first-round vote) and subsequently Environment Minister in the 1991-92 government led by Édith Cresson of the →Socialist Party (PS). Then more sympathetic to the Socialists than the rival →Greens, the GE nonetheless refused to enter the subsequent Bérégovoy administration headed by the PS. The GE won 7% of the vote at the March 1992 regional elections, before slipping to less than 1% in the 1993 Assembly elections, despite a reciprocal support agreement with the Greens. Contesting the June 1994 European Parliament poll as an independent list, the GE recovered to just over 2% of the vote, without winning a seat. Following the victory of Jacques Chirac of the →Rally for the Republic (RPR) in the April-May 1995 presidential elections, a former GE member, Corinne Lepage, accepted appointment as Environment Minister in the new centre-right government. In the mid-1997 Assembly elections the GE again failed to win representation, but in the June 1999 European Parliament elections the GE won one seat on the list headed by the RPR, its representative joining the European People's Party/European Democrats group. *Address.* 22 rue Daguerre, 75014 Paris; *Telephone.* (+33-1) 4427-1166; *Fax.* (+33-1) 4327-0555

Federalist Party (*Parti Fédéraliste*, PF), led by Jean-Philippe Allenbach, advocates creation of a federal European state. *Address.* 18 place du 8 Septembre, BP 76222, 25015 Besançon 6; *Telephone/Fax.* (+33-3) 8121-3233; *Email.* pfed.allen@wanadoo.fr; *Website.* http://www.dalmatia.net/parti-federaliste

Federation for a New Solidarity (*Fédération pour une Nouvelle Solidarité*, FNS), a rightist formation derived from the European Labour Party (*Parti Ouvrier Européen*, POE), created by Argentine-born Jacques Chéminade to support his candidacy in the 1995 presidential elections, in which he finished last of nine first-round candidates, with only 0.3% of the vote.

French and European Nationalist Party (*Parti Nationaliste Français et Européen*, PNFE), a far-right group led by Claude Cornilleau.

French Nationalist Party (*Parti Nationaliste Français*, PNF), far-right grouping formed in 1983 by a faction of the →National Front opposed to the leadership of Jean-Marie Le Pen.

French Royalist Movement (*Mouvement Royaliste Français*, MRF), led by Jean de Beauregard, anti-left grouping aiming to restore a French monarchy.

Independent Ecological Movement (*Mouvement Ecologiste Indépendant*, MEI), led by Antoine Waechter, the 1988 presidential candidate of the →Greens, from which he broke away in 1993; critical of the Greens' participation in the post-1997 government headed by the →Socialist Party, Waechter headed an MEI list for the 1999 European Parliament elections which obtained 267,853 votes (1.5%) without winning a seat. *Address.* 7 rue du Vertbois, 75003 Paris; *Telephone.* (+33-1) 4027-8536; *Fax.* (+34-1) 4027-8544; *Email.* mei@novomundi.com; *Website.* http://www.novomundi.com/mei

Internationalist Communist Party (*Parti Communiste Internationaliste*, PCI), led by Pierre Lambert and Daniel Gluckstein, Trotskyist grouping founded in 1944, subsequently undergoing various name changes, broke with Fourth International in 1952 and helped to found the rival Fourth International–International Centre of Reconstruction, embraced electoral politics in the 1980s, with minimal impact. *Address.* 87 rue du Faubourg Saint-Denis, 75010 Paris; *Telephone.* (+33-1) 4801-8820

Liberal Christian Right (*Droite Libérale Chrétienne*, DLC), led by former Defence Minister Charles Millon, launched at a Paris conference in November 1999 on the basis of "The Right" (*La Droite*) created by Millon in April 1998 following his expulsion from the UDF (→New Union for French Democracy) for having accepted →National Front (FN) support to secure re-election as president of the Rhône-Alpes regional council; claiming a membership of 20,000, the DLC aspired to become the French equivalent of Germany's ⇒Christian Democratic/Social Union (CDU/CSU). *Address.* 21 rue de Bourgogne, 75007 Paris; *Telephone.* (+33-1) 5359-5300. *Email.* La-Droite@wanadoo.fr; *Website.* http://www.la-droite.org

Liberal Party for the Economy, Regions and Environment (*Parti Libéral pour l'Économie, la Région et l'Environment*, PLERE), founded after the 1997 Assembly elections in opposition to the "false right" of the outgoing government and the new left-wing coalition. *Address.* 61 rue Falguière, 75015 Paris; *Telephone.* (+33-1) 4320-9498; *Fax.* (+33-1) 4320-6560; *Email.* arbidou@micronet.fr; *Website.* http://persoweb.francenet.fr/~arbidou

Modern France (*France Moderne*, FM), political association headed by Alain Juppé, former Prime Minister and former leader of the →Rally for the Republic (RPR), aiming to provide "dynamic opposition" to the post-1997 left-wing government and supportive of President Chirac's aim to be re-elected in 2002. *Address.* 10 rue Royale, 75008 Paris; *Telephone.* (+33-1) 4296-8586; *Website.* http://www.france-moderne.asso.fr

Movement of Communist Renovators (*Mouvement des Rénovateurs Communistes*, MRC), led by Claude Llabrès, a reformist splinter group of the →French Communist Party.

Movement of Democrats (*Mouvement des Démocrates*, MdD), founded in 1974 by former Gaullist Foreign Minister Michel Jobert, backed →Socialist Party candidate François Mitterrand in 1981 presidential election. *Address.* 96 ave de Nantes, 86000 Poitiers; *Telephone.* (+33-5) 4988-8035: *Fax.* (+33-5) 4988-9143

National Communitarian Party (*Parti Communautaire National*, PCN), French section of European-wide network of such parties. *Address.* 38 rue Marceau, 72600 Mamers; *Telephone/Fax.* (+33-2) 4334-1613; *Email.* pcn@wanadoo.fr; *Website.* http://www.pcn.isicom.fr

National Restoration (*Restauration Nationale*, RN), led by Guy Steinbach, right-wing pro-monarchy formation supporting the claim of the Count of Paris, weakened in 1971 by a breakaway that led to the creation of →New Royalist Action.

Natural Law Party (*Parti de la Loi Naturelle*, PLN), led by Benoît Frappé and Gérard Laporte, French version of worldwide network of such parties, contested 1994 and 1999 Euro-elections without success. *Address.* 19 rue des Écoles, 95680 Montlignon; *Telephone.* (+33-1) 3959-7051; *Fax.* (+33-1) 3959-3835; *Website.* http://members.aol.com/partiloina

New Royalist Action (*Nouvelle Action Royaliste*, NAR), led by Bertrand Renouvin and Yvan Aumont, founded in 1971 as a splinter group of →National Restoration, advocating the restoration of a progressive monarchy. *Address.* 17 rue des Petits-Champs, 75001 Paris; *Telephone.* (+33-1) 4297-4257; *Website.* http://www.mygale.org/10/francesc/royaliste

Red and Green Alternatives (*Alternatifs Rouge et Verte*, ARV), founded in November 1989 as a merger of the rump Unified Socialist Party (*Parti Socialiste Unifié*, PSU) and the New Left (*Nouvelle Gauche*, NG), espousing anarcho-syndicalism, internationalism, environmentalism and feminism; dating from 1960, the PSU had remained in existence when a minority faction led by Michel Rocard had joined the →Socialist Party in 1975, while the NG had been founded in 1987 by an expelled "renovator" of the →French Communist Party, Pierre Juquin, who won 2.1% in the 1988 presidential elections. *Address.* 40 rue de Malte, 75011 Paris; *Telephone.* (+33-1) 4357-4480; *Fax.* (+33-1) 4357-6450; *Email.* alternatifs@wanadoo.fr; *Website.* http://perso.wanadoo.fr/alternatifs

Reformers' Movement (*Mouvement des Réformateurs*, MdR), led by Jean-Pierre Soisson, founded in 1992 as a new centre-left formation aligned with the →Socialist Party, taking the name of the main centrist umbrella organization of the 1970s; sought to attract centrist voters from what became the →New Union for French Democracy in subsequent elections. *Address.* 7 rue de Villersexel, 75007 Paris; *Telephone.* (+33-1) 4544-6150

Republican Initiative (*Initiative Républicaine*, IR), led by André Bellon. *Address.* 27 rue de la Réunion, 75020 Paris; *Telephone.* (+33-1) 4370-9049; *Fax.* (+34-1) 4370-9072; *Website.* http://www.multimania.com/inirepub

Revolutionary Communist League (*Ligue Communiste Révolutionnaire*, LCR), led by Alain Krivine, a Trotskyist party founded in 1973 as successor to the Communist League, as whose candidate Krivine won 1.1% of the vote in the 1969 presidential elections; contested

Assembly and European elections of the 1970s in alliance with the →Workers' Struggle (LO), which became the stronger of the two. Krivine on his own won 0.4% in the 1974 presidential contest, while in 1988 the LCR backed Pierre Juquin of the New Left (which later joined the →Red and Green Alternative. Having contributed to LO leader Arlette Laguiller's 5.3% first-round vote in the 1995 presidential elections, the LCR joined with the LO in the June 1999 Euro-elections, their joint list winning 5.2% and five seats, Krivine being elected as one of two successful LCR candidates, who joined the European United Left/Nordic Green Left group. *Address.* 2 rue Richard Lenoir, 93198 Montreuil; *Telephone.* (+33-1) 4870-4230; *Fax.* (+33-1) 4859-2328

Social and Democratic Renewal (*Rénovation Sociale et Démocratique*, RSD), founded in 1997 by Jean-Louis Laurence. *Email.* info@rsd.org; *Website.* http://www.rsd.org

Social and Liberal Rally (*Rassemblement Social et Libéral*, RSL), led by Corinne Barrière, progressive centrist formation. *Address.* 10 rue Gracieuse, 75005 Paris; *Telephone.* (+33-1) 4331-0953; *Fax.* (+33-1) 4331-0954; *Email.* rsl@worldnet.fr; *Website.* http://www.rsl.asso.fr

Workers' Party (*Parti des Travailleurs*, PT), led by Yannick Giou, extreme left-wing grouping. *Address.* 87 rue du Faubourg Saint-Denis, 75010 Paris; *Telephone.* (+33-1) 4801-8829

Regional Parties

Alsace-Lorraine National Forum (*Nationalforum Elsass-Lothringen/Forum Nationaliste d'Alsace-Lorraine*), led by Gerald Müller, based in the German-speaking population of Alsace-Lorraine. *Email.* geraldmueller@nfel.org; *Website.* http://www.geocities.com/~bfel

Union of the Alsatian People (*Union du Peuple Alsacien/Elsass Volksunion*, UPA/EVU), political movement favouring autonomy for Alsace within the European Union. *Address.* BP 75, 67402 Illkirch Graffenstaden; *Fax.* (+33-3) 8907-9024; *Website.* http://www.multimania.com/elsassnet

Breton Democratic Union (*Unvaniezh Demokratel Breizh/Union Démocratique Bretonne*, UDB), led by Christian Guyonvarc'h, left-oriented party founded in 1964 in quest of complete autonomy for Brittany in the French Republic and European Union by non-violent means; has obtained representation on most main city councils in Brittany, including Nantes, Rennes, Lorient and Saint-Malo, but remains a regional minority party; a member of Democratic Party of the Peoples of Europe–European Free Alliance. *Address.* BP 203, 56102 Lorient, Brittany; *Telephone/Fax.* (+33-2) 9784-8523; *Email.* christian_guyonvarch@yahoo.fr; *Website.* http://www.geocities.com/CapitolHill/2177

Party for the Organization of a Free Brittany (*Parti pour l'Organisation d'une Bretagne Libre*, POBL), proclaiming "the inalienable right of the Breton people freely to rule itself and to become independent again". *Address.* BP 4518, 22045 Saint-Brieuc 2; *Email.* pobl@wordnet.fr; *Website.* http://rafale.wordnet.net/~pobl

Corsican Nation (*Corsica Nazione*, CN), led by P. Andreucci, nationalist movement with linked trade union and social organizations, claims to have won around 20% of vote in recent Corsican regional elections. *Address.* c/o Assemblée de Corse, 22 cours Grandval, BP 215, 20187 Ajaccio Cedex 1; *Website.* http://www.corsica-nazione.com

A Cuncolta, political wing of the banned Front for the National Liberation of Corsica–Historic Wing (FLNC-CH); weakened by the arrest of several leaders in 1996-97 on charges of involvement in terrorism.

Union of the Corsican People (*Unione di u Populu Corsu*, UPC), legal pro-autonomy party which has obtained minority representation in the Corsican regional assembly, sometimes in alliance with more militant nationalist groups. *Address.* BP 165, 20293 Bastia, Corsica; *Telephone.* (+33-4) 9532-2787; *Fax.* (+33-4) 9531-6490

Party for Independent Normandy (*Parti pour la Normandie Indépendante*, PNI), led by Jéremy Lefèvre and Sylvain Bion, seeks an independent Normandy with its political capital at Caen, its industrial capital at Le Havre and its military capital at Cherbourg, to which end it has set up a "provisional government". *Website.* http://www.multimania.com/pni

Occitania Party (*Partit Occitan*, POC), led by Gustave Alirol, founded in Toulouse in 1987 to seek "self-government" for the region of southern France where Occitan is spoken; won up to 1.8% of the vote in southern constituencies in 1997 Assembly elections. *Address.* Sant Ostian, 43260 Saint Julien Chapteuil; *Telephone/Fax.* (+33-4) 7157-6413; *Email.* poc@multimania.com/poc; *Website.* http://www.multimania.com/poc

Savoy League (*Ligue Savoisienne/Liga de Saboya*, LS), led by Patrice Abeille, founded in 1995 with aim of reversing French annexation of Savoy in 1860 and re-establishing it as a sovereign independent state. *Address.* 2 ave de la Mavéria, 74940 Annecy le Vieux, Savoy; *Telephone.* (+33-4) 5009-8713; *Fax.* (+33-4) 5009-9580; *Email.* ligue@savoie.com; *Website.* http://www.ligue.savoie.com

French Overseas Possessions
Overseas Departments

Under decentralization legislation enacted in 1982 by the then Socialist-led government in Paris, the four French overseas departments (*départements d'outre-me*, DOM) of French Guiana, Guadeloupe, Martinique and Réunion each have the additional status of a region of France. Each therefore has a regional council (*conseil régional*) that is directly elected for a six-year term from party lists by proportional representation and has increased powers as compared with the previous indirectly-elected bodies. At the same time, the traditional departmental council (*conseil général*) remained in being in each overseas department, these bodies also being directly elected for a six-year term but by majority voting over two rounds in constituent cantons. Each overseas department elects representatives to the National Assembly and the Senate in Paris according to the procedures applicable in metropolitan France (the precise number depending on size of population) and the DOM electorates also participate in French elections to the European Parliament. Political parties active in the overseas departments include local sections of metropolitan parties as well as a number of formations specific to particular departments.

French Guiana

Situated on the northern South American littoral between Suriname and Brazil, French Guiana (*capital*: Cayenne; *population*: 155,000) has been under French control since the 17th century and a recognized French possession since 1817, being accorded departmental status in 1946. Elections to the 31-member regional council on March 15, 1998, resulted as follows: Guianese Socialist Party 11 seats, Rally for the Republic 6, Walawari 2, others 12.

Democratic Socialist Union (*Union Socialiste Démocratique*, USD), led by Théodore Roumillac.

Guianese Democratic Action (*Action Démocratique Guyanaise*, ADG), led by André Lecante, left-wing pro-independence party founded c.1981, represented in the regional council in 1986-92 and subsequently in the departmental council, of which Lecante became president. *Address*. ave d'Estrées, Cayenne

Guianese Democratic Forces (*Forces Démocratiques Guyanaises*, FDG), led by Georges Othily, founded in 1989 by a dissident faction of the →Guianese Socialist Party, became second-largest party in the regional council in 1992 but lost ground sharply in May 1998, though Othily was re-elected to the French Senate in September 1998. *Address*. c/o Conseil Régional, Cayenne

Guianese National Popular Party (*Parti National Populaire Guyanais*, PNPG), led by José Dorcy, leftist party founded in 1985, supportive of independence for French Guiana, was represented in the regional council in the 1980s. *Address*. BP 265, Cayenne

Guianese Socialist Party (*Parti Socialiste Guyanais*, PSG), led by Antoine Karam, founded in 1956, consistently the strongest party in the department, for long led by Elie Castor, once officially the departmental section of the metropolitan ⇒Socialist Party, now autonomous and supportive of autonomy for French Guiana leading to full independence; won 16 regional council seats in 1992, subsequently providing the presidents of both the regional council and the general council, although it lost its National Assembly seat to an independent leftist in 1993; slipped to 11 regional council seats in March 1998 and to five out of 19 departmental council seats, Karam being nevertheless re-elected to the council presidency, whereas Stéphan Phinéra-Horth of the PSG lost the departmental council presidency. *Address*. 1 cité Césaire, Cayenne

Movement for Decolonization and Social Emancipation (*Mouvement pour la Décolonisation et l'Émancipation Sociale*, MDES), led by Maurice Pindard, advocates independence for French Guiana.

New Union for French Democracy (*Nouvelle Union pour la Démocratie Française*, NUDF), led by R. Chow-Chine, departmental section of the metropolitan party, has made little electoral impact despite essaying alliances with the local →Rally for the Republic.

Rally for the Republic (*Rassemblement pour la République*, RPR), led by Roland Ho-Wen-Sze, departmental section of the metropolitan RPR, supports the constitutional status quo, took a distant third place in the 1992 regional council elections, but retained its National Assembly seat in 1993 and 1997; advanced to six seats in the 1998 regional council elections. *Address*. 84 ave Léopold Héder, Cayenne

Socialist Party (*Parti Socialiste*, PS), led by Pierre Ribardière, departmental section of the metropolitan party, but eclipsed locally by the autonomous →Guianese Socialist Party.

Walawari, led by Christiane Taubira-Delannon, left-wing movement emphasizing non-French aspects of departmental society, won two regional council seats in 1998. *Address*. c/o Conseil Régional, Cayenne

Guadeloupe

A group of islands located in the Caribbean south-east of Puerto Rico, Guadeloupe (*capital*: Basse-Terre; *population*: 430,000) has been a French possession since the 17th century and was annexed in 1815. Elections to the 41-member regional council on March 15, 1998, resulted as follows: Guadeloupe Objective (OG) 25 seats, Socialist Party 12, Guadeloupe Communist Party 2, various right 2.

Guadeloupe Communist Party (*Parti Communiste Guadeloupéen*, PCG), led by Christian Céleste, founded in 1944 as the departmental section of the ⇒French Communist Party, became independent in 1958, for long favoured retention of departmental status, moved to cautious support for eventual independence in the 1980s as it steadily lost former electoral dominance; weakened by the formation of the →Guadeloupe Progressive Democratic Party, it managed only fifth place in the 1992 regional council elections with three seats and slipped to two in 1998. *Address*. 119 rue Vatable, Pointe-à-Pitre

Guadeloupe Objective (*Objectif Guadeloupe*, OG), led by Lucette Michaux-Chevry, an eventually victorious centre-right alliance formed for the 1992 regional council elections, consisting of the departmental →Rally for the Republic, →Union for French Democracy and other conservative elements; increased its regional majority from 22 to 25 in March 1998, so that Michaux-Chevry was re-elected president.

Guadeloupe Progressive Democratic Party (*Parti Progressiste Démocratique Guadeloupéen*, PPDG), led by Marcellin Lubeth and Ernest Moutoussamy, founded in 1991 by dissident members of the →Guadeloupe Communist Party (PCG) and others, outpolled the PCG in the 1992 regional council elections but took only fourth place; despite retaining a National Assembly seat in mid-1997, it lost its representation in the regional council in 1998, although Lubeth was elected president of the departmental council.

New Union for French Democracy (*Nouvelle Union pour la Démocratie Française*, NUDR), led by Marcel Esdras, departmental section of the centre-right metropolitan formation; after serious strains in the 1980s it resumed alliance with the →Rally for the

Republic for the 1992 regional council elections, participating in the eventual victory of the →Guadeloupe Objective alliance and its further triumph in 1998.

Popular Movement for an Independent Guadeloupe (*Konvwa pou Liberayson Nasyon Gwadloup/Mouvement Populaire pour une Guadeloupe Indépendante*, KLNG/MPGI), led by Simone Faisans-Renac, founded in 1982 as a radical pro-independence movement, later handicapped by the imprisonment in 1985 of then leader Luc Reinette, who was implicated in violent activities (and who later escaped).

Popular Union for the Liberation of Guadeloupe (*Union Populaire pour la Libération de la Guadeloupe*, UPLG), led by Roland Thesaurus, founded in 1978 as a semi-underground pro-independence movement, later operating legally in favour of greater autonomy, took a poor sixth place in the 1992 regional council elections.

Rally for the Republic (*Rassemblement pour la République*, RPR), led by Lucette Michaux-Chevry and Aldo Blaise, departmental federation of the metropolitan party, supportive of French status, suffered electorally from the defection of the RPR regional council president to the Union for French Democracy in 1986 (⇒New Union for French Democracy), but recovered in 1992 as the leading component of the →Guadeloupe Objective (OG) alliance, which won a narrow overall majority in re-run elections in January 1993, although the party took only one of Guadeloupe's four National Assembly seats in 1993 and 1997; the RPR-led GO won an overall majority of 25 regional council seats in March 1998, Michaux-Chevry being re-elected council president. *Address.* 1 rue Baudot, Basse-Terre

Socialist Party (*Parti Socialiste*, PS), led by Georges Louisor, departmental federation of the metropolitan party, held the presidency of the regional council from 1986, but was split into two factions for the 1992 elections, the main party winning nine seats and a dissident group led by Dominique Larifla seven; went into regional council opposition after the December 1993 re-run election, but returned one National Assembly deputy (out of four) in March 1993 and retained its dominance of the general council in March 1994 elections; won 12 seats in the 1998 regional council elections. *Address.* rés. Collinette 801, Grand Camp, Les Abymes

Martinique

Located in the Caribbean, Martinique (*capital*: Fort-de-France; *population*: 400,000) came under French control in the 17th century and was annexed in 1790, achieving departmental status in 1946. Elections to the 41-member regional council on March 15, 1998, resulted as follows: Independent Martinique Movement 13, Martinique Progressive Party 7, Rally for the Republic 6, Martinique Forces of Progress 5, Martinique Socialist Party 3, others 7.

Independent Martinique Movement (*Mouvement Indépendantiste Martiniquais*, MIM), led by Alfred Marie-Jeanne, pro-independence formation that once aimed to seize power through revolution, obtained increasing support through the 1980s, taking second place in the 1992 regional council election campaigning as the Martinique Patriots (*Patriotes Martiniquais*); after Marie-Jeanne had been returned to the French National Assembly in 1997, the MIM headed the poll with 13 seats in 1998 regional council elections, Marie-Jeanne being elected president. *Address*. Mairie de Rivière-Pilote, Martinique

Martinique Communist Party (*Parti Communiste Martiniquais*, PCM), led by Georges Erichot, founded in 1957 when the departmental federation of the ⇒French Communist Party split and the socialist pro-autonomy →Martinique Progressive Party (PPM) was formed; the PCM itself later favoured autonomy, especially after its pro-independence wing broke away in 1984; from 1974 co-operated with the PPM and other left-wing parties, often in government in the department; shared in the electoral decline of French communism in the 1980s, taking fourth place in the 1992 regional council election standing as For a Martinique of Labour; left-wing voting discipline secured the election of Émile Capgras of the PCM as council president, but he lost the post following the further PCM decline in the 1998 regional elections. *Address*. rue Émile Zola, Fort-de-France

Martinique Forces of Progress (*Forces Martiniquaises de Progrès*, FMP), late 1998 successor to the departmental federation of the centre-left metropolitan ⇒New Union for French Democracy; as the UDF, had been junior partner to the →Rally for the Republic (RPR), their combined forces consistently proving inferior to those of the Martinique left, as after the 1992 regional council elections, in which the RPR/UDF Union for a Martinique of Progress list won the most seats but remained in opposition; the UDF took one of the four Martinique seats in the 1993 French National Assembly elections but lost it in 1997, before winning five seats in the March 1998 regional council elections.

Martinique Progressive Party (*Parti Progressiste Martinique*, PPM), led by Aimé Césaire and Camille Darsières, founded in 1957 by a splinter group of the →Martinique Communist Party, eventually overtaking the parent party, Césaire being elected president of the first directly-elected regional council in 1983, retaining the post in 1986; dissension between the PPM pro-autonomy and pro-independence wings weakened the party thereafter, third place being achieved in the 1992 regional council elections; won one of Martinique's four National Assembly seats in 1993 and 1997, as well as holding both departmental seats in French Senate; slipped to seven seats in 1998 regional council elections, but Claude Lise of the PPM was re-elected president of departmental council. *Address*. rue André Aliker, Fort-de-France

Martinique Socialist Party (*Parti Martiniquais Socialiste*, PMS), led by Louis Joseph Dogué and Ernest Wan Ajouhu, won three seats in 1998 regional council elections.

Rally for the Republic (*Rassemblement pour la République*, RPR), led by Anicet Turinay and Pierre Petit, departmental federation of the metropolitan party and of similar conservative persuasion, formerly the strongest single party in Martinique but usually in opposition to left-wing alliances; allied with the Union for French Democracy (UDF) in the 1992 regional council elections, their Union for a Martinique of Progress list winning a substantial plurality, although not enough to obtain the council presidency; won two of the department's four National Assembly seats in 1993 and 1997 but slipped to six seats in the 1998 regional council elections standing independently of the UDF (→Martinique Forces of Progress).

Socialist Federation of Martinique (*Fédération Socialiste de Martinique*, FSM), led by Jean Crusol, departmental section of the metropolitan ⇒Socialist Party, but consistently surpassed electorally by other left-wing parties, securing a poor fifth place for its New Socialist Generation list in the 1992 regional contest and declining further in 1998. *Address*. cité la Meynard, 97200 Fort-de-France

Socialist Revolution Group (*Groupe Révolution Socialiste*, GRS), led by Gilbert Pago, pro-independence Trotskyist formation founded in 1973, has made little electoral impact despite seeking to build a regional alliance against "colonialist represssion".

Réunion

The Indian Ocean island of Réunion (*capital*: Saint-Denis; *population*: 700,000) has been a French possession since the 17th century and an overseas department since 1946. Elections to the 45-member regional council on March 15, 1998, resulted as follows: New Union for French Democracy 8 seats, Réunion Communist Party 7, Socialist Party 6, FreeDOM 5, Rally for the Republic 4, various right 15.

FreeDOM, led by Camille Sudre (formerly a member of the →Socialist Party) and Marguerite (Margie) Sudre, pro-autonomy but conservative movement whose use of English in its title has raised eyebrows in Paris; polled strongly in the 1991 general council and 1992 regional council elections, Camille Sudre (a medical doctor and well-known pirate broadcaster) being elected president of the latter body but later being obliged to face new elections in 1993 because of illegal broadcasts; again returned as the largest single party, FreeDOM secured the election of Margie Sudre (wife of Camille) as regional council president, to which post she added that of metropolitan State Secretary for Francophone Affairs following the advent of a centre-right government in Paris in 1995; in some disarray after the defeat of the metropolitan centre-right in mid-1997, FreeDOM candidates retained only five seats in the 1998 regional council elections.

Left Radical Party (*Parti des Radicaux de Gauche*, PRG), led by Jean-Marie Finck, departmental section of the metropolitan party, supportive of independence for Réunion (unlike the other main left-wing parties).

Movement for the Independence of Réunion (*Mouvement pour l'Indépendance de la Réunion*, MIR), pro-autonomy formation dating from 1981.

National Front (*Front National*, FN), led by Alix Morel, departmental section of the radical right-wing metropolitan party.

New Union for French Democracy (*Nouvelle Union pour la Démocratie Française*, NUDF), led by Gilbert Gérard and Jean-Luc Poudroux, departmental section of the centre-right metropolitan formation, favouring retention of French status, has been allied with the larger →Rally for the Republic (RPR) in recent elections; won eight regional council seats in March 1998, when Poudroux was elected president of the departmental council with some left-wing support.

Rally for the Republic (*Rassemblement pour la République*, RPR), led by André-Maurice Pihouée and Tony Manglou, departmental section of the conservative metropolitan party, favouring retention of French status, for long the leading electoral formation in alliance with what became the →New Union for French Democracy (NUDF), but in local opposition in the 1980s to the combined forces of the left; lost ground in the 1992 and 1993 regional council elections to the new →FreeDOM movement, and to the left in the 1994 general council elections; returned one of Réunion's five National Assembly deputies in 1993 and 1997; won four regional council seats in 1998. *Address.* BP 11, 97400 Saint-Denis

Réunion Communist Party (*Parti Communiste Réunionnaise*, PCR), led by Paul Vergès and Elie Hoarau, founded as an autonomous party in 1959 by the departmental branch of the ⇒French Communist Party, disavowed pro-Soviet orthodoxy of metropolitan party, has consistently been the leading left-wing electoral force in Réunion, supporting the successful →Socialist Party (PS) candidate for general council president in 1994; returned one of Réunion's five National Assembly deputies in 1993 and three in 1997; allied with the PS and some conservative elements in the *Rassemblement* for the 1998 regional council elections, it slipped from nine to seven seats, but Vergès (also a metropolitan senator) became council president. *Address.* 21bis rue de l'Est, Saint-Denis

Socialist Party (*Parti Socialiste*, PS), led by Jean-Claude Fruteau and Christophe Payet, departmental federation of the metropolitan ⇒Socialist Party, supports retention of departmental status, consistently allied with the stronger →Réunion Communist Party (PCR) against the departmental right, Payet being elected general council president in 1994 with PCR support; returned one of Réunion's five National Assembly deputies in 1993 and 1997; won six seats in March 1998 regional council elections, allied with the PCR and some conservative elements in the *Rassemblement. Address.* 85 rue d'Après, Saint-Denis

Overseas Territories and Collectivities

The French overseas territories (*territoires d'outre-mer*, TOM), namely French Polynesia, the French Southern and Antarctic Territories (with no permanent population), New Caledonia and the Wallis and Futuna Islands, are regarded as integral parts of the French Republic under present arrangements, the three with permanent populations electing representatives to the National Assembly and Senate in Paris and also participating in French elections to the European Parliament. They differ from the overseas departments in that their representative body is the territorial assembly (*assemblée territoriale*) elected by universal adult suffrage) and that they have a greater, although varying, degree of internal autonomy. Also covered below are the two French overseas territorial collectivities (*collectivités territoriales*), namely Mayotte and St Pierre and Miquelon, whose status is explained in the relevant introductions.

French Polynesia

French Polynesia (*capital*: Papeete, Tahiti; *population*: 220,000) consists of some 120 South Pacific islands, including Tahiti, which became a French protectorate in 1847 and a colony in 1860, with the other island groups being annexed later in the 19th century. The territory includes the former French nuclear testing site of Mururoa Atoll.

Elections to the 41-member territorial assembly on May 13, 1996, and by-elections in 11 seats on May 25, 1998, produced the following representation: People's Front/Rally for the Republic 23 seats, Liberation Front of Polynesia 11, New Land 5, others 2.

Autonomous Patriotic Party (*Pupu Here Ai'a Te Nuina'a Ia Ora*), pro-autonomy rural party formed in 1965, contested 1991 assembly elections as part of the Polynesian Union, by the end of the year joining the territorial government; won one of the two French Polynesia seats in the National Assembly in 1993 but lost it in 1997. *Address*. BP 3195, Papeete, Tahiti

Liberation Front of Polynesia (*Tavini Huiraatira/Front de Libération de la Polynésie*, FLP), led by Oscar Temaru, pro-independence movement, won four seats in 1991 assembly elections, advancing strongly to 10 in May 1996 and to 11 in May 1998, remaining in opposition.

New Land (*Ai'a Api*), led by Émile Vernaudon, centrist pro-autonomy party founded in 1982, was briefly in territorial government with the →People's Front in 1991, having taken third place in that year's territorial elections; retained five seats in 1996 territorial elections, Vernaudon being elected to the French National Assembly in mid-1997 with support from the People's Front. *Address*. BP 11055, Mahina, Tahiti

New Star (*Fe'tia Api*), led by Boris Léontieff, won one seat in May 1996 territorial assembly elections.

People's Front (*Tahoeraa Huiraatira*, TH), led by Gaston Flosse and Jacques Teuira, territorial branch of the conservative ⇒Rally for the Republic (RPR), founded in 1971 as a merger of various groups; under assorted names led the territorial government through most of the 1970s and early 1980s, in opposition from 1986, but returned to office under Flosse on winning a plurality in 1991, first with the support of →New Land and then backed by the →Autonomous Patriotic Party (also linked with the RPR), whose leader became president of the territorial assembly; Flosse survived a 1992 conviction for illegal use of authority, being re-elected to the French National Assembly in 1993 and later to the Senate; TH gained an overall majority in the May 1996 territorial elections, so that Flosse remained head of government. *Address*. BP 471, Papeete, Tahiti

Power to the People (*Ia Mana Te Nunaa*), led by Jacques Drollet, leftist pro-independence party founded in 1976, represented in the territorial assembly in the 1980s. *Address*. BP 1223, Papeete, Tahiti

Rally of Liberals (*Rassemblement des Libéraux/Pupu Taina*), led by Michel Law, linked to the metropolitan ⇒New Union of French Democracy, favouring the retention of French status. *Address*. BP 169, Papeete, Tahiti

Te Henua Enata Kotoa, led by Lucien Kimitete, won one territorial assembly seat in May 1996.

Te Tiaraama, led by Alexandre Léontieff, founded in 1987 by a faction of the →People's Front, contested the 1991 territorial elections as part of the Polynesian Union headed by the →Autonomist Patriotic Party.

True Path (*Te Avel'a Mau*), led by Tinomana Ebb, won one territorial assembly seat in May 1996.

Mayotte

The Indian Ocean island of Mayotte or Mahoré (*capital*: Dzaoudzi; *population*: 132,000) has been a French possession since the mid-19th century, remaining such when the other Comoro Islands declared independence from France in 1975. In two referendums in 1976 its mainly Christian population opted for maintenance of the French connection rather than incorporation into the Muslim-dominated Comoros, being granted the special status of "territorial collectivity" pending possible elevation to that of a French overseas department. The island's representative body is its 19-member general council. Elections in March 1994 and by-elections in March 1997 gave the Mahoré People's Movement 8 seats, the Rally for the Republic (RPR) 5, the Socialist Party 1, various right 5.

Mahoré People's Movement (*Mouvement Populaire Mahorais*, MPM), led by Younoussa Bamana (president of the Mayotte general council) and Marcel Henry (member of the French Senate), articulated majority resistance to incorporation into a Comoro state in the mid-1970s, favouring permanent overseas departmental status; dominant in the local general council, although the party's 1994 overall majority was reduced to a plurality in March 1997 by-elections.

New Union for French Democracy (*Nouvelle Union pour la Démocratie Française*, NUDF), led by Henri Jean-Baptiste, local section of the centre-right metropolitan formation, unrepresented in the island's general council, but has returned Mayotte's National Assembly deputy in recent elections.

Party for the Mahoran Democratic Rally (*Parti pour le Rassemblement Démocratique des Mahorais*, PRDM), led by Darouèche Maoulida, founded in 1978, favours Mayotte's incorporation into the Comoro Republic, finding little local support for this aim.

Rally for the Republic (*Rassemblement pour la République*, RPR), led by Mansour Kamardine, local federation of the conservative metropolitan party, favouring departmental status, rose to five seats in the general council in March 1997 by-elections.

Socialist Party (*Parti Socialiste*, PS), local branch of the metropolitan PS.

New Caledonia

The New Caledonia archipelago of Pacific islands (*capital*: Nouméa; *population*: 200,000) has been a French possession since 1853. In recent years local politics have been dominated by a demand for the severance of the French connection by groups representing indigenous Melanesians (Kanaks), forming about 45% of the population, and the equally insistent demand of French and other settler groups that French status should be retained. Under complex and frequently changing arrangements instituted to accommodate local aspirations, there are currently three autonomous provincial assemblies (North, South and Loyalty Islands), whose members make up an overall territorial congress. In a November 1998 referendum New Caledonian voters gave 71.9% approval to an accord between the French government and the main territorial parties providing for a gradual transfer of powers to local bodies and for a referendum on independence within 15 to 20 years. Elections on July 9, 1995, resulted in the 54 seats in the territorial congress becoming distributed as follows: Rally for Caledonia in the Republic 22, Kanak Socialist National Liberation Front 12, A New Caledonia for All 7, National Union for Independence 5, Develop Together to Construct the Future 2, National Front 2, Rally for Caledonia in France 2, Kanak Future 1, Front for the Development of the Loyalty Islands 1.

A New Caledonia for All (*Une Nouvelle Calédonie pour Tous*, NCPT), led by Didier Leroux, founded in 1995 to support retention of French status on the basis of reconciliation of competing aspirations, took second place in South province elections of July 1995 and third place overall.

Caledonia Tomorrow (*Calédonie Demain*, CD), led by Bernard Marant, right-wing grouping created by dissidents of the →Rally for Caledonia in the Republic and the →National Front.

Caledonian Generation (*Génération Calédonienne*, GC), led by Jean Renaud Posap, founded in 1995 to rally the younger generation in opposition to corruption.

Develop Together to Construct the Future (*Développer Ensemble pour Construire l'Avenir*, DEPCA), pro-reconciliation grouping that won two seats in North province in 1995.

Federation for a New Caledonian Society (*Fédération pour une Nouvelle Société Calédonienne*, FNSC), led by Jean-Pierre Aïfa, founded in 1979 as moderate pro-autonomy alliance of Caledonian Republican Party (PRC), Democratic Union (UD), New Caledonian Union (UNC) and Wallis and Futuna Movement (MWF).

Front for the Development of the Loyalty Islands (*Front pour le Développement des Îles Loyautés*, FDIL), won one seat in Loyalty Islands province in 1995 elections.

Kanak Socialist Liberation (*Libération Kanak Socialiste*, LKS), led by Nidoïsh Naisseline, pro-independence Melanesian grouping based in the Loyalty Islands, where it won one seat in 1995 on a list called Kanak Future.

Kanak Socialist National Liberation Front (*Front de Libération Nationale Kanak Socialiste*, FLNKS), led by Rock Wamytan and Paul Neaoutyine, established in 1984 by radical elements of a pre-existing Independence Front, including the Caledonian Union (UC) and Kanak Liberation Party (PALIKA), prominent in pro-independence agitation in late 1980s and early 1990s, helped to secure restoration of New Caledonia to UN list of non-self-governing territories in 1986; accepted 1988 proposals of Socialist government in Paris for New Caledonia to be divided into three autonomous regions (two dominated by

Kanaks), but assassination in 1989 of then FLNKS leader Jean-Marie Tjibaou and his deputy by a Kanak militant demonstrated perils of compromise; called in 1993 for immigration controls to prevent further dilution of Melanesians in advance of status referendum scheduled for 1998; won pluralities in North and Loyalty Islands provinces in 1995 elections, but dominance of the →Rally for Caledonia in the Republic in the populous South province confined the FLNKS to second place in territorial congress.

National Front (*Front National*, FN), led by Guy George, territorial section of radical right-wing metropolitan party, won two South province seats in 1995.

National Union for Independence (*Union Nationale pour l'Indépendance*, UNI), pro-independence competitor of the →Kanak Socialist National Liberation Front in North province, where it won five seats in July 1995 elections.

Oceanic Union (*Union Océanienne*, UO), led by Michel Hema, conservative formation founded in 1989, based in community originating from Wallis and Futuna Islands.

Popular Congress of the Kanak People (*Congrès Populaire du Peuple Kanak*, CPPK), led by Yann Céléné Uregeï, pro-independence grouping founded in 1992 as successor to United Kanak Liberation Front (*Front Uni de Libération Kanak*, FULK), which had been associated with numerous acts of violence and had rejected 1988 accord with Paris government establishing provincial structure.

Provisional Committee for the Defence of Republican Principles of French New Caledonia (*Comité Provisoire pour la Défense des Principes Républicains de la Nouvelle Calédonie Française*, CPDPRNCF), founded in September 1998 by pro-French elements opposed to the constitutional accord approved by referendum two months later.

Rally for Caledonia in France (*Rassemblement pour une Calédonie dans la France*, RCF), strongly supportive of French status, won two South province seats in 1995.

Rally for Caledonia in the Republic (*Rassemblement pour la Calédonie dans la République*, RPCR), led by Jacques Lafleur and Pierre Frogier, territorial section of the conservative metropolitan ⇒Rally for the Republic, allied with local branches of component parties of centre-right ⇒New Union for French Democracy, represents both *caldoches* (established settlers) and *métros* (recent immigrants), favours retention of French status, has consistently been the leading electoral force, currently providing not only the territorial congress president but also the islands' representatives in the French National Assembly and Senate. *Address.* BP 306, Nouméa

United Kanak Liberation Front (*Front Uni de Libération Kanak*, FULK), led by Yann Céléné Uregei, activist wing of the Melanesian liberation movement, associated with numerous acts of violence, rejected 1988 accord with Paris government establishing provincial structure; in 1992 launched Popular Congress of the Kanak People (*Congrès Populaire du Peuple Kanak*, CPPK) in quest for complete independence for New Caledonia.

St Pierre and Miquelon

St Pierre and Miquelon are a group of eight islands off the Canadian Newfoundland coast (*capital*: Saint-Pierre; *population*: 6,750) that have been French possessions since the 17th century and have a population of French stock. Their elevation in 1976 from the status of overseas territory to that of overseas department generated a local campaign for reversion to territorial status with special elements, leading to legislation in 1984 converting the islands into an overseas territorial collectivity with effect from June 1985. Under these arrangements the islands' 19-member general council is the principal representative body, its members also serving as the territorial assembly. Elections on March 20, 1994, ended the long dominance of the local Socialist Party, with allied centre-right lists headed by the New Union for French Democracy winning 15 seats.

New Union for French Democracy (*Nouvelle Union pour la Démocratie Française*, NUDF), led by Gérard Grignon, local section of centre-right metropolitan formation, for long overshadowed electorally by the local →Socialist Party, turned the tables in March 1994 with its Archipelago Tomorrow (*Archipel Demain*) list in Saint-Pierre, which together with the allied Miquelon Objectives (*Objectifs Miquelonnais*) list won 15 of the 19 council/assembly seats; elected president of the council, Crignon resigned in June 1996 and was succeeded by Bernard Le Soavec, defined politically as "various right"; the NUDF has held the islands' National Assembly seat since 1986, Crignon being the deputy.

Rally for the Republic (*Rassemblement pour la République*, RPR), led by Victor Reux, local section of conservative metropolitan formation, participated in victorious centre-right coalition in March 1994 elections; Reux retained the islands' seat in French Senate in 1998.

Socialist Party (*Parti Socialiste*, PS), led by Marc Plantagenest, local section of the metropolitan ⇒Socialist Party, for long the majority party in the general council, led the successful campaign against departmental status; but in March 1994 its SPM 2000 list in Saint-Pierre and the allied Future Miquelon (*Miquelon Avenir*) list led by Jean de Lizarraga won only four general council/territorial assembly seats and went into opposition.

Wallis and Futuna Islands

Situated in the Pacific Ocean north of Fiji and west of Western Samoa, the Wallis and Futuna Islands (*capital*: Mata-Utu; *population*: 15,000) became a French protectorate in 1842 but were never formally annexed. The islands are governed by a French administrator assisted by a 20-member territorial assembly elected by universal adult suffrage for a five-year term. There are also three traditional kingships, of Wallis, Sigave and Alo, exercising limited local powers. Assembly elections on March 16, 1997, and by-elections on Sept. 6, 1998, resulted in the Rally for the Republic holding 11 seats and leftists and independents 9.

Left Radical Party (*Parti des Radicaux de Gauche*, PRG), led by Kamilo Gata, territorial section of the centre-left metropolitan party, held the islands' seat in the French National Assembly until 1997.

New Union for French Democracy (*Nouvelle Union pour la Démocratie Française*, NUDF), territorial section of metropolitan centre-right party, known locally as *Luakaetahi*.

Rally for the Republic (*Rassemblement pour la République*, RPR), led by Clovis Logologofolau and Victor Brial, territorial section of the conservative metropolitan formation, dominant in recent territorial elections; Brial was elected president of territorial assembly following March 1997 elections and also won the islands' National Assembly seat later that year; the RPR's 1997 tally of 14 assembly seats was reduced to 11 in September 1998 by-elections called because of irregularities in 11 constituencies.

Union for Wallis and Futuna (*Union pour Wallis et Futuna*, UWF), alliance of Bright Future (*Taumu'a Lelei*) led by Soane Mani Uhila and the Local Popular Union (*Union Populaire Locale*, UPL) founded in 1985 by Falakiko Gata (hitherto a member of the territorial →New Union for French Democracy and before that of the territorial →Rally for the Republic).

Germany

Capital: Berlin

Population: 83,000,000

The Federal Republic of Germany (FRG) was established in 1949 in the three Western zones of post-World War II occupation (British, US and French), achieving full sovereignty in May 1955. The FRG's Basic Law (constitution) defined it as "a democratic and social federal state" with a bicameral parliament consisting of (i) a lower house (*Bundestag*) directly elected for a four-year term by universal adult suffrage, and (ii) an upper house (*Bundesrat*) indirectly constituted by representatives of the legislatures of the FRG's constituent states (*Länder*). Executive power was vested in the federal government headed by a Chancellor elected by the *Bundestag*, while the largely ceremonial President (head of state) is

Elections to the *Bundestag* on Sept. 27, 1998, resulted as follows:				
	Seats		Percentage	
	1999	*(1995)*	*1999*	*(1995)*
Social Democratic Party of Germany (SPD)	298	(252)	40.9	(36.4)
Christian Democratic Union (CDU)	198	(244)	28.4	(34.2)
Christian Social Union (CSU)	47	(50)	6.7	(7.3)
Alliance 90/The Greens	47	(49)	6.7	(7.3)
Free Democratic Party (FDP)	43	(47)	6.2	(6.9)
Party of Democratic Socialism (PDS)	36	(30)	5.1	(4.4)

elected for a five-year term by a Federal Assembly (*Bundesversammlung*) made up of the *Bundestag* deputies plus an equal number of delegates nominated by the *Länder* parliaments. The reunification of Germany in October 1990 was achieved by the FRG's absorption of the five eastern *Länder* (Brandenberg, Mecklenburg-West Pomerania, Saxony, Saxony-Anhalt and Thuringia) of the former Soviet-occupied and Communist-ruled German Democratic Republic, and also of Berlin (previously under four-power administration). The post-1990 FRG thus consists of 16 *Länder*, with a federal structure still governed by the 1949 Basic Law, under which each *Länder* has a parliament exercising substantial powers in the economic and social fields. The FRG was a founder member of what is now the European Union, its membership being extended to the five eastern *Länder* at reunification. Germany elects 99 members of the European Parliament.

The *Bundestag* is formed by a combination of direct elections from 328 single-member constituencies and the proportional allocation of a theoretically equal number of seats to party lists according to their share of the vote. Proportional seats are only allocated to parties winning at least 5% of the national vote or to those returning three deputies directly in any one electoral district (i.e. *Länd*). In the 1994 *Bundestag* elections the 328 directly-elected seats were supplemented by 344 proportional seats (for a total complement of 672), the 16 additional "supra-proportional" mandates being required to achieve overall proportionality.

In 1954 Germany became the first West European country to introduce direct public funding of political parties. Under legislation enacted in July 1967, political parties are defined as being a constitutionally necessary element of a free democratic order and as contributing to the formation of the national political will, by influencing public opinion, encouraging participation in public life and training citizens for public office. On these grounds, state funding is granted to political parties or independent candidates obtaining at least 0.5% of the national party-list vote or 10% in any electoral district, payable retrospectively in the next electoral period. Under an amendment to the 1967 law effective from January 1994, parties and independent candidates receive DM1.30 per annum for each vote received up to 5 million votes and DM1 for each additional vote above that figure. They are also allocated DM0.50 to match every DM1 that they receive from members' contributions or donations. In 1998 the global sum available in state aid to parties was DM245 million (about $148 million), of which the Social Democratic Party of Germany obtained DM96,756,243 (about $58 million) and the Christian Democratic Union DM73,817,137 (about $44 million). Separate state aid is paid to foundations associated with the main parties, although such bodies must maintain their organizational independence and not use such funding for party political purposes.

Each of the 16 *Länder* has its own parliament (*Landtag*, or *Bürgerschaft* in the case of Bremen and Hamburg), elected for a four- or five-year term, the most recent results (to end-1999) being as follows:

Baden-Württemberg (March 24, 1996)—CDU 69, SPD 39, Greens 19, FDP 14, Republicans 14
Bavaria (Sept. 13, 1998)—CSU 123, SPD 67, Greens 14

Berlin (Oct. 10, 1999)—CDU 76, SPD 42, PDS 33, Greens 18

Brandenburg (Sept. 5, 1999)—SPD 37, CDU 25, PDS 22, German People's Union 5

Bremen (June 6, 1999)—SPD 47, CDU 42, Greens 10, German People's Union 1

Hamburg (Sept. 21, 1997)—SPD 54, CDU 46, Greens 21

Hesse (Feb. 7, 1999)—CDU 50, SPD 46, Greens 8, FDP 6

Lower Saxony (March 1, 1998)—SPD 83, CDU 62, Greens 12

Mecklenburg-West Pomerania (Sept. 27, 1998)—SPD 27, CDU 24, PDS 20

North Rhine–Westphalia (May 14, 1995)—SPD 108, CDU 89, Greens 24

Rhineland-Palatinate (March 24, 1996)—SPD 43, CDU 41, FDP 10, Greens 7

Saarland (Sept. 5, 1999)—CDU 26, SPD 25

Saxony (Sept. 19, 1999)—CDU 76, PDS 30, SPD 14

Saxony-Anhalt (April 26, 1998)—SPD 47, CDU 28, PDS 25, German People's Union 16

Schleswig-Holstein (March 24, 1996)—SPD 33, CDU 30, Greens 6, FDP 4, South Schleswig Voters' Union 2

Thuringia (Sept. 12, 1999)—CDU 49, PDS 21, SPD 18

Alliance 90/The Greens
Bündnis 90/Die Grünen

Address. Platz vor dem Neuen Tor 1, 10115 Berlin
Telephone. (+49–30) 284-420
Fax. (+49–30) 2844-2210
Email. info@gruene.de
Website. http://www.gruene.de
Leadership. Gunda Röstel, Antje Radcke (spokespersons); Kerstin Müller, Rezzo Schlauch (parliamentary leaders); Reinhard Bütikhofer (general secretary)

The Greens first emerged in West Germany in the 1970s at state and local level. A number of these disparate groups came together at a Frankfurt conference in March 1979 to form the Alternative Political Union, The Greens (*Sonstige Politische Vereinigung, Die Grünen*), which was given a federal structure under the rubric The Greens at a Karlsrühe congress in January 1980. A programme adopted in March 1980 called for a worldwide ban on nuclear energy and on chemical and biological weapons, the non-deployment of nuclear missiles in Europe, unilateral disarmament by West Germany, the dismantling of NATO and the Warsaw Pact, and the creation of a demilitarized zone in Europe. It also advocated the dismantling of large economic concerns into smaller units, a 35-hour week and recognition of the absolute right of workers to withdraw their labour.

Having taken only 1.5% of the vote in the 1980 federal elections, the Greens broke through to representation in 1983, winning 5.6% and 27 lower house seats. They progressed to 8.2% in the 1984 European Parliament elections and to 8.3% in the 1987 federal elections, winning 42 seats. Prominent in the Greens' rise was Petra Kelly, whose charismatic leadership attracted national publicity and acclaim. However, opposition within the party to "personality politics" contributed to her departure from the joint leadership in April 1984, together the other two members. (Some years later, in October 1992, Kelly and her partner, former army general turned pacifist Gert Bastian, were found dead in their Bonn apartment; according to the German police, Kelly had been shot by Bastian, who had then killed himself.)

Divisions also surfaced between the Greens' "realist" wing (*Realos*), favouring co-operation with the →Social Democratic Party of Germany (SPD), and the "fundamentalists" (*Fundis*), who rejected any compromises with other formations. In December 1985 the "realist" Greens of Hesse joined a coalition government with the SPD (the first such experience for both parties), but this collapsed in February 1987 after the Green environment minister, Joschka Fischer, had unsuccessfully demanded that the state government should halt plutonium processing at a plant near Frankfurt. The Hesse experience strengthened the "fundamentalist" wing at the Greens' annual congress in May 1987, when it obtained eight of the party's 11 executive seats. By 1989, however, the *Realos* had regained the initiative, in alliance with a "Fresh Start" (*Aufbruch*) group led by Antje Vollmer which had sought to mediate between the contending factions.

In late 1989 a Green Party (*Grüne Partei*) was launched in East Germany, being at that stage opposed to German reunification. It joined with the Independent Women's League (*Unabhängige Frauenbund*) in contesting the March 1990 *Volkskammer* elections, winning 2.2% of the vote and eight seats. Unwilling to join forces with the West German Greens, the eastern Greens instead joined Alliance 90, which had been founded in February 1990 by a number of East German grass-roots organizations, including the New Forum (*Neues Forum*) and Democracy Now (*Demokratie Jetzt*), on a platform urging "restructuring" of the GDR along democratic socialist lines, rather than German unification or the importation of capitalism. In the all-German *Bundestag* elections of December 1990 Alliance 90 secured eight seats by surmounting the 5% threshold in the former GDR, even though its overall national vote was only 1.2%. In contrast, the western Greens, with an overall 3.9% share, failed to retain representation.

With German reunification a fact, the western Greens and Alliance 90 gradually resolved their differences, until parallel congresses in Hannover in January 1993 voted to unite under the official name Alliance 90 but with the suffix "The Greens" being retained for identification purposes. The merger was formalized at a Leipzig congress in May 1983. The Greens' Mannheim congress in February 1994 opted in principle for a "red-green" coalition with the Social Democrats at federal level, although without modifying policies (such as opposition to NATO membership) that were unacceptable to the SPD leadership. In the June 1994 European Parliament elections the Green list took third place with a 10.1% vote share, winning 12 of the 99 German seats. In the October 1994 *Bundestag* elections the Greens achieved a further federal advance, to 7.3% and 49 seats. The new parliamentary arithmetic precluded a coalition with the SPD, but the Green presence was acknowledged by the election of a Green deputy (Antje Vollmer) as one of the *Bundestag*'s four vice-presidents.

In 1995 the Greens registered significant advances in *Länder* elections in Hesse (February), North Rhine–Westphalia and Bremen (May) and Berlin (October), winning a vote share of 10–13% in the four contests. At a Green party conference in Bremen in December 1995, a majority of delegates endorsed the party's traditional opposition to any external military role for Germany, although an unprecedented 38% backed a motion by Joschka Fischer (by now a leading Green deputy in the *Bundestag*) to the effect that German troops could be deployed on UN peacekeeping missions. Further divisions were in evidence at the Greens' March 1998 congress, where delegates responded to Fischer's appeal for "discipline and realism" by calling for Germany's withdrawal from the NATO-led peacekeeping force in Bosnia and by adopting a raft of radical proposals, including the trebling of the price of petrol over a 10-year period.

Ousted from the Saxony-Anhalt parliament in April 1998, the Greens also lost ground in the federal elections in September, slipping to 6.7% of the vote and 47 seats. It nevertheless entered into Germany's first "red-green" federal coalition (in which Fischer became Foreign Minister and Vice-Chancellor, Jürgen Trittin Environment Minister and Andrea Fischer

Health Minister), on the basis of a pact with the SPD which included commitments to "ecological tax reform" and withdrawal from nuclear power generation. Strains quickly appeared in the coalition, notably over the SPD's insistence on a 20-year time-span for the phasing-out of nuclear plants. A Green congress in Leipzig in December 1998 approved the lifting of the party ban on members holding both public and party offices and set up a 30-member council to defuse internal policy disputes. But it rebuffed a proposal that the Greens should have a recognized chairperson, so that Fischer's aim of establishing a "normal" organizational structure for the party remained unrealised. On the other hand, at Fischer's urging, a special Green conference in Bielefeld in May 1999 defeated by 444 votes to 318 a proposal from the party's pacifist wing that the Green ministers should not support the NATO military action against Yugoslavia over Kosovo, thus effectively backing the deployment of German troops outside the NATO area.

In the June 1999 European Parliament elections the Greens fell back to 6.4% of the vote, losing five of their 12 seats, and also lost ground in a series of state elections in 1999, being eliminated from the Saarland parliament in September. At end-1999 the Greens participated in state-level coalition governments with the SPD in Hamburg, North Rhine–Westphalia and Schleswig-Holstein.

With an official membership of c.50,000, the German Greens are affiliated to the European Federation of Green Parties. The party's representatives in the European Parliament are members of the Greens/European Free Alliance group.

Christian Democratic Union
Christlich-Demokratische Union (CDU)
Address. Konrad-Adenauer-Haus, Friedrich-Ebert-Allee 73–75, 53113 Bonn
Telephone. (+49–228) 5440
Fax. (+49–228) 544216
Email. post@cdu.de
Website. http://www.cdu.de
Leadership. Wolfgang Schäuble (chair and parliamentary leader); Angela Merkel (general secretary)

The moderate conservative CDU was established in October 1950 as a federal organization uniting autonomous groups of Christian Democrats (both Catholic and Protestant) which had re-emerged in all parts of Germany after World War II, descended in part from the Centre Party founded in the 19th century and prominent in the pre-Hitler Wiemar Republic. Following a strong showing in the first *Länder* elections held in West Germany in 1947, an alliance of these groups, including the →Christian Social Union (CSU) of Bavaria, had become the strongest element in the first *Bundestag* elections in 1949 under the leadership of Konrad Adenauer, who became the first West German Chancellor. On the formation of the CDU in 1950, the CSU remained a separate though allied party in Bavaria, and has generally been regarded as the more right-wing of the two.

The CDU remained in government until 1969, presiding over the blossoming of the "German economic miracle" under the successive chancellorships of Adenauer (until 1963), Ludwig Erhard (1963–66) and Kurt-Georg Kiesinger (until 1969). From 1959, moreover, Heinrich Lübke of the CDU served two five-year terms in the federal presidency. During this period the CDU/CSU tandem was in coalition with the →Free Democratic Party (FDP) until 1957, governed with an absolute *Bundestag* majority until 1961, returned to a coalition with the FDP in 1961–66 and then formed a "grand coalition" with the →Social Democratic Party of Germany (SPD). Having slipped to 46.1% in the 1969 elections, the CDU/CSU went into opposition to an SPD/FDP coalition that was to endure until 1982. The CDU/CSU share of the vote fell to 44.9% in 1972, rose to 48.6% in 1976 and then fell to 44.5% in 1980, when a joint electoral list was headed by Franz-Josef Strauss of the CSU, who had threatened a rupture with the CDU unless he was accepted as the alliance's Chancellor-candidate. Meanwhile, Karl Carstens of the CDU had been elected President of West Germany in May 1979.

The FDP's desertion of the SPD-led coalition in October 1982 enabled the CDU/CSU to form a new government with the FDP under the leadership of Helmut Kohl. In *Bundestag* elections in March 1983 the CDU advanced strongly to 38.2% and 191 seats (and the CSU also gained ground), so that the CDU/CSU/FDP coalition continued in office. In May 1984 Richard von Weizsächer of the CDU, a former mayor of West Berlin, was elected to succeed Carstens as President. In the January 1987 lower house elections the CDU declined to 34.5% and 174 seats (and the CSU also lost ground), but gains by the FDP enabled Kohl to continue as Chancellor with the same coalition partners. Criticism of Kohl's leadership surfaced at the CDU's congress of November 1987, when he was re-elected chair (as the only candidate) by his lowest-ever number of delegates' votes. In the June 1989 European Parliament elections the CDU slipped to 29.5% of the national vote.

Confidence in Kohl's leadership was restored by his performance as government leader through the process of German reunification in 1990, after which his position in the CDU was unassailable. In the all-German elections of December 1990 the CDU won 36.7% of the vote overall and took 268 seats in the enlarged 662-member *Bundestag*. Although the combined CDU/CSU share of the vote was the lowest since 1949, an SPD decline enabled Kohl to form a further CDU/CSU/FDP coalition. In the 1990 contest the CDU was confirmed as the strongest party in the eastern *Länder*, although it later lost ground because the Kohl government was blamed for the problems of economic transition. As a dedicated pro-European party, the CDU strongly supported German ratification of the Maastricht Treaty on European union (which was finally completed in October 1993); it also backed moves to amend the German constitution so that German forces could be deployed on UN-approved peacekeeping missions outside the NATO area. In May 1994 Roman Herzog of the CDU was elected President, while in the following month's European Parliament elections the CDU registered 32.0% of the vote, winning 39 of the 99 German seats.

In the October 1994 *Bundestag* elections the CDU slipped to 34.2% and 244 seats (out of 672), sufficient to underpin a further CDU/CSU/FDP coalition under the continued chancellorship of Kohl (who was re-elected CDU chair in November 1994 with over 94% of delegates' votes at a special congress). However, CDU setbacks in *Länder* elections in 1993–94 meant that the SPD established a majority in the indirectly-elected *Bundesrat* (federal upper house). Further setbacks followed in state elections, but Kohl nevertheless announced in April 1997 that he would stand for a fifth term as Chancellor and was confirmed as the CDU (and CSU) candidate at a party congress in October 1997, when he at last designated CDU/CSU parliamentary leader Wolfgang Schäuble as his preferred successor.

The September 1998 *Bundestag* elections produced a widely-predicted defeat for Kohl and the CDU, whose vote share fell sharply to 28.2% and seat total to 198, with the result that it went into opposition after 17 years in continuous power. In November 1998 Kohl was succeeded as CDU chair by Schäuble, who was elected unopposed. In the June 1999 European Parliament elections the CDU advanced strongly to 39.3% of the vote and 43 of the 99 German seats, while state elections in 1999 produced some notable successes for the CDU, as the party orchestrated a nationwide campaign against government plans to abolish Germany's 100-year-old law restricting right of citizenship to those with German blood. However, the party was tainted in late 1999 by the opening of an official investigation into the alleged receipt by Kohl as CDU leader of secret donations and the prospect that the former Chancellor, now a back-bench deputy, would face criminal proceedings over such illegal funding. At end-1999 the CDU governed alone in Saarland, Saxony and Thuringia; it was in coalition with the FDP in Baden-Württemberg and Hesse, and with the SPD in Berlin, Brandenburg and Bremen.

With an official membership of 635,000, the CDU is a member of the Christian Democrat International and the International Democrat Union. Its European Parliament representatives sit in the European People's Party/European Democrats group.

Christian Social Union
Christlich-Soziale Union (CSU)
Address. Nymphenburger Strasse 64-66, 80335 Munich
Telephone. (+49–89) 1243-243
Fax. (+49–89) 1243-279
Email. landesleitung@csu-bayern.de
Website. http://www.csu.de
Leadership. Edmund Stoiber (chair and minister-president of Bavaria); Thomas Goppel (general secretary)

The CSU was established in Bavaria in January 1946 by various Catholic and Protestant political groups with the aim of rebuilding the economy on the basis of private initiative and property ownership and of restoring the rule of law in a federal Germany. Led by Josef Müller, it won an absolute majority in the first Bavarian *Landtag* elections in December 1946 (with 52.3% of the vote), although the emergence of the separatist →Bavaria Party in the 1950 elections reduced the CSU to a relative majority, obliging it to form a coalition with the state →Social Democratic Party of Germany (SPD). The CSU continued in being on the formation of the →Christian Democratic Union (CDU) in October 1950, it being agreed that the CSU would be the CDU's sister party in Bavaria and that neither would oppose the other at elections. While both parties have espoused essentially the same policies, the CSU is generally reckoned to be more conservative than the CDU. It is also less enthusiastic than the CDU leadership about plans for European monetary union and favours retention of the Deutsche Mark for the foreseeable future rather than German participation in a single European currency.

The post-war CSU/SPD coalition in Bavaria lasted until 1954, when the CSU went into opposition to a four-party government headed by the SPD. Under the leadership of Hanns Seidel, the CSU returned to office in 1957 at the head of a three-party coalition and in 1962 regained an absolute majority in the Bavarian *Landtag*, which it has held ever since. Seidel was succeeded as CSU leader by Franz-Josef Strauss in 1961 and as Bavarian minister-president by Alfons Goppel, who held office from 1962 until 1978. Strauss became the CSU's dominant figure in the CDU-led federal government, serving as Defence Minister from 1956 until being forced to resign in 1963 over the *Spiegel* affair. He returned to government as Finance Minister in the 1966–69 "grand coalition" between the CDU, the CSU and the SPD, but in 1978 opted to become head of the CSU government of Bavaria. Strauss was the unsuccessful CDU/CSU candidate for the chancellorship in the 1980 *Bundestag* elections, in which the CSU vote slipped to 10.3% (from 10.6% in 1976) and its seat total to 52.

Having been in federal opposition since 1969, the CSU returned to government in 1982 as part of a coalition headed by the CDU and including the →Free Democratic Party (FDP). In the 1983 *Bundestag* elections that confirmed the coalition in power the CSU improved to 10.6% and 53 seats, although two CSU deputies later departed to join the far-right →Republicans. In the 1987 elections the CSU slipped to 9.8% and 49 seats but continued its participation in the federal government. Strauss died in October 1988 and was succeeded as CSU leader by Theo Waigel and as Bavarian minister-president by Max Streibl. In the June 1989 European Parliament elections the CSU list took 8.2% of the overall West German vote.

In Bavarian state elections in October 1990 the CSU maintained its absolute majority, winning 54.9% of the vote and 127 of the 204 seats.

As Germany moved towards reunification in 1990 the →German Social Union (DSU) was set up in the re-established eastern *Länder* as a would-be sister party of the CSU. However, in the all-German *Bundestag* elections of December 1990 the DSU made minimal impact, while the percentage vote of the Bavaria-based CSU inevitably fell, to 7.1% (8.8% in western Germany), yielding 51 seats out of 662 and enabling the CSU to continue as part of the federal coalition. In the June 1994 European Parliament elections the CSU list took 6.8% and eight of the 99 German seats, while in the Bavarian *Landtag* elections of September 1994 the party won its customary overall majority, although its seat total slipped to 120 and its vote share to 52.8%. The party therefore suffered little from a corruption scandal which had caused the resignation of Steibl as Bavarian minister-president in May 1993 and his replacement by Edmund Stoiber.

The CSU improved its vote share slightly to 7.3% in the October 1994 *Bundestag* elections (although its representation fell to 50 seats) and obtained three portfolios in the re-formed CDU/CSU/FDP federal coalition. In February 1998 it suffered a major defeat when a Bavarian referendum yielded an overwhelming majority in favour of abolition of the state's second chamber, despite CSU advice to the contrary. The party shared in the federal coalition's defeat in September 1998, slipping to 6.7% of the national vote and to 47 *Bundestag* seats, but retained its overall majority in that month's Bavarian state elections, winning 123 seats on a vote share of 52.9%. Having announced his resignation after the elections, Waigel was succeeded as CSU chair by Stoiber in January 1999. The party improved to 9.4% of the vote in the June 1999 European Parliament elections, taking 10 seats.

The CSU is affiliated to the Christian Democrat International and the International Democrat Union. Its representatives in the European Parliament sit in the European People's Party/European Democrats group.

Free Democratic Party
Freie Demokratische Partei (FDP)
Address. Reinhardtstrasse 14, 10117 Berlin
Telephone. (+49–30) 284-9580
Fax. (+49–30) 2849-5822
Email. fdp@fdp.de
Website. http://www.fdp.de
Leadership. Wolfgang Gerhardt (chair); Hermann Otto Solms (parliamentary chair); Guido Westerwelle (secretary-general)

Strongly based in the farming community, the centrist and secular FDP was founded in December 1948 at a conference in Heppenheim (near Heidelberg) as a fusion of various liberal and democratic *Länder* organizations descended from the German State Party (*Deutsche Staatspartei*) and the more right-wing German People's Party (*Deutsche Volkspartei*, DVP) of the Weimar Republic (1918–33), and more distantly from the People's Party (*Volkspartei*) founded in 1866. The DVP had been revived in Baden-Württemberg in 1945 under the leadership of Reinhold Maier (who became the state's first premier and was later FDP leader in 1957–60) and Theodor Heuss (who became the first FDP leader and was then West Germany's first President, from 1949 until 1959). An attempt in 1947 to create an all-German liberal party had foundered on the opposition of the East German Communists to the participation of the Berlin-based Liberal Democratic Party (LDP), whose enforced support for socialism impelled prominent members, notably Hans-Dietrich Genscher, to flee to the West to join the FDP.

The FDP secured representation in the first West German *Bundestag* elected in 1949, with an 11.9% vote share, and joined a coalition government headed by what became the →Christian Democratic Union (CDU) and also including the Bavarian →Christian Social Union (CSU). It slipped to 9.5% in the 1953 elections and was in opposition in 1956–61, declining further to 7.7% of the vote in the 1957 federal elections. A major advance in 1961, to 12.8%, brought it back to office in a new coalition with the CDU/CSU that lasted until 1966, when the FDP again went into opposition, this time to a "grand coalition" of the CDU/CSU and the →Social Democratic Party of Germany (SPD). Having declined to 9.5% in the 1965 elections, FDP fell back sharply to 5.8% in 1969, but nevertheless joined a centre-left coalition with the SPD. Having succeeded Erich Mende as FDP chair in 1968, Walter Scheel served as Vice-Chancellor and Foreign Minister from 1969 until being elected West German President in 1974. During this period opposition within the party to the government's *Ostpolitik* caused several FDP deputies, including Mende, to desert to the opposition Christian Democrats. Scheel was succeeded in his party and government posts by Genscher, under whose leadership the FDP slipped to 7.9% in the 1976 elections (from 8.4% in 1972), before recovering to 10.6% in 1980.

The SPD/FDP federal coalition finally collapsed in September 1982 when the Free Democratic ministers resigned rather than accept the proposed 1983 budget deficit. The following month the party joined a coalition with the CDU/CSU, this switch to the right causing internal dissension and the exit of some FDP left-wingers. The party slumped to 6.9% in the 1983 federal elections and failed to secure representation in the 1984 European Parliament contest, its problems including the steady decline of its traditional farming constituency. The election of Martin Bangemann as FDP chair in 1985 in succession to Genscher (who nevertheless remained Foreign Minister) resulted in the party taking a more conservative tack, on which basis it revived to 9.1% in the 1987 *Bundestag* elections and continued its coalition with the CDU/CSU. In 1988 Bangemann opted to become a European commissioner and was succeeded as FDP chair by Count Otto Lambsdorff, who won a tight party election despite having been forced to resign from the government in 1984 after being convicted of illegal party financing activities. Having recovered some ground in state elections in the late 1980s, the FDP regained representation in the European Parliament in 1989 (winning 5.6% of the German vote).

On the collapse of Communist rule in East Germany, an eastern FDP sister party was formally established in February 1990. In the East German elections of March 1990 this party was part of the League of Free Democrats (together with the Communist-era LDP under new leadership and the German Forum Party), which took a 5.3% vote share. On the reunification of Germany in October 1990 these eastern elements were effectively merged into the western FDP, enabling the party to make a major advance in the all-German *Bundestag* elections in December 1990, to 11.0% of the overall vote and 79 seats out of 662. Maintaining its federal coalition with the CDU/CSU, the FDP showed electoral buoyancy in 1991 but encountered new difficulties following Genscher's resignation from the government in April 1992, as highlighted by the enforced resignation in January 1993 of the FDP Vice-Chancellor and Economics Minister, Jürgen Möllemann, over a corruption scandal.

In June 1993 Genscher's successor as Foreign Minister, Klaus Kinkel, replaced Lambsdorff as FDP chair, but he failed to halt a series of electoral failures at state level, while the party slumped to 4.1% in the June 1994 Euro-elections and thus failed to win any seats. Kinkel obtained a reprieve when the FDP unexpectedly retained a *Bundestag* presence in the October 1994 federal elections, winning 47 out of 672 seats on a 6.9% vote share. Despite previous strains over issues such as overseas German troop deployment (which the FDP opposed), the party opted to continue the federal coalition with the CDU/CSU and was rewarded with further electoral failures in Bremen and North Rhine–Westphalia in May 1995, whereupon Kinkel vacated the FDP leadership while remaining Foreign Minister. Elected as his successor at a special party congress in June, Wolfgang Gerhardt distanced himself from Chancellor Kohl on various policy issues, but a further FDP failure in Berlin elections in October 1995 served to intensify internal divisions on the party's future course. In December 1995 the FDP Justice Minister, Sabine Leutheusser-Schnarrenberger, resigned after her party colleagues had backed a government plan to institute electronic surveillance of suspected criminals.

After relaunching itself with a more right-wing orientation in January 1996, the FDP polled strongly in state elections in Baden-Württemberg, Rhineland-Palatinate and Schleswig-Holstein in March, winning representation in all three contests. A party congress in June 1996 confirmed the shift to the right, adopting a new programme which placed less emphasis on civil liberties than previous texts. The FDP shared in the defeat of the ruling coalition in the September 1998 federal elections, slipping to 6.3% of the vote and 43 seats. In opposition, it again failed to secure European representation in June 1999, winning only 3.0% of the national vote, and also fared badly in state elections. At end-1999 the FDP held office only in Baden-Württemberg and Hesse (in coalition with the CDU) and in Rhineland-Palatinate (in coalition with the SPD).

Claiming a membership of 70,000, the FDP is a member party of the Liberal International.

German People's Union
Deutsche Volksunion (DVU)
Address. Postfach 600464, 81204 Munich
Telephone. (+49-89) 896-0850
Fax. (+49-89) 834-1534
Email. info@dvu.net
Website. http://www.dvu.net
Leadership. Gerhard Frey (chair)
The extreme right-wing DVU claims not to be a neo-fascist party but has been prominent in anti-foreigner and anti-immigration agitation, contending that the majority of Germans want a "racially pure" country. In 1987 Frey launched a DVU/List D movement (the D signifying *Deutschland* as an electoral alliance which included elements of the →National Democratic Party and which won one seat in the Bremen state elections of September 1987. In January 1990 the DVU participated in the creation of the →German Social Union in East Germany, although with minimal lasting electoral impact. Following unification the DVU increased its Bremen representation to six seats in September 1991 (with 6.2% of the vote) and also won six seats in Schleswig-Holstein in April 1992 (with 6.3%).

The DVU backed the unsuccessful →Republicans in the October 1994 federal elections in the wake of reports that the two groups might overcome their longstanding rivalry for the far-right vote. In the May 1995 Bremen elections the DVU declined to 2.5% and lost its representation in the state assembly. It also failed to retain any seats in the Schleswig-Holstein state election on March 1996, taking only 4.3% of the vote. It had more success in the depressed eastern state of Saxony-Anhalt in April 1998, producing the best post-war performance for a far-right party by winning 12.9% of the vote and 16 of the 116 seats.

The DVU obtained only 1.2% of the vote standing in its own right in the September 1998 federal elections; but it returned to the Bremen state parliament in June 1999, winning only 3% of the vote but being awarded one seat because its vote in Bremerhaven was 6%. In September 1999 it returned five members in elections in Brandenburg, taking 5.3% of the vote, so that it then had representation in three state parliaments.

Party of Democratic Socialism
Partei der Demokratischen Sozialismus (PDS)
Address. Karl-Liebknecht-Haus, Kleine Alexanderstrasse 28, 10178 Berlin
Telephone. (+49–30) 240-090
Fax. (+49–30) 241-1046
Email. pdspv@pds-online.de
Website. http://www.pds-online.de
Leadership. Lothar Lisky (chair); Hans Modrow (honorary chair); Sylvia-Yvonne Kaufmann (deputy chair); Gregor Gysi (parliamentary leader); Wolfgang Gehrcke (general secretary)
The PDS was established under its present name in February 1990 amid the collapse of Communist rule in East Germany, being descended from the former ruling Socialist Unity Party of Germany (*Sozialistische Einheitspartei Deutschlands*, SED), although it sought to throw off this provenance by espousing a commitment to multi-party democracy. The SED itself had been created in April 1946 as an enforced merger of the East German →Social Democratic Party of Germany (SPD) with the dominant Soviet-backed Communist Party of Germany (*Kommunistische Partei Deutschlands*, KPD). The KPD had been founded in December 1918 by the left-wing minority of the SPD and other leftist elements and had played an important opposition role in the inter-war Weimar Republic, usually in conflict with the SPD, until being outlawed on the advent to power of Hitler's Nazi regime in 1933. During the Third Reich many German Communists had taken refuge in Moscow, returning to Germany at the end of World War II to assume power in the eastern Soviet-occupied zone.

In what became the German Democratic Republic (GDR), the SED was effectively the sole ruling party for over four decades, operating through the familiar device of a National Front that included four other "democratic" parties supportive of socialism, namely the Christian Democratic Union, the Democratic Farmers' Party, the Liberal Democratic Party and the National Democratic Party. Walter Ulbricht was elected SED leader in 1950, in which year several leading party members were expelled in the wake of Yugoslavia's break with the Cominform; other were purged in consequence of the major anti-government uprising in East Berlin in 1953. Some of these expellees were rehabilitated in 1956, but further purges followed the Hungarian Uprising later that year. Economic difficulties and the nationalization of agriculture served to increase the exodus of East Germans to the West, to staunch which the authorities erected the Berlin Wall in 1961, extending it along the entire length of the border with West Germany. In August 1968 East German troops participated in the Soviet-led military intervention that crushed the "Prague Spring" in Czechoslovakia.

In May 1971 Ulbricht was replaced as SED leader by Erich Honecker, under whom East Germany normalized its relations with West Germany in 1972 and became a UN member in 1974. In the 1980s Honecker maintained rigid orthodoxy, showing no enthusiasm for the post-1985 reform policies of Mikhail Gorbachev in the USSR. In 1989, however, a rising tide of protest and renewed flight of East German citizens to the West via Hungary resulted in Honecker being replaced in October by Egon Krenz, who himself resigned in December after the historic opening of the Berlin Wall on Nov. 9 had unleashed irresistible pressure for change. Later in December an emergency SED congress abandoned Marxism, added the suffix "Party of Democratic Socialism" to the party's name and elected Gregor Gysi as leader. A government of "national responsibility" appointed in February 1990 contained a minority of Communists for the first time in East Germany's history, although Hans Modrow of the SED-PDS retained the premiership. Having dropped the SED component from its name, the PDS polled better than expected in multi-party elections in March 1990 (winning 16.4% of the vote), assisted by the personal standing of Modrow. It nevertheless went into opposition to a broad coalition of parties committed to German reunification.

In the all-German *Bundestag* elections of December 1990 the PDS won only 2.4% of the overall vote but scored 11.1% in the eastern *Länder* and was therefore allocated 17 of the 662 seats by virtue of the separate application of the 5% theshold rule to the two parts of Germany. Thereafter the PDS suffered from a tide of disclosures about the evils of the former SED regime, but retained a substantial following among easterners disadvantaged by rapid economic and social change. In February 1993 Gysi was succeeded as PDS leader by Lothar Bisky, under whom the party polled strongly in elections in the eastern *Länder* in 1993–94. Although the PDS failed to win representation in the June 1994 Euro-elections, in the October 1994 federal elections it increased its national vote share to 4.4% and its eastern share to around 18%, being allocated 30 *Bundestag* seats from the proportional pool by virtue of having returned three candidates in a single electoral district (Berlin).

In January 1995 a PDS congress voted in favour of a "left-wing democratic" programme and voted down the party's Stalinist faction led by Sarah Wagenknecht. In June 1995 the PDS received a financial boost when an independent commission agreed that it could retain a proportion of the former SED's assets. In Berlin legislative elections in October 1995 the PDS advanced to 14.6% of the vote (giving it 34 of the 206 seats), mainly at the expense of the SPD. Whereas the SPD's then leader, Rudolf Scharping, had consistently rejected any co-operation with the PDS, his successor elected in November 1995, Oskar Lafontaine, envisaged building a broad progressive front, including the PDS, to challenge the Kohl government in the next federal elections. The PDS was the only major party to oppose the proposed merger of Berlin and Brandenburg, which voters of the latter rejected in a referendum in May 1996.

Having polled strongly in Saxony-Anhalt in April 1998 (winning 19.6% and 25 seats), the PDS for the first time surmounted the national 5% barrier in the September 1998 federal elections, winning 5.1% of the vote and 36 seats. In simultaneous state elections in Mecklenburg–West Pomerania, moreover, the PDS advanced to 25.5% and 20 seats, on the strength of which it entered government for the first time in the new Germany, as junior coalition partner to the SPD. Having become a supporter of European integration, the PDS entered the European Parliament for the first time in June 1999, winning a 5.8% vote share and six seats. It then registered major advances in eastern state elections, benefiting from the unpopularity of the SPD-led federal coalition and continuing high unemployment in eastern Germany. In polling in Thuringia and Saxony in September 1999 it pushed the SPD into third place by taking, respectively, 21.4% and 22.2% of the vote. In the Berlin elections in October 1999 the PDS won 17.7% and 33 seats. The party was also strengthened in the *Bundestag* by the defection of a left-wing SPD deputy in late 1999, with the result that PDS representation increased to 37 seats.

The PDS members of the European Parliament sit in the European United Left/Nordic Green Left group. The party has an official membership of 100,000.

The Republicans
Die Republikaner
Address. Schmidt-Ott-Strasse 10/A, 12165 Berlin
Telephone. (+49-30) 7909-8310
Fax. (+49-30) 7909-8315
Email. republikaner-bgs@t-online.de
Website. http://www.rep.de
Leadership. Rolf Schlierer (federal chair)
The far-right anti-immigration Republicans were established as a party in November 1983 by two former *Bundestag* deputies of the Bavarian →Christian Social Union (CSU) who had criticized the alleged dictatorial style of the then CSU leader, Franz Josef Strauss, particularly

as regards the latter's involvement in developing relations with East Germany in contravention of CSU policy. Standing for German reunification, lower business taxes and restrictions on foreigners, the new party was also joined by the small Citizens' Party (*Bürgerpartei*) of Baden-Württemberg. Having won only 3% in their first electoral contest, for the Bavarian *Landtag* in 1986, the Republicans did not contest the 1987 federal elections. Under the leadership of former SS officer Franz Schönhuber, however, the party won 7.5% and 11 seats in the January 1989 Berlin legislative elections. It also did well in the June 1989 European Parliament elections, winning 7.1% and six seats (on a platform of opposition to European integration).

Amid the progression to reunification in 1990, the Republicans' electoral appeal waned. They obtained less than 2% in state elections in North Rhine-Westphalia and Lower Saxony in May 1990, whereupon Schönhuber was briefly ousted from the party chairmanship, recovering the post in July. In the December 1990 all-German elections the party managed only 2.1% (and no seats), while in simultaneous polling it lost its representation in Berlin, falling to 3.1%. The party made a comeback in the Baden-Württemberg state elections in April 1992, winning 10.9% of the vote and 15 seats. In May 1993, moreover, it secured *Bundestag* representation for the first time when it was joined by a right-wing deputy of the →Christian Democratic Union (CDU), Rudolf Krause. In June 1994, however, it failed to retain its European Parliament seats (falling to a 3.9% vote share), while in the October 1994 *Bundestag* elections the Republicans won only 1.9% (and no seats). Prior to the federal polling Schönhuber was again deposed as leader, officially because of an unauthorized meeting with the leader of the →German People's Union, but also because of his negative media image.

In state elections in March 1996, the Republicans again polled strongly in Baden-Württemberg, winning 9.1% and 14 seats, while in Rhineland-Palatinate they improved to 3.5%, without gaining representation. In the September 1998 federal elections, however, the Republicans managed only 1.8% of the vote, subsequently falling back to 1.7% in the June 1999 European Parliament elections.

Social Democratic Party of Germany
Sozialdemokratische Partei Deutschlands (SPD)
Address. Willy-Brandt-Haus, Wilhelmstrasse 140, 10963 Berlin
Telephone. (+49-30) 259-910
Fax. (+49-30) 2599-1720
Email. parteivorstand@spd.de
Website. http://www.spd.de
Leadership. Gerhard Schröder (chair); Rudolf Scharping, Renate Schmidt, Wolfgang Thierse, Heidemarie Wieczorek-Zeul (deputy chairs); Peter Struck (parliamentary leader); Franz Müntefering (secretary-general)
The origins of the SPD lie in the reformist General Association of German Workers (*Allgemeiner Deutscher Arbeiterverein*, ADA) founded by Ferdinand Lassalle in 1863 and the Social Democratic Labour Party (*Sozialdemokratische Arbeiterpartei*, SDAP) founded by the Marxists Wilhelm Liebknecht and August Bebel in 1869. In 1875 these two forerunners merged to form the Socialist Labour Party of Germany (*Sozialistische Arbeiterpartei Deutschlands*, SAPD), which was outlawed from 1878 under Chancellor Bismarck's anti-socialist laws. Relegalized in 1890, the SAPD became the SPD at the 1891 Erfurt congress, when the party reaffirmed its Marxist belief in inevitable socialist revolution, although in practice it was already following the reformist line advocated by Eduard Bernstein. Representing the rapidly expanding industrial working class and benefiting from

universal manhood suffrage, the SAPD became the largest party in the *Reichstag* in 1912, although it played no part in Germany's unrepresentative government before 1914.

Ideological divisions within the SPD were intensified by World War I, during which the party split into a "majority" reformist wing supportive of the German war effort and the anti-war "Independent Social Democrats" led by Liebknecht and Rosa Luxemburg. Most of the latter faction joined the Communist Party of Germany founded in December 1918, while the main SPD became a key supporter of the post-war Weimar Republic, of which party leader Friedrich Ebert was the first Chancellor and the first President (from 1919 to 1925). SPD participation in most Weimar coalition governments was accompanied by theoretical criticism of capitalism, notably in the Heidelberg Programme of 1925, but thereafter the party was identified as a defender of the status quo against Soviet-backed Bolshevism on the left and the rising tide of fascism on the right. In the July 1932 elections the SPD was overtaken as the largest party by Hitler's National Socialist German Workers' Party (the Nazis), the latter winning 37.4% and the SPD 24.3%. In further elections in November 1932 the Nazis fell back to 33.2% and the SPD to 20.7%, while the Communists increased from 14.3% to 17%. Nevertheless, Hitler was appointed Chancellor in January 1933 and was granted emergency powers following the burning of the *Reichstag* the following month. In new elections in March 1933 the Nazis won 43.9% against 18.3% for the SPD and 12.1% for the Communists, whereupon an enabling act approved by the non-Nazi centre-right parties (but not by the SPD) gave Hitler absolute power to ban his political opponents, including the SPD.

After World War II the SPD was re-established in both the Western and the Soviet occupation zones, headed in the former by Kurt Schumacher and in the latter by Otto Grotewohl. The East German SPD was quickly constrained to merge with the Communists in the Socialist Unity Party of Germany (SED), founded in April 1946. In the first elections to the West German *Bundestag* in August 1949 the SPD came a close second to the Christian Democrats, with a 29.2% vote share, and was the principal opposition party until 1966, under the leadership of Schumacher until his death in 1952, then of Erich Ollenhauer and from 1958 of Willy Brandt (the mayor of West Berlin). During this opposition phase, the SPD's federal vote slipped to 28.8% in 1953 but then rose steadily, to 31.8% in 1957, 36.2% in 1961 and 39.3% in 1965. Faced with the evidence of West Germany's economic miracle of the 1950s, the SPD in 1959 adopted its celebrated Godesberg Programme, which jettisoned Marxist theory, embraced private ownership within the context of an equitable social order and industrial co-determination (*Mitbestimmung*), and reversed the party's previous opposition to NATO and the European Community.

In October 1966 the SPD entered a West German federal government for the first time, in a coalition headed by the →Christian Democratic Union (CDU) and the Bavarian →Christian Social Union (CSU). Brandt became Vice-Chancellor and Foreign Minister, in which capacity he pursued an *Ostpolitik* seeking normalization of relations with the Communist-ruled East European states, including East Germany. In March 1969 Gustav Heinemann became West Germany's first SPD President, elected with the backing of the →Free Democratic Party (FDP). In the September 1969 federal elections the SPD at last broke the 40% barrier, winning 42.7% of the vote and forming a centre-left coalition with the FDP. Brandt became West German Chancellor and led the SPD to a further advance in the 1972 *Bundestag* elections, to a post-war high of 45.8% of the vote. Brandt continued as head of an SPD/FDP coalition until 1974, when the discovery that a close aide was an East German spy forced him to resign. He was succeeded as Chancellor by Helmut Schmidt (although Brandt remained SPD chair) and the SPD/FDP coalition under Schmidt's leadership continued in power through the 1976 and 1980 federal elections, in which the SPD vote was 42.6% and 42.9% respectively.

The SPD/FDP government finally collapsed in September 1982, when the FDP withdrew and opted to join a coalition headed by the CDU/CSU. The SPD remained in opposition after the March 1983 and January 1987 *Bundestag* elections, in which its support fell back to 38.2% and 37.0% respectively, eroded in particular by the advancing Greens. Brandt finally resigned as SPD chair in March 1987, when the party objected to his appointment of a non-SPD Greek lady as his spokesperson. He was succeeded by Hans-Jochen Vogel, a prominent SPD moderate, who launched a major reappraisal of the party's basic policy programme, although without achieving a definitive resolution of the vexed question of whether the SPD should formally commit to a future federal coalition with the Greens. In the latter context, however, the "red–green" coalition formed in 1985 between the SPD and the Greens in the state of Hesse set a trend of co-operation between the SPD and what was later named the →Alliance 90/The Greens.

The sudden collapse of East European communism from late 1989 caught the opposition SPD on the back foot, with the result that it tended to follow in the wake of events leading to German reunification in October 1990. Launched in October 1989, an East German SPD led by Ibrahim Böhme won 21.9% of the vote in multi-party elections in March 1990 and joined an eastern "grand coalition" government. Böhme quickly resigned on being found to have been a Stasi agent and was succeeded by Markus Meckel (then East German Foreign Minister), who was himself replaced by Wolfgang Thierse in June 1990. In September 1990 the East and West German SPDs were merged, but the party found it difficult to recover its pre-war strength in the east. Oskar Lafontaine was the SPD's Chancellor-candidate in the December 1990 all-German *Bundestag* elections, in which the party won only 33.5% of the overall vote (35.7% in the western *Länder*, 24.3% in the east), which yielded 239 of the 662 seats.

The SPD therefore continued in opposition and Vogel immediately resigned as SPD chair, being succeeded by Bjoern Engholm, then premier of Schleswig-Holstein. In November 1992 a special SPD conference endorsed a leadership recommendation that the party should give qualified backing to government-proposed constitutional amendments which would end the automatic right of entry to asylum-seekers and would allow German forces to be deployed outside the NATO area on UN-approved peacekeeping missions. Damaged by the revival of an old political scandal, Engholm resigned as SPD leader in May 1993 and was succeeded by Rudolf Scharping (then premier of Rhineland-Palatinate). In the June 1994 European Parliament elections the SPD slipped to 32.2% of the vote (from 37.3% in 1989) and won 40 of the 99 German seats. Scharping then led the SPD to its fourth successive federal election defeat in October 1994, although its share of the vote improved to 36.4% and its representation in the *Bundestag* rose to 252 seats out of 672. Concurrent SPD advances at state level gave it a majority in the *Bundesrat* (upper house), although in May 1995 the party lost ground in North Rhine-Westphalia and Bremen, and in October went down to a heavy defeat in Berlin (once an SPD stronghold).

In November 1995 an SPD conference in Mannheim elected Oskar Lafontaine (then premier of Saarland) as SPD chair in succession to Scharping, who remained the SPD leader in the *Bundestag*. Located ideologically on the SPD left, Lafontaine had opposed the Maastricht Treaty on European union, on the grounds that it contained inadequate provisions for real political union, and was also an advocate of a political alliance between the SPD, the Greens and the (ex-communist) →Party of Democratic Socialism (PDS). He took the SPD into a stance of opposition to any speedy adoption of a single European currency and to the automatic granting of citizenship to ethnic German immigrants from Russia. The party suffered further setbacks in three state elections in March 1996 and also lost ground in Hamburg in September 1997.

In March 1998 the SPD executive elected Gerhard Schröder, an ideological pragmatist who had just won a third term as minister-president of Lower Saxony, as the party's Chancellor-candidate in preference to Lafontaine, who continued as party chair. Gains for the SPD in Saxony-Anhalt in April were followed by a significant advance in the September 1998 federal elections, in which the SPD vote increased to 40.9% and its *Bundestag* representation to 298 seats. The following month Schröder formed an historic "red-green" federal coalition with the Greens, on the basis of a government programme setting the fight against unemployment as the main priority and also including Green objectives such as an "ecological tax reform" and the phasing-out of nuclear power generation.

SPD-Green strains quickly developed on the nuclear and other issues, but more damage was done to the government by divisions between Schröder and Finance Minister Lafontaine, the former advocating a "New Middle" (*Neue Mitte*) course, the latter preferring a traditional social democratic line. In March 1999 Lafontaine resigned from the government and also as SPD chair, following a major disagreement with the Chancellor, who was elected as SPD party leader in April. The following month Johannes Rau (former SPD minister-president of North Rhine–Westphalia) was elected as President of Germany by 690 votes in the 1,338-member Federal Assembly.

In European Parliament elections in June 1999 the SPD slipped to 30.7% of the vote, losing seven of its 40 seats. Amid growing public disquiet about the federal government's performance, state elections in September-October 1999 saw the SPD being relegated to third place in Saxony and Thuringia, being ousted from power in Saarland and losing ground in Brandenburg and Berlin. The losses meant that the SPD-led federal government commanded only 26 out of 69 votes in the *Bundesrat* (the upper legislative house representing the states). At end-1999 the SPD was in sole governmental control in Lower Saxony and Saxony-Anhalt; in coalition with the Greens in Hamburg, North Rhine–Westphalia and Schleswig-Holstein; in coalition with the CDU in Berlin, Brandenburg and Bremen; in coalition with the FDP in Rhineland–Palatinate; and in coalition with the PDS in Mecklenburg-West Pomerania.

With an official membership of 800,000, the SPD is a member party of the Socialist International. Its European Parliament representatives sit in the Party of European Socialists group.

Other Parties

Around 80 other parties are officially registered in Germany. The following selection focuses on those which obtained a degree of support in the 1998 federal or 1999 European elections.

Anarchist Pogo Party of Germany (*Anarchistische Pogo Partei Deutschland*, APPD), led by Markus Gäthke in association with the "The Unknown Ape" (*Der Unbekannte Affe*); leftist alternative formation in whose title "Pogo" signifies "wild and mindless dance", won 0.1% of the vote in 1998 federal elections. *Address.* Zenettistrasse 49, 80337 Munich; *Email.* kontakt@appd.de; *Website.* http://www.appd.de

Animal Rights Party (*Tierschutzpartei*, TP), led by Gisela Bulla, won 0.3% in 1998 federal elections and 0.7% in 1999 Euro-elections. *Address.* Frankfurter Strasse 7, 65825 Schwalbach; *Telephone.* (+49-6796) 888-007; *Fax.* (+49-6196) 889-7306; *Website.* http://www.tierschutzpartei.de

Bavaria Party (*Bayernpartei*, BP), led by Dorn Hubert, founded in 1946 to seek the restoration of an independent Bavarian state, represented in the *Bundestag* in 1949–53 (but not since) and influential in the Bavarian *Landtag* until the mid-1960s, won 0.1% in 1994 and 1998 federal elections and 0.1% in 1999 Euro-elections. *Address.* Unter Weidenstrasse 14,

81543 Munich; *Telephone.* (+49-89) 651-8051; *Fax.* (+49-89) 654-259; *Email.* bayernpart@aol.com

Car-Drivers' Party of Germany (*Autofahrer Partei Deutschlands*, APD), led by Dr E. Hörber, promotes drivers' rights and citizens' interests, won 0.7% of national vote in 1994 European elections, falling to 0.4% in 1999. *Address.* Emilstrasse 71A, 44869 Bochum; *Telephone/Fax.* (+49-2327) 59391; *Email.* apdberlin@aol.com

Car Taxpayers' Party (*Automobile Steuerzahler Partei*, ASP), led by Bernd Bräuer, founded in 1993, won 0.1% in 1999 European elections. *Address.* Georg-Knorr-Strasse 25B, 85662 Hohenbrunn; *Telephone.* (+49-8102) 6836; *Fax.* (+49-8102) 72129; *Email.* info@as-partei.de; *Website.* http://www.as-partei.de

Chance 2000, led by Alexander Karschnia, Matthias Riedel and Herbert Rusche, won 0.1% in 1998 federal elections. *Address.* Eckenheimer Landstrasse 160, 60318 Frankfurt; *Telephone.* (+49-69) 597-4575; *Fax.* (+49-69) 9552-0199; *Email.* chance2000@freunde.de; *Website.* http://www.chance2000.com

Christian Middle (*Christliche Mitte*, CM), won 0.2% in 1994 European elections, falling to 0.1% in 1999. *Address.* Lippstädter Strasse 42, 59329 Liesborn; *Telephone.* (+49-2523) 8388; *Fax.* (+49-2523) 6138; *Email.* christliche-mitte@t-online.de

Citizens' Rights Solidarity Movement (*Bürgerrechtsbewegung Solidarität*, BüSo), led by Helga Zepp-LaRouche, inspired by US civil rights campaigner Lyndon H. LaRouche, won 0.1% in 1994 European elections and less than 0.1% in 1998 federal and 1999 European elections. *Address.* Postfach 3366, 55023 Mainz; *Telephone.* (+49-6131) 237-384; *Fax.* (+49-6131) 237-387; *Email.* info@bueso.de; *Website.* http://www.bueso.de

Democratic Party of Germany (*Demokratische Partei Deutschlands*, DPD), led by Sedat Sezgin, founded in October 1995 to represent foreigners in Germany and to oppose racism, based in the two-million-strong Turkish immigrant community (most of whom do not have German citizenship and are therefore not entitled to vote); won negligible vote in 1998 federal elections. *Address.* Marktstrasse 41, 71254 Ditzingen; *Telephone.* (+49-7156) 959-688; *Fax.* (+49-7156) 959-698

Ecological Democratic Party (*Ökologisch–Demokratische Partei*, ÖDP), led by Susanne Bachmeier, standing for sustainable development and protection of the environment, won 0.4% in both the 1990 and 1994 federal elections, rising to 0.8% in 1994 Euro-elections, but slipping to 0.2% in 1998 federal elections and 0.4% in June 1999 Euro-elections, when it had some 300 municipal councillors. *Address.* Bohnesmühlgasse 5, 97070 Würzburg; *Telephone.* (+49-931) 12031; *Fax.* (+49-931) 14087; *Email.* geschaeftsstelle@oedp.de; *Website.* http://www.oedp.de

Family Party of Germany (*Familienpartei Deutschlands*, FPD), won 0.1% in 1998 federal elections and less than 0.1% in 1999 Euro-elections. *Address.* Postfach 4122, 66376 St Ingbert; *Telephone.* (+49-6894) 4209; *Fax.* (+49-6894) 382-362; *Email.* familien.partei@t-online.de

Feminist Party (*Feministische Partei*, FP), campaigns as "Women" (*Die Frauen*), won 0.1% in 1998 federal elections and 0.4% in 1999 Euro-elections. *Address.* Hausdorffstrasse 99,

53129 Bonn; *Telephone.* (+49-228) 231-455; *Fax.* (+49-228) 235-529; *Email.* w-pomper@t-online.de

German Communist Party (*Deutsche Kommunistische Partei*, DKP), founded in West Germany in 1969 some 13 years after the banning of its predecessor, for long led by Herbert Mies, had close links with the then ruling Socialist Unity Party of East Germany, but lost any impetus on the collapse of the East German regime in 1989; Mies resigned in October 1989 and was replaced by a four-member council at the party's 10th congress in March 1990; won negligible vote in 1994 and 1998 federal elections. *Address.* Hoffnungstrasse 18, 45127 Essen; *Telephone.* (+49-201) 225-148; *Fax.* (+49-201) 202-467; *Email.* dkp.pv@t-online.de

German Social Union (*Deutscher Sozialer Union*, DSU), led by Roberto Rink, launched in East Germany in January 1990 as an umbrella organization of 12 conservative groups including the far-right →German People's Union, then allied with the →Christian Social Union (CSU) of West Germany; won only 0.2% in December 1990; its decision in April 1993 to campaign throughout Germany caused a breach with the CSU; won negiligible vote in 1994 and 1998 federal elections. *Address.* Zur Wetterwarte 27/127, 01109 Dresden; *Telephone.* (+49-351) 886-4487; *Fax.* (+49-351) 886-4486; *Email.* dsu@dotexpress.com

The Greys (*Die Grauen*), led by Trude Unruh, also known as the Grey Panthers, formerly a pensioners' group within the West German Greens, became a separate party in mid-1989 to represent the interests of older citizens; it won 0.8% of the federal vote in 1990, 0.5% in 1994 and 0.3% in 1998, recovering to 0.4% in 1999 Euro-elections. *Address.* Kothener Strasse 1-5, 42285 Wuppertal; *Telephone.* (+49-202) 280-700; *Fax.* (+49-202) 280-7070; *Email.* grauepanther@t-online.de

Instead of a Party (*Unabhängen Statt Partei*, SP), led by Markus Ernst Wegner and Mike Bashford, subtitled set up in July 1993 to promote "a different kind of politics", including a reduction in government bureaucracy, the introduction of popular referendums and more voting according to conviction rather than by party discipline; main founder and lawyer Wegner had previously been a member of the →Christian Democratic Union (CDU) and attracted support not only from Hamburg CDU branches but also from other parties; in 1993 Hamburg elections the SP won 5.6% of the vote and eight seats (out of 121) and entered into a "co-operation" agreement with the new minority government of the →Social Democratic Party of Germany; obtained only 0.01% of the vote in 1994 federal elections and lost its Hamburg seats in 1997. *Address.* Postfach 600247, 22202 Hamburg; *Telephone/Fax.* (+49-40) 5149-1661

League of Free Citizens (*Bund der Freie Bürger*, BFB), sub-titled "Offensive for Germany", led by Heiner Kappel, right-wing party founded in 1994 by Manfred Brunner, a former *chef de cabinet* to one of Germany's European Union commissioners; relaunched in January 1998 to oppose further moves towards European political and economic union; won 0.2% in 1998 federal elections. *Address.* Haupstrasse 31, 65812 Bad Soden; *Telephone.* (+49-6196) 527-809; *Fax.* (+49-6196) 527-811; *Email.* kappel@bfb-kappel.de; *Website.* http://www.bfb-kappel.de

Marxist-Leninist Party of Germany (*Marxistisch-Leninistische Partei Deutschlands*, MLPD), led by Stefan Engel, Maoist formation whose belief in Marxist-Leninist precepts has survived their collapse in European countries where they were once practised. *Address.*

Kostrasse 8, 45899 Gelsenkirchen; *Telephone*. (+49-209) 951-940; *Fax*. (+49-209) 951-9460; *Email*. mlpd_zk@compuserve.com; *Website*: http://www.mlpd.de

National Democratic Party (*Nationaldemokratische Partei Deutschlands*, NPD), led by Udo Voigt, far-right formation founded in 1964, reached high of 4.3% in the 1969 federal elections and won seats in several state parliaments in the late 1960s, but declined thereafter, being supplanted by the →Republicans; in April 1995 Deckert received a prison sentence for incitement to racial hatred and other offences; won 0.3% in 1998 federal elections and 0.4% in 1999 Euro-elections. *Address*. Postfach 103528, 70030 Stuttgart; *Telephone*. (+49-711) 610-605; *Fax*. (+49-711) 611-716; *Email*. pressenpd@aol.de

Natural Law Party (*Naturgesetz Partei*, NP), the German branch of a worldwide network of such parties, won 0.2% in the 1994 federal elections and 0.1% in 1998 federal and 1999 Euro-elections. *Address*. Leuterstal 2, 74249 Jagsthausen; *Telephone/Fax*. (+49-7943) 8657; *Email*. vorstand@naturgesetz.de

New Liberal Party Pro-Deutschmark (*Neue Liberale Partei Pro-Deutsche Mark*, NLP Pro-DM), free-market movement opposed to German participation in the single European currency, won 0.9% in 1998 federal elections. *Address*. Tiergartenstrasse 17, 40237 Düsseldorf; *Telephone/Fax*. (+49-721) 567-458

Party of Bible-Believing Christians (*Partei der Bibeltreuen Christen*, PBC), won vote share of 0.1% in 1994 and 1998 federal elections and 0.3% in 1999 Euro-elections. *Address*. Postfach 410810, 76208 Karlsrühe; *Telephone*. (+49-721) 495-596; *Fax*. (+49-721) 494-125; *Email*. pbc.de@t-online.de

Party of the Unemployed and Socially-Excluded (*Partei der Arbeitlosen und Sozial Schwachen*, PASS), led in Berlin by Andreas Lüdecke and in Hesse by Herbert Schleiermacher, won 0.4% in 1994 European elections and 0.3% in 1999, rising to 0.5% in October 1999 Berlin state elections. *Address*. Babelsberger Strasse 5, 10715 Berlin; *Telephone*. (+49-30) 853-8104; *Fax*. (+49-30) 834-4695; *Email*. bund@passpartei.de; *Website*. http://passpartei.de

South Schleswig Voters' Union (*Südschleswigscher Wählerverband*, SSW/*Sydslesvigk Vaelgerforening*, SSV), led by Wilhelm Klüver, representing ethnic Danes in Schleswig-Holstein, won one seat in the 1992 state elections with 1.9% of the vote (being exempt from the 5% threshold rule), increasing to two seats in 1996 (with 2.5%); *Address*. Norderstrasse 74, 24939 Flensburg; *Telephone*. (+49-461) 1440-8300; *Fax*. (+49-461) 1440-8305; *Email*. info@ssw-sh.de; *Website*. http://www.ssw-sh.de

Work for Bremen (*Arbeit für Bremen*, AfB), a left-wing splinter group of the →Social Democratic Party of Germany, formed prior to the May 1995 state elections, in which it won 10.7% and 12 seats, losing them all in 1999. *Address*. Sögestrasse 43, 28195 Bremen; *Telephone*. (+49-421) 320-707; *Fax*. (+49-421) 320-708; *Email*. roland2801@aol.de

Greece

Capital: Athens

Population: 10,500,000

Officially called the Hellenic Republic, Greece is a parliamentary democracy with a largely ceremonial President as head of state, elected by vote of the parliamentary deputies for a five-year term. Predominant executive power resides in the Prime Minister and members of the Cabinet, who must enjoy the confidence of the 300-member unicameral Parliament (*Vouli*). The latter is elected for a four-year term by universal adult suffrage under a system of proportional representation based on electoral constituencies returning between one and 26 deputies depending on their population size. Voting is compulsory for citizens aged 18 years and over (unless they are ill or incapacitated). By-elections are held to fill any vacancies, except during the final year of a parliamentary term. Political parties are required by the 1975 constitution to "serve the free functioning of democratic government". Greece joined what became the European Union on Jan. 1, 1981, and elects 25 members to the European Parliament.

A law of May 1984 provides for public funding of political parties to cover organizational and electoral expenses, an amount equivalent to 0.001% of GDP being allocated for this purpose. Eligible parties are those with parliamentary representation which have obtained at least 3% of the total vote in the most recent election and which have presented lists in at least two-thirds of the electoral constituencies. Coalitions of parties are also eligible, those of two parties requiring 5% of the vote to qualify and those of three or more 6%. Of the annual total subsidy available, 10% is shared equally between the qualifying parties and the other 90% is allocated in proportion to votes received at the most recent election.

Parliamentary elections held on Sept. 22, 1996, resulted as follows:

	Seats 1996 (1993)	Percentage 1996 (1993)
Pan-Hellenic Socialist Movement … … …	162 (170)	41.5 (46.9)
New Democracy … … … … … … … …	108 (111)	38.2 (39.3)
Communist Party of Greece … … … … …	11 (9)	5.6 (4.5)
Coalition of the Left and Progress … … …	10 (–)	5.1 (–)
Democratic Social Movement … … … …	9 (–)	4.4 (–)

Coalition of the Left and Progress
Synaspismos tis Aristeras kai tis Proodou
Address. Plateia Eleftherias 1, 10553 Athens
Telephone. (+30–1) 337–8400
Fax. (+30-1) 321-9914; 321-7003
Email. intrelations@syn.gr
Website. http://www.syn.gr

Leadership. Nicos Constantopoulos (president); Stergios Pitsiorlas (co-ordinator of secretariat)
Synaspismos was created prior to the June 1989 general elections as an alliance of the
orthodox →Communist Party of Greece (KKE) "exterior", the Greek Left Party (*Elleniki
Aristera*, EAR) and a number of minor leftist formations. The EAR had been launched in
April 1987 by the majority wing of the KKE "interior", itself founded in 1968 by resident
Communists opposed to the pro-Soviet orthodoxy of the exiled leadership of the KKE, which
became known as the "exterior" party. Following the restoration of democracy in 1974, the
Eurocommunist KKE "interior" had been part of the United Democratic Left (EDA), then
including the KKE "exterior", and had won two of the EDA's eight seats in the November
1974 elections. In 1977 it had obtained one of the two seats won by an Alliance of
Progressive and Left Forces (the precursor of *Synaspismos*), but had failed to win
representation in 1981, before regaining one seat in 1985, when its share of the vote was
1.8%. In the 1984 European Parliament elections the KKE "interior" had again won one seat,
on a 3.4% vote share.

Reuniting many of the Greek Communist factions, *Synaspismos* polled strongly in the
June 1989 national elections, winning 28 seats out of 300 and 13.1% of the vote. In
concurrent European Parliament elections a *Synaspismos* list won four of the 24 Greek seats
with 14.3% of the vote. However, the decision of the *Synaspismos* leadership to join a
temporary coalition government with the conservative →New Democracy (ND) generated
rank-and-file unrest, with the result that the alliance fell back to 21 seats and 11.0% in the
November 1989 elections. The subsequent participation of *Synaspismos* in another temporary
coalition, this time with ND and the →Pan-Hellenic Socialist Movement (PASOK), was also
controversial, and the alliance slipped again in the April 1990 elections, to 19 seats and 10.2%
of the vote. The upshot was that in February 1991 the orthodox faction regained control of the
KKE "exterior", which in June 1991 withdrew from *Synaspismos* and expelled elements that
opted to remain in the alliance. The following month the prominent Communist reformer
Maria Damanaki was re-elected *Synaspismos* chair.

In opposition to an ND government, *Synaspismos* endeavoured to transform itself into a
unified party, to which end the EAR was dissolved in June 1992. However, the local
organizational strength of the KKE (now the sole Communist Party) proved decisive in the
October 1993 general election victory of PASOK, in which *Synaspismos* failed to win
representation (on a 2.9% vote share), whereas the KKE won nine seats. Damanaki thereupon
resigned as *Synaspismos* leader and was succeeded by Nicos Constantopoulos. In the June
1994 European Parliament elections *Synaspismos* recovered to 6.3% (only narrowly behind
the KKE) and took two of the 25 Greek seats.

Benefiting from disenchantment among some PASOK voters with the incumbent
government, *Synaspismos* returned to the Greek parliament in the September 1996 elections,
winning 5.1% of the vote and 10 seats. In opposition to a further PASOK government and
economic austerity measures in preparation for the desired entry of Greece into the single
European currency, *Synaspismos* polled strongly local elections in October 1998. In the June
1999 European Parliament elections it again won two seats, on a 5.2% vote share.

The *Synaspismos* members of the European Parliament sit in the European United
Left/Nordic Green left group, as do the KKE representatives. The party is a member of the
New European Left Forum (NELF).

Communist Party of Greece
Kommounistiko Komma Elladas (KKE)
Address. Leoforos Irakliou 145, 14231 Athens
Telephone. (+30–1) 259-2111
Fax. (+30–1) 259-2298

Email. cpg@kke.gr
Website. http://www.kke.gr
Leadership. Aleka Papariga (general secretary); Harilaos Florakis (honorary president)

For long known as the "exterior" Communist Party because many of activists were forced into exile after World War II, the present KKE is directly descended from the Socialist Workers' Party of Greece (SEKE) founded in November 1918, which joined the Communist International (Comintern) in 1924 and changed its name to KKE. The party secured its first parliamentary representation in 1926 and in 1936 held the balance of power between the Monarchists and the Liberals, the resultant deadlock provoking a military coup by Gen. Metaxas in August 1936, following which all political parties were banned. During World War II popular resistance to the occupying Axis powers was organized by the Communists in the National Liberation Front (EAM) and the guerrilla Greek People's Liberation Army (ELAS), which gained control of the countryside. Following the liberation, however, ELAS was suppressed by British (and later US) troops after civil war had broken out between the Communists and centre-right forces favouring restoration of the monarchy. The KKE was officially banned in July 1947 and by 1949 had been defeated, its leadership and thousands of members fleeing to Communist-ruled countries.

The banned KKE became the dominant force within the Democratic Party (which won 9.7% of the vote in 1950) and then within the legal United Democratic Left (EDA), which won 10.4% of the vote in 1951, rising to 24.4% and 79 seats in 1958, before falling back to 11.8% and 22 seats in the the 1964 elections won by the centre-left Centre Union. During this period the KKE remained an orthodox Marxist-Leninist party whose pro-Soviet line was unaffected by the suppression of the Hungarian Uprising in 1956. In 1967–74 the KKE took a leading role in the opposition to the Greek military junta, but factional conflict not only within the exiled party but also between it and Communist forces in Greece culminated in a decision by the latter in February 1968 to form an independent "interior" KKE. The "exterior" KKE's support for the Soviet-led suppression of the Czechoslovak "Prague Spring" later in 1968 and the gravitation of the KKE "interior" towards reformist Eurocommunism served to widen the ideological gap between the two factions. Accused of prime responsibility for the split, the KKE "exterior" leader, Constantine Kolliyannis, was replaced by Harislaos Florakis in 1973.

Legalized after the fall of the military regime, the KKE "exterior" contested the November 1974 elections as part of the EDA, which also included the "interior" Communists, winning five of the EDA's eights seats. Standing on its own in subsequent elections, the KKE "exterior" advanced to 11 seats in 1977 (with 9.4% of the vote) and to 13 in 1981 (10.9%), when it also secured three of the 24 Greek seats in the European Parliament (with a 12.8% vote share). After its overtures for representation in the new government of the →Pan-Hellenic Socialist Movement (PASOK) had been rejected, the KKE "exterior" subsequently adopted a critical attitude towards PASOK, accusing it of betraying its election promises, notably its pledge to take Greece out of the European Community and NATO. For its part, the PASOK government allowed tens of thousands of KKE supporters, exiled since the late 1940s, to return to Greece.

Concurrently, the party's rigid pro-Moscow orthodoxy, which included support for the Soviet intervention in Afghanistan, caused some internal dissension and defections. In the 1984 Euro-elections the KKE "exterior" vote slipped to 11.6% (although it again won three seats), while in the June 1985 national elections it achieved 9.9% of the vote and 12 seats. On the latter occasion the deputies elected on the KKE "exterior" list included a former PASOK Finance Minister and nominees of the Agrarian Party (AKE) and the →United Socialist Alliance of Greece (ESPE), the latter launched by PASOK dissidents in 1984. In the October 1986 municipal elections the KKE "exterior" withheld crucial second-round support from

PASOK candidates, thus ensuring their defeat in Athens, Piraeus and Salonika (the three largest cities).

Influenced by the formation of the Greek Left Party (EAR) by the KKE "interior" the previous month, the 12th congress of the KKE "exterior" in May 1987 issued a call for a new left-wing alliance committed to socialism. The eventual result was the →Coalition of the Left and Progress (*Synaspismos*) between the KKE "exterior", the EAR (including the KKE "interior") and other groups, the alliance winning 28 seats in the June 1989 general elections on a 13.1% vote share. In simultaneous European Parliament elections a joint Communist list won 14.3% and four seats. However, the subsequent participation of *Synaspismos* in two temporary governments, the first with the conservative →New Democracy (ND) and the second with ND and PASOK (after further elections in November 1989 in which *Synaspismos* slipped to 21 seats and 11.0%), generated unrest in the KKE "exterior", leading to some defections. The party remained in *Synaspismos* for the April 1990 elections, in which the alliance fell back to 19 seats and 10.2% of the vote. However, the 13th KKE "exterior" congress in February 1991 resulted in the party's orthodox wing narrowly gaining control and in the election as general secretary of Aleka Papariga, who in June 1991 took the party out of *Synaspismos*. By then the "exterior" suffix was no longer required as an identifier, in that the "interior" party had ceased to be a distinct formation.

Having opted for independence, the KKE experienced further internal turmoil, involving the expulsion or departure of various elements that preferred the reformist line of *Synaspismos*. In the October 1993 elections, however, the KKE retained appreciable support, winning 4.5% of the vote and nine seats, whereas *Synaspismos* failed to obtain representation. In the June 1994 Euro-elections the KKE advanced to 6.3%, taking two of the 25 Greek seats, and thereafter maintained a critical stance on the policies of the PASOK government. In the September 1996 general elections the KKE advanced to 5.6% of the vote and 11 seats, remaining in opposition to a further PASOK administration. In the June 1999 European Parliament elections the KKE won an additional seats on the strength of a vote share of 8.7%.

The three KKE representatives in the European Parliament sit in the European United Left/Nordic Green left group, as do the *Synaspismos* representatives.

Democratic Social Movement
Dimokratiko Kinoniko Kinima (DIKKI)
Address. Odos Xalkokondili 9, 10677 Athens
Telephone. (+30-1) 380-1712
Fax. (+30-1) 383-9047
Email. dikki@otenet.gr
Website. http://www.dikki.gr
Leadership. Dimitris Tsovolas (president)
DIKKI originated in 1995 in a breakaway from the ruling →Pan-Hellenic Socialist Movement (PASOK) opposed in particular to the government's policy of participating in closer European Union integration and of preparing Greece for membership of the single European currency by austerity measures. In the September 1996 general elections DIKKI achieved 4.4% of the popular vote and won nine parliamentary seats. In the June 1999 European Parliament elections it advanced to 6.8%, taking two of the 25 Greek seats.

The DIKKI members of the European Parliament sit in the European United Left/Nordic Green Left group.

New Democracy
Nea Dimokratia (ND)
Address. Odos Rigillis 18, 10674 Athens

Telephone. (+30–1) 729-0071
Fax. (+30–1) 725-1491
Email. valinak@otenet.gr
Website. http://www.nd.gr
Leadership. Costas Karamanlis (president); Dimitrios Sioufas (parliamentary spokesman); Ioannis Vartholomeos (director-general)

The moderate conservative ND was founded in October 1974 by Constantine Karamanlis, who had been Prime Minister in 1956–63 as leader of the National Radical Union (ERE) and had opposed the colonels' regime of 1967–74 from exile in Paris. The new party won an absolute majority in the November 1974 elections, securing 220 of the 300 seats on a 54.4% vote share. It was confirmed in power in the November 1977 elections, although it slipped to 172 seats and 41.8% of the vote, with Karamanlis continuing as Prime Minister until being elected President in May 1980, when he was succeeded as government and party leader by George Rallis. In January 1981 a key ND policy aim was achieved when Greece became a member of the European Community, but in the October 1981 elections the party was heavily defeated by the →Pan-Hellenic Socialist Movement (PASOK), retaining only 115 seats and 35.9% of the vote.

In the wake of ND's 1981 defeat Rallis was ousted as leader and replaced by right-winger Evangelos Averoff-Tossizza, but the latter resigned in August 1984 following the ND's poor showing in the European Parliament elections two months earlier. He was succeeded by the moderate Constantine Mitsotakis, who led ND to another election defeat in June 1985, although it improved to 126 seats and 40.8% of the vote. Mitsotakis's leadership then came under strong criticism from "new right" elements led by Constantine Stephanopoulos, who in September 1985 broke away to form the Democratic Renewal Party (DIANA). Mitsotakis reasserted his authority at a February 1986 ND congress, when "new right" policy theses were rejected, and in October 1986 the party made significant gains in municipal elections, taking control from PASOK in the three largest cities (Athens, Piraeus and Salonkia). Nevertheless, internal strains resurfaced in May 1987 when Rallis resigned from the party in protest against the earlier expulsion of his son-in-law for criticizing the ND leadership for its alleged departure from the policies of Karamanlis.

ND won a relative majority of 145 seats in the June 1989 general elections, the parliamentary arithmetic obliging it to form a temporary coalition with the →Coalition of the Left and Progress (*Synaspismos*). Another election in November 1989 produced another stalemate, with ND representation edging up to 148 seats (on a 46.2% vote share), so that a temporary three-party coalition of ND, PASOK and *Synaspismos* representatives plus non-party technocrats was formed. Yet more general elections in April 1990 gave ND exactly half the seats (150) with 46.9% of the vote, so that Mitsotakis was able to form a single-party government with the external support of the single DIANA deputy. In May 1990 Karamanlis was returned for another term as President, securing parliamentary election as the ND candidate although at 82 he was no longer a party politician.

Amid a deteriorating economic situation, the Mitsotakis government experienced growing internal rifts in 1992–93, culminating in the formation of the breakaway →Political Spring (PA) in June 1993. Deprived of a parliamentary majority, Mitsotakis resigned in September 1993, precipitating early elections in October, in which ND was heavily defeated by PASOK, falling to 111 seats and 39.3% of the vote. Mitsotakis immediately resigned as ND leader and was succeeded by Miltiades Evert, who had been dismissed from the ND government in October 1991 for criticizing its free-market policies. ND took second place in the June 1994 European Parliament elections, winning 32.7% of the vote and nine of the 25 Greek seats, one of which went to the singer Nana Mouskouri despite (or perhaps because of) her self-admitted ignorance of politics. In October 1994 the ND candidate registered a notable

117

victory in the Athens mayoral contest, while remaining much weaker than PASOK in local government.

In January 1995 the Greek parliament voted to drop phone-tapping and various corruption charges against Mitsotakis arising from his term as Prime Minister; the former ND leader complained that the decision denied him the opportunity of proving his innocence in court. In March 1995 the ND candidate, Athanasios Tsaldaris, failed to secure parliamentary election as President, being defeated by Constantine Stephanopoulos, who was nominated by the PA (and backed by PASOK in the interests of avoiding a general election), having disbanded his DIANA party following its failure in the 1994 Euro-elections.

In the September 1996 general elections the ND failed to fulfil expectations that it would oust the PASOK government, winning only 108 seats and 38.2% of the vote. Evert speedily announced his resignation as leader, but secured re-election in October after a power-struggle in which Mitsotakis had advanced the claims of his daughter, former Culture Minister Dora Bakoyiannis. Evert's victory was short-lived, however, because in March 1997 was replaced by Costas Karamanlis (nephew of the ND founder), who at 40 became the youngest ever leader of a major Greek political party. His election was seen as drastic action by a party fearing marginalization and concerned at having lost business community support to PASOK.

Under new leadership, ND made a strong showing in the October 1998 local elections, retaining the mayorships of Athens and Salonika, athough it was potentially weakened by the launching in May 1999 of the →Liberals by a former ND deputy. The ND won 36.0% of the vote in the June 1999 European Parliament elections, thus overtaking PASOK, although its representation remained at nine seats.

With an official membership of 400,000, ND is a member party of the Christian Democrat International, the International Democrat Union and the European Democrat Union. Its members of the European Parliament sit in the European People's Party/European Democrats group.

Pan-Hellenic Socialist Movement
Panellenio Sosialistiko Kinema (PASOK)
Address. Odos Charilaou Tricoupi 50, 10680 Athens
Telephone. (+30–1) 368-4037
Fax. (+30–1) 368-4042
Email. pasok@pasok.gr
Website. http://www.pasok.gr
Leadership. Costas Simitis (president); Costas Skandalidis (general secretary)
PASOK was founded in 1974, being derived from the Pan-Hellenic Liberation Movement (PAK) created by Andreas Papandreou in 1968 to oppose the military dictatorship which held power in Greece from 1967 to mid-1974. Having worked in the USA as an economics professor (and become a US citizen), Papandreou had returned to Greece in 1959 and had held ministerial office in pre-1967 Centre Union governments headed by his father George. Briefly imprisoned after the 1967 colonels' coup, he had been allowed to go into exile and had founded PAK, becoming convinced of the need for an unequivocally socialist party that would follow a "third road" distinct from West European social democracy and East European communism. According to Papandreou, the absence of a socialist tradition in Greece meant that PASOK had its roots in the wartime resistance and in the post-war National Liberation Front (EAM), which had been Communist-led, with a later centre-left admixture deriving from the Centre Union. PASOK was originally committed to the socialization of key economic sectors and also to withdrawal from the then European Community (EC) and NATO, but was later to revise such policies when it came into government.

PASOK emerged from the November 1974 elections as the third strongest party, with 12 of 300 seats and 13.6% of the vote. In the November 1977 elections it became the strongest opposition party, with 93 seats and 25.3%, and in October 1981 it won an absolute majority of 170 seats (with 48.1% of the vote) and formed its first government under Papandreou's premiership. Four years later, in June 1985, PASOK was returned for a second term, although with its representation reduced to 161 seats on a 45.8% vote share. Prior to the 1985 contest, the PASOK candidate, Christos Sartzetakis, had been elected President in acrimonious parliamentary balloting in March. In office, PASOK experienced considerable internal divisions over the government's foreign and economic policies, including a new five-year agreement signed in September 1983 allowing US bases to remain in Greece, the dropping of opposition to EC and NATO membership, and the introduction of an economic austerity programme in 1985. Various critics of the leadership were expelled from PASOK in the 1980s and a number of breakaway groups were formed, although none had any enduring impact. In the October 1986 municipal elections PASOK suffered sharp reverses, losing the three largest cities to the conservative →New Democracy (ND), although it remained by far the strongest party at local level.

In the June 1989 parliamentary elections PASOK was damaged by the Koskotas affair, involving financial malpractice in the Bank of Crete, and by Papandreou's extramarital affair with a young air hostess called Dimitra Liani, with whom he later contracted his third marriage. The party's representation slumped to 125 seats (on a 39.2% vote share) and it went into opposition to a temporary coalition between ND and the →Coalition of the Left and Progress (*Synaspismos*). Further elections in November 1989 produced another statemate, with PASOK improving slightly to 128 seats and 40.7% of the vote, well behind ND, although the latter's lack of an overall majority dictated the formation of another temporary coalition, this time of the three main parties (but not including their leaders). Meanwhile, Papandreou had been indicted on corruption charges arising from the Koskotas affair. Greece's third general elections in less than a year, held in April 1990, broke the deadlock, with PASOK slipping to 123 seats and 38.6% and going into opposition to an ND government.

Continuing divisions within PASOK were highlighted during its second congress in September 1990, when Papandreou's nominee for the new post of party general secretary, Apostolos Tsokhatzopoulos, was approved by a bare one-vote majority. Papandreou nevertheless remained unchallenged as PASOK leader, and in January 1992 was finally acquitted of the various corruption charges against him. In the October 1993 elections PASOK stood on a manifesto which jettisoned much of the left-wing rhetoric of the 1980s and instead professed a "social democratic" identity, supportive of EC and NATO membership and of good relations with the USA. It won an overall majority of 170 seats (on a 46.9% vote share) and returned to government with Papandreou once again Prime Minister. Also reappointed (as Minister of Culture) was the famous actress and 1967–74 pro-democracy campaigner Melina Mercouri, although she was to die in office in March 1994. In the June 1994 European Parliament elections PASOK headed the poll, winning 37.6% of the vote and 10 of the 25 Greek seats. In October 1994 PASOK maintained its dominance in local elections, although losing the Athens mayoral contest to an ND candidate.

Growing unrest within PASOK over the ageing Papandreou's continued leadership and the undisguised political ambitions of his wife Dimitra developed into a fullscale succession struggle when the Prime Minister fell seriously ill in November 1995. Papandreou eventually resigned in January 1996 and was succeeded as PASOK political leader and Prime Minister by Costas Simitis, who defeated acting Prime Minister Apostolos Tsokhatzopoulos in a runoff ballot of PASOK deputies by 86 votes to 75. Simitis had resigned from the government in September 1995 in protest against alleged sabotage of his reform plans by the PASOK hierarchy. Following the death of Papandreou on June 22, 1996, Simitis prevailed over strong internal opposition by securing election to the PASOK presidency at a special party congress at the end of the month.

Simitis consolidated his position in the September 1996 general elections, rather unexpectedly securing a further mandate for PASOK, which won 162 seats on a 41.5% vote share. Nevertheless, his government's economic austerity measures to prepare Greece for the single European currency were resisted by the PASOK "old guard", three of whose members were expelled from the parliamentary group in December 1997 for opposing the 1998 budget. Early in 1998, moreover, 10 PASOK deputies voted against a government bill aimed at cutting the deficits of many public-sector enterprises. Having lost ground in the October 1998 local elections, PASOK was relegated to second place in the June 1999 European Parliament elections, obtaining only 32.9% of the vote and nine seats.

PASOK is a member party of the Socialist International. Its representatives in the European Parliament sit in the Party of European Socialists group.

Other Parties

Communist Party of Greece–Renovating Left (*Kommunistiko Komma Ellados–Ananeotiki Aristera*, KKE-AA), led by Yiannis Banias, created in 1987 by a minority faction of the "interior" Communist Party opposed to the majority's decision to join a broader Greek Left Party (which later became part of the →Coalition of the Left and Progress).

Green Party (*Prassini Politiki*, PP), pro-environment formation that has made minimal electoral impact, affiliated to European Federation of Green Parties. *Address.* Koloktroni 31, 10562 Athens; *Telephone.* (+30-1) 251-1304; *Fax.* (+30-1) 322-4344; *Email.* ecorec@ath.forthnet.gr

Hellenic Front (*Elliniko Metopo*, EM), right-wing party seeking to promote Greek national interests. *Email.* elliniko@metopo.gr; *Website.* http://www.metopo.gr

Hellenic Liberal Party, mainstream liberal formation led by Nikitas Venizelos, grandson of former Prime Minister Eleftherios Venizelos (1864–1936), from whose historic Liberal Party (founded 1910) the present party claims direct descent. *Address.* Vissarionos 1, 10672 Athens; *Telephone.* (+30-1) 360-6111

Hellenic Women's Party (*Komma Ellinidon Gynaikon*, KEG), founded in 1998 by Emmanuel Economakis, aiming to promote the political, economic and social rights of women. *Address.* Rostan 37, Ano Patisia, 11141 Athens; *Telephone.* (+30-1) 202-1828; *Fax.* (+30-1) 223-5823; *Email.* emmanecon@vip.gr

The Liberals (*Oi Fileleftheroi*), launched in April 1999 by Stephanos Manos, a former National Economic and Finance Minister who had been expelled from →New Democracy (ND) in 1998 for not following the party line of opposition to legislation tabled by the government of the →Pan-Hellenic Socialist Movement (PASOK) aimed at making state enterprises more competitive. Calling for fundamental reforms to prepare Greece for the 21st century, the new formation was the latest attempt to create a modern political party that could claim the mantle of the historic Greek Liberal Party of Eleftherios Venizelos (1864–1936). *Address.* Anastasiou Tshoa 15-17, 11521 Athens; *Telephone.* (+30-1) 645-5070; *Fax.* (+30-1) 645-8946; *Email.* liberals@otenet.gr; *Website.* http://www.liberals.gr

National Political Union (*Ethniki Politiki Enosis*, EPEN), led by Chryssanthos Dimitriades, far-right party founded in 1984, at first led by ex-Col. George Papadopoulos (military dictator in 1967–73), held one European Parliament seat in 1984–89.

Natural Law Party (*Komma Fisikoi Nomoi*, KFN), Greek branch of worldwide network of such parties, has made minimal electoral impact. *Email.* nlp@otenet.gr; *Website.* http://www.natural-law-party.org/greece

Political Spring (*Politiki Anixi*, PA), right-wing populist party established in June 1993 by Antonis Samaras, a dissident member of the then ruling →New Democracy (ND) who had been dismissed as Foreign Minister in April 1992 because of his hardline opposition to the recognition of the ex-Yugoslav republic of Macedonia under that name. The new party attracted three other ND deputies into defection, so that the government lost its narrow parliamentary majority and was forced to resign. In early general elections in October 1993 Samaras (42) campaigned for an end to rule by the "dinosaurs" of ND and the →Pan-Hellenic Socialist Movement (PASOK), winning 10 seats with a vote share of 4.9%, becoming part of the parliamentary opposition to the new PASOK government. In the European Parliament elections of June 1994 the PA advanced to 8.7% of the vote, giving it two of the 25 Greek seats, and in March 1995 it successfully nominated the veteran conservative politician Constantine Stephanopoulos as President. But it failed to retain representation in the September 1996 national elections (winning only 2.9% of the vote) and the June 1999 Euro-elections (2.3% of the vote)

Union of the Democratic Centre (*Enosi Dimokratikou Kentrou*, EDIK), led by Ioannis G. Zighdis, centre-left formation founded in 1974 as a merger of pre-1967 parties (including the Centre Union), won 60 seats in 1974, 15 in 1977 and none in 1981 (suffering from the left-right polarization of Greek politics); its leader was elected a deputy in 1985 with the backing of the →Pan-Hellenic Socialist Movement.

United Socialist Alliance of Greece (*Eniaea Sosialistiki Parataxi Ellados*, ESPE), left-wing party founded in 1984 by Stathis Pagagoulis, previously a deputy minister in the government of the →Pan-Hellenic Socialist Movement, who was elected a deputy in 1985 on the list of the →Communist Party of Greece.

Ireland

Capital: Dublin   **Population:** 3,700,000

The Irish Republic's 1937 constitution expressly stated that it applied to the whole of Ireland (Éire), not just to the 26 counties actually comprising the Republic, and was therefore seen as containing an implicit territorial claim to the six counties of Northern Ireland under UK sovereignty. However, following the signature of the Good Friday Agreement on Northern Ireland in April 1998, constitutional amendments approved by referendum in the Republic on May 22, 1998, formally enshrined the principle of popular consent to any change in the status of the North. These amendments were promulgated on Dec. 2, 1999, on the establishment of a power-sharing Executive in the North and the inauguration of a consultative North-South Ministerial Council (see United Kingdom, Northern Ireland, chapter).

   The Irish parliament (*Oireachtas*) consists of (i) the President (*Uachtará na hÉireann*) directly elected for a seven-year term (once renewable); (ii) a

166–member lower house (*Dáil Eireann*) elected by universal adult suffrage for a five-year term); and (iii) a 60–member indirectly-elected Senate (*Seanad*), including 11 prime ministerial appointees, with power to delay, but not to veto, lower house legislation. The cabinet, which is responsible to the *Dáil*, is headed by a Prime Minister (*Taoiseach*), who is the leader of the majority party or coalition. Members of the *Dáil* are elected by the single transferable vote (STV) version of proportional representation, from multi-member constituencies. Ireland joined what became the European Union in 1973 and elects 15 members of the European Parliament.

Under legislation governing the remuneration of public representatives, leaders of parties which have seven or more seats in the *Dáil* are eligible for allowances from public funds to help them carry out their parliamentary duties.

Elections to the *Dáil* on June 6, 1997, resulted as follows:		
	Seats	Percentage*
	1997 (1992)	*1997 (1992)*
Fianna Fáil	77 (68)	39.3 (39.1)
Fine Gael...	54 (45)	27.9 (24.5)
The Labour Party	17 (33)	10.4 (19.3)
Progressive Democrats	4 (10)	4.7 (4.7)
Democratic Left	4 (4)	2.5 (2.8)
Green Party	2 (1)	2.8 n/a
Sinn Féin	1 (0)	2.5 n/a
Socialist Party	1 (0)	0.7 (–)
Independent *Fianna Fáil*	1 (1)	n/a n/a
Others...	5 (4)	n/a n/a
*First-preference votes		

Democratic Left (DL)
Address. 69 Middle Abbey Street, Dublin 1
Telephone. (+353–1) 872–9550
Fax. (+353–1) 872–9238
Email. dlhead@indigo.ie
Website. http://www.connect.ie/users/dl
Leadership. Proinsías de Rossa (president); Catherine Murphy (executive committee chair); John Gallagher (general secretary)
The DL was launched by a reformist faction of the Marxist →Workers' Party which broke away in February 1992. Committed to democratic socialism, the DL won four *Dáil* seats and 2.8% of first-preference votes in November 1992 (when the parent party failed to win representation). In December 1994 the DL agreed to join a coalition government with →*Fine Gael* and the →Labour Party, its leader becoming Minister of Social Welfare. In the June 1997 elections the DL slipped to 2.5% of first-preference votes but retained four *Dáil* seats, going into opposition to a new government headed by →*Fianna Fáil*. The party is a member of the New European Left Forum (NELF).

IRELAND

Fianna Fáil

Address. 13 Upper Mount Street, Dublin 2
Telephone. (+353–1) 676–1551
Fax. (+353–1) 678–5690
Email. fiannafáil@iol.ie
Website. http://www.fiannafail.ie
Leadership. Bertie Ahern (president); Rory O'Hanlon (parliamentary chair); Martin Mackin (general secretary)

Republican, nationalist and populist, *Fianna Fáil* seeks the peaceful reunification by consent of Ireland, national self-sufficiency, social justice and the preservation of the Irish language and culture. It strongly supports the European Union's common agricultural policy but opposes any extension of the powers of the European Parliament. It favours nuclear disarmament and wants all of Ireland to be a nuclear-free zone.

Fianna Fáil (literally "Soldiers of Destiny" but officially known in English as The Republican Party) was founded in 1926 by Éamon de Valera, who was the sole surviving leader of the 1916 rebellion as well as the leading opponent of the 1921 treaty with Britain, boycotted the Free State *Dáil* (because of a required oath of allegiance to the British monarchy) until 1927; in 1932 it came to power in general elections. De Valera then became *Taoiseach* (and was President of Ireland from 1959 until his death in 1973).

Fianna Fáil remained in government until 1948, introducing the autonomist (and strongly Catholic) constitution of 1937 and maintaining neutrality during World War II, at the end of which De Valera outraged many in Britain and the USA by sending a message of condolence to Germany on the death of Hitler. The party was again in power in 1951-54, 1957-73, 1977-81 and in 1982. Charles Haughey became party leader and *Taoiseach* in 1979, his ministerial career having survived gun-running allegations in 1970. *Fianna Fáil* maintained its status as usually the largest in the *Dáil*, although only once (in 1965) secured an overall majority. It returned 75 TDs in the November 1982 elections (with 47.3% of the vote) and 81 in 1987 (with 44.1%), when Haughey returned as Prime Minister

In the June 1989 elections FF parliamentary strength was reduced to 77 seats. The result was the first really serious political impasse in independent Ireland's history. It was resolved by Haughey agreeing the following month to the inclusion of the →Progressive Democrats (PDs) in *Fianna Fáil*'s first-ever experience of coalition government. Subsequently, the FF deputy leader and Defence Minister, Brian Lenihan, began as favourite to win the November 1990 presidential election, but lost public confidence when he was dismissed from the government a month before voting over a scandal, the consequence being that he was heavily defeated by Mary Robinson, the nominee of the →Labour Party.

Haughey finally bowed out in January 1992, being succeeded as *Fianna Fáil* leader and therefore as Prime Minister by his old party adversary, Albert Reynolds. In November 1992 the party experienced its poorest election result since World War II (its *Dáil* representation falling to 68 seats and its first-preference vote to 39.1%), but Reynolds managed to entice the resurgent Labour Party into a majority coalition. Less than two years later, however, the coalition collapsed over the affair of an allegedly paedophile Catholic priest, which forced Reynolds's resignation in November 1994. *Fianna Fáil* then went into opposition to a three-party coalition headed by →*Fine Gael*, although it remained the largest parliamentary party under the new leadership of Bertie Ahern.

Fianna Fáil returned to power after the June 1997 elections, in which it recovered to 77 *Dáil* seats, while improving only marginally, to 39.3%, in first-preference votes. As incoming *Taoiseach*, Ahern formed a minority coalition with the →Progressive Democrats (PDs), his government being dependent on independents for a parliamentary majority. He quickly lost his Foreign Minister, Ray Burke, who resigned in October 1997 after being named in a financial corruption case. In the same month, however, *Fianna Fáil* candidate Mary McAleese was elected Irish President with 58.7% of the vote on the second count.

Ahern played a major role in the conclusion of the potentially historic Good Friday Agreement in Northern Ireland in April 1998 and the following month successfully recommended resultant constitutional revisions to Republic voters, involving formal acceptance that Irish unity could only be achieved by consent of the people north and south of the border. At the same time, the Ahern government secured popular endorsement for the EU's Amsterdam Treaty. The surfacing in February 1999 of another alleged financial corruption case damaged *Fianna Fáil* in the June 1999 European Parliament elections, in which the party slipped from seven to six of the 15 Irish seats, on a vote share of 38.6%.

The *Fianna Fáil* members of the European Parliament sit in the Union for a Europe of Nations group, the largest component of which is the French "Eurosceptic" ⇒Rally for France and the Independence of Europe.

Fine Gael
Address. 51 Upper Mount Street, Dublin 2
Telephone (+353–1) 676-1573
Fax. (+353–1) 662-5046
Email. finegael@finegael.com
Website. http://www.finegael.com
Leadership. John Bruton (leader); Nora Owen (deputy leader); Phil Hogan (*Dáil* group chair); Tom Curran (general secretary)
Of Christian democratic orientation, *Fine Gael* advocates free enterprise, social justice, decentralization, reconciliation with the North, participatory democracy, tax equity and the improvement of education and welfare provision. It also supports an active Irish role in strengthening the European Union and the constructive use of Irish neutrality in addressing international issues such as peace, disarmament, human rights and self-determination for peoples.

Fine Gael (literally "Tribe of the Gael", but officially known in English as the United Ireland Party) was created in 1933 by the merger of *Cumann na nGaedhale* (Society of the Gales), the ruling party of the Irish Free State in 1923-32, with the Centre Party and the fascist Blueshirt Movement of Gen. Eoin O'Duffy, who briefly led the new party. Although it was the main party in favour of the treaty which established the state, *Fine Gael* supported the 1949 declaration of a republic and has since retained nationalist ideals. Since the 1970s the party has been involved in efforts to make Irish society more pluralistic, supporting the lifting of the constitutional prohibitions on divorce and abortion.

The party ruled through coalitions when it was in power in the post-war decades, all involving the →Labour Party, heading governments in 1948-51, 1954-57, 1973-77, 1981-82 and 1982-87, latterly under the premiership of Garret FitzGerald, who became *Fine Gael* leader in 1977. In the February 1987 elections, however, *Fine Gael* was reduced to 27.1% and 51 *Dáil* seats (from 37.3% and 70 seats in November 1982), which resulted in the resignation of FitzGerald. The new *Fine Gael* leader, Alan Dukes, maintained the party's strong commitment to the 1985 Anglo-Irish Agreement whereby the Republic's government recognized the partition of Ireland but secured a consultative role in the administration of the North.

In the June 1989 elections *Fine Gael* increased its parliamentary representation to 55, but remained in opposition. In November 1990 Dukes resigned as party leader and was replaced by his more right-leaning deputy, John Bruton. In the November 1992 *Dáil* elections *Fine Gael* slumped to 45 seats and 24.5% of first-preference votes, its worst showing since 1948. Nevertheless, a political crisis in late 1994 resulted in the resignation of the →*Fianna*

Fáil Prime Minister and enabled Bruton to form a three-party coalition government with Labour and the →Democratic Left. Meanwhile, *Fine Gael* had taken 24.3% of the vote and four seats in the June 1994 European Parliament elections.

In the June 1997 *Dáil* elections *Fine Gael* recovered to 54 seats and 27.9% of first-preference votes but went into opposition to a centre-right coalition headed by *Fianna Fáil*. In the June 1999 European Parliament elections *Fine Gael* improved slightly to 24.5% of the vote, again taking four of Ireland's 15 seats.

With an official membership of 23,000, *Fine Gael* is affiliated to the Christian Democrat International. Its members of the European Parliament sit in the European People's Party/European Democrats group.

Green Party
Comhaontás Glas
Address. 5A Upper Fownes Street, Dublin 2
Telephone. (+353–1) 679-0012
Fax. (£353-1) 679–7168
Email. greenpar@iol.ie
Website. http://www.greenparty.ie
Leadership. John Gormley, Trevor Sargent (parliamentary representatives)
The Green Party stands internationally for a globally-sustainable economic system and the redistribution of resources to the world's poor, and nationally for political, economic and social decisions to be taken at the lowest possible level and the promotion workers' co-operatives and small family businesses. The party was established as the Ecology Party of Ireland (EPI) in December 1981 with support from what became the UK ⇒Green Party and from members of anti-nuclear and environmental protection groups in Ireland. It became the Green Alliance in 1983 and the Green Party in 1987.

The party won its first *Dáil* seat in the June 1989 election, retaining it in 1992. Like other Green parties in the European Union, it made a greater impact in the June 1994 European Parliament elections, winning two of Ireland's 15 seats with 7.9% of the vote. The party improved to two seats in the June 1997 national elections (taking 2.8% of first-preference votes), one of its successful candidates, John Gormley, having in 1994 become Dublin's first Green lord mayor. The Greens again won two seats in the June 1999 European Parliament elections, although its vote share slipped to 6.7%.

The Green Party is affiliated to the European Federation of Green Parties. Its representatives in the European Parliament sit in the Greens/European Free Alliance group.

Labour Party
Páirtí Lucht Oibre
Address. 17 Ely Place, Dublin 2
Telephone. (+353–1) 661–2615
Fax. (+353–1) 661–2640
Email. head_office@labour.ie
Website. http://www.labour.ie
Leadership. Ruairí Quinn (leader); Jim Kemmy (chair); Ray Kavanagh (general secretary)
The social democratic Labour Party seeks the peaceful transformation of Irish society into a socialist republic. It calls for the resolution of economic problems by means which will not impoverish weaker sections of society, favouring public-sector job creation and taxation equity between wage-earners and the self-employed, especially farmers. It advocates the reunification of Ireland by consent, as well as the maintenance of strict Irish neutrality in international relations.

Founded in 1912 by James Connolly and Jim Larkin, the Labour Party was the main opposition party in the *Dáil* of the Irish Free State in 1922-26, becoming independent of the Irish trade unions in 1930. It supported the →*Fianna Fáil* minority government under Éamon de Valera in 1932-33 but opposed the 1937 constitution, while supported its main effect, which was to create a republic outside the British Empire. The party participated in coalition governments in 1948-51 with four other parties, in 1954-57 with →*Fine Gael* and a farmers' party, and with *Fine Gael* alone in 1973-77, 1981-82 and 1982-87, providing the *Tánaiste* (Deputy Prime Minister) in these governments.

A Labour conference decided in 1986 to end its participation in coalitions, which had been consistently opposed by its left wing and which had resulted in a steady loss of electoral support (from 17% in 1969 to 9.1% in 1982 and to 6.5% in 1987). The party accordingly withdrew from government in early 1987 in opposition to proposed cuts in the health budget, thus precipitating general elections in which it dropped to 12 seats (from 16 in 1982). Labour's recovery began at the June 1989 elections, when it increased its *Dáil* representation from 12 to 15 seats. The following year it joined with the →Workers' Party in backing the successful presidential candidacy of Mary Robinson, who had twice been a Labour parliamentary candidate but was no longer a party member.

In the November 1992 elections Labour achieved its best election result to date, more than doubling its *Dáil* representation to 33 seats (from 19.3% of first-preference votes) after a campaign focusing on the shortcomings of the *Fianna Fáil* government. Nevertheless, in January 1993 the party entered into a majority coalition with FF, which lasted until November 1994, when Labour ministers took exception to *Fianna Fáil* conduct in the case of a Catholic priest accused of paedophilia. The party promptly rediscovered its sympathies with *Fine Gael*, joining a three-party coalition which also included the →Democratic Left. Meanwhile, Labour had won one of Ireland's 15 European Parliament seats in June 1994 with 11.0% of the vote.

The Labour Party was punished in the June 1997 national elections, being reduced to 17 seats and 10.4% of first-preference votes and remaining in opposition. In October 1997 Labour candidate Adi Roche came a poor fourth in presidential election, with only 6.9% of the vote. The following month Spring resigned as Labour leader and was succeeded by Ruairí Quinn, hitherto deputy leader. The party also lost ground in the June 1999 European Parliament elections, taking 8.8% of the vote, although retaining its single seat.

The Labour Party is a member of the Socialist International. Its member of the European Parliament sits in the Party of European Socialists group.

Progressive Democrats (PDs)
Address. 25 South Frederick Street, Dublin 2
Telephone. (+353–1) 679–4399
Fax. (+353–1) 679-4757
Email. jackm@iol.ie
Website. http://ireland.iol.ie/pd
Leadership. Mary Harney (parliamentary leader); Garvan McGinley (general secretary)
The PDs are a centre-right grouping calling for reduced government spending, privatization, a secular state and acceptance of the reality of the partition of Ireland. The party was founded in December 1985 under the leadership of former cabinet minister Desmond O'Malley following a split in the then opposition →*Fianna Fáil* which led four TDs to break away. The PDs campaigned mainly for fiscal responsibility, to which end they supported what they regarded as "essential and balanced" measures by successive governments, while opposing those seen as "ill-thought-out and unjust". In its first electoral test in February 1987, the party secured 11.8% of the vote and 14 seats in the *Dáil*, thus displacing the →Labour Party as the third strongest parliamentary formation.

The PDs then experienced a loss of its initial momentum, falling to only six seats at the 1989 election, after which the party opted to join a coalition government headed by *Fianna Fáil*. Its withdrawal three years later precipitated the November 1992 *Dáil* elections, in which PD representation rose to 10 seats but the party remained in opposition. O'Malley resigned as PD leader in October 1993 and was succeeded by the first female head of a significant Irish party, Mary Harney. In the June 1997 national elections the PDs slumped to only four seats and opted to join a coalition led by *Fianna Fáil* in which it was awarded one post, Harney becoming Ireland first-ever woman Deputy Prime Minister. In the June 1999 European Parliament elections the PDs failed to gain representation.

Sinn Féin (SF)

Address. 44 Parnell Square, Dublin 1
Telephone. (+353–1) 872–6100
Fax. (+353–1) 873–3074
Email. sinnfein@iol.ie
Website. http://www.sinnfein.ie
Leadership. Gerry Adams (president)
Republican, revolutionary and nationalist, *Sinn Féin* (literally "Ourselves") supports the Irish Republican Army (IRA) campaign in Northern Ireland and seeks the establishment of a unitary democratic socialist state. The party was founded in 1905 by Arthur Griffith and was radicalized by the popular impact of the 1916 rebellion in Dublin. In 1918 it won (but did not take up) 72 of the 105 Irish seats in the UK House of Commons; instead, it set up the *Dáil* in Dublin, whereupon Northern loyalists organized resistance to Irish independence. After a three-year guerrilla war the 1922 Treaty partitioned Ireland into the autonomous Irish Free State in 26 counties and British-ruled Northern Ireland in the other six. The anti-treaty *Sinn Féin* under Éamon de Valera supported the IRA in a subsequent civil war with Free State forces. De Valera left *Sinn Féin* in 1926 to form →*Fianna Fáil*, following which *Sinn Féin* was left on the margins of Irish politics, supporting IRA campaigns conducted mainly in Britain and on the Northern border. *Sinn Féin* won (but did not take up) four seats in the *Dáil* in 1957 but lost them in 1961.

The movement split in 1969-70, the left wing envolving into the →Workers' Party, while the nationalist faction became known as Provisional *Sinn Féin* and had as its military wing the Provisional IRS ("the Provos"). By the 1980s *Sinn Féin* had become involved in community and electoral politics in the South, winning some local council seats, although not in the *Dáil*. A younger, more radical leadership was elected in 1983. In 1986 the party ended its policy of non-participation in the *Dáil*. The policy change proved to be somewhat academic, since *Sinn Féin* continued to be signally unsuccessful in Irish Republic elections, winning no seats in 1987, 1989 or 1992. In the June 1997 contest, however, it returned one member to the *Dáil*, winning 2.5% of first-preference votes overall. In the June 1999 European Parliament election

Socialist Party (SP)

Address. 141 Thomas Street, Dublin 8
Telephone. (+353-1) 677-2686
Email. dublinsp@clubi.ie
Website. http://www.dojo.ie/socialist
Leadership. Joe Higgins (leader)
The SP was formed prior to the June 1997 national elections as a party seeking "to fight for the interests of working-class people" and contending that the →Labour Party and the →Democratic Socialists "have embraced the dictates of the market". Opposed to the EU's Maastricht Treaty and Irish participation in the single European currency, the SP returned Joe Higgins as its sole member of the *Dáil*.

Other Parties

Christian Solidarity Party (CSP–*Comhar Críostaí*), led by Patrick D. Smyth, founded in 1994; fielded eight candidates in 1997 elections, winning 0.5% of first-preference votes but no seats. *Address.* 52 Foxrock Ave, Dublin 18; *Telephone.* (+353–1) 289-1040; *Fax.* (+353–1) 289-1042; *Email.* comharcriostai@tinet.ie

Communist Party of Ireland (CPI), led by James Stewart (general secretary) and Eugene McCartan (chair), all-Ireland formation founded in 1921 by Roddy Connolly, reestablished in 1933, split during the World War II over a 1941 decision to suspend activities in the Republic with reunification of its southern and northern elements not occurring until 1970; staunchly pro-Soviet right up to the demise of the USSR (though harbouring a reformist minority), it has never won a *Dáil* seat and has only limited industrial influence. *Address.* 43 East Essex Street, Dubblin 2; *Telephone/Fax.* (+353–1) 671-1943

Independent Fianna Fáil, founded in 1970 by Neil Blaney following his dismissal as *Fianna Fáil* Agriculture Minister because of his strong anti-partition views; he remained a member of the *Dáil* (and was elected to the European Parliament), but the party had little following outside his Donegal constituency, so that from 1977 Blaney became its only parliamentary representative.

Irish Republican Socialist Party (IRSP–*Pairtí Poblachtach Sósialach na hÉirean*), founded in 1974 by left-wing militarist members of the Official IRA/*Sinn Féin* (now the →Workers' Party), led by Seamus Costello until his murder by the Official IRA in 1977; functioned as the political wing of the Irish National Liberation Army (INLA) in the North and never gained *Dáil* representation in its own right in the Republic, although two members were elected in 1981 for the ephemeral H-Block–Armagh Committee formed by paramilitary prisoners in the North; feuding by INLA factions in 1986-87 placed a question-mark over the IRSP's survival, but the party later re-emerged in both the Republic and the North, although without making any electoral impact. *Address.* 392 Falls Road, Belfast; *Website.* http://www.irsm.org/irsp

National Party (NP), led by Nora Bennis, conservative formation founded in 1995, committed to traditional Irish values and culture, stressing the importance of the family; fielded 16 candidates in 1997 elections, taking 1.1% of first-preference votes but no seats. *Address.* 41 Dalysfort Road, Salthill, Co. Galway; *Telephone.* (+353-61) 364-172; *Website.* http://wwwcastletown.com/national

Natural Law Party (NLP), Irish branch of worldwide network of such parties, fielded 10 candidates in 1997 elections, taking 0.1% of first-preference votes.

People of Ireland Party (*Muintir na hÉireann*), led by local councillor Richard Greene (a former →Green Party member), anti-abortion formation founded in 1995. *Address.* 58 The Palms, Roebuck Road, Dundrum, Dublin 14; *Telephone/Fax.* (353-1) 283-1484; *Email.* muintir@indigo.ie; *Website.* http://aoife.indigo.ie/~muintir

Socialist Workers' Party (SWP), leftist formation rejecting what it sees as the revisionism of the →Labour Party and the →Democratic Left; nominated four candidates in 1997 elections, winning 0.1% of first-preference votes. *Address.* PO Box 1648, Dublin 8; *Telephone.* (+353-1) 872-2682; Email. swp@clubi.ie; Website. http://www.clubi.ie/swp

The Workers' Party (WP–*Pairtí na nOibri*), led by Pat Quearney (general secretary) and Tom French (president), standing for a united democratic socialist Irish republic; claims descent from the historic →*Sinn Féin* following the 1969-70 split producing the Official IRA/*Sinn Féin* and the Provisionals, the former disbanding as an active military organization and from 1971 pursuing a parliamentary strategy; called *Sinn Féin* The Workers' Party from 1977, it adopted its present name in 1982, having returned one *Dáil* member in 1981; rising to four seats in 1987, the party advanced to seven seats in 1989, although six of these deputies, including leader Proinsías de Rossa, resigned after their proposal to abandon Leninism in favour of democratic socialism had been narrowly rejected at a party conference, the result being the →Democratic Left; the rump WP failed to secure parliamentary representation in November 1992 and June 1997 elections, nominating seven candidates in the latter and winning 0.4% of first-preference votes. *Address.* 23 Hill Street, Dublin 1; *Telephone.* (+353–1) 874–0716; *Fax.* (+353–1) 874–8702; *Email.* pqloc@indigo.ie; *Website.* http://www.workers-party.org

Workers' Solidarity Movement (WSM), minimally-supported anarchist formation founded in 1984. *Address.* PO Box 128, Dublin 8; *Email.* wsm_ireland@geocities.com; *Website.* http://flag.blackened.net/revolt/wsm

Italy

Capital: Rome   **Population:** 58,000,000

Under its 1948 constitution, Italy is "a democratic republic founded on work", with a system of parliamentary democracy. The head of state is the President, who is elected for a seven-year term by an electoral college of the two houses of parliament (plus delegates named by the regional assemblies) and who appoints the Prime Minister and, on the latter's recommendation, other ministers. The President has the important power of being able to dissolve parliament at any time except in the last six months of its full term. Legislative authority and government accountability are vested in a legislature of two houses with equal powers, namely (i) the upper 315–member Senate of the Republic (*Senato della Repubblica*), whose members are directly elected for a five-year term on a regional basis, except that life senators (numbering nine in mid-1996) may be appointed by the President; and (ii) the lower 630–member Chamber of Deputies (*Camera dei Deputati*), which is also directly elected for a five-year term subject to dissolution. Under electoral system modifications approved by referendum in April 1993, proportional representation by share of vote gave way to a predominantly "first-past-the-post" system for both houses. In the case of the Chamber, 475 of its 630 members are elected by plurality voting in constituencies and the other 155 by a system of proportional representation, subject to a requirement that at least 4% of the national vote must be won to obtain seats. A founder member of what is now the European Union, Italy elects 87 members of the European Union.

Italian parties have been eligible for state financial subventions since a referendum on the issue in 1976 produced a 56.4% majority in favour of parties being subsidized from public funds. There are two state funds on which parties can draw, one relating to campaign expenses in an election year and the other for defraying ongoing organizational costs. From the first fund some Lit30,000 million (about $19 million) was distributed to parties that won at least one parliamentary seat in 1996. From the second fund a total of some Lit110,000 million (about $67 million) was payable in 1998, about three-quarters being allocated to parties in proportion to their seat totals, just under a quarter equally to parties that presented candidates in at least two-thirds of constituencies in the most recent election, and 2% equally to all represented parties.

The established post-war party structure came under increasing challenge in the 1980s, before effectively disintegrating in the early 1990s amid a torrent of scandals mostly concerning illegal party financing and other graft. The party establishments reacted by creating new party names and alliances, thus giving a new facade to Italian party politics whilst maintaining underlying orientations.

Elections to the Chamber on April 21, 1996, resulted as follows:

	Seats	Percentage*
Olive Tree Movement	284	34.8
Freedom Alliance	246	44.0
Northern League	59	10.1
Communist Refoundation Party...	35	8.6
Others...	6	2.5

*For the 155 seats elected by proportional representation

Christian Democratic Centre
Centro Cristiana Democratica (CCD)
Address. Via Due Macelli 66, 00187 Rome
Telephone. (+39-6) 697-9100
Fax. (+39-6) 679-1586
Email. infoccd@ccd.it
Website. http://www.ccd.it
Leadership. Pier Ferdinando Casini (president)
The CCD was established by a right-wing group of the former ruling Christian Democratic Party when the majority wing of the latter opted to become the →Italian Popular Party in January 1994. As a member of the victorious →Freedom Alliance (PL) coalition in the March 1994 election, the CCD was allocated one portfolio in the short-lived Berlusconi government. Remaining part of the PL, it contested the April 1996 parliamentary elections in close alliance with the →United Christian Democrats, their joint list taking a 5.8% vote share and both parties going into opposition.

The CCD finally broke with the PL in February 1998, aligning itself instead with the new →Democratic Union of Republic (UDR) led by former President Francesco Cossiga, which in October 1998 joined a centre-left government headed by the →Democrats of the Left. In the June 1999 European Parliament elections the CCD took two of Italy's 87 seats on a vote share of 2.6%, its representatives joining the European People's Party/European Democrats group. The CCD is a member of the Christian Democrat International.

Communist Refoundation Party
Partito della Rifondazione Comunista (PRC)
Address. Viale Policlinico 131, 00161 Rome
Telephone. (+39–6) 441-821
Fax. (+39–6) 4423-9490
Email. esteri.prc@rifondazione.it
Website. http://www.rifondazione.it
Leadership. Fausto Bertinotti (secretary-general); Franco Giordano (Chamber group chair)
The PRC came into being at a session held in Rome in February 1991 of dissident members of the Italian Communist Party (PCI) opposed to the latter's majority preference for conversion into the democratic socialist Democratic Party of the Left (PDS), renamed the →Democrats of the Left (DS) in 1998. After legal proceedings, the PRC was awarded the right to use the traditional hammer and sickle symbol of the PCI and was formally launched at a Rome conference in May 1991. Having won 5.6% of the vote in the 1992 general elections, the PRC advanced to 6.0% in 1994, when it was part of the left-wing Progressive Alliance (AP) headed by the PDS. Subsequently distancing itself from the AP, the PRC contested the June 1994 European Parliament elections on a joint list with other ex-PCI elements, winning 6.1% of the vote and five seats, while the April-May 1995 regional elections yielded an 8.4% vote share.

In June 1995 the PRC was weakened by the defection of 14 of its 35 lower house deputies in protest at the alleged "isolationism" of the party leadership, the defectors becoming the Unitary Communists (*Comunisti Unitari*), most of whom later joined the DS. Undeterred, the rump PRC contested the April 1996 parliamentary elections independently and increased its vote share to 8.6%, which restored its Chamber representation to 35 seats. Although it had, by mutual agreement, remained outside the centre-left →Olive Tree Movement, the PRC opted to give qualified parliamentary backing to the Olive Tree minority government of Romano Prodi. However, after the PRC had polled strongly in local elections in April-May 1997, persistent strains over PRC opposition to government economic policies eventually resulted in the collapse of the Prodi government in October 1998 and its replacement by a majority coalitioon headed by the DS. Now deprived of its leverage in parliament, the PRC was also weakened by the concurrent launching of the →Party of Italian Communists (PdCI) under the leadership of Armando Cossutta, until then president of the PRC.

The fourth national PRC congress in Rimini in March 1999 reaffirmed the party's "class opposition to centre-left, now and forever". Standing alone in the June 1999 European elections, the PRC slipped to 4.3% of the vote and four seats. Its representatives in the European Parliament sit in the European United Left/Nordic Green Left group and the party is also a member of the New European Left Forum (NELF).

Democratic Union for the Republic
Unione Democratica per la Repubblica (UDR)
Address. Piazza de Gesù 46, 00186 Rome
Telephone. (+39-6) 67751
Email. info@udr.org
Website. http://www.udr.org
Leadership. Francesco Cossiga (president); Rocco Buttiglione (co-ordinator)
The centre-right UDR was launched in February 1998 by Francesco Cossiga, who had been President of Italy in 1985-92, elected as candidate of the then Christian Democratic Party (now the →Italian Popular Party). The new initiative was endorsed by the →Christian Democratic Centre and the →United Christian Democrats, which thereby effectively left the umbrella →Freedom Alliance of conservative parties. In October 1998 the UDR joined the

new →Olive Tree coalition headed by the →Democrats of the Left, receiving three cabinet portfolios. In the June 1999 European elections, the UDR list, called the Democratic Union for Europe (UdeuR), won 1.6% of the vote and one of Italy's 87 seats, its victorious candidate joining the European People's Party/European Democrats group.

Democrats for the New Olive Tree
I Democratici per il Nuovo Ulivo
Address. Piazza SS Apostoli 73, Rome
Telephone. (+39-6) 607-0379
Fax. (+39-6) 6680-2766
Email. info@democraticiperlulivo.it
Website. http://www.democraticiperlulivo.it
Leadership. Arturo Parisi (executive president)
This grouping was launched in February 1999 by Romano Prodi, formerly of the →Italian Popular Party (PPI), who had been Prime Minister of the centre-left →Olive Tree coalition government formed after the June 1996 elections but who had been ousted in October 1998 and replaced by Massimo D'Alema of the →Democrats of the Left (DS). Described by Prodi as intended to strengthen the centre-left, the new initiative was seen as the former Prime Minister's attempt to redress the balance in the Olive Tree alliance back to the centre and to counter the new dominance of the DS. Groupings backing the new party included the →Network Movement for Democracy (*La Rete*); the Italy of Values (*Italia dei Valori*) movement formed by Antonio Di Pietro following his exit from the Prodi government in November 1996 in contentious circumstances; and the Hundred Cities for a New Italy (*Centocittá per un Italia Nuova*) movement of mayors, environmentalists and voluntary groups.

A joint list put forward by the Democrats for the New Olive Tree and *La Rete* in the June 1999 European elections won seven of Italy's 87 seats with 7.7% of the vote, the representatives joining the European Liberal, Democratic and Reformist group. However, the Democrats' future was cast into some doubt by Prodi's subsequent appointment as president of the European Commission and his resultant withdrawal from Italian party politics for the duration.

Democrats of the Left
Democratici di Sinistra (DS)
Address. Via delle Botteghe Oscure 4, 00186 Rome
Telephone. (+39-6) 67111
Fax. (+39-6) 679-8376
Email. posta@democraticidisinistra.it
Website. http://www.democraticidisinistra.it
Leadership. Massimo D'Alema (political leader); Walter Veltroni (national secretary)
The DS is directly descended organizationally, but not ideologically, from the Italian Communist Party (*Partito Comunista Italiano*, PCI), delegates to the March 1990 extraordinary congress of which voted to abandon the traditional name of the PCI. Formal adoption of "Democratic Party of the Left" (PDS) as the party's new title followed in February 1991, at a final congress (*ultimo congresso*) of the PCI. A further change in February 1998, when the party was joined by most of the Unitary Communists (*Comunisti Unitari*) who had defected from the →Communist Refoundation Party in 1995, produced the shortened DS title.

Formed as a result of the split in the Italian Socialist Party (→Italian Democratic Socialists, SDI) at the 1921 Livorno congress, the PCI went underground during the Mussolini period, its then leader, Palmiro Togliatti, escaping to Moscow, where he worked for the Comintern until his return to Italy in 1944. In the early 1940s the PCI played a leading role in the struggle against the fascist regime and the German Nazi occupation forces. Under Togliatti's leadership the PCI participated in the post-war coalition government until being excluded in May 1947, after which it mounted a violent campaign of political and industrial opposition. Following the decisive election victory of the Christian Democrats in April 1948 the PCI took the road of democratic opposition and subsequently developed into the largest and most influential non-ruling Communist party in Europe. Throughout the post-war period the PCI was consistently the second strongest party (after the Christian Democrats) in terms of both votes and seats in parliament.

From 1975 the PCI governed a large number of regions, provinces and municipalities (particularly in the "red belt" of Emilia-Romagna, Umbria and Tuscany), usually in coalition with other left-wing parties. At national level, the PCI's claims for admission to government responsibility were resisted, although following the sharp increase in the party's vote in the June 1976 elections (to over 34%) successive Christian Democrat-led governments accepted parliamentary support from the PCI, initially through abstention and subsequently, from March 1978, on the basis of the PCI being included in the official parliamentary majority. The PCI withdrew from this arrangement in January 1979 and reverted to a position of full opposition; in the elections of that year its vote share fell to 30.4%.

In 1980 the PCI adopted a new "democratic alternative" strategy based on an alliance with the Socialists, but the latter remained committed to centre-left coalitions. In the 1983 general elections the PCI again lost ground, winning 198 seats and 29.9% of the vote, although in the June 1984 European Parliament elections it emerged as the largest party for the first time in its history, winning 33.3% of the vote. Under the new leadership of Alessandro Natta (who had succeeded Enrico Berlinguer on the latter's death in June 1984), the PCI was strengthened in November 1984 by absorbing the Party of Proletarian Unity for Communism (originally founded in 1972). However, it lost ground in the May 1985 regional and local elections (surrendering Rome to the Christian Democrats) and suffered a further setback in the June 1987 general elections, when its Chamber representation fell to 177 seats and its share of the vote to 26.6%.

A post-election reorganization of the PCI leadership bodies included the appointment of Achille Occhetto as deputy general secretary and thus as potential successor to Natta. Meanwhile, Natta had paid an official visit to Moscow in January 1986 (the first by a PCI leader since 1978) and had reportedly healed the breach caused by Berlinguer's and his outspoken criticism of the Soviet role in Afghanistan and Poland. Nevertheless, the 17th PCI congress in April 1986 reaffirmed the party's rejection of the Soviet model and its "Eurocommunist" orientation as part of the European democratic left.

In June 1988 Natta was succeeded as PCI leader by Occhetto, who promised a "new course" for Italian communism. This process turned out to be the abandonment of much of the traditional party line and the transformation of the PCI into the PDS in February 1991, with a democratic socialist orientation. Having won 16.1% of the national vote in the 1992 elections, the PDS advanced to 20.4% in the March 1994 contest, although it failed to make the hoped-for breakthrough to political power as a member of the left-wing Progressive Alliance. In the June 1994 European Parliament elections PDS support slipped to 19.1%, which gave the party 16 seats. This setback precipitated the resignation of Occhetto as general secretary and the succession of Massimo D'Alema. In late 1994 and April-May 1995 the PDS made major advances in local and regional elections, on the latter occasion heading the poll with 24.6% of the vote.

In July 1995 the PDS took the momentous decision to enter a structured centre-left alliance, called the →Olive Tree Movement, which registered a major victory in the April

1996 parliamentary elections. The PDS secured 21.1% of the vote and 156 seats in its own right, being awarded nine posts in the resultant centre-left coalition of Romano Prodi. D'Alema and his renamed DS were the main political beneficiaries of the collapse of the Prodi government in October 1998, the DS leader becoming Prime Minister of a centre-left coalition which also included the →Italian Popular Party, →Italian Renewal, the →Italian Democratic Socialists, the →Party of Italian Communists and the →Green Federation.

The DS slipped to 17.4% of the vote and 15 seats in the June 1999 European elections. Its representatives in the European Parliament sit in the Party of European Socialists group, the party having been admitted to the Socialist International in 1992.

Federation of Liberals
Federazione dei Liberali (FdL)
Address. Via Frattina 89, 00187 Rome
Telephone. (+39–6) 679–0801
Website. http://www.luda.it/~liberali
Leadership. Valerio Zanone (president); Raffaello Morelli (secretary)
The FLI acts as the umbrella body of liberalism in Italy following the effective demise of the historic Italian Liberal Party (*Partito Liberale Italiano*, PLI) amid the party corruption scandals of the early 1990s. The PLI had its roots in the 19th-century liberal movement of Count Camillo di Cavour, the diplomatic architect of Italian unification. In the period following World War II the party increased its representation in the Chamber of Deputies from 13 members in 1953 to 39 in 1963, participating in several coalition governments in this period and subsequently. It declined to five seats by 1976, although it won nine seats in June 1979 and 16 in June 1983, following which it participated in the Socialist-led government of 1983-87 and its successor headed by a Christian Democrat. In June 1987 the PLI slipped to 11 Chamber seats and 2.1% of the vote, but continued to be a centre-left coalition partner. In November 1987 it caused a brief crisis by withdrawing from the government in protest against the 1988 draft budget, but after five days the coalition was reconstituted with identical composition.

In the April 1996 parliamentary elections the Liberal remnants formed part of the Democratic Union, itself a member of the victorious →Olive Tree alliance of centre-left parties. In the June 1999 European elections a joint list of the Liberals and the →Italian Republican Party (PRI) won 0.5% of the vote and one of the 87 Italian seats. The list's representative in the European Parliament joined the European Liberal, Democratic and Reformist group.

Forza Italia (FI)
Address. Via dell'Umiltà 36, 00100 Rome
Telephone. (+39–6) 67311
Fax. (+39–6) 5994–1315
Email. lettere@forza-italia.it
Website. http://www.forza-italia.it
Leadership. Silvio Berlusconi (president); Beppe Pisanu (Chamber group chair); Claudio Scajola (chief of organization)
The FI was launched in January 1994, its Italian title being variously translated into English as "Go Italy!" and "Come On Italy!", as being the English equivalent of the traditional chant of supporters of the Italian football team which provided the party's title. The FI was created by Berlusconi, Italy's most powerful media tycoon (and owner of the leading Milan football club), who identified the prevention of an electoral victory by the ex-Communist Democratic Party of the Left (PDS), later renamed →Democrats of the Left (DS), as the new formation's

principal objective. To this end, it organized the right-wing →Freedom Alliance (PL), which secured an absolute parliamentary majority of 366 seats in the March 1994 general elections and accordingly formed a new government.

In the June 1994 European Parliament elections the PL won a narrow majority of 44 of Italy's 87 seats, 27 of which were credited to the FI on a vote share of 30.6%. However, growing strains between the coalition parties culminated in the collapse and ejection of the Berlusconi government in December 1994 as a result of the withdrawal of the →Northern League. There followed strong FI pressure for fresh general elections, despite disappointing local election results for the party in late 1994 and April-May 1995. Berlusconi had greater success in a multiple referendum exercise in June 1995, when there were majorities for propositions effectively maintaining the dominance of his media interests. But the FI leader was increasingly tainted by financial corruption allegations in the run-up to the April 1996 general elections, in which the FI remained at 21% within a reduced PL alliance and the centre-left →Olive Tree alliance came to power.

In opposition, the FI was damaged by further court proceedings against Berlusconi in 1997-98, while the PL was weakened in February 1998 by defections to the →Democratic Union of the Republic (UDR). Nevertheless, in April 1998 was formally elected FI president, whilst in June 1998 the FI achieved wider respectability by being accepted as a member of the European People's Party group in the European Parliament, having previously been part of the Union for a Europe of Nations group. Although he had been convicted several times (without going to prison), Berlusconi's acquittal in March 1999 on a tax fraud charge helped the FI to head the poll again in the June 1999 European elections, in which it took 25.2% of the vote and 22 seats. By the end of the year, however, Berlusconi faced a new trial on charges of bribing judges in a controversial company sale case in 1985.

The FI representatives in the European Parliament were readmitted to what had become the European People's Party/European Democrats group. The FI is also affiliated to the International Democrat Union and the European Democrat Union.

Freedom Alliance
Polo delle Libertà (PL)
Address. c/o Camera dei Deputati, Piazza Montecitorio, 00186 Rome
Leadership. Silvio Berlusconi (→*Forza Italia*) and Gianfranco Fini (→National Alliance)
The PL was formed in 1994 as effectively the umbrella of two alliances of right-wing parties, namely the main Freedom Alliance, consisting of →*Forza Italia* and the →Northern League (LN) in the north, and the Good Government Alliance (*Polo del Buon Governo*, PBG), encompassing the →National Alliance (AN) and the →Christian Democratic Centre (CCD) in the south. Loosely, however, all four, plus the →Radical Party, were then components of the overarching PL. Having taken power after the March 1994 general elections under the premiership of Silvio Berlusconi, the component PL parties quickly experienced dissension, which resulted in the exit of the LN in December 1994 and the resultant collapse of the PL government.

The aggregate vote of the reduced PL in regional elections in April-May 1995 slipped to 40.7%, from 43% in the 1994 parliamentary elections. The PL structure remained largely in place for the April 1996 general elections, although personal rivalry and public disputation between Berlusconi and AN leader Fini did the alliance little good at the polls. Although the PL's overall share of the proportional vote rose to some 44%, about 10% higher than that obtained by the centre-left →Olive Tree Movement, the latter's relative majority of seats meant that the PL parties became the principal opposition to the new Prodi government and to its successor under Massimo D'Alema of the →Democrats of the Left, appointed in October 1998.

Green Federation
Federazione dei Verdi
Address. Via Catalana 1A, 00186 Rome
Telephone. (+39–6) 6880–2879
Fax. (+39–6) 6880–3023
Email. notizie@verdi.it
Website. http://www.verdi.it
Leadership. Luigi Manconi (spokesperson)
Officially called the National Federation for the Green List, the Italian branch of the European Federation of Green Parties was founded as a national electoral movement at a constituent assembly held in Florence in December 1984. The formation won some 1.8% of the vote overall in regional and local elections in May 1985, when it was backed by the →Radical Party, and made a significant breakthrough in the July 1987 general elections, winning 2.5% of the vote and returning 13 Chamber deputies and one member of the Senate.

The Greens improved further in 1992, winning four Senate and 16 Chamber seats on a vote share of 2.8%. For the 1994 general elections the Greens joined the Progressive Alliance, headed by what later became the →Democrats of the Left (DS), their vote share slipping to 2.7%. In a recovery in the June 1994 European Parliament elections, the Greens won three seats on a 3.2% vote share. Joining the centre-left →Olive Tree Movement for the April 1996 parliamentary elections, the Greens won 2.5% of the proportional vote and had the satisfaction of seeing party member Edo Ronchi appointed Environment Minister in the new Olive Tree government. He was joined by Laura Balbo as Equal Opportunities Minister when a new coalition was formed in October 1998 under the leadership of the DS.

Damaged by the rival appeal of the →Emma Bonino List in the June 1999 European elections, the Greens slipped to 1.8% of vote and two seats. The party's representatives in the European Parliament joined the Greens/European Free Alliance group.

Italian Democratic Socialists
Socialisti Democratici Italiani (SDI)
Address. Piazza San Lorenzo in Lucina 26, 00186 Rome
Telephone. (+39–6) 6830–7666
Fax. (+39–6) 6830–7659
Email. socialisti@nexus.it
Website. http://www.socialisti.org
Leadership. Enrico Bosselli (president)
The SDI resulted from the merger in 1998 of the Italian Socialists (SI), a designation adopted by the historic Italian Socialist Party (*Partito Socialista Italiano*, PSI) in 1994, with the Italian Democratic Socialist Party (*Partito Socialista Democratico Italiano*, PSDI), which itself had derived from a left–right split in the PSI in 1947.

Founded in 1892, the PSI had first split at its Livorno congress in 1921 when a pro-Bolshevik group broke away to form the Italian Communist Party (→Democrats of the Left, DS). At the Rome congress in January 1947 Giuseppe Saragat's right-wing PSI faction, opposed to the majority Pietro Nenni wing's policy of alliance with the Communists, broke away to form the Workers' Socialist Party (PSLI), which in 1952 merged with other factions to become the PSDI. Whereas the Democratic Socialists took part in successive coalitions in 1947-63 headed by the Christian Democrats (→Italian Popular Party, PPI), the rump PSI remained in opposition, its Chamber representation rising to 87 seats in 1963.

Following the 1963 "opening to the left", the PSI repeatedly co-operated with the dominant Christian Democrats, either by joining coalition governments or by giving external support. The PSI and PSDI signed a reunification agreement in 1966, a combined PSI/PSDI list called the *Partito Socialista Unificato* winning 91 Chamber seats in 1968. The following year, however, the merger attempt broke down and the two parties re-established their separate identities, although both usually continued to be part of the centre-left majority. Having resigned from the Fanfani government, the PSI advanced from 62 to 73 seats in the June 1983 Chamber elections, with the result that party leader Bettino Craxi formed Italy's first-ever Socialist-led government, based on a coalition with the Christian Democrats, the PSDI and two other parties.

The Craxi administration lasted an unprecedented four years, eventually resigning in March 1987 over a dispute with the Christian Democrats about the application of a rotation pact under which a Christian Democrat was to take over the premiership early in 1987. In the June 1987 elections the PSI gained further ground, to 94 seats and 14.3% of the vote, subsequently joining a further five-party coalition headed by the Christian Democrats and including the PSDI (which declined from 23 to 17 seats and 3% in 1987). In the April 1992 elections the PSI slipped to 92 seats and 13.6% of the popular vote, but remained in the government coalition, as did the PSDI, which had won 17 seats and 2.7%. Craxi then came under judicial investigation on numerous charges of financial corruption and illegal party funding, with the consequence that he resigned as PSI leader in February 1993, having served 17 years in the post. In the wake of charges against many other PSI representatives, the party slumped to 2.2% in the March 1994 Chamber elections, in which the PSDI failed to win any Chamber seats at all. Some PSI elements contested the elections under the banner of the Democratic Alliance, doing the same in the European Parliament elections in June 1994, in which the PSI and PSDI managed only one seat each. The following month Craxi received a long prison sentence, and still faced other charges, along with several dozen other former PSI officials.

Seeking to recover its former constituency, the PSI transformed itself into the SI in November 1994, believing that dropping the discredited descriptor "party" from its title would improve its public image. In the April 1996 parliamentary elections the SI and the PSDI were both components of the victorious →Olive Tree Movement, in close alliance with the new →Italian Renewal formation. Reunification of the SI and PSDI was finally accomplished in 1998, the resultant SDI obtaining one portfolio in the government formed in October 1998 by Massimo D'Alema of the DS. In the June 1999 European elections the SDI won only two seats with 2.1% of the vote, its representatives in the European Parliament sitting in the Party of European Socialists group. The SDI inherited the Socialist International membership held by both the PSI and the PSDI.

Italian Popular Party
Partito Popolare Italiano (PPI)
Address. 46 piazza de Gesù, 00186 Rome
Telephone. (+39–6) 67751
Fax. (+39–6) 6775–3951
Email. ppidirnaz@pronet.it
Website. http://www.popolari.it
Leadership. Gerardo Bianco (president); Franco Marini (secretary-general)
The PPI is the successor to the post-war Christian Democratic Party (DC), for long Italy's dominant formation, which in January 1994, beset by corruption scandals, reverted to the PPI title of an earlier age. The PPI had been founded by Don Luigi Sturzo before World War I and had functioned as Italy's Catholic party until the rise of fascism in 1922. It was revived as the DC towards the end of World War II, taking part in January 1944 in the first congress of (six) democratic parties for over 20 years (in Bari). It participated in coalition governments from April 1944 and in the formation of the National Consultative Council in 1945. Its post-war

leader, Alcide De Gasperi, was Prime Minister from December 1945 until August 1953, overseeing the post-war reconstruction programme and Italy's participation in the creation of what later became the European Union.

In general elections to a Constituent Assembly in June 1946 the DC emerged as the strongest party with 35.2% of the votes and 207 (out of 556) seats. In elections to the Chamber of Deputies held in April 1948 it gained 48.7% of the votes and 307 (out of 574) seats. In June 1953, however, the DC's strength in the Chamber was reduced to 262 seats (based on 40.1% of the votes). From August 1953 onwards the DC continued in office either as the sole government party or in coalition, at first with Liberals and Democratic Socialists, and later also with Republicans. In the 1958 elections it obtained 42.2% of the votes and 273 seats in the Chamber. In elections held after 1963 the DC maintained its position as the strongest party until the 1990s.

At a Naples congress early in 1962 the DC had approved a policy of "opening to the left" *(apertura a sinistra)* involving the formation of administrations relying on Socialist support. The DC formed coalition governments including Socialists from July 1964 to June 1968 and from December 1968 to July 1969; it accepted other coalition partners between March 1970 and February 1971 and from June 1972 to July 1973. Thereafter it again included Socialists in its government from July 1973 to November 1974, when it formed a coalition with Republicans only. From July 1976 onwards it was in power as a minority government, until in March 1977 the DC concluded an agreement with five other parties, including the Communist Party (PCI), which undertook to give external support to the DC government. In March 1978 the DC entered into a limited policy agreement with the PCI, but the latter withdrew from both agreements in January 1979, whereupon the DC formed a coalition government with the Democratic Socialists and Republicans. This administration fell at the end of March 1979 after losing a confidence vote, whereupon premature elections in June 1979 resulted in the DC retaining its position as the largest parliamentary party (although its percentage declined slightly). In August 1979 the DC formed a coalition with the Democratic Socialists and Liberals under the premiership of Francesco Cossiga.

There followed further DC-led coalition governments until June 1981, when the DC joined a coalition headed by Giovanni Spadolini of the Italian Republican Party, the first non-Christian Democrat to head a post-war Italian administration. In December 1982 the DC resumed the leadership of a coalition government, but after the June 1983 general elections in which the DC's representation in the Chamber of Deputies was reduced from 262 to 225 members, it agreed to join the first coalition government to be led by a Socialist (Bettino Craxi). After lasting for an unprecedented four years, the Craxi government ended in March 1987 amid recriminations from the DC that the PSI leader was reluctant to honour a pact of August 1986 specifying that a DC Prime Minister should take over early in 1987. An "institutional" DC government followed until early general elections in June 1987, when the DC increased its representation in the Chamber to 234 seats. The party accordingly resumed the government leadership, forming a five-party coalition with the Socialist, Republican, Democratic Socialist and Liberals parties, with Giovanni Goria as Prime Minister followed by Ciriaco De Mita from March 1988.

De Mita resigned in May 1989 and was succeeded as DC Prime Minister by the indispensable Giulio Andreotti, who formed another five-party centre-left coalition government. In July 1990 the coalition was rocked by the resignations of five ministers from the De Mita DC faction, but Andreotti survived until the Socialists withdrew from the government in March 1991. He bounced back yet again to form his seventh centre-left cabinet headed by the DC, this one including three other parties. The DC then became a leading victim of the political corruption cases which resulted in a melt-down of the Italian party system, the most prominent DC casualty being Andreotti himself, who was accused of maintaining links with the Mafia (and later brought to trial on such charges, although eventually acquitted). The party slumped to a post-war low of 29.7% and 206 seats in the April 1992 parliamentary elections, being obliged therefore to cede the premiership to a Socialist, although it remained a government party.

The DC's plummeting fortunes were revealed in local elections in June 1993, when only one of 47 DC candidates prevailed in mayoral contests. Having reverted to the historical PPI name in January 1994, the party contested the March 1994 general elections as part of a centrist alliance called the Pact for Italy (*Patto per l'Italia*, PI), which had been launched in January by Mario Segni, leader of the →Segni Pact. As the leading component of the PI, the PPI won only 11.1% of the vote in the March 1994 general election, slipping further to 10% in the June elections to the European Parliament, in which the party took only eight of Italy's 87 seats.

In opposition, the PPI experienced deep divisions over whether to form an alliance with Silvio Berlusconi's then ruling →Freedom Alliance. The controversy resulted in an open split in March 1995, when the anti-Berlusconi "Democratic" wing elected Gerardo Bianco as PPI leader in the absence of the previously dominant right-wing faction, which disputed the election's legitimacy. In local elections in April-May 1995 the two factions competed separately, the "Democrats" winning 6% and the pro-Berlusconi faction 3%. In July 1995 the pro-Berlusconi faction finally broke away, forming the →United Christian Democrats, while the rump PPI became the second largest component of the victorious centre-left →Olive Tree Movement in the April 1996 general elections, its list of candidates featuring Olive Tree leader Romano Prodi. The PPI accordingly obtained substantial representation in the resultant Prodi government and also, following the collapse of the latter in October 1998, in the succeeding coalition headed by the →Democrats of the Left.

Weakened by Prodi's formation of the →Democrats for the New Olive Tree in February 1999, the PPI slumped to 4.3% of the vote and four seats in the June 1999 European Parliament elections. Its representatives in the European Parliament sit in the European People's Party/European Democrats group. The party is also a member of the Christian Democrat International and the International Democrat Union.

Italian Republican Party
Partito Repubblicano Italiano (PRI)
Address. Piazza dei Caprettari 70, 00186 Rome
Telephone. (+39–6) 683–4037
Fax. (+39-6) 654-2990
Website. http://www.netart.it/voce
Leadership. Bruno Visentini (president); Giorgio La Malfa (secretary)
Founded as such in 1894, the PRI has its origins in the *Fiovine Italia* of 1831, who as republicans fought, under the leadership of Giuseppe Mazzini, for national unity and independence. The party's still-influential daily newspaper, *La Voce Repubblicana*, was founded in 1921. The PRI was dissolved by the Facist regime and reconstituted in 1943, taking part in the Resistance. Under the republican constitution introduced in January 1948 the PRI was a partner in numerous coalition governments led by Christian Democrats from 1948 to 1981.

In June 1981 the then PRI leader, Giovanni Spadolini, became the first non-Christian Democrat to head an Italian government since the war, forming a five-party centre-left Cabinet which lasted until November 1982. In the June 1983 Chamber elections the PRI's vote increased to 5.1% and its representation to 29 seats, however, in those of June 1987 it fell back to 3.7% and 21 seats. Meanwhile, the PRI had participated in the Socialist-led centre-left coalition of 1983-87, while after the 1987 elections it joined a similar coalition headed by the

Christian Democrats. Thereafter the PRI continued its participation in centre-left coalitions until going into opposition in April 1991.

Then a PRI member, Antonio Maccanico accepted the post of Cabinet Secretary in the Ciampi government formed in May 1993, although the party itself remained in opposition. Having won 4.4% of the national vote in 1992, the PRI contested the March 1994 poll as a member of the Democratic Alliance (AD), and thus also of the broader Progressive Alliance (AP). In the June 1994 European balloting a specifically PRI list secured 0.7% of the vote, its one seat going to Giorgio La Malfa. Having resigned the party leadership in 1988 and been reinstated in January 1994, La Malfa again resigned in October 1994 and was again reinstated in March 1995.

The PRI contested the April 1996 general elections within Maccanico's new (and short-lived) Democratic Union, and therefore as part of the victorious →Olive Tree Movement of centre-left parties. In the resultant Prodi coalition government Maccanico became Minister of Posts and Telecommunications, but was not reappointed when Prodi gave way in October 1998 to a more left-tilted coalition headed by the →Democrats of the Left (DS). The PRI contested the June 1999 European elections on a joint list with the Liberals (→Federation of Italian Liberals) that obtained 0.5% of the vote and one seat. The list's representative in the European Parliament sits in the European Liberal, Democratic and Reformist group.

Italian Renewal
Rinnovamento Italiano (RI)
Address. Via di Ripetta 142, 00186Rome
Telephone. (+39–6) 6880-8380
Fax. (+39–6) 6880-8480
Email. informa@rinnovamento.it
Website. http://www.rinnovamento.it
Leadership. Lamberto Dini (president); Paolo Ricciotti (organization secretary)
The formation of the RI was announced by Prof. Dini in February 1996, a month after the fall of his year-old government of technocrats. The new formation formed part of the victorious →Olive Tree Movement in the April 1996 elections, obtaining three posts in the resultant government of Romano Prodi, in which Dini became Foreign Minister. He retained the post in the succeeding coalition headed by the →Democrats of the Left (DS) formed in October 1998.

The RI won one of Italy 87 seats in the June 1999 European elections with a 1.1% vote share, its representative joining the European People's Party/European Democrats group.

National Alliance
Alleanza Nazionale (AN)
Address. Via della Scrofa 39, 00186 Rome
Telephone. (+39–6) 6880–3014
Fax. (+39–6) 654–8256
Email. uffintan@tin.it
Website. http://www.alleanza-nazionale.it
Leadership. Gianfranco Fini (secretary-general); Maurizio Gaspari (co-ordinator)
The radical right-wing AN is the direct descendant of the post-war Italian Social Movement (MSI), which was founded in 1946 as a successor to the outlawed Fascist Party of the late dictator Benito Mussolini. The MSI first contested parliamentary elections in 1948, winning six seats in the Chamber of Deputies. Between 1953 and 1972 its representation in the Chamber fluctuated between 29 and 24 members. It contested the 1972 general elections in an alliance *(Destra Nazionale,* DN) with the Italian Democratic Party of Monarchical Unity,

the joint list winning 56 seats in the Chamber. The two parties formally merged as the MSI-DN in January 1973, but in the 1976 elections the new party obtained only 35 seats in the Chamber.

The MSI-DN did not rule out the use of violence in its activities, and its extremist members were involved in numerous clashes and other acts of violence, which were not approved by the party as a whole. In December 1976 a total of 26 MSI-DN parliamentarians (17 deputies and nine senators) broke away from the party to form a group known as *Democrazia Nazionale* (DN), which was led by Ernesto De Marzio, it repudiated all fascist tendencies and announced that it would support the Christian Democrats. However, in the 1979 elections this group won no seats, while the rump MSI-DN retained 30 seats in the Chamber of Deputies.

In the 1983 elections the party made significant gains both at national and at regional and provincial level, gaining 42 seats in the Chamber of Deputies (with 6.8% of the vote). In the June 1987 elections, however, it slipped back to 35 seats (5.9% of the vote). The party's veteran leader, Giorgio Almirante (who had been a member of Mussolini's government), retired in December 1987 and was succeeded by Gianfranco Fini, regarded as a representative of the young "new face" of the party. Meanwhile, the party had decided in October 1987 to mount an active campaign in South Tyrol/Bolzano in support of the Italian speaking minority and against the political aspirations of the German-speaking majority.

In the 1992 parliamentary elections the MSI-DN slipped to 34 Chamber seats and 5.4% of the vote, one of the party's successful candidates in Naples being Alessandra Mussolini, grand-daughter of the former dictator. It then sought to capitalize on the massive corruption scandals that engulfed the centre-left parties so long in government. The AN designation was used by the MSI-DN from January 1994 as part of a strategy to attract support from former Christian Democrats and other right-wing groups, including Italian monarchists, and the party joined the →Freedom Alliance (PL) of conservative parties headed by Silvio Berlusconi's new →*Forza Italia* party, becoming the leading force in the PL's southern arm, designated the Good Government Alliance (*Polo del Buon Governo*). In the March 1994 elections the AN advanced strongly to 13.5% of the proportional vote as part of the PL, its support being concentrated in southern Italy. Six AN ministers were included in the Berlusconi government appointed in May 1994. In the following month's European Parliament elections the AN won 12.5% of the vote and 11 seats. The party's first post-war experience of national office ended with the collapse of the Berlusconi government in December 1994.

The AN title was officially adopted by the party in January 1995 at a Rome congress which also decided to delete most references to fascism in basic AN policy documents. Thereafter party spokesmen became even more insistent in rejecting the "neo-fascist" label commonly appended by the media and others, especially since a hardline minority which saw no discredit in the term "fascist" had in effect broken away by forming what became the →Tricolour Flame Social Movement. The regional elections of April-May 1995 showed a modest increase in the AN vote to 14.1%, which rose appreciably to 15.7% in the April 1996 general elections, for which the AN remained within the PL alliance, winning 91 Chamber seats in its own right. In the 1996 contest Fini added to his reputation as a keen debater and effective campaigner, rather overshadowing Berlusconi.

In opposition to the centre-left →Olive Tree government, the AN in March 1998 relaunched itself as a "modern, open right-wing party" in which fascist ideology was said to have no place, adopting the ladybird as its new logo symbol. In the June 1999 European elections the AN was allied with the →Segni Pact, but the joint list secured only 10.3% of the vote and nine seats. Those elected joined the Union for a Europe of Nations in the European Parliament.

The Network Movement for Democracy
Movimento per la Democrazia La Rete (MpD–*La Rete*)
Address. Lungotevere Marzio 3, 00186 Rome
Telephone. (+39–6) 6830–0447
Fax. (+39–6) 6830–0446
Website. http://www.larete.it
Leadership. Leoluca Orlando
This anti-Mafia movement was founded as *La Rete* (The Network) at Palermo, Sicily, in 1991 and became the city's leading party in the 1992 general elections, winning three Senate and 12 Chamber seats. As a member of the left-wing Popular Alliance in the March 1994 elections it won 1.9% of the national vote. In the June European Parliament poll it obtained one seat on a 1.1% vote share. By now also using the MpD label, the party contested the April 1996 general elections as part of the victorious →Olive Tree Movement.

In February 1999 *La Rete* backed the launching of the →Democrats for the New Olive Tree to strengthen the centre within the centre-left. A joint list of the two formations won 7.7% and seven seats in the June 1999 European elections.

Northern League
La Lega Nord (LN-IF)
Address. Via Arbe 63, 20125 Milan
Telephone. (+39–2) 607–0379
Fax. (+39–2) 6680–2766
Email. info@leganord.org
Website. http://www.leganord.org
Leadership. Umberto Bossi (federal secretary); Stefano Stefani (federal president); Giancarlo Pagliarini (Chamber group chair)
The Northern League (LN) "for the independence of Padania" originated in February 1991 as a federation of the Lombardy League (*Lega Lombarda*, LL) and fraternal parties in Emilio Romagna, Liguria, Piedmont, Tuscany and Venice. The LL had been launched in 1979, named after a 12th-century federation of northern Italian cities. It had achieved prominence in the 1980s as the most conspicuous of several regional groups to challenge the authority of the government in Rome, in particular its use of public revenues from the rich north to aid the impoverished south. Adopting the same stance, the LN called at its foundation for a move to a federal system with substantial regional autonomy in most areas except defence and foreign policy. More fundamentally, the eventual LN objective was the full independence of the lands north of the Po, which it called "Padania". Party leaders subsequently denied that the LN's attitude to southern Italians was tantamount to racism but made no apology for the League's advocacy of a strong anti-immigration policy, including resolute action against illegal immigrants and against criminality in immigrant communities.

Having won 8.7% of the national vote and 55 Chamber seats in the 1992 general elections, the LN made political capital out of popular disgust over the bribery scandals engulfing Italy's political establishment, winning a record 40% of the vote in the Milan mayoral election of June 1993. For the March 1994 parliamentary elections the LN joined the →Freedom Alliance (PL), winning 8.4% of the national vote; in June 1994 it won six European Parliament seats on a 6.6% vote share. Having joined the Berlusconi government in May 1994, the LN withdrew six months later because of chronic policy and personality clashes with other PL components, notably with Berlusconi's →*Forza Italia* party.

Contesting the April 1996 general elections independently, the LN increased its share of the national vote to 10.1%, taking 59 Chamber seats, and became the strongest single party in northern Italy. In opposition to the resultant centre-left government in Rome, the League convened a "parliament" in Mantua in May 1996, when party leader Umberto Bossi reasserted the League's secessionist objective and announced the creation of a "Committee for the Liberation of Padania" to act as a "provisional government". However, such schemes received a knock in local elections the following month, when the LN-IF polled poorly throughout "Padania" and managed only third place in Mantua, seat of its "parliament". Bossi also came under criticism by moderates within the LN, responding in August 1996 by expelling their leader, former Chamber president Irene Pivetti.

Also in August 1996, Bossi came under pressure from local investigating magistrates, who requested the Rome parliament to lift his parliamentary immunity so that he could face charges of inciting political violence at LN rallies in the north. Contending that he was not answerable to judges of "colonial Italy", Bossi in September 1996 led a three-day march along the River Po which culminated in a Venice rally and the declaration of the independent "Republic of Padania". An accompanying "transitional constitution" provided that the declaration would not come into effect for up to 12 months, during which the LN "provisional government" would negotiate a "treaty of agreed separation" with the Rome government. Bossi announced at the same time that a "national guard" would be set up to protect "Padania's interests". The reaction of the Prime Minister in Rome was that the country and the government "will not be troubled by political projects that have no roots in the past and no future", whilst police raided the NL headquarters in Milan to search for evidence of the party's alleged unconstitutional activities.

The third LN congress in February 1997 featured some moderation of the party's demand for speedy independence, with Bossi now calling for "consensual secession" and dialogue with the Italian authorities. Local elections in April-May 1997 were disappointing for the LN and an unofficial referendum organized by the party on May 25, when 99% of participants were said to have supported independence for "Padania", was dismissed by the government as a political stunt. Nevertheless, in October 1997 the LN proceeded to organize "elections" for a 200-member "constituent assembly of the Republic of Padania", the body holding its inaugural meeting in November, when the guests included Russian nationalist leader Vladimir Zhirinovsky.

In January 1998 a Bergamo court gave Bossi a one-year prison sentence and fined him Lit170 million after he had been convicted of inciting criminal acts at an LN rally in 1995. In July 1998, moreover, Bossi and another NL leader were given suspended sentences of seven and eight months respectively for offenses committed in a clash with police in 1996. In the June 1999 European elections the LN slipped to 4.5% of the national vote and from six seats to four.

Olive Tree Movement
Movimento per l'Ulivo (MpU)
Address. c/o Camera dei Deputati, Piazza Montecitorio, 00186 Rome
Email. info@perlulivo.it
Website. http://www.perlulivo.it
Leadership. Leaders of constituent parties
The MpU dates from July 1995, when a Rome conference of the main centre-left parties endorsed economics professor Romano Prodi of the liberal wing of the Christian democratic →Italian Popular Party (PPI) as their standard-bearer in the forthcoming general elections. In addition to the PPI, the constituent parties of the new movement, which adopted the olive tree as its symbol and title, included what later became the (ex-Communist) →Democrats of the Left (DS); what later became the →Italian Democratic Socialists (SDI); the →Green Federation; →Italian Renewal (RI); the →Network Movement for Democracy (*La Rete*); the →Italian Republican Party (PRI); and the →Federation of Liberals (FdL). Aiming to reverse

the victory of the right-wing parties in the 1994 Chamber elections, the MpU drew up a programme of constitutional and economic reform, including a commitment to preparing Italy for participation in the single European currency (euro).

In the April 1996 Chamber elections the MpU won 34.8% of the vote for the 155 proportional seats, well behind the →Freedom Alliance (PL), but dominated polling for the 475 directly elective seats, ending up with a relative majority of 284 seats, of which the DS held more than half. Prodi accordingly formed an Olive Tree minority government, dependent on external parliamentary support from the →Communist Refoundation Party (PRC). The new administration succeeded in manœuvring Italy into being accepted for founder membership of the new euro (from Jan. 1, 1999), but its constitutional reform proposals made little progress in face of PL opposition. The government also upset the PRC with its economic austerity measures, the constant aggravation on that score culminating in the PRC's withdrawal of support and the ousting of Prodi in October 1998. Widely seen as having helped to engineer the government's defeat, the DS was the main beneficiary. The DS leader, Massimo D'Alema, became Prime Minister of a new centre-left coalition tilted more to the left and including the non-MpU →Party of Italian Communists (PdCI).

Ex-Premier Prodi responded in February 1999 by launching the →Democrats for the New Olive Tree, with the declared aim of strengthening the centre-left as a whole but also clearly seeking to move the MpU balance back towards the centre. Following the June 1999 European elections, Prodi's appointment as president of the European Commission, and his resultant withdrawal from Italian party politics, meant that the future of the new initiative to preserve the MpU became uncertain. Nevertheless, in October 1999 leaders of the main Olive Tree parties, including the Democrats and the DS, declared their support for "the relaunching of the spirit of the Olive Tree and its opening to new political forces, all in support of the D'Alema government".

Party of Italian Communists
Partito dei Comunisti Italiani (PdCI)
Address. Corso Vittorio Emanuele II 209, 00186 Rome
Telephone. (+39-6) 686-271
Fax. (+39-6) 6862-7230
Email. direzionenazionale@comunisti-italiani.it
Website. http://www.comunisti-italiani.it
Leadership. Armando Cossutta (president)

The PdCI was formally launched in October 1998 under the leadership of Armando Cossutta, until then president of the →Communist Refoundation Party (PRC). The new party grouped elements deriving from the historic Italian Communist Party (PCI) in its "Eurocommunist" later phase who rejected the PCI's transformation into the left-of-centre →Democrats of the Left (DS) but who also opposed the "unreconstructed" line of the PRC. On its formation, the PdCI joined the new coalition government headed by Massimo D'Alema of the DS, receiving two cabinet portfolios.

In the June 1999 European elections the PdCI won two of Italy's 87 seats with a vote share of 2.0%. Its two representatives in the European Parliament joined the European United Left/Nordic Green Left group.

Radical Party
Partito Radicale (PR)
Address. Via di Torre Argentina 76, 00186 Rome
Telephone. (+39-6) 689-791
Fax. (+39-6) 880-5396

Email. radical.party@radicalparty.org
Website. http://www.radicalparty.org
Leadership. Marco Pannella (president); Emma Bonino (leader of Radical MEPs)

The PR was founded in December 1955 on a platform of non-violence, anti-militarism, human and civil rights, and the construction of a "socialist and democratic society". It has also campaigned for women's and homosexual rights, against nuclear energy and against "extermination by famine" in the Third World. Originally formed by a left-wing faction of the Italian Liberal Party (→Federation of Italian Liberals), the PR became concerned with civil rights from 1962. It sponsored the legalization of divorce in 1970 and subsequently campaigned against the use of the referendum to change the law. It successfully supported legislation on conscientious objection, the lowering of the age of majority to 18 years, more liberal laws on drug offences and family relations, and the partial legalization of abortion. The Radicals were the first Italian party to have a woman secretary (in 1977-78).

Having obtained four Chamber seats in 1976, the Radicals achieved a significant success in the 1979 elections, in which they won 18 in the Chamber (with 3.4% of the vote) and two in the Senate. The party initially announced that it would not take part in the 1983 general elections, but later campaigned for the casting of blank or invalid ballot papers. In the event 11 Radicals were returned to the Chamber by 2.2% of the voters. At its annual congresses in 1985 and 1986 the PR considered a proposal that the party should be disbanded, in protest against the "autocracy" of the larger parties. However, the congress in late 1986 decided against dissolution provided that paid-up membership rose to at least 15,000 by January 1987. Although this target was apparently not achieved, the party remained in being and in the July 1987 elections increased its Chamber representation to 13 seats and its share of the vote to 2.6%. Prominent among the new PR deputies was Ilona Staller, a pornographic film actress better known as Cicciolina. A further congress in Bologna in January 1988 decided that the party would not take part in any future Italian elections.

Meanwhile, in November 1979 the then PR secretary-general, Jean Fabre (a French national), had been sentenced by a Paris court to a month in prison for evading conscription. More serious was the 30–year prison sentence passed in 1984 on a PR deputy, Antonio Negri, following his conviction for complicity in terrorist acts, although he and seven others were acquitted in January 1986 of being "moral leaders" of extremist groups such as the Red Brigades.

Marco Pannella's return to the PR leadership in 1992 served to end the electoral non-participation policy and also shifted the party to the right. Contesting the March 1994 elections as part of the →Freedom Alliance, the PR presented a "Pannella" List but won no seats in its own right. Running as "Pannella Reformers" in the June 1994 European Parliament elections, it won two seats with a 2.1% vote share. In June 1995 referendum approval was given to three out of four proposals presented by the PR leader with the aim of restricting trade union powers. The PR presented the "Pannella List" in the June 1996 national elections, failing to win representation in the Chamber (with 1.9% of the proportional vote) but returning one member to the Senate. It contested the June 1999 European elections as the "Emma Bonino List", headed by the popular former European commissioner, which secured 8.5% of the national vote and seven of Italy's 87 seats. One of those elected was Pannella (then 70), who in November 1999 was given a four-month prison sentence for distributing marijuana to draw attention to what he called "the absurdity of the law".

The Radical/Bonino representatives in the European Parliament are among the "non-attached" contingent. The PR has spawned the Transnational Radical Party, with members in 43 countries and office in four.

Segni Pact
Patto Segni (PS)
Address. Via Belsiana 100, 00187 Rome
Telephone. (+39-6) 6994-1838
Fax. (+39-6) 6994-1840
Email. patto.segni@pattosegni.it
Website. http://www.pattosegni.it
Leadership. Mario Segni (leader)
The PS leader, Mario Segni, had been a leading anti-corruption campaigner within the then Christian Democratic Party (later the →Italian Popular Party, PPI), until breaking away in 1992 to advocate reform of the Italian political system. For the March 1994 general elections he launched the Pact for Italy, drawing in the PPI to assume the dominant role. Having received only 4.6% of the national vote on that occasion, the PS fell back to 3.3% in the June 1994 European Parliament elections, in which it won three seats.

Segni was an initial supporter of the centre-left →Olive Tree Movement formed in 1995, but withdrew before the April 1996 general elections, which his forces did not contest. He then launched a grass-roots movement for political reform (*Comitatidi Base per la Costituente*, COBAC), calling for the election of a constituent assembly to write a new constitution. In the June 1999 European elections the Segni Pact was allied with the right-wing →National Alliance, their joint list winning 10.3% of the vote and nine of Italy's 87 seats.

Tricolour Flame Social Movement
Movimiento Sociale Fiamma Tricolore (MSFT)
Address. Via Simone De Saint Bon 89, 00195 Rome
Telephone. (+39-6) 370-1756
Fax. (+39-6) 372-0376
Email. fiamma@msifiammatric.it
Website. http://www.msifiammatric.it
Leadership. Pino Rauti (national secretary); Manlio Sargenti (honorary president)
The MSFT originated in the opposition of a minority pro-fascism faction of the former Italian Social Movement–National Right (MSI-DN) to the party's decision in January 1995 to convert itself into the →National Alliance (AN). Having made little impact in the 1996 general elections, the splinter group adopted the "Tricolour Flame" logo and won one of Italy's 87 seats in the June 1999 European elections, receiving 1.6% of the vote.

United Christian Democrats
Cristiani Democratici Uniti (CDU)
Address. Piazza del Gesù 46, 00146 Rome
Telephone. (+39-6) 6775-3265
Fax. (+39-6) 6775-3267
Email. cdu@axnet.it
Website. http://www.axnet.it/cdu
Leadership. Rocco Buttiglione (president)
The CDU was launched in July 1995 by a right-wing minority group of the →Italian Popular Party (the former Christian Democratic Party) which favoured participation in the →Freedom Alliance (PL) rather than the centre-left →Olive Tree Movement. As part of the PL, the CDU contested the proportional section of the April 1996 parliamentary elections in close co-operation with the →Christian Democratic Centre, their joint list securing 5.8% of the vote. In the June 1999 European elections the CDU list obtained 2.1% of the vote and elected

two candidates, who joined the European People's Party/European Democrats group in the European Parliament. The CDU is also affiliated to Christian Democrat International and the European Democrat Union.

Regional Parties

Free Emilia Alliance (*Aleanza Lebbera Emegliena*, ALE), led by Sergio La Canna, Farouk Ramadana and Matteo Incerti, successor to Emilian Freedom/Emilia Nation (*Libertà Emiliana/Nazione Emilia*), itself dating from 1994 breakaway by an Emilian faction of the →Northern League opposed to the latter's participation in the →Freedom Alliance; a centre-left liberal formation, ALE seeks self-government for Emilia-Romagna within a European Union of historic regions; has some local council representation and contested 1999 Euro-elections jointly with →Sardinian Action Party; ALE is an observer member of the Democratic Party of the Peoples of Europe–European Free Alliance. *Address.* CP 112, 40124 Bologna; *Telephone.* (+39-51) 432-566; *Fax.* (+39-51) 841-530; *Email.* matteoincerti@hotmail.com; *Website.* http://utendi.tripod.it/libertaemiliana

Lombard Alpine League (*Lega Alpina Lombarda*, LAL), seeks to articulate local aspirations in Italy's border regions in the Alps, won one Senate seat in March 1994 and 0.3% of the vote in the June 1994 European Parliament elections.

North-Eastern Union (*Unione Nord-Est*), advocating autonomy for the historic lands of Lombardy and Venezia within a "Europe of regions". *Address.* Via Rella 1/4, 17100 Savona; *Telephone.* (+39-198) 485-032; *Fax.* (+39-198) 487-352; *Email.* alpazur@geocities.com; *Website.* http://www.geocities/capitolhill/3004

Romagna Autonomy Movement (*Movimento per l'Autonomia della Romagna*, MAR), led by Lorenzo Cappelli and Stefano Servadei, founded in 1991. *Address.* Via C. Battisti 149, 47023 Cesena; *Telephone.* (+39-547) 20876; *Email.* mar@cyberforli.it; *Website.* http://mbox.cyberforli.it/mar

Sardinian Action Party (*Partito Sardo d'Azione*, PsdA), favouring autonomy for the island of Sardinia, took four Chamber seats in 1996 elections as part of →Olive Tree Movement, strongly represented in Sardinian regional council; member of Democratic Party of the Peoples of Europe–European Free Alliance. *Address.* Via Roma 231, 09100 Cagliari; *Telephone.* (+39-70) 657-599; *Fax.* (+39-70) 657-779; *Email.* psdaz@sol.dada.it; *Website.* http://www.mediamundi.it/partidus

Sicilian Action Party (*Partito Siciliano d'Azione*, PsdA), led by Nino Italico Amico, seeking the full implementation of Sicily's regional statute. *Address.* Via Malta 10, 93100 Caltanissetta; *Telephone.* (+39-934) 592-470; *Fax.* (+39-934) 459-796; *Email.* euratolo@tin.it; *Website.* http://www.sicilianet.it/partitosiciliano

Two Sicilies (*Due Sicilie*), movement seeking autonomy for the area once covered by the Kingdom of the Two Sicilies and the creation of a "new Europe" based on historic regions. *Email.* info@duesicilie.org; *Website*, http:www.duesicilie.org

South Tyrol People's Party (*Südtiroler Volkspartei*, SVP), led by Siegfried Brugger (president) and Hartmann Gallmetzer (general secretary), Christian democratic party of the German-speaking population of Bolzano province (South Tyrol). From 1948 onwards it consistently held three seats in the Italian Chamber of Deputies, and from 1979 one directly elective seat in the European Parliament. The party's struggle for equal rights for the German-speaking and Ladin-speaking population of South Tyrol led to Austro-Italian agreements on the status of the province in 1969-71 and a new statute for the Trentino–Alto Adige region in 1971. The SVP became the strongest party in the South Tyrol *Landtag* and the second-strongest in the regional council of Trentino–Alto Adige, winning 22 seats out of 70 in November 1983. Normally securing representation in the Rome parliament thereafter, the SVP again won one seat in the June 1994 European Parliament elections. For the April 1996 general elections the SVP was part of the victorious centre-left →Olive Tree Movement. The SVP is affiliated to the European Democrat Union. *Address.* Brennerstrasse 7, 39100 Bozen/Bolzano; *Telephone* (+39–471) 304-000; *Fax.* (+39–471) 981473; *Email.* info@svpartei.org; *Website.* http://www.svpartei.org

Union for South Tyrol (*Union für Südtirol*, UfS), led Eva Klotz and Andreas Pöder, deriving from the radical Fatherland Union (*Heimatbund*), advocates a South Tyrol "free state" able to opt for union with Austria; has challenged the regional dominance of the →South Tyrol People's Party in seeking enhanced rights for the German-speaking majority; member of Democratic Party of the Peoples of Europe–European Free Alliance. *Address.* Garibaldistrasse 6, 39100 Bozen/Bolzano; *Telephone.* (+39-471) 975-696; *Fax.* (+39-471) 978-559; *Email.* union@unionfs.com; *Website.* http://www.unionfs.com

Southern League (*Lega Meridionale*, LM), a *Mezzogiorno* formation, won 0.7% in June 1994 European Parliament elections.

For Trieste (*Per Trieste*), led by Manlio Cecovini, founded in opposition to the 1975 Osimo Treaty settling the Trieste territorial dispute between Italy and the then Yugoslavia, autonomist group advocating special status for Trieste within the special statute region of Friuli–Venezia Giulia.

Valdostan Union (*Union Valdôtaine/Unione Valdostana*, UV), led by August Rollandin, pro-autonomy grouping founded in 1945 to further the interests of the French-speaking minority in the special statute region of Val d'Aosta, represented in the regional assembly from 1959, winning 17 of 35 seats (40.1% of vote) in May 1998 elections; usually represented in the national parliament, retaining one seat in 1999. *Address.* Ave des Maquisards, 11100 Aoste; *Telephone.* (+39-165) 235-181; *Fax.* (+39-165) 364-289; *Email.* peuple@aostanet.com; *Website.* http://www.unionvaldotaine.org

Venetian Republic League (*Liga Veneta Repubblica*), led by Ettore Beggiato, also known as Venetians for Europe (*Veneti d'Europa*), seeks the restoration of the historic Republic of Venice (which fell to Napoleon Bonaparte without resistance in 1797) within a region-based European Union; has six representatives in Veneto regional council. *Address.* c/o Consiglio Regionale Veneto, Venice; *Email.* venetideuropa@consiglio.regione.veneto.it; *Website.* http://www.consiglio.regione.veneto.it/gruppipolitici/lvr

Other Parties

Fascism and Liberty Movement (*Movimento Fascismo e Libertà*, MFL), led by Giorgio Pisano, far-right grouping founded in 1991. *Address.* Piazza Chiaradia 9, Milan; *Telephone.* (+39-2) 5681-4233; *Fax.* (+39-2) 5681-5402

Humanist Party (*Partito Umanista*, PU), led by Giorgio Schultze, civil rights formation founded in 1984, affiliated to Humanist International. *Address.* Via la Nebbia 9, 00168 Rome; *Telephone/Fax.* (+39-2) 481-4092; *Email.* info@partitoumanista.org; *Website.* http://www.partitoumanista.org

Italian Marxist-Leninist Party (*Partito Marxista-Leninista Italiano*, PMLI), led by Giovanni Scuderi, Maoist formation founded in 1977 from earlier grouping dating from 1969, advocates abstention in all elections. *Address.* Via Gioberti 101, 50121 Florence; *Telephone/Fax.* (+39-55) 234-7272; *Email.* pmli@dada.it; *Website.* http://www.dadacase.com/pmli

Italian Monarchist Movement (*Movimento Monarchico Italiano*, MMI), led by Francesco Garofalo Modica, seeks the restoration of the monarchy to cement national unity and territorial integrity; opposed to all regional separatism. *Address.* Via Roma 108, 97100 Ragusa; *Telephone/Fax.* (+39-932) 245-075; *Email.* movimento.monarchico@monarchici.org; *Website.* http://www.monarchici.org

Monarchist Alliance (*Alleanza Monarchica*, AM), umbrella organization for a number of pro-monarchy groupings. *Address.* Via Mercanti 30/C, 10121 Turin; *Telephone.* (+39-11) 540-720; *Email.* anmitaly@geocities.com; *Website.* http://www.geocities.com/anmitaly

National Front (*Fronte Nazionale*, FN), radical right-wing formation modelled on the ⇒National Front of France. *Email.* info@frontenazionale.org; *Website.* http://www.frontenazionale.org

Pensioners' Party (*Partito Pensionati*, PP), led by Carlo Fatuzzo, created to oppose any reduction in Italy's generous pensions provisions, especially for civil service employees; won 0.7% in June 1999 European elections, its one seat going to Fatuzzo, who joined the European People's Party/European Democrats group.

Luxembourg

Capital: Luxembourg-Ville   **Population:** 405,000

Fully independent since 1867, the Grand Duchy of Luxembourg is, under its 1868 constitution as amended, a constitutional hereditary monarchy in which the head of state (the Grand Duke) exercises executive power through a government headed by a Prime Minister and accountable to the legislature. The latter is the Chamber of Deputies (*Chambre des Députés*), whose 60 members are elected for a five-year term by citizens aged 18 and over (voting being compulsory). A system of proportional representation is based on four electoral districts, in which each voter has the same number of votes as there are seats and may cast them all for a single party list or may select candidates of more than one party. There is also an advisory Council of State, whose 21 members are appointed for life, seven directly by the Grand Duke and the other 14 by him on the recommendation of the Council itself or of the Chamber of Deputies. A founder member of what became the European Community, Luxembourg elects six members of the European Parliament.

Since political parties in Luxembourg do not have a legal personality, there is no law providing for state funding of parties. However, groups represented in the Chamber of Deputies receive subsidies from public funds according to their size for the purposes of financing their parliamentary activities. Parties also have the benefit of certain free postal services during election campaigns.

Elections to the Chamber on June 13, 1999, resulted as follows:				
	Seats		Percentage	
	1999	*(1994)*	*1999*	*(1994)*
Christian Social People's Party	19	(21)	30.1	(31.4)
Democratic Party	15	(12)	22.4	(18.9)
Luxembourg Socialist Workers' Party	13	(17)	22.3	(24.8)
Action Committee for Democracy and Justice ...	7	(5)	11.3	(n/a)
The Greens	5	(5)	9.1	(10.9)
The Left	1	(–)	3.3	(–)

Action Committee for Democracy and Justice
Aktiounskomitee fir Demokratie a Gerechtegkeet (ADR)
Comité d'Action pour la Démocratie et la Justice (CADJ)
Address. BP 365, L-4004 Esch sur Alzette
Telephone. (+352) 463-742
Fax. (+352) 463-745
Email. adr@chd.lu
Website. http://www.adr.lu
Leadership. Robert (Roby) Mehlen (president); Fernand Greisen (secretary-general)
The ADR was launched in March 1987 as the "Five-Sixths Action Committee" to campaign for universal entitlement to pensions worth five-sixths of final salary. Benefiting from the increasing number of pensioners on electoral rolls, the right-leaning formation won four Chamber seats in the 1989 elections and five in 1994. In the June 1999 elections it advanced to seven seats, with a vote share of 10.5%, but failed to gain representation in simultaneous elections for the European Parliament, in which it won 8.99% of the vote.

Christian Social People's Party
Chrëschtlech-Sozial Volkspartei (CSV)
Parti Chrétien Social (PCS)
Address. 4 rue de l'Eau, BP 826, L-2018 Luxembourg
Telephone. (+352) 225-731
Fax. (+352) 472-716
Email. csv@csv.lu
Website. http://www.csv.lu
Leadership. Erna Hennicot-Schoepges (president); Lucien Weiler (Chamber group chair); Claude Wiseler (secretary-general)
Committed to the promotion of "a policy of solidarity and social progress under the guidance of Christian and humanist principles" and the preservation of the constitutional status quo, the

CSV has long been Luxembourg's strongest party, drawing its support from the conservative middle class, Catholic workers and the farming community. The party is a keen proponent of European economic and monetary union via the European Union (EU), with the proviso that Luxembourg's special banking secrecy laws must be maintained against any EU encroachment. Founded as the *Parti de la Droite*, the CSV adopted its present name in December 1914. Since 1919 the party has taken part in coalition government with various other parties and has supplied Prime Ministers as follows: Émile Reuter (1919-25), Joseph Bech (1926-37), Pierre Dupong (1937-53), Joseph Bech (1953-58), Pierre Frieden (1958-59), Pierre Werner (1959-74 and 1979-84), Jacques Santer (1984-94) and Jean-Claude Juncker (from 1995).

The party formed a coalition with the →Luxembourg Socialist Workers' Party (LSAP) following the June 1984 elections, prior to which it had been in coalition with the →Democratic Party. Its share of the vote in June 1984 was 34.9%, while in simultaneous elections to the European Parliament it retained three of Luxembourg's six seats. In the June 1994 elections the CSV's Chamber representation fell back to 21 seats (with 31.4% of the vote), while in simultaneous European elections it lost one of its three seats. Having formed another coalition with the LSAP, CSV Prime Minister Jacques Santer was unexpectedly appointed president of the European Commission from January 1995, being succeeded as head of the Luxembourg government and CSV leader by Juncker, hitherto Finance Minister.

In the June 1999 elections the CSV slipped further to 19 seats (and 30.1% of the vote) but remained the biggest Chamber party, so that Juncker was able to form a new coalition government, this time with the DP. In simultaneous European elections, the CSV again won two of Luxembourg's six seats, with a vote share of 31.7%. One of the CSV seats was taken by Santer, who had resigned as European Commission president in March 1999, together with his fellow commissioners, after an inquiry set up by the European Parliament had found evidence of corruption and fraud in the Commission.

The CSV is a member of the Christian Democrat International and the International Democrat Union. Its two representatives in the European Parliament sit in the European People's Party/European Democrats group.

Democratic Party
Demokratesch Partei (DP)
Parti Démocratique (PD)
Address. 46 Grand'rue, L-1660 Luxembourg
Telephone. (+352) 221-021
Fax. (+352) 221-013
Email. dp@dp.lu
Website. http://www.dp.lu
Leadership. Lydie Polfer (president); Henri Grethen (secretary-general)
Dating from the origins of parliamentary democracy in Luxembourg in the 1840s, the DP became an established party in the 19th century, unsuccessfully resisting the introduction of universal suffrage and suffering a major defeat in 1919 in consequence. After a process of adaptation, the party became one of the three major national parties represented in the post-1945 Chamber, taking part in many coalition governments: in the national unity administration of 1945-47; in coalition with the →Christian Social People's Party (CSV) in 1947-51 (when the PD was known as the *Groupement Patriotique et Démocratique*) and in 1959-64 and 1968-74; with the →Luxembourg Socialist Workers' Party (LSAP) in 1974-79; and with the CSV again in 1979-84.

In the June 1984 elections the DP slipped to 14 seats (and from 21.3 to 18.7% of the vote) and went into opposition to a coalition of the CSV and LSAP. At the same time, it retained one of Luxembourg's six seats in the European Parliament. The DP remained in opposition after the 1989 elections, in which it fell back to 11 seats, and also after 1994 elections, in which it improved 12 seats, taking 18.9% of the vote. It retained its European Parliament seat on both occasions.

By Luxembourg standards the June 1999 elections brought a breakthrough for the DP, to the status of second-strongest Chamber party with 15 seats, from a 22.4% vote share. It accordingly returned to government after 15 years in opposition, taking half of the portfolios in a new coalition headed by the CSV, with Lydie Polfer of the DP becoming Deputy Prime Minister. In the simultaneous European elections, the DP retained its single seat with a 20.5% vote share.

The DP is affiliated to the Liberal International, its member of the European Parliament sitting in the European Liberal, Democratic and Reformist group.

The Greens
Déi Gréng
Les Verts
Address. BP 454, L-2014 Luxembourg
Telephone. (+352) 463-740
Fax. (+352) 463-741
Email. greng@greng.lu
Website. http://www.greng.lu
Leadership. Marthy Thull, Carlo De Toffoli (spokespersons); Abbès Jacoby, Félix Braz (joint secretaries)
The organized Greens date from June 1983, when a number of individuals and groups, including former Socialists, founded the Green Alternative (*Di Gráng Alternativ/Parti Vert Alternatif*, GA/PVA). The new party won two seats and 5.2% of the vote in the June 1984 national elections, while in European Parliament elections the same month it achieved 6.1% without winning representation. In accordance with the "rotation principle" established by the German Greens (⇒Alliance 90/The Greens Party), the party's two elected deputies were replaced by alternatives half way through the parliamentary term The GA/PVA again won two seats in the 1989 elections, before making a major advance in the 1994 contest, to five seats. Concurrent elections to the European Parliament were contested jointly with the less radical Green Ecologist Initiative List (*Gréng Lëscht Ekologesch Initiativ/Initiative Vert Écologiste*, GLEI/IVE), the alliance achieving 10.9% of the vote and one of the Grand Duchy's six seats.

A long-contemplated merger between the GA/PVA and most of the GLEI/IVE was eventually consummated in advance of the June 1999 elections, although the Greens' then representative in the European Parliament launched the separate →Green and Liberal Alliance. In the elections the Greens retained five seats, although their vote share slipped to 9.1%. In the simultaneous European elections the Greens took 10.7% of the vote and again won one seat, the party's representative joining the Greens/European Free Alliance group. The party is also affiliated to the European Federation of Green Parties.

The Left
Déi Lénk
La Gauche
Address. BP 1228, L-1012 Luxembourg
Telephone. (+352) 426-193
Fax. (+352) 426-193
Email. info@dei_lenk.lu
Website. http://www.dei-lenk.lu

Leadership. There is a 46-member national co-ordination committee which has no declared leaders

This party was launched prior to the June 1999 elections by leftist groups and individuals and with the backing of the →Communist Party of Luxembourg, which had failed to win parliamentary representation in 1994. The new formation achieved 3.3% of the vote and won one Chamber seat, while taking only 2.8% in the simultaneous European Parliament elections.

Luxembourg Socialist Workers' Party
Lëtzebuerger Sozialistesch Arbechterpartei (LSAP)
Parti Ouvrier Socialiste Luxembourgeois (POSL)

Address. 16 rue de Crécy, L-1364 Luxembourg

Telephone. (+352) 455-991

Fax. (+352) 456-575

Email. info@lsap.lu

Website. http://www.lsap.lu

Leadership. Jean Asselborn (president); Paul Bach (secretary-general)

Founded in 1902 as the Luxembourg Social Democratic Party, the party made little initial progress because of the qualified franchise. After a minority had broken away in 1921 to form the →Communist Party of Luxembourg, the party first took part in government from the end of 1937, after which the Socialist ministers laid the basis for modern social legislation. During the Nazi occupation the party was dismembered, but after World War II it re-emerged under its present name and took part in a government of national union until 1947, when it returned to opposition. Following renewed government participation in 1951-59 and 1964-68, the party was defeated in the 1968 legislative elections, after which it was temporarily weakened by the formation of the breakaway Social Democratic Party (which later became defunct).

A reconstructed LSAP made gains in the 1974 elections, after which it joined a coalition government with the →Democratic Party (DP). It returned to opposition after losing ground in the June 1979 elections, but returned to government (in coalition with the →Christian Social People's Party, CSV) after making a major advance in the June 1984 national elections, in which it rose from 14 to 21 seats and from 24.3 to 33.6% of the vote. In European Parliament elections the same month the LSAP retained two of the six Luxembourg seats. The LSAP won 18 seats (25.5% of the vote) in a smaller Chamber in 1989 and slipped to 17 (24.8%) in 1994, retaining two European Parliament seats on both occasions and continuing as the junior coalition partner.

The LSAP was the principal loser in the June 1999 elections, falling to third place in the Chamber behind the CSV and the DP, winning only 13 seats on a slightly reduced vote share of 24.3%. In simultaneous European elections, the LSAP retained two seats with 23.6% of the vote. The LSAP is a member party of the Socialist International, its two representatives in the European Parliament being members of the Party of European Socialists group.

Other Parties

Communist Party of Luxembourg (*Kommunistesch Partei vu Letzeburg/Parti Communiste Luxembourgeois*, KPL/PCL), led by Aloyse Bisdorff, formed as a result of a split in the →Luxembourg Socialist Workers' Party (LSAP) at the 1921 Differdange congress. It first obtained a Chamber seat in 1934 but the result was annulled by the Chamber majority (though a proposal to ban the party was defeated in a referendum in 1937). The party was represented in the Chamber from 1945, its number of seats fluctuating between three in 1954-64 and six in 1968-74, and declining to two in 1979. It took part in the national unity government of 1945-47, after which it went into opposition, but co-operated with the LSAP at local level. In the June 1979 elections the KPL obtained 5.8% of the vote (compared with 10.4% in 1974), while in 1984 its share fell to 5.0%. The KPL's representation fell to a single seat in the 1989 elections, while the death in 1990 of veteran leader René Urbany (son of the party's previous leader) was a further blow. Having in 1994 experienced its first post-war failure to win Chamber representation, the party did not contest the 1999 elections directly, instead backing the →Left list, which won one seat. *Address.* 16 rue Christophe Plantin, L-2339 Luxembourg; *Telephone.* (+352) 492-095; *Fax.* (+352) 496-920; *Email.* jlredondo@homemail.com; *Website.* http://ourworld.compuserve.com/homepages/kpllux

Green and Liberal Alliance (*Gréng a Liberal Allianz*, GaL), centrist ecology party led by Jup Weber, who had been elected to the European Parliament in 1994 but who opposed the subsequent merger which created the →Greens (and also backed Jacques Santer prior to his resignation as European Commission president in March 1999. The GaL failed to gain representation in the June 1999 elections, winning only 1.1% of the vote for the Chamber and 1.8 in the European contest. *Email.* info@gal.lu; *Website.* http://www.gal.lu

Taxpayers' Party (*De Steierzueler*), middle-class formation advocating lower state expenditure, won 0.4% of the vote in the 1999 national elections.

Third Age Party (*Partei vum 3. Alter*), aspiring to represent the interests of pensioners, more centrist than the right-inclined →Action Committee for Democracy and Justice, won 0.1% of the vote in the 1999 national elections.

Netherlands

Capital: Amsterdam
Seat of Government: The Hague   **Population:** 15,600,000

The Kingdom of the Netherlands (consisting of the Netherlands in Europe and the Caribbean territories of Aruba and the Netherlands Antilles) is a constitutional and hereditary monarchy whose two non-European parts enjoy full autonomy (see next section). Under its 1815 constitution as amended, the Netherlands in Europe has a multi-party parliamentary system of government employing proportional representation to reflect the country's religious and social diversity. Executive authority is exercised on behalf of the monarch by a Prime Minister and other ministers, who are accountable to the States-General (*Staten-Generaal*). The latter consists of (i) the 75–member First Chamber (*Eeerste Kamer*) elected by the members of the country's 12 provincial councils for a four-year term; and (ii) the 150–member Second Chamber (*Tweede Kamer*), also elected for a four-term but by universal suffrage of those aged 18 and over by a system of "pure" proportional representation with no minimum percentage threshold requirement. A founder member of what is now the European Union, the Netherlands elects 31 members of the European Parliament.

While political parties in the Netherlands have traditionally relied on members' subscriptions and donations, since 1972 state funding has been available for policy research and educational foundations attached to parties represented in the Second

Chamber. Parties also receive certain concessions to defray expenses during election campaigns, including a limited amount of free media access.

Elections to the Second Chamber on May 6, 1998, resulted as follows:	Seats		Percentage	
	1998	(1994)	1998	(1994)
Labour Party　… … … … … … … … … … …	45	(37)	29.0	(24.0)
People's Party for Freedom and Democracy　…	38	(31)	24.7	(19.9)
Christian Democratic Appeal　… … … … … …	29	(34)	18.4	(22.2)
Democrats 66　… … … … … … … … … … …	14	(24)	9.0	(15.5)
Green Left　… … … … … … … … … … … …	11	(5)	7.3	(3.5)
Socialist Party … … … … … … … … … … …	5	(2)	3.5	(1.3)
Reformational Political Federation　… … … …	3	(3)	2.0	(1.8)
Reformed Political Party… … … … … … … …	3	(2)	1.8	(1.7)
Reformed Political Association　… … … … …	2	(2)	1.3	(1.3)

Christian Democratic Appeal
Christen-Democratisch Appèl (CDA)
Address. Dr Kuyperstraat 5, 2514 BA The Hague
Telephone. (+31–70) 342–4888
Fax. (+31–70) 364–3417
Email. bureau@cda.nl
Website. http://www.cda.nl
Leadership. M.L.A. van Rij (chair); Jaap de Hoop Scheffer (parliamentary leader); Cees Bremmer (general secretary)
The right-of-centre Christian-inspired CDA was founded in April 1975 as a federation of (i) the Anti-Revolutionary Party *(Anti-Revolutionaire Partij,* ARP) founded in 1878 by Abraham Kuyper; (ii) the Christian Historic Union (*Christelijk Historische Unie*, CHU*)* established by ARP dissidents in 1908; and (iii) the Catholic People's Party *(Katholieke Volkspartij*, KVP*)* dating from 1928 and renamed in 1945. The new CDA formation represented an attempt by these confessional parties to reverse the steady decline in their vote since 1945. The CDA was constituted as a unified party in October 1980, after a five-year preparatory phase. It gained 49 seats in the Second Chamber in 1977, 47 in 1981 and 45 in 1982.

From 1977 the CDA headed several coalition governments: with the →People's Party for Freedom and Democracy (VVD) until September 1981, with the →Labour Party and the →Democrats 66 (D66) until May 1982, with D66 only until November 1982, and with the VVD after that under Ruud Lubbers. Having slipped from 48 to 45 Second Chamber seats in the September 1982 elections, the CDA subsequently experienced some internal dissension over the government's economic and defence policies. Nevertheless, in May 1986 it staged a sharp recovery, to 54 seats, and continued in government with the VVD.

The CDA retained 54 seats in the 1989 Second Chamber elections (with 35.3% of the vote), after which it formed a centre-left coalition with the PvdA, under the continued premiership of Lubbers, who became the Netherlands' longest-serving post-war Prime Minister. In advance of the May 1994 election, however, Rubbers announced his retirement from Dutch politics, with the result that the CDA campaigned under the new leadership of Elco Brinkman, amid difficult economic and social conditions. The outcome was that the party suffered its worst-ever electoral defeat, losing a third of its 1989 support and slumping to 22.2% and 34 seats, three less than the PvdA. The CDA recovered somewhat in the June 1994 European Parliament elections, to 30.8%, which yielded 10 of the 31 Dutch seats; nevertheless, Brinkman resigned as CDA leader in August 1994, as the party went into opposition to a PvdA-led coalition.

The CDA lost even more ground in the May 1998 general elections, winning only 18.4% of the vote for the Second Chamber and falling to 29 seats. It therefore remained in opposition to another PvdA-led coalition. In the June 1999 European elections the party slipped to 26.9% of the national vote, losing one of the 10 seats it held previously.

The CDA is a member of the Christian Democrat International. Its representatives in the European Parliament sit in the European People's Party/European Democrats group.

Democrats 66
Democraten 66 (D66)
Address. Noordwal 10, 2513 EA The Hague
Telephone. (+31–70) 356-6066
Fax. (+31–70) 364-1917
Email. lsd66@d66.nl
Website. http:/www.d66.nl
Leadership. Tom Kok (chair); Thom de Graaf (parliamentary leader); Jan-Diek Sprokkereef (general secretary)

D66 was founded in 1966 as a left-of-centre progressive non-socialist party with "a commitment to change inspired by a sense of responsibility for the future", favouring pragmatism over ideology and strongly libertarian in inclination. Long-term leader Hans van Mierlo recorded that both liberalism and socialism were sources of inspiration for D66, both movements having "taken responsibility for a part of the whole truth" but then having erected their part into "the whole truth", so that false antetheses had been engendered, such as liberty against equality, individual against community and the free market against state control.

D66 won seven seats in the Second Chamber in 1967 and 11 in 1971, but only six seats in 1973 and eight in 1977. In 1981 the party increased its electoral support significantly, gaining over 11% of the vote and 17 seats in the Second Chamber. A downward trend reappeared in 1982, when the party was reduced to six seats. However, in May 1986 it recovered to nine seats and 6.1 % of the votes. D66 has usually regarded the →Labour Party (PvdA) as its most obvious partner for participation in government. It took part in a coalition government with the PvdA (and three other parties) in 1973-77, but subsequently joined in coalition with the →Christian Democratic Appeal (CDA) in 1982. This last experience of government was seen as contributing to the party's setback in the September 1982 elections, in light of which Jan Terlouw resigned as leader and was eventually replaced by his predecessor, Hans van Mierlo.

D66's lower house representation rose from nine seats in 1986 to 12 in 1989, the latter tally being doubled to 24 in a major advance in May 1994 on a vote share of 15.5%, on the basis of which the party joined a coalition government with the PvdA and the →People's Party for Freedom and Democracy (VVD). In the June 1994 European Parliament elections D66 slipped back to 11.7%, taking four of the 31 Dutch seats. A key condition of D66 participation in the government was that the constitution should be amended to make provision for "corrective referendums" in which parliamentary legislation on some subjects could be overturned by the people. After VVD ministers had opposed the proposal and Labour had expressed doubts, the version given cabinet approval in October 1995 excluded more subjects from referendum correction than D66 had originally proposed.

The May 1998 general elections delivered a major setback to D66, which slumped to 9.0% of the vote and 14 seats. The party nevertheless joined a further coalition with the PvdA and VVD. The November 1998 D66 conference in Gouda adopted a proposal by a group of young activists called "Upheaval" (*Opschudding*) that the party should officially identify itself as a "social liberal" formation, a committee being set up to draft a new mission statement to that effect. In the June 1999 European elections the D66 vote was halved, to 5.8%, and its representation reduced from four to two seats.

With an official membership of 13,500, D66 is a member party of the Liberal International. Its representatives in the European Parliament sit in the European Liberal, Democratic and Reformist group.

Green Left
GroenLinks (GL)
Address. PO Box 8008, 3503 RA Utrecht
Telephone. (#31-30) 239-9900
Fax. (+31-30) 230-0342
Email. info@groenlinks.nl
Website. http://www.groenlinks.nl
Leadership. Mirjam de Rijk (chair); Paul Rosenmuller (parliamentary leader)
The GL was founded prior to the 1989 Second Chamber elections as an alliance of the Evangelical People's Party (*Evangelische Volkspartij*, EVP), the Radical Political Party (*Politieke Partij Radikalen*, PPR), the Pacifist Socialist Party (*Pacifistisch Socialistische Partij*, PSP) and the Communist Party of the Netherlands (*Communistische Partij van Nederland*, CPN). It became a unitary party in 1991, when each of its constituent groups voted to disband.

Of the component parties, the EVP had been formed in 1978 and had held one seat in the 1982-86 Second Chamber. The PPR had been founded in 1968 by a left-wing faction of the Catholic People's Party (later the mainstay of the →Christian Democratic Appeal), had won seven seats in 1972 and had participated in a centre-left coalition in 1973-77. The PSP had dated from 1957 and had won between one and four seats in subsequent elections. The CPN had been founded in 1918 by left-wing Social Democrats, had held 10 seats in post-1945 Second Chamber but had steadily declined to zero representation in 1986.

Having won six seats and 4.1% of the vote in its first general election contest in 1989, the GL slipped to five seats and 3.5% in May 1994. In the following month's European Parliament elections it recovered slightly to 3.7%, retaining one of the two seats it had won in 1989. It registered major gains in the May 1998 national elections, more than doubling its vote share to 7.3% and its Second Chamber representation to 11 seats. It continued its advance in the June 1999 European elections, winning 11.9% of the vote and four seats.

With an official membership of 14,000, the GL is affiliated to the European Federation of Green Parties. Its representatives in the European Parliament sit in the Greens/European Free Alliance group.

Labour Party
Partij van de Arbeid (PvdA)
Address. Herengracht 54, 1000 BH Amsterdam
Telephone. (+31–20) 551–2155
Fax. (+31–20) 551–2250
Email. pvda@pvda.nl
Website. http://www.pvda.nl
Leadership. Willem (Wim) Kok (leader); Marijke van Hees (chair); A.P.W. Melkert (parliamentary leader); Annie Brouwer-Korf (general secretary)

The PvdA was founded in 1946 as the post-war successor to the Social Democratic Workers' Party, founded in 1894 by P.J. Troelstra and other dissidents of the Social Democratic Union (created by F.D. Nieuwenhuis in 1881). From its establishment in 1946 as a broader-based party including many former Liberals, the PvdA engaged in the reconstruction of the Netherlands after the German occupation. Its leader, Willem Drees, was Prime Minister of a Labour-Catholic coalition government from 1948 to 1958, whereafter the PvdA was in opposition for 15 years—except briefly in 1965–66, when it took part in a coalition government with the Catholic People's Party (KVP) and the Anti-Revolutionary Party (ARP). The PvdA was weakened in 1970 by a right-wing breakaway by followers of Dr Willem Drees (son of the former Prime Minister), who formed the Democratic Socialists 1970 (DS-70) party. Although DS-70 gained eight seats in the 1971 elections, thereafter its representation declined and the party was dissolved in January 1983.

In 1971 and 1972 the PvdA contested elections on a joint programme with the →Democrats 66 (D66) and the Radical Political Party, and in 1973 it formed a coalition government with these parties and also the KVP and the ARP, with the then PvdA leader, Joop den Uyl, becoming Prime Minister. This was the first Dutch government with a left-wing majority of ministers. However, after the 1977 elections, in which the PvdA increased its seats in the Second Chamber from 43 to 53, the party went into opposition to a centre-right government led by the →Christian Democratic Appeal (CDA). From September 1981 to May 1982 the party took part in a coalition government with the CDA and D66. The PvdA was then in opposition, despite achieving a significant advance in the May 1986 Second Chamber elections, from 47 to 52 seats. Following those elections, Wim Kok (hitherto leader of the Netherlands Trade Union Confederation) became PvdA leader in succession to den Uyl (who died in December 1987).

Although it fell back to 49 seats on a 31.9% vote share, the PvdA returned to government after the 1989 elections, as junior coalition partner to the CDA. In August 1991 Marjanne Sint resigned as PvdA chair because of the party's acceptance of cuts in the state social security system, introduced by the CDA–PvdA coalition. In the May 1994 lower house elections the PvdA slipped again, to 24.0% and 37 seats, but overtook the CDA as the largest party and therefore became the senior partner in a new three-party coalition, this time with the →People's Party for Freedom and Democracy (PVV) and D66. In the June 1994 elections to the European Parliament, support for Labour declined further, to 22.9%, giving it eight of the Netherlands' 31 seats.

Helped by the popularity of Prime Minister Kok, the PvdA staged a major recovery in the May 1998 general elections, winning 45 seats on a 29.0% vote share. Kok accordingly formed a further coalition with the PVVand D66. In the June 1999 European elections, however, the PvdA fell back to 20.1% of the vote, its representation falling from eight to six seats.

With an official membership of 60,000, the PvdA is a member party of the Socialist International. Its European Parliament representatives sit in the Party of European Socialists group.

People's Party for Freedom and Democracy
Volkspartij voor Vrijheid en Democratie (VVD)
Address. Koninginnegracht 57, PO Box 30836, 2500 GL The Hague
Telephone. (+31–70) 361–3061
Fax. (+31–70) 360–8276
Email. alg.sec@vvd.nl
Website. http://www.vvd.nl

Leadership. Frits Bolkestein (leader); Hans F. Dijkstal (parliamentary leader); Willem Hoekzema (chair); Jan Korff (general secretary)

Founded in 1948, the VVD is descended from the group of Liberals led by J.R. Thorbecke who inspired the introduction of constitutional rule in 1848. Organized as the Liberal Union from 1885, the Dutch Liberals (like their counterparts elsewhere in Europe) lost influence as the move to universal suffrage produced increasing electoral competition on the left, with the result that after World War II many Liberals joined the new →Labour Party. However, other Liberal elements under the leadership of P.J. Oud founded the VVD, which remained in opposition to Labour-Catholic coalitions until 1959, when an electoral advance enabled the party to join a coalition with the Catholics.

After languishing electorally in the 1960s, the VVD made steady advances in the 1970s under the leadership of Hans Wiegel, winning 28 seats in the Second Chamber in 1977 and joining a coalition headed by the new →Christian Democratic Appeal (CDA). Reduced to 26 seats in 1981, the VVD went into opposition, but under the new leadership of Ed Nijpels made a big advance to 36 seats the following year and joined a further coalition with the CDA. This was continued after the 1986 elections, although the VVD slipped back to 27 seats and from 23.1 to 17.4% of the vote.

The VVD lost ground in both the 1986 and the 1989 elections, on the latter occasion going into opposition for the first time since 1982. In the May 1994 contest, however, the VVD made a major advance by Dutch standards, from 14.6 to 19.9% of the vote, while the June European Parliament elections gave it a 17.9% tally and six of the 31 Dutch seats. In August 1994 the VVD returned to government, joining a coalition with the PvdA and →Democrats 66 (D66). In provincial elections in March 1995 the VVD struck a popular chord with its tough policy prescriptions on immigration and asylum seekers, overtaking the CDA as the strongest party at provincial level and therefore increasing its representation in the First Chamber to 23 seats. Within the national government, VVD ministers urged cuts in government spending to reduce the deficit to the Maastricht criterion for participation in a single European currency, thereby coming into conflict with the PvdA, which preferred to raise taxes.

In the May 1994 national elections the VVD overtook the CDA as the second-strongest party, winning 24.7% of the vote and 38 Second Chamber seats and subsequently joining a further coalition with the PvdA and D66. In the June 1999 European elections, moreover, it advanced to 19.7% and retained six seats.

The VVD is a member of the Liberal International. Its European Parliament representatives sit in the European Liberal, Democratic and Reformist group.

Reformational Political Federation
Reformatorische Politieke Federatie (RPF)

Address. PO Box 302, 8070 AH Nunspeet

Telephone. (+31-341) 256744

Fax. (+31-341) 260348

Email. rpf@rpf.nl

Website. http://www.rpf.nl

Leadership. A. van den Berg (chair); Leen C. van Dijke (parliamentary leader); A.L. Langius (secretary)

Founded in March 1975, the RPF seeks a reformation of political and social life in accordance with the Bible and Calvinistic tradition and creed. The party was formed by the National Evangelical Association, dissenters from the AntiRevolutionary Party (ARP) and the Associations of Reformed (Calvinist) Voters. It won two seats in the Second Chamber in 1981 and again in 1982, when it also obtained 10 seats in provincial elections and about 100 in municipal elections. In 1986 it was reduced to one seat, which it retained in 1989, but trebled this tally in May 1994 on a 1.8% vote share. For the following month's European Parliament elections the RPF presented a joint list with the →Reformed Political Association (GPV) and the →Reformed Political Party (SGP), which took a 7.8% vote share and elected two members (neither from the RPF).

The RPF improved to 2.0% in the May 1998 national elections, retaining three Second Chamber seats. In the June 1999 European Parliament elections it again presented a joint list with the GPV and SGP, which improved to 8.7% of the vote and three seats, one of which went to the RPF. All three representatives joined the Europe of Democracies and Diversities group.

Reformed Political Association
Gereformeerd Politiek Verbond (GPV)
Address. Berkweg 46, PO Box 439, 3800 AK Amersfoort
Telephone. (+31-33) 461-3546
Fax. (+31-33) 461-0132
Email. bureau@gpv.nl
Website. http://www.gpv.nl
Leadership. S.J.C. Cnossen (chair); Gert J. Schutte (parliamentary leader)
On its creation in April 1948, the founders of the GPV claimed to represent the continuation of the ideas of the Dutch national Calvinists of the 16th and 17th centuries, but on the basis of recognition of the separation of church and state and of spiritual and fundamental freedoms. Before World War II the Anti-Revolutionary Party had claimed to represent these ideas, but the founders of the GPV objected to the "partly liberal and partly socialistic" tendencies which they believed to be developing in that party.

Having won one Second Chamber seat in 1986, the GPV recovered to two seats in 1989 and retained them in the 1994 and 1998 elections, with 1.3% of the vote in each contest. In the 1994 and 1999 European Parliament elections the GPV presented a joint list with the →Reformational Political Federation (RPF) and the →Reformed Political Party (SGV), which took 7.8% of the vote and two seats in 1994, rising to 8.7% and three seats in 1999, one for each constituent party. All three representatives joined the Europe of Democracies and Diversities group. The GPV has an official membership of 13,912.

Reformed Political Party
Staatkundig Gereformeerde Partij (SGP)
Address. Laan van Meerdervoort 165, 2517 AZ The Hague
Telephone. (+31-70) 345-6226
Fax. (+31-70) 365-5959
Email. partijbureau@sgp.nl
Leadership. Bastiaan Johannis (B.J.) van der Vlies (leader); Rev. D.J. Budding (chair); A. de Boer (secretary)
Founded in 1918, the right-wing Calvinist SGP bases its political and social outlook on its interpretation of the Bible. It advocates strong law enforcement, including the use of the death penalty, and is opposed to supranational government on the grounds that it would expose the Netherlands to corrupting influences. It has consistently attracted somewhat under 2% of the vote, which gave it three Second Chamber seats through the 1980s, slipping to two in May 1994 on a vote share of 1.7%. For the following month's European Parliament elections the SGP presented a joint list with the →Reformed Political Association (GPV) and the →Reformational Political Federation (RPF), which took a 7.8% vote share and two seats (one for the SGP and one for the GPV).

The SGP improved to 1.8% of the vote in the May 1998 national elections, sufficient to increase its Second Chamber representation to three seats. In the June 1999 European Parliament elections it again presented a joint list with the GPV and RPF, which improved to 8.7% of the vote and three seats, one of which went to the SGP. All three representatives joined the Europe of Democracies and Diversities group. The SGP has an official membership of 24,000.

Socialist Party
Socialistische Partij (SP)
Address. Vijverhofstraat 65, 3032 SC Rotterdam
Telephone. (+31-10) 243-5555
Fax. (+31-10) 243-5566
Email. sp@sp.nl
Website. http://www.sp.nl
Leadership. Jan Marijnissen (chair and parliamentary leader); Tiny Kox (general secretary)
The left-wing SP derives from a Maxist-Leninist party founded in 1971 and has latterly obtained electoral support from former adherents of the Communist Party of the Netherlands, which disbanded in 1991 to become part of the →Green Left. The SP increased its vote share from 0.4% in 1989 to 1.3% in the May 1994 Second Chamber elections, returning two deputies.

Contending in the May 1998 elections that the incumbent coalition led by the →Labour Party had done little to alleviate poverty and had allowed wealth differentials to grow, the SP almost trebled its vote, to 3.5%, and won five Second Chamber seats. It registered a further advance in the June 1999 European Parliament elections, taking 5.0% of the vote and winning its first seat. Its representative joined the European United Left/Nordic Green Left group. The party has an official membership of 26,000.

Other Parties

55+ Union (*Unie 55+*), led by Bert Leerks, one of several Dutch pensioners' parties, being more inclined to radicalism than the →General Union of the Elderly (AOV); obtained 0.9% of the vote and one Second Chamber seat in the May 1994 elections, but a joint list with the AOV in May 1998 won only 0.5% and no seats. *Address*. PO Box 111, 7450 AC Holten; *Telephone*. (+31-548) 362422; *Fax*. (+31-548) 363422

Centre Democrats (*Centrumdemocraten*, CD), led by Hans Janmaat, radical right-wing party created in 1986 by the majority "moderate" wing of the Centre Party (CP). Established on an anti-immigration platform mainly by former members of the ultra-nationalist Dutch People's Union (NVU), the CP had succeeded in attracting significant support among white working-class voters in inner city areas with heavy immigrant concentrations. In the 1982 Second Chamber elections it had obtained over 68,000 votes (0.8%) and one seat, while in the 1984 local elections it won 10% of the vote in Rotterdam and eight seats on the city council. Violent incidents occurred at several CP meetings prior to the May 1986 Second Chamber elections, in which the party failed to secure representation. Eight days before polling the CP had been declared bankrupt by a Dutch court after failing to pay a fine of 50,000 guilders imposed for forgery of election nominations. Re-emerging as the CD, the party regained one Second Chamber seat in 1989 and advanced to three seats in May 1994, winning 2.5% of the vote. It slumped to 0.6% in May 1998 and failed to win a seat. *Address*. PO Box 84, 2501 CB The Hague; *Telephone*. (+31-70) 346-9264;

Dutch Middle Class Party (*Nederlandse Middenstands Partij*, NMP), led by Martin Dessing, conservative formation founded in 1970, won 0.3% in 1998 lower house elections. *Address.* PO Box 285, 1250 AG Laren; *Email.* info@nmp.nl; *Website.* http://www.nmp.nl

European Party (*Europese Partij*, EP), led by Kees Nieuwenkamp and Roel Nieuwenkamp, founded in 1998 to advocate "global subsidiarity" and "democratic European governance" for its citizens and to oppose the "wasteful bureaucracy" of the present European Union. *Address.* PO Box 136, 2501 CC The Hague; *Telephone.* (+31-10) 213-6218; *Email.* info@europeanparty.org; *Website.* http://www.europeanparty.org

Frisian National Party (*Fryske Nasjonale Partij*, FNP), led by Rindert Straatsma, founded in 1962 to seek autonomy for northern province of Friesland within a federal Europe; affiliated to Democratic Party of the Peoples of Europe–European Free Alliance. *Address.* Obrechtstrjitte 32, 8916 EN Ljouwert; *Telephone.* (+31-58) 213-1422; *Fax.* (+31-58) 213-1420; *Email.* fnp@eboa.com; *Website.* http://www.eboa.com/fnp

General Union of the Elderly (*Algemeen Ouderen Verbond*, AOV), led by Martin Batenburg and W.J. Verkerk, pledged to opposing cuts in the state pension and other benefits for the elderly; won 3.6% of the vote in the May 1994 Second Chamber elections, giving it six seats, but then damaged by internal dispute, which resulted in three deputies breaking away or being expelled from the group; a joint list with →55+ Union in May 1998 won only 0.5% and no seats. *Address.* Louis Kookenweg 12, 5624 KW Eindhoven; *Telephone.* (+31-40) 433-961; *Fax.* (+31-40) 124765

The Greens (*De Groenen*), led by Ron van Wonderen, founded in 1984 as a conservative church-oriented environmentalist party, opposed to leftist radicalism of →Green Left; won one upper house seat in March 1995 but failed to gain lower house representation in 1994 or 1998, its vote share in the latter contest being 0.2%; member of European Federation of Green Parties. *Address.* PO Box 6192, 2001 HD Haarlem; *Telephone.* (+31-23) 542-7370; *Fax.* (+31-23) 514-4176; *Email.* info@degroenen.nl; *Website.* http://www.degroenen.nl

Natural Law Party (*Natuurwetpartij*, NWP), Netherlands branch of wordwide network of such parties. *Address.* Rivierenlaan 164, 8226 LH Lelystad; *Telephone.* (+31-320) 258-181; *Fax.* (+31-320) 258-858; *Email.* info@natuurwetpartij.nl; *Website.* http://www.natuurwetpartij.nl

Netherlands Mobile (*Nederland Mobiel*), led by J.H.van Laar and Alphen aan de Rijn, conservative pro-motorist party founded in 1997, won 0.5% in 1998 lower house elections. *Address.* PO Box 65712, 2506 EA The Hague; *Website.* http://www.nederland-mobiel.nl

New Dutch Communist Party (*Nieuwe Communistische Partij Nederland*, NCPN), leftist formation. *Address.* Donker Curtiusstraat 7/325, 1051 JL Amsterdam; *Telephone.* (+31-20) 682-5019; *Fax.* (+31-20) 682-8276; *Email.* 106057.1021@compuserve.com; *Website.* http://www.ncpn.nl

Political Party of the Elderly (*Politieke Partij voor Ouderen*, PPO), led by K. Blokker, contested 1998 elections as Seniors 2000 (*Senioren 2000*), winning only 0.4% of vote.

Socialist Workers' Party (*Socialistiese Arbeiderspartij*, SAP), led by H.E.W. Lindelauff, Trotskyist formation founded in 1974. *Address.* Sint Jacobstraat 10-20, 1012 NC Amsterdam; *Telephone.* (+31-20) 625-9272; *Fax.* (+31-20) 620-3774

Portugal

Capital: Lisbon　　　　　　　　　　　　　　　**Population:** 10,00,000

Under Portugal's 1976 constitution as amended, legislative authority is vested in the unicameral Assembly of the Republic (*Assembléia da República*), currently consisting of 230 members elected for a four-year term (subject to dissolution) by universal adult suffrage of those aged 18 and over according to a system of proportional representation in multi-member constituencies. The head of state is the President, who is popularly elected for a five-year term (once renewable) by absolute majority, a failure to achieve which in a first round of voting requires the two leading candidates to contest a second round. The President appoints the Prime Minister, who selects his or her ministerial team, all subject to approval by the Assembly. There is also a Supreme Council of National Defence, a 13–member Constitutional Tribunal and an advisory Council of State chaired by the President. Portugal joined what became the European Union on Jan. 1, 1986, and elects 25 members of the European Parliament.

Portuguese political parties and parliamentary groups are eligible for annual subsidies from public funds, on the following basis: (i) a sum equivalent to 1/225th of the minimum national salary is payable on each vote obtained at the most recent Assembly elections; (ii) a sum equivalent to four times the minimum salary, plus one-third of the minimum national salary multiplied by the number of deputies in an Assembly group, is payable to defray deputies' secretarial costs.

Elections to the Assembly on Oct. 10, 1999, resulted as follows:		
	Seats	Percentage
	1999 (1995)	*1999 (1995)*
Socialist Party (PS)	115　(112)	44.1 (43.9)
Social Democratic Party (PSD)	81　(88)	32.3 (34.0)
United Democratic Coalition (CDU)	17　(15)	9.0 (8.6)
Popular Party (PP)	15　(15)	8.3 (9.1)
Left Bloc (BE)	2　(–)	2.4　(–)

A presidential election on Jan. 14, 1996, resulted in Jorge Sampaio (PS) winning a 53.8% first-round victory over Aníbal Cavaco Silva (PSD).

Ecologist Party The Greens
Partido Ecologista Os Verdes (PEV)
Address. Calçada Salvador Correia de Sá 4–0° Dt, 1200 Lisbon
Telephone. (+351-1) 343-2763
Fax. (+351-1) 343-2764
Email. osverdes@mail.telepac.pt
Leadership. Maria Santos and Isabel Castro (spokespersons)

The left-leaning PEV joined the Communist-dominated →United Democratic Coalition (CDU) prior to the 1987 Assembly elections, obtaining representation in that and subsequent contests. In the October 1999 elections the PEV took two of the 17 Assembly seats won by the CDU. The party is affiliated to the European Federation of Green Parties.

Left Bloc
Bloco do Esquerda (BE)
Address. Rua de S. Bento 698-1°, 1250-223 Lisbon
Telephone. (+351-1) 388-5034
Fax. (+351-1) 388-5035
Email. udp@esoterica.pt
Website. http://www.bloco-de-esquerda.pt
Leadership. Luís Fazenda (president)
The BE was formed for the 1999 elections by three far-left parties, namely the Marxist-Leninist Popular Democratic Union (*União Democrática Popular*, UDP), the Trotskyist Revolutionary Socialist Party (*Partido Socialista Revolucionario*, PSR) and Politics XXI (*Politica XXI*). In the June 1999 European Parliament elections the alliance took 1.8% of the vote and no seats. Standing on a platform of opposition to the "anti-working class" policies of the incumbent →Socialist Party government, the alliance won 2.4% of the vote and two Assembly seats in the October 1999 national elections.

Popular Party
Partido Popular (PP)
Address. Largo Adelino Amaro da Costa 5, 1196 Lisbon
Telephone. (+351–1) 886–9730
Fax. (+351–1) 886–0454
Email. cds-pp@esoterica.pt
Website. http://www.partido-popular.pt
Leadership. Paulo Portas (president)
Advocating a social market economy, the conservative Christian democratic PP was established in 1974 as the Democratic Social Centre (*Centro Democrático Social*, CDS). It quickly began using the suffix "Popular Party" to distinguish itself from the main →Social Democratic Party (PSD), being formally known as the CDS-PP until opting for the shorter PP title in the 1990s.

The CDS was founded on the basis of an earlier Manifesto Association, *(Associação Programa)* by Prof. Diogo Freitas do Amaral, who had been a member of the Council of State under the quasi-fascist Salazarist regime overthrown in 1974. The CDS was attacked by left-wing groups in 1974-75. In the April 1975 constituent elections, in which it allied with the Christian Democrats, it won 16 of the 250 seats. In 1976 it became the largest party in the new Assembly, with 15.9% of the vote and 42 of the 263 seats. The CDS joined a government headed by the →Socialist Party (PS) in January-July 1978, but fought the 1979 and 1980 elections as part of the victorious Democratic Alliance, led by the PSD; Freitas do Amaral became Deputy Prime Minister in the ensuing coalition government.

The coalition ended in April 1983, and the CDS, standing alone, won only 12.4% and 30 seats in that month's Assembly elections; it then elected a new leader, Dr Francisco Antonio Lucas Pires. In 1985 the CDS declined further, to 9.8% and 22 seats. The leadership of the CDS passed in 1985 to a former Salazarist minister, Prof. Adriano Alves Moreira. Freitas do Amaral, endorsed by the CDS and PSD, narrowly lost the second round of the 1986 presidential elections to Mário Soares of the PS. The CDS continued to decline, securing only

4.4% and four seats in the 1987 Assembly elections, and Freitas do Amaral was re-elected leader at a congress in January 1988.

What was now known as the PP won only five Assembly seats in the 1991 elections (again with a 4.4% vote share), after which Freitas do Amaral finally resigned the party leadership and was succeeded by Manuel Monteiro. In the European Parliament elections of June 1994, the party regained support, winning three of Portugal's 25 seats on a 12.5% vote share. This European success did not moderate the party's deep reservations about Portuguese membership of the European Union, which struck something of a chord with voters in the October 1995 Assembly elections, when the PP advanced to 9.1% of the vote and 15 seats.

Internal divisions in the PP from September 1996 eventually resulted in Monteiro being succeeded as leader by Paulo Portas. After an attempted alliance with the PSD had collapsed in March 1999, the PP contested the June 1999 European elections on its own, slipping to 8.2% of the vote and two seats. The party also lost ground in the October 1999 Assembly elections, winning a vote share of 8.3% and 15 seats.

The PP is an affiliate of the International Democrat Union. Its two European Parliament members sit in the Europe of Nations group.

Portuguese Communist Party
Partido Comunista Português (PCP)
Address. Rua Soeiro Pereira Gomes 3, 1600 Lisbon
Telephone. (+351–1) 781-3800
Fax. (+351–1) 796–9126
Email. pcp.dep@mail.telepac.pt
Website. http://www.pcp.pt
Leadership. Carlos Carvalhas (secretary-general); Octávio Teixeira (parliamentary leader)
The PCP was founded in March 1921 by the pro-Bolshevik wing of the →Socialist Party (PS) and was banned from May 1926 until April 1974. Its leader from the 1940s was Alvaro Barreirinhas Cunhal, a charismatic Stalinist who was imprisoned throughout the 1950s and was then in exile until 1974. The PCP took part in interim governments between May 1974 and July 1976. In April 1975 it won 30 seats (out of 250) in constituent elections, with 12.5% of the vote; in April 1976 it won 40 seats in the Assembly, with 14.6%, but in June its presidential candidate took only 7.6%. From 1979 to 1986 the PCP was in an electoral front—the Popular Unity Alliance (APU)—with the small Portuguese Democratic Movement (MDP/CDE). The PCP itself won 44 seats in the Assembly in 1979, 39 in 1980 and 44 in 1983. In 1985 the APU won 15.4% and 38 seats, almost all for the PCP. In the 1986 presidential elections the PCP at first backed Dr Francisco Salgado Zenha, but in the second round it reluctantly endorsed Mário Soares of the PS.

In the 1987 elections the PCP formed a new front, the →United Democratic Coalition (CDU), along with a minority section of the MDP known as the Democratic Intervention (ID), some independent left-wingers and the →Ecologist Party The Greens (PEV). The CDU secured 31 seats with 12.1% of the vote, but the PCP-led parliamentary bloc rose from fourth to third place as a result of the eclipse of the Democratic Renewal Party (PRD); it also retained its three seats in Portugal's first direct elections to the European Parliament held simultaneously. In early 1988 the PCP experienced internal divisions as it prepared for a congress, some members calling for "democratization" and the Cunhal leadership insisting on maintaining rigid pro-Soviet orthodoxy.

In the event, the 12th PCP congress in December 1988 showed some awareness of developments in the Soviet Union by making a formal commitment to freedom of the press and multi-party politics, the CDU) being rewarded in the June 1989 European Parliament elections with four seats and 14.4% of the vote. Yet even as communism was collapsing all over Eastern Europe in 1989–90, the PCP majority maintained a hardline view of events, showing no sympathy with the popular aspirations to multi-party democracy. The electoral consequence was that the PCP-dominated CDU fell back to 17 seats (8.8% of the vote) in the 1991 elections and to 15 seats (8.6%) in October 1995. In between, the CDU slipped to three seats and an 11.2% vote share in the June 1994 European elections.

The June 1999 European elections brought a further reverse for the CDU, to 10.3% of the vote and two seats. In the October 1999 Assembly elections, however, the CDU reversed its long decline, winning 9.0% of the vote and 17 seats, of which the PCP took 15 and the PEV two. The PCP has an official membership of around 160,000.

Social Democratic Party
Partido Social Democrata (PSD)
Address. Rua de São Caetano 9, 1296 Lisbon
Telephone. (+351–1) 395–2140
Fax. (+351–1) 397–6967
Email. psd@mail.telepac.pt
Website. http://www.psd.pt
Leadership. José Manuel Durão Barroso (leader); Artur Torres Pereira (secretary-general)
Centre-right rather than social democratic in orientation, the PSD was founded in May 1974 as the Popular Democratic Party (*Partido Popular Democrático*, PPD) and adopted the PSD label in 1976, when the Portuguese political scene created by the 1974 revolution was heavily tilted to the left. The party took part in five of the first six provisional governments established after the April 1974 revolution. It was in opposition in June-September 1975 and in 1976-79; it supported the election of Gen. Antonio Ramalho Eanes as President in 1976. It was the second largest party in the April 1975 constituent elections, with 27% of the vote, and in the April 1976 legislative elections, in which it took 24%.

Having supported the non-party government of November 1978-June 1979, the PSD fought the 1979 elections along with the Democratic Social Centre (CDS, later the →Popular Party, PP) as the Democratic Alliance, winning 79 seats for itself. The then PSD leader (and party co-founder), Dr Francisco Sa Carneiro, became Prime Minister and continued in office after fresh elections in October 1980, in which PSD representation increased to 82 seats. Sa Carneiro died in December 1980 at the age of 46 and was succeeded by Dr Francisco Pinto Balsemão, also a co-founder of the PSD, who brought the Popular Monarchist Party (PPM) into the coalition in September 1981. The PSD held 75 seats in the April 1983 elections, which it fought alone, and in June it joined the →Socialist Party (PS) in a new coalition government, with a new PSD leader, former Prime Minister (1978-79) Carlos Mota Pinto, as Deputy Prime Minister.

In October 1985 the PSD increased its vote share to 29.9% and won 88 seats—the largest bloc—in the Assembly, allowing it to form a minority government under Aníbal Cavaco Silva, who had been elected party leader in May 1985. He subsequently strengthened his control over the party and after the presidential elections of 1986, in which the PSD endorsed the losing CDS candidate, he opposed all suggestions of alliance with other parties. On April 3, 1987, his government lost a vote of confidence concerning the integration of Portugal into what became the European Union. In early elections in July 1987 the PSD greatly increased its vote, to 50.2% and 148 seats, giving it an absolute majority (the first in the Assembly since 1974). In simultaneous elections to the European Parliament, the nine PSD members appointed in January 1986 were replaced by 10 popularly-elected PSD members (from the total of 24 Portuguese representatives). In August 1987 Cavaco Silva was reappointed Prime Minister of an almost wholly PSD government.

The PSD retained governmental office in the October 1991 parliamentary elections, although with a slightly reduced majority of 135 of 230 seats on a 50.4% vote share. In the June 1994 European Parliament elections the party fell to 34.4%, taking only nine of the 25 Portuguese seats. This result and the PSD's negative opinion poll ratings impelled Cavaco Silva to resign from the party leadership in January 1995, although he remained Prime Minister until the October elections to prepare for a presidential challenge. Under the new leadership of Joaquim Fernando Nogueira, the PSD lost the October contest, although its retention of 88 seats on a 34% vote share was a better performance than many had predicted. Cavaco Silva's presidential ambitions were also thwarted by the swing of the political pendulum to the left. Standing as the PSD candidate in January 1996, he was defeated by the Socialist candidate in the first voting round, winning only 46.2% of the vote. The PSD's somewhat drastic response to these twin setbacks was to elect a new leader, namely Marcelo Rebelo de Sousa, a popular media pundit who had never held ministerial office.

Rebelo de Sousa lasted as PSD leader until March 1999, when the acrimonious collapse of plans for an alliance with the PP precipitated his resignation. He was succeeded by José Manuel Durão Barroso, under whom the PSD retained nine European Parliament seats in June 1999 (on a reduced vote share of 31.1%). In the October 1999 national elections the PSD slipped to 81 Assembly seats on a vote share of 32.3%.

The PSD is affiliated to the International Democrat Union and the European Democrat Union. Its nine European Parliament representatives belong to the European People's Party/European Democrats group.

Socialist Party
Partido Socialista (PS)
Address. Largo do Rato 2, 1200 Lisbon
Telephone. (+351–1) 382-2021
Fax. (+351–1) 382-2023
Email. info@ps.pt
Website. http://www.ps.pt
Leadership. António Guterres (general secretary); António Almeida Santos (president); Francisco Assis (parliamentary group chair)
Founded in 1875, the early Socialist Party was a member of the Second International and played a minor role in the first period of democratic government in Portugal (1910-26). Forced underground during the period of the fascistic "New State" (1928-74), Socialists were active in various democratic movements. In 1964 Dr Mario Alberto Nobre Lopes Soares and others formed Portuguese Socialist Action *(Accão Socialista Portuguesa, ASP)*, which led to the reconstruction of the Socialist Party (PS) among exiles in West Germany in 1973.

Soares was repeatedly arrested and banished from Portugal, but the April 1974 revolution permitted his return and the PS took part in the coalition government formed in May 1974. In April 1975 the party won 116 of the 250 seats in a Constituent Assembly which drew up a constitution aspiring to a "transition to socialism", although in July-September the PS was excluded from the government, along with other parties except the →Portuguese Communist Party (PCP). In April 1976 the PS won 35% of the vote and 107 of the 263 seats in the new Assembly. In June it supported the successful presidential candidate, Gen. Antonio Ramalho Eanes, who in July appointed Soares as Prime Minister of a minority PS government including independents and military men. That was followed in January-July 1978 by a coalition, also led by Soares, of the PS and the Democratic Social Centre (CDS, later the Popular Party, PP). The PS subsequently supported a government of independents formed in October 1978.

The PS later suffered numerous defections, was decisively defeated in the 1979 Assembly elections, and went into opposition. In June 1980 it formed the Republican and

Socialist Front *(Frente Republicana* e *Socialista,* FRS) electoral coalition with the (now defunct) Independent Social Democratic Action party (ASDI) and the Left Union for a Socialist Democracy (UEDS, formed in 1978 by Antonio Lopes Cardoso, a former PS Agriculture Minister). The FRS won 74 seats in the October 1980 Assembly elections. Reforms in 1981 (since reversed) increased the power of the PS general secretary, leading to dissent within the party. In the April 1983 elections the PS obtained 36.2% of the valid vote and 101 (out of 250) seats; it then formed a coalition government with the →Social Democratic Party (PSD). In 1985 that government lost a vote of confidence and in the ensuing elections the PS fell to 20.7% and 57 seats, being excluded from the minority government formed by the PSD. In February 1986, however, Soares was elected as the country's first civilian President in over 50 years, whereupon he resigned his PS posts. His 1986 opponents included two former PS ministers—Maria de Lourdes Pintasilgo, backed by the Popular Democratic Union (UDP) and Dr Francisco Salgado Zenha, backed by the PCP.

The sixth PS congress in June 1986 elected Manuel Vitor Ribeiro Constâncio (a former Finance Minister and central bank governor, regarded as a pragmatic left-winger) as party leader. It also significantly moderated the party's programme and altered its structure. A minority faction developed around Dr Jaime Gama, a former Foreign Minister close to Soares, but he was later reconciled with the leadership, whereafter the *Soaristas* (who wanted more active opposition to the PSD, including co-operation with the Communists) were led by the President's son, João Soares. Elections in July 1987 gave the PS 22.3% of the vote and 60 seats, so that it remained the leading opposition party; it also held its six European Parliament seats, which were subject to direct election for the first time. The October 1991 parliamentary elections resulted in the PS advancing to 72 seats (on a 30% vote share), but the party remained in opposition, with its leadership passing in February 1992 from Jorge Sampaio to António Gutteres, a young technocrat with a non-ideological approach to politics. The party achieved an all-time high national vote in the December 1993 local elections and again outpolled the ruling PSD in the June 1994 European Parliament elections, in which its vote share was 34.9% and its seat tally 10 of the 25 allocated to Portugal.

In the October 1995 Assembly elections Gutteres led the PS back to governmental office, albeit in a narrow minority position in terms of strict parliamentary arithmetic, its seat tally being 112 out of 230 (on a 43.9% vote share). The new minority PS government, which was expected to obtain the external support of the →United Democratic Coalition on most key issues, announced a programme of accelerated privatization of state enterprises, combined with introduction of a guaranteed minimum wage, social and educational improvements and regional devolution for mainland Portugal. In January 1996 Socialist political authority was consolidated when PS presidential candidate Sampaio (who had become mayor of Lisbon) was elected to the top state post with a commanding 53.8% of the first-round vote.

The PS polled strongly in local elections in December 1997 and also in the June 1999 European Parliament elections, in which it advanced to 43.1% of the national vote and 12 seats. In the October 1999 national elections the PS retained power, winning exactly half of the 230 Assembly seats with a 44.1% vote share.

The PS is a member of the Socialist International. Its representatives in the European Parliament sit in the Party of European Socialists group.

United Democratic Coalition
Coligação Democrático Unitária (CDU)
Address. Rua Soeiro Pereira Gomes 3, 1600-196 Lisbon
Telephone. (+351–1) 793–6272
Fax. (+351–1) 796–9126
Leadership. Vested in the leaderships of component parties.

The CDU is the electoral front organization of the →Portuguese Communist Party (PCP), effectively dating from prior to the 1979 Assembly elections, in which the PCP presented a joint list with the Portuguese Democratic Movement (MDP) called the United People's Alliance (APU). The APU won 47 seats in 1979, before falling to 41 in 1980 and to 38 in 1985, its constituent formations having campaigned separately in 1983. In the 1986 presidential election the APU backed the independent candidacy of former Prime Minister Maria de Lourdes Pintasilgo in the first round, switching with reluctance in the second to Mario Soares of the →Socialist Party (PS). Following the MDP's withdrawal in November 1986, the pro-Soviet PCP converted the APU into the CDU, which also included a group of MDP dissidents, the →Ecologist Party The Greens (PEV) and a number of independent leftists.

The new CDU won 31 Assembly seats in 1987, seven less than the APU in 1985. In the October 1991 elections, with the Soviet Union in its death throes, CDU representation was further reduced to 17 seats (from 8.8% of the vote). In the June 1994 European Parliament elections the CDU list (in which the PEV was prominent) improved to 11.2% and won three of Portugal's 25 seats. In the October 1995 Assembly elections the CDU slipped further to 15 seats (from 8.6% of the vote), thereafter offering qualified parliamentary backing to the new PS minority government. Having lost one of its three seats in the June 1999 European elections (with a vote share of 10.3%), the CDU improved to 9.0% in the October 1999 Assembly elections, winning 17 seats (15 for the PCP and two for the PEV).

The three CDU representatives in the European Parliament sit in the European United Left/Nordic Green Left group.

Other Parties

Communist Party of Portuguese Workers (*Partido Comunista dos Trabalhadores Portugueses*, PCTP), led by Garcia Pereira, a Maoist faction, won 0.9% vote share in June 1999 European Parliament elections.

Humanist Party (*Partido Humanista*, led by Luís Filipe Guerra, affiliated to Humanist International. *Address*. Rua de Santa Catarina 818–3°, 4000-446 Porto; *Telephone*. (+351-2) 2332-0570; *Email*. lfguerra@mail.telepac.pt; *Website*. http://members.xoom.com/_XMCM/humanista

Liberal Party (*Partido Liberal*, PL), led by João Paulo P.R. Santos. *Address*. Apdo 14061, 1064 Lisbon; *Website*. http://www.cidadevirtual.pt/liberal

National Solidarity Party (*Partido Solidariedade Nacional*, PSN), led by Manuel Sergio, pensioners' party founded in 1990, won one Assembly seat on 1991, but none in 1995 or 1999; obtained 0.3% in June 1999 European Parliament elections.

Popular Monarchist Party (*Partido Popular Monárquico*, PPM), led by Gonçalo Ribeiro Telles and Augusto Ferreira do Amaral, pro-market monarchist formation, won six Assembly seats in 1980, but none in subsequent elections; took 0.5% in June 1999 European Parliament elections.

Socialist Struggle (*Luta Socialista*) left-wing faction affiliated to Committee for a Workers' International. *Address*. Apdo 27018, 1201-950 Lisbon. *Email*. is_cit@hotmail.com; *Website*. http://members.xoom.com/ls_cpio

Workers' Party of Socialist Unity (*Partido Operário de Unidade Socialista*, POUS), Trotskyist cell formed in 1979 by →Socialist Party dissidents; won 0.2% in June 1999 European Parliament elections.

Spain

Capital: Madrid **Population:** 40,000,000

The Kingdom of Spain's 1978 constitution rescinded the "fundamental principles" and organic legislation under which General Franco had ruled as Chief of State until his death in 1975 and inaugurated an hereditary constitutional monarchy. Executive power is exercised by the Prime Minister and the Council of Ministers nominally appointed by the King but collectively responsible to the legislature, in which they must command majority support. Legislative authority is vested in the bicameral *Cortes Generales*, both houses of which are elected for four-year terms (subject to dissolution) by universal adult suffrage of those aged 18 and over. The upper Senate (*Senado*) currently has 256 members, of whom 208 were directly elected in 1996 (four from each of the 47 mainland provinces, six from Santa Cruz de Tenerife, five from the Balearic Islands, five from the Canary Islands and two each from the North African enclaves of Ceuta and Melilla), the other 48 senators being designated by the 19 autonomous regional legislatures. The lower Congress of Deputies (*Congreso de los Diputados*) consists of 350 deputies elected from party lists by province-based proportional representation, with each of the 50 provinces being entitled to a minimum of three deputies. Spain joined what became the European Union on Jan. 1, 1986, and elects 64 members of the European Parliament.

Pursuant to the constitutional description of political parties as the expression of pluralism and an essential instrument of political participation, subsidies are available from state funds for parties represented in the Congress of Deputies, in proportion to number of seats and votes obtained at the most recent general elections. Parties are also eligible for state subsidies to defray election campaign expenses, again in proportion to representation obtained, and to certain benefits

Elections to the Congress on March 3, 1996, resulted as follows:

	Seats 1996 (1993)	Percentage 1996 (1993)
Popular Party	156 (141)	38.9 (34.8)
Spanish Socialist Workers' Party	141 (159)	37.5 (38.7)
United Left	21 (18)	10.6 (9.6)
Convergence and Union	16 (17)	4.6 (4.9)
Basque Nationalist Party	5 (5)	1.3 (1.2)
Canarian Coalition	4 (4)	0.9 (0.9)
Galician Nationalist Bloc	2 (0)	0.9 (n/a)
United People (*Herri Batasuna*)*	2 (2)	0.7 (0.9)
Catalan Republican Left	1 (1)	0.7 (0.8)
Basque Solidarity/Basque Left	1 (1)	0.5 (0.6)
Valencian Union	1 (2)	0.4 (0.5)

*Renamed We Basques (*Euskal Herritarrok*) in 1998

during campaigns, such as free advertising space in the media. A separate channel of public subsidy is the entitlement of parliamentary groups in the national and regional legislatures to financial assistance according to their number of members.

Communist Party of Spain
Partido Comunista de España (PCE)

Address. Calle Toronga 27, 28043 Madrid
Telephone. (+34–91) 300-4969
Fax. (+34–91) 300-4744
Email. internacional@pce.es
Website. http://www.pce.es
Leadership. Francisco Frutos (secretary-general)

The PCE was founded in April 1920 by dissident members of the youth wing of the →Spanish Socialist Workers' Party (PSOE) who wished to join the Third (Communist) International and who united in November 1921 with the *Partido Comunista Obrero Español* (PCOE), formed by further defections from the PSOE. The PCE held its first congress in 1922 but was forced underground by the Primo de Rivera dictatorship and had only 800 members by 1929. The party formed part of the republican Popular Front from January 1936, winning 17 seats in the Congress in that year. During the Francoist uprising the PCE policy was "victory first, then revolution", in contrast to the Trotskyists and anarcho-syndicalists. Under the subsequent Franco regime, the PCE was active in the clandestine resistance, its general secretaries (in exile) being Dolores Ibárruri Gómez ("*La Pasionaria*") in 1942–60 and Santiago Carrillo Solares from 1960 (when Ibárruri was appointed honorary president of the party). Undergoing various splits during the 1960s, the PCE developed links with the Italian Communist Party (PCI), sharing the latter's opposition to Moscow's leadership and the 1968 Czechoslovakia intervention, and its support for co-operation with other democratic parties.

In July 1974 the exiled PCE leadership joined other anti-Franco parties in the *Junta Democrática*, which in March 1976 joined the Socialist-led Democratic Platform to form the Democratic Co-ordination. Legalized in April 1977, when it had some 200,000 members, the PCE supported the restoration of a constitutional monarchy and won 20 seats in the Congress of Deputies elected in June 1977 (and three in the Senate). The ninth (1978) PCE congress was the first to be held in Spain for 46 years. The party's congressional strength increased to 23 in the elections of March 1979, but it became internally divided between two large and broadly Euro-communist factions and two smaller and broadly pro-Soviet factions. The weakened party was reduced to 4.1% of the vote and four deputies in the October 1982 elections, whereupon Carrillo resigned and was succeeded as PCE secretary-general (in November) by a more committed Euro-communist, Gerardo Iglesias Argüelles.

In local elections in May 1983 the PCE vote recovered to 7.9%, but in the following months it suffered a series of splits, mainly between "*gerardistas*" favouring a broad left alliance and "*carrillistas*" opposed to such a strategy. In March 1985 Carrillo was forced out of the PCE leadership, his supporters being purged from the central committee. In April 1986 the PCE was a founder-member of the →United Left (IU), which secured 4.6% of the vote and seven lower house seats in the June general elections. The then deputy general secretary, Enrique Curiel, resigned in December 1987, and Iglesias himself resigned in February 1988 after losing the support of the large Madrid, Catalan and Andalusian sections. Later that month the 12th PCE congress elected Julio Anguita (a former mayor of Córdoba) as his successor. Meanwhile, the PCE had become involved in sporadic efforts to reunify the Spanish communist movement following the establishment by Ignacio Gallego of the People's

Communist Party of Spain (PCPE) and by Carrillo of what became the Workers' Party of Spain (PTE).

PCE president Dolores Ibárruri died in November 1989, whereafter the PCE continued its "broad left" strategy in the 1993 and 1996 elections, deriving some benefit from the troubles of the ruling PSOE and the broadly conservative policies of the González government. At the 15th PCE congress in December 1998, Anguita was succeeded as secretary-general by Francisco Frutos.

Popular Party
Partido Popular (PP)
Address. Génova 13, 28004 Madrid
Telephone. (+34–91) 557-7300
Fax. (+34–91) 308–4618
Email. pp@pp.es
Website. http://www.pp.es
Leadership. José María Aznar López (president); Javier Arenas Bocanegra (secretary-general)
The moderate conservative PP was established in its present form in January 1989 as successor to the Popular Alliance (*Alianza Popular*, AP), which been created in October 1976 as a distinctly right-wing grouping embracing the dominant political forces of the Franco era. The AP had been formed as a coalition of seven right-wing and centre-right parties: *Reforma Democrática* (RD), led by a former Francoist minister Manuel Fraga Iribarne; *Acción Regional* (AR), led by Laureano López Rodó; *Acción Democrática Española* (ADE), formed in 1976 and led by Federico Silva Muñoz; *Democracia Social* (DS), led by Licinio de la Fuente; *Unión del Pueblo Español* (UDPE), led by Cruz Martínez Esteruelas; *Unión Nacional Española* (UNE), led by Gonzalo Fernández de la Mora, and *Unión Social Popular* (USP), led by Enrique Thomas de Carranza. In March 1977 five of these parties merged as a single organization named the *Partido Unido de Alianza Popular* (PUAP) led by Fraga Iribarne as secretary-general. The two non-participating parties were the ADE and the UNE, both led by former Francoist ministers, but they remained in alliance with the PUAP until late 1979.

In the June 1977 general elections the AP, then widely regarded as a Francoist grouping, won 8.2% of the vote, giving it 16 seats in the Congress of Deputies and two in the Senate. Divided over whether to endorse the 1978 constitution (which Fraga Iribarne in the event supported), the AP lost support. In the March 1979 general elections the Democratic Coalition which it had formed with other right-wing groups, including *Acción Ciudadana Liberal*, the *Partido Popular de Cataluña*, *Renovación Española* (RE) and the Popular Democratic Party (PDP), won only 6% of the vote, giving it nine seats in the Congress and three in the Senate. At the 1979 and 1980 party congresses, the AP leadership moved the party, with some difficulty, towards a mainstream conservative orientation, a leading advocate of which was Fraga Iribarne, who was elected AP president in 1979. In mid-1980 the AP merged with the PDP and RE; the combined party, projecting a moderate image (and denouncing the 1981 coup attempt), doubled its membership in 1981–82.

The Galician elections of October 1981 enabled the AP to form a minority government in that region, where it secured a majority in 1983 by recruiting members of the by then dissolved Union of the Democratic Centre (UCD). Meanwhile, in the national parliamentary elections of October 1982 the AP-led bloc won 26.6% of the vote and 106 seats in the lower chamber (and 54 in the upper), so eclipsing the UCD and becoming the main opposition formation. From 1983 the AP led a regional and national electoral alliance, the Popular Coalition (*Coalición Popular*, CP), including the PDP, the Liberal Union (UL) and regional formations such as the →Union of the Navarrese People (UPN), the →Aragonese Party and the →Valencian Union. The CP came under severe strain following the June 1986 general elections, in which it secured 26% of the vote and 105 seats in the lower house (and 63 in the Senate). In July 1986 the PDP broke away. In December, after an electoral rout in the Basque Country, Fraga resigned as AP president. In January 1987 the national AP broke with the Liberal Party (PL, as the UL had become) although the AP-PL alliance remained in existence in some regions. The 8th AP congress, in February 1987, installed a new youthful party leadership headed by Antonio Hernández Mancha, who had been AP leader in Andalusía. During 1987 the AP contested elections at various levels, securing 231 seats in autonomous parliaments, over 13,000 local council seats and 17 seats in the European Parliament (for which its list was led by Fraga Iribarne). However, by late 1987 defections resulting from chronic internal infighting had reduced the party's strength in the national Congress of Deputies to 67.

The conversion of the AP into the PP at a party congress in January 1989 reflected the wish of most AP currents to present a moderate conservative alternative to the ruling →Spanish Socialist Workers' Party (PSOE) and to eschew any remaining identification with the Franco era. The congress was preceded by a power struggle between Hernández and Fraga Iribarne, the latter having been persuaded by supporters that he should try to regain the leadership. In the event, Hernández opted out of the contest shortly before the congress, so that Fraga Iribarne resumed the leadership of a more united party, which subsequently made particular efforts to build alliances with regional conservative parties. In the October 1989 general elections it advanced marginally to 106 seats and 30.3% of the vote, but remained far behind the PSOE. In December 1989 the PP won an absolute majority in the Galician assembly, whereupon Fraga Iribarne became regional president, being succeeded as PP leader by José María Aznar López.

In the early 1990s the PP was not immune from scandals concerning irregular party financing, of the type affecting most of Latin Europe; but it remained relatively untarnished compared with the ruling PSOE. In general elections in June 1993 the party increased its Chamber representation to 141 seats and its vote share to 34.8%, less than four points behind the PSOE. Continuing in opposition, the PP registered major victories in the October 1993 Galician regional election and in the June 1994 European Parliament elections, on the latter occasion overtaking the PSOE by winning 40.6% of the vote and 28 of the 64 seats. Further advances followed in regional and local elections in May 1995, although in actual voting the PP failed to match its large opinion poll lead over the PSOE. Aznar's public standing was boosted by a car-bomb assassination attempt against him in Madrid in April 1995.

In early general elections in March 1996 the PP at last overtook the PSOE as the largest Chamber party, but its 156 seats (from 38.9% of the vote) left it well short of an overall majority. Aznar was accordingly obliged to form a minority government, which received qualified pledges of external support from the Catalan →Convergence and Union, the →Basque Nationalist Party (PNV) and the →Canarian Coalition in return for concessions to their regional agendas. His government programme promised urgent economic austerity measures to achieve the "national objective" of meeting the Maastricht treaty criteria for participation in a single European currency. The PNV withdrew its support from the PP government in September 1997, without affecting its ability to survive. It did so again in June 1999 following municipal and regional elections in which the PP maintained its status as the leading political formation, retaining control in nine of the 13 autonomous regions where elections were held. In simultaneous European Parliament elections the PP slipped to 39.8% of the national vote and 27 seats.

The PP is affiliated to the Christian Democrat International and the International Democrat Union. Its representatives in the European Parliament sit in the European People's Party/European Democrats group.

Spanish Socialist Workers' Party
Partido Socialista Obrero Español (PSOE)
Address. Ferraz 68-70, Madrid 28008
Telephone. (+34–91) 582–0444
Fax. (+34–91) 582–0525
Email. internacional@psoe.es
Website. http://www.psoe.es
Leadership. Joaquín Almunia Amann (secretary-general)
Of social democratic orientation, the PSOE seeks a fairer and more united society based on social, economic and political democracy. It supports Spanish membership of the European Union (EU) and of the Atlantic Alliance, having opposed the latter until 1986. It defined itself as Marxist in 1976, but since 1979 has regarded Marxism as merely an analytical tool. It defends divorce and the decriminalization of abortion in certain circumstances.

Originally founded in 1879 from socialist groups in Madrid and Guadalajara, the PSOE held its first congress in 1888 and became a leading party of the Second International. It was allied with the Republicans from 1909, as a result of which its founder, Pablo Iglesias, was elected to the Congress of Deputies in 1910. The party had some 40,000 members when its left wing broke away in 1920–21 to form the →Communist Party of Spain (PCE). The PSOE doubled its membership during the 1920s and returned about one third of the deputies in the Congress in 1931. It played an important role in the history of the Spanish Republic until the end of the Civil War in 1939, when it was banned by the Franco regime. The exiled leadership, based in Toulouse (France), refused to ally with other anti-Franco forces, but a more radical internally-based "*renovador*" faction began to organize in the late 1960s. The internal section gained control at a congress in Paris in 1972, and in 1974 it elected Felipe González as first secretary (although a rival "*historico*" faction survived in France and evolved into the →Socialist Action Party). Both the PSOE and various regional socialist parties experienced rapid growth in Spain at about this time, partly due to the death of Franco.

In June 1975 the PSOE joined other non-Communist opposition parties in the *Plataforma Democrática* alliance, which in March 1976 merged with the PCE-led *Junta Democrática*. The latter had been created in 1974 and included the Popular Socialist Party (*Partido Socialista Popular*, PSP), which had been formed in 1967 as the *Partido Socialista del Interior* (PSI). The PSOE was also a component of the even broader *Coordinación Democratica*, which negotiated with the post-Franco government for the restoration of civil and political rights, regional autonomy and popular consultation on the future form of government. During 1976 the PSOE formed the *Federación de Partidos Socialistas* along with groups such as the →Party of Socialists of Catalonia (PSC), *Convergencia Socialista Madrileña*, the *Partit Socialiste des Illes*, the *Partido Socialista Bilzarrea* and the Aragonese and Galician Socialist parties.

In December 1976 the PSOE, the largest socialist group with about 75,000 members, held its first congress inside Spain for 44 years, the venue being in Madrid. It was formally legalized on Feb. 17, 1977, along with a number of other parties. The PSOE participated in the June 1977 general elections together with the PSC and the Basque Socialist Party (PSE-PSOE), winning a total of 118 seats in the Congress of Deputies and 47 in the Senate. In February 1978 the PSC formally affiliated to the national party, as the PSC-PSOE, and in April the PSOE absorbed the PSP, which had six deputies and four senators. The Aragonese and Galician parties were similarly absorbed in May and July 1978. In the March 1979 general elections the PSOE, with its Basque and Catalan affiliates, won 121 seats in the Congress and 68 in the Senate, therefore remaining in opposition. At a centennial congress in May 1979 González unexpectedly stepped down as party leader after a majority of delegates refused to abandon a doctrinal commitment to Marxism. His control was re-established during a special congress in late September 1979, the hard-liners being defeated by a 10 to 1 majority.

The PSOE made further gains in the October 1982 general elections, in which it won 48.7% of the vote (passing the 10 million mark for the first time) and gained an absolute majority in both chambers (with 202 of the 350 deputies and 134 of the 208 senators). A PSOE government was formed on Dec. 1, with González as Prime Minister; it subsequently negotiated Spain's entry into what became the European Union (EU) with effect from Jan. 1, 1986. In January 1983 the PSOE absorbed the Democratic Action Party (*Partido de Acción Demócrata*, PAD), which had been formed in March 1982 by centre-left defectors from the then ruling Union of the Democratic Centre (UCD). In 1985 the PSOE experienced serious internal divisions over the government's pro-NATO policy, which ran counter to the party's longstanding rejection of participation in any military alliance. The issue was resolved by a referendum of March 1986 which delivered a majority in favour of NATO membership on certain conditions, including reduction of the US military presence in Spain.

The PSOE retained power in the June 1986 general elections with a reduced vote share of 43.4% but a renewed majority of 184 lower house seats and 124 in the Senate. It thereafter pursued what were generally seen as moderate and somewhat conservative policies, particularly in the economic sphere. The PSOE's narrow loss of an overall majority in the October 1989 general elections (in which it slipped to 175 seats in the lower house on a 39.6% vote share) was attributed in part to internal divisions, highlighted by the prior emergence of the dissident →Socialist Democracy splinter group and by the defection of a substantial PSOE group to the →United Left (IU). In the early 1990s the PSOE's standing was damaged further by a series of financial scandals involving prominent party figures, combined with familiar left/right tensions. At the 32nd PSOE congress in November 1990 the left-leaning Deputy Prime Minister and deputy party leader, Alfonso Guerra, was able to block a move by the party's right to strengthen its base in leadership bodies. However, a corruption scandal involving his brother compelled Guerra to resign from the government in January 1991; although he remained deputy leader of the party, the PSOE right became increasingly dominant thereafter.

In early general elections in June 1993 the party retained a narrow relative majority of 159 Chamber seats (on a 38.7% vote share), sufficient for González to form a minority government with regional party support. Held amid further disclosures about irregular party financing, the 33rd PSOE congress in March 1994 resulted in the transfer of the party's controversial organization secretary, José María ("Txiki") Benegas, to another post. In the June 1994 European Parliament elections PSOE support slumped to 31.1%, so that the party took only 22 of the 64 Spanish seats, while in simultaneous regional elections the PSOE lost overall control of its stronghold of Andalusia. Further setbacks followed in Basque Country elections in October 1994 and in regional/municipal polling in May 1995, although the PSOE retained control of Madrid and Barcelona.

The tide of corruption and security scandals rose inexorably through 1995, with the CESID phone-tapping disclosures in June, causing the small Catalan →Convergence and Union party to withdraw its external support from the PSOE government the following month. The eventual upshot was another early general election in March 1996 in which the PSOE finally lost power, although the margin of its defeat was less wide than many had predicted: it retained 141 seats with 37.5% of the vote, only slightly down on its 1993 showing and only 1.5% behind the →Popular Party, which was therefore obliged to form a minority government.

González finally vacated the PSOE leadership at the 34th party congress in Madrid in June 1997, being succeeded by Joaquín Almunia Amann, an uncharismatic Basque politician. On Almunia's proposal the first-ever "primary" elections were held in April 1998 to choose

175

the party's prime ministerial candidate, the unexpected victor being not Almunia but articulate former minister Josep Borrell Fontelles. An uneasy dual leadership ensued, until Borrell resigned as Prime Minister-candidate in May 1999 over a controversial financial investment by his now-estranged wife in the 1980s. In the June 1999 European Parliament elections the PSOE presented a joint list with the →Democratic Party of the New Left (PDNI), advancing to 35.3% of the vote and 24 of the 64 Spanish seats. The following month Almunia was elected unopposed as the PSOE candidate for Prime Minister in the 2000 general elections.

The PSOE is a member party of the Socialist International and its European Parliament representatives sit in the Party of European Socialists group.

United Left
Izquierda Unida (IU)

Address. Olimpo 35, 28043 Madrid
Telephone. (+34–91) 300-3233
Fax. (+34–91) 388-0405
Email. cendoc@izquierda-unida.es
Website. http://www.izquierda-unida.es
Leadership. Julio Anguita González (co-ordinator); Fernando Perez Royo (parliamentary leader); Víctor Ríos (secretary)

The radical left-wing (mainly Marxist) IU was founded in April 1986 as an electoral alliance, originally consisting of the →Communist Party of Spain (PCE), the Peoples' Communist Party of Spain (PCPE), the Progressive Federation (FP), the →Socialist Action Party (PASOC), the Communist Union of Spain (UCE) and the Republican Left (IR). It was later joined by the →Carlist Party and the →Humanist Party (PH), although the latter quickly withdrew, and it formed a local alliance with the →Unity of the Valencian People (UPV). The first president of the IU was the then PCE leader, Gerardo Iglesias.

In the June 1986 general elections the IU won seven seats in the Congress of Deputies and none in the Senate. The FP left the IU in late 1987, partly as a result of the unilateral decision of the PCE to sign a parliamentary accord against political violence without consulting the other IU parties. In December 1987 the IU leadership adopted a strategy seeking to make the IU a permanent rather than *ad hoc* alliance, and to broaden its base during 1988 beyond the member parties to incorporate independent left-wingers and pressure groups. The IU was expanded in 1988–89 to include the →Republican Left (IR) and the Unitarian Candidature of Workers (*Candidatura Unitaria de Trabajadores*, CUT), led by Juan Manuel Sánchez Gordillo. In the October 1989 general elections the IU increased its lower house representation to 18 seats (on a 9.1% vote share) and also won one Senate seat.

Proposals for a formal merger between the IU parties caused dissension in 1991–92, the outcome being that component formations retained their autonomous identity. In the June 1993 general elections the IU made only marginal headway, again winning 18 lower house seats but with 9.6% of the vote. It fared substantially better in the June 1994 European Parliament elections, obtaining nine of the 64 Spanish seats on a 13.5% vote share. In simultaneous regional elections in Andalusia, it won 19.2% of the vote. In the March 1996 general elections the IU derived some benefit from the defeat of the →Spanish Socialist Workers' Party, winning 10.6% of the national vote and 21 lower house seats (although none in the Senate). However, the June 1999 European elections brought a sharp reverse for the IU, to only 5.8% of the vote and four seats.

The IU representatives in the European Parliament sit in the European United Left/Nordic Green Left group. The IU has an official membership of 68,000.

Other National Parties

Alliance for National Union (*Alianza por l'Unión Nacional*, AUN), led by Ricardo Saenz de Ynestrillas, radical far-right formation seeking the preservation of the unity of the Spanish state and a halt to immigration.

Carlist Party (*Partido Carlista*, PC), formed in 1934, a left-wing group which arose from a 19th-century Catholic monarchist movement; strongest in the north of Spain, the Carlists turned against the Franco regime after 1939 and many of its leaders were exiled; in the post-Franco era it became a component of the →United Left alliance.

Centrist Union (*Unión Centrista*, UC), led by Fernando García Fructuoso, launched in early 1995 by elements that included former members of the Democratic and Social Centre (*Centro Democrático y Social*, CDS), which had been founded prior to the 1982 elections by Adolfo Suárez González, who had vacated the leadership of the Union of the Democratic Centre (*Unión de Centro Democrático*, UCD) on resigning as Prime Minister in January 1981 and had been rebuffed when he tried to regain the party leadership in July 1982; allied regionally and locally with the →Popular Party (PP) and an affiliate of the Liberal International, the CDS had won 14 lower house seats and five European Parliament seats in 1989, although the resignation of Suárez González in September 1991 had heralded virtual extinction in the 1993 national and 1994 European elections; the new UC fared little better in the 1996 general elections. *Address*. Jorge Juan 30, 28001 Madrid

Democratic Party of the New Left (*Partido Democrático de la Nueva Izquierda*, PDNI), led by Cristina Almeida (president) and Diego López Garrido (secretary-general), founded in 1996 by dissident faction of the →United Left; contested June 1999 European election in alliance with the →Spanish Socialist Workers' Party, winning two seats. *Address*. San Bernardo 23/4°, 28015 Madrid; *Telephone*. (+34-91) 559-5893; *Fax*. (+34-91) 547-3867; *Email*. pdni@nuevaizquierda.es

European Alternative (*Alternativa Europea*, AE), advocating a Europe liberated for socialism and the workers. *Address*. Apdo 877, 08080 Barcelona; *Email*. ae-lsr@mixmail.com

Feminist Party of Spain (*Partido Feminista de España*, PFE), led by Lidia Falcón O'Neill, founded in 1979, aiming to spread the gospel of women's liberation at the political and social levels, but not making much headway in Catholic and socially conservative Spain. *Address*. Magdalena 29/1A, 28012 Madrid

The Greens (*Los Verdes*), confederation resulting from ecologist conferences in Tenerife in May 1983 and in Malaga in June 1984, legally registered in November 1984, inaugurated at a congress in Barcelona in February 1985; the resultant Green Alternative (*Alternativa Verde*) electoral alliance won less than 1% of the vote in the 1986 general elections, and subsequent assorted electoral variants (sometimes simultaneous and competing) have made no further progress, although the movement has gained some representation at local level and won 1.4% in the June 1999 European Parliament elections. *Address*. Calle Navellos 9/2°, 46003 Valencia; *Telephone/Fax*. (+34-96) 392-1314; *Email*. verdspv@xarxaneta.org; *Website*. http://www.xarxaneta.org/losverdes

Humanist Party of Spain (*Partido Humanista de España*, PHE), formed in 1984 and led by Rafael de la Rubia, a member of the →United Left electoral coalition (IU) at the time of the 1986 general elections, subsequently independent. *Website*. http://www.mdnh.org

Liberal Party (*Partido Liberal*, PL), led by José Antonio Segurado, founded in 1977, absorbed the small Liberal Union (*Unión Liberal*, UL) in 1985, closely allied with the →Popular Party from 1989, although retaining independent party status. *Address.* Plaza de las Cortes 4, 28014 Madrid; *Website.* http:www.website.es/liberal

National Democracy (*Democracia Nacional*, DN), led by Francisco Pérez Corrales, right-wing formation founded in 1995. *Email.* demnac@arrakis.es; *Website.* http://www.ecomix.es/~demnac

National Front (*Frente Nacional*, FN), led by Blas Piñar López, far-right party founded in October 1986 aiming to rally Francoist forces against the then ruling →Spanish Socialist Workers' Party.

Republican Left (*Izquierda Republicana*, IR), led by Albert Vela Antón (president) and Isabelo Herreros Martín-Maestro (secretary-general), left-wing formation dating from 1934, became a component of the →United Left (IU) in 1988. *Address.* Calle Príncipe de Vergana 55/4°/A, 28006 Madrid; *Telephone.* (+34-91) 564-8719; *Fax.* (+34-91) 564-8655; *Email.* ir@bitmailer.net; *Website.* http://www.izqrepublicana.es

Socialist Action Party (*Partido de Acción Socialista*, PASOC), led by Pablo Castellano and Alonso Puerta, founded in January 1983 by left-wing socialists who regarded the then ruling →Spanish Socialist Workers' Party (PSOE) as having betrayed the working class; succeeded the PSOE *Histórico*, which arose from the 1974 split between the *renovadores* ("renewal") group based inside Spain (led by Felipe González) and the *historicos* loyal to the exiled leadership of Rodolfo Llopis; having absorbed some even smaller socialist formations, PASOC was a founder member of the →United Left alliance in 1986, through which it gained representation at national, regional and European levels. *Address.* Espoz y Mina 5, 28012 Madrid

Socialist Democracy (*Democracia Socialista*, DS), led by Ricardo García Damborenea, founded in 1990 by a left-wing dissident faction of the then ruling →Spanish Socialist Workers' Party.

Spanish Falange (*Falange Española*), led by Carmen Franco and Diego Marquez Jorrillo, residual survival of the ruling formation of the Franco era, won one lower house seat in 1979 in a National Union (*Unión Nacional*) with other neo-fascist groups; other far-right formations appeared to supersede the Falange in the 1980s, notably the →National Front; in the 1990s it has sought to articulate right-wing sentiment among those damaged by free-market government policies. *Address.* Calle Silva 2, 4-3, 28015 Madrid; *Telephone.* (+34-91) 541-9699; *Fax.* (+34-91) 559-9210; *Website.* http://www.falange.es

Workers' Revolutionary Party (*Partido Obrero Revolucionario*, POR), Trotskyist formation founded in 1974. *Email.* por@pangea.org; *Website.* http://www.pangea.org/por

Regional Parties

As the leading national formations, the →Popular Party (PP), →Spanish Socialist Workers' Party (PSOE) and →United Left (IU) are organized in most of Spain's autonomous regions, either under their own name or in alliance with autonomous regional parties. There are also many regional parties without national affiliation.

ANDALUSIA

Regional assembly elections on March 3, 1996, resulted as follows: PSOE 52 seats, PP 20, a joint list of the IU, Greens and local progressives (the *Convocatoria por Andalucía*) 13, Andalusianist Party 4.

Andalusianist Party
Partido Andalucista (PA)
Address. Av. San Francisco Javier 24, Edificio Seville 1/9A-2, 41005 Seville
Telephone. (+34–95) 422–6855
Fax. (+34–95) 421–0446
Leadership. Alejandro Rojas-Marcos (president); Antonio Ortega (secretary-general)
The PA was founded in 1976 (as the Socialist Party of Andalusia) on a progressive nationalist platform, seeking self-determination for Andalusia on terms more concessionary than those of the 1981 autonomy statute. Legalized in 1977, the party fought the 1979 general elections on a moderate regionalist manifesto, securing five seats in the Congress of Deputies (which it failed to hold in 1982). It won two seats in the Catalan assembly in March 1980 and three seats in the Andalusian assembly in May 1982 (with 5.4% of the vote). The party adopted its present name at its fifth congress in February 1984. In the 1986 Andalusian elections it was reduced to two seats, but it slightly raised its vote in the 1987 local elections. The party regained national representation in 1989, winning two lower house seats, and advanced strongly to 10 seats in the Andalusian regional assembly in 1990. However, its lost its national seats in 1993 and fell back to three regional seats in 1994. In the 1996 contests it again failed at national level, while improving to four seats in the Andalusian assembly. It contested the June 1999 European elections as part of the European Coalition (*Coalición Europea*, CE) of regional parties, winning one of the CE's two seats.

ARAGON

Regional assembly elections on June 13, 1999, resulted as follows: PP 28 seats, PSOE 23, Aragonese Party 10, Aragonese Junta 5, IU 1.

Aragonese Party
Partido Aragonés (PAR)
Address. Coso 87, 50001 Zaragoza, Aragon
Telephone. (+34–976) 200-616
Fax. (+34–976) 200-987
Leadership. José María Mur Bernad (president); Emilio Eiroa García (secretary-general)
Officially called the Aragonese Regionalist Party (*Partido Aragonés Regionalista*) until 1990, the PAR was founded in January 1978 to campaign for greatly increased internal autonomy for the provinces of Aragon within the Spanish state. Having its main strength in Zaragoza, it secured one of the region's 13 seats in the national lower house in 1977, retaining it in 1979. In the 1982 general elections the PAR was allied with the conservative Popular Alliance (later the →Popular Party) and lost its seat. It became the third-largest bloc in the regional assembly in the May 1983 elections, which gave it 13 seats. Standing alone in the 1986 national elections, it regained a lower house seat. After the 1987 regional elections, which produced no overall majority, the then PAR president, Hipólito Gómez de las Roces, was elected regional premier. The party retained its one national seat in 1989 and 1993, but lost it in 1996 (despite being allied with the PP). In the interim, it won 14 seats in the regional assembly in March 1995. It contested the June 1999 European elections as part

of the European Coalition (*Coalición Europea*, CE) of regional parties, failing to win representation.

Aragonese Union (*Chunta Aragonesista*, ChA), led by Bizén Fuster Santaliestra and Chesús Bernal Bernal, of socialist and ecological orientation, advanced from two to five seats in June 1999 regional elections in Aragon; claims about 1,000 members. *Address*. Conde Aranda 14/1°, 5003 Zaragoza; *Telephone*. (+34-97) 628-4242; *Fax*. (+34-97) 628-131; *Email*. sedenacional@chunta.com; *Website*. http://www.chunta.com

ASTURIAS

Regional assembly elections on June 13, 1999, resulted as follows: PSOE 24 seats, PP 15, IU 3, Asturian Renewal Union 3.

Asturian Renewal Union (*Unión Renovadora Asturiana*, URAS), led by Sergio Marqués Fernández, founded in 1998 by dissident faction of regional Popular Party (PP), won three seats in June 1999 regional elections.

BALEARIC ISLANDS

Regional assembly elections on June 13, 1999, resulted as follows: PP 28 seats, PSOE 13, Socialist Party of Majorca-Nationalists of Majorca 5, IU 3, Majorcan Union 3, others 7.

Majorcan Union
Unió Mallorquina (UM)
Address. Av. de Joan March 1/3/3, 07004 Palma de Mallorca
Telephone. (+34-971) 726-336
Fax. (+34-971) 728-116
Email. um@ctv.es
Leadership. María Antonia Munar (president); Bartomeu Vicens (secretary-general)
The regionalist UM has a centrist political orientation. It won six of the 52 regional assembly seats in 1983, so that it held the balance of power between the PP and the PSOE. By 1995 it had slipped to only two seats, recovering to three in June 1999. On the latter occasion it contested the European elections as part of the Nationalist Coalition/Europe of the Peoples (*Coalición Nacionalista/Europa de los Pueblos* alliance, without winning representation.

Socialist Party of Majorca–Nationalists of Majorca (*Partit Socialista de Mallorca-Nacionalistes de Mallorca*, PSM-NM), left-oriented nationalist formation, won six out of 59 regional assembly seats in 1995, falling to five in 1999.

BASQUE COUNTRY (EUSKADI)

Regional assembly elections on Oct. 25, 1998, resulted as follows: Basque Nationalist Party 21 seats, PP 16, We Basques 14, Basque Socialist Party-Basque Left 14, Basque Solidarity 6, IU 2, Alavan Unity 2.

Alavan Unity
Unidad Alavesa (UA)
Address. c/o Basque Parliament, Vitoria, Euzkadi
Leadership. José Luis Añúa (president); Pablo Mosquera (secretary-general)

The UA is a →Popular Party splinter group founded in 1989 campaigning for recognition of the rights of the province of Alava within the Basque Country. It won three seats in the 1990 Basque parliament elections, five in 1994 and two in 1998.

Basque Left
Euskal Ezkerra (EuE)
Address. Jardines 5/1°, 48005 Bilbao, Euzkadi
Leadership. Xabier Gurrutxaga (secretary-general)
The EuE was formed by militant pro-independence elements of the previous Basque Left grouping who rejected the 1993 merger with the Basque federation of the →Spanish Socialist Workers' Party to create the →Basque Socialist Party–Basque Left. The militant rejectionists have a slightly different Basque title than that of the previous Basque Left, but it apparently translates the same in English. In the March 1996 national elections the EuE presented a joint list with →Basque Solidarity, returning one deputy to the lower house.

Basque Nationalist Party
Partido Nacionalista Vasco (PNV)
Euzko Alderdi Jeltzalea (EAJ)
Address. Ibáñez de Bilbao 16, 48001 Bilbao, Euzkadi
Telephone. (+34–94) 435-9400
Fax. (+34–94) 435-9415
Email. ebb@eaj-pnv.com
Website.
Leadership. Xabier Arzallus Antía (president); Juan José Ibarretxe Markuartu (*lendakari* of Basque government); Ricardo Ansotegui (secretary)
Dating from 1895, the Christian democratic PNV stands for an internally autonomous Basque region (including Navarra) within Spain and is opposed to the terrorist campaign for independence. It opposes unrestrained capitalism and supports a mixed economy. The PNV developed from the Basque Catholic traditionalist movement led by its founder, Sabino Arana y Goiri. It returned seven deputies to the Spanish *Cortes* in 1918, 12 in 1933 and nine in 1936, succeeding in the latter year in establishing an autonomous Basque government under José Antonio Aguirre. Allied with the republican regime in the Spanish civil war, its leadership was forced into exile by Gen. Franco's victory, and the party was suppressed throughout the Franco era. Aguirre died in 1960 and the Basque "government in exile" nominated Jesus María de Leizaola to succeed him as *lendakari* (president of the Basque government).

In the 1977 Spanish general elections the PNV won seven seats in the Congress of Deputies and eight in the Senate; its representatives abstained in the parliamentary vote on the 1978 constitution, and its supporters were among the 56% of voters in Guipúzcoa and Vizcaya (the two largest Basque provinces) who abstained in the ensuing referendum. It lost one of its seats in Congress in 1979, but in that year's elections to the Basque general junta the PNV won 73 of the 171 seats in the two main provinces, whereupon de Leizaola returned from France, ending the 43–year-old "government in exile". In the March 1980 elections to the new Basque parliament it won 37.6% of the vote and 25 of the 60 seats. The then PNV leader, Carlos Garaikoetxea, became *lendakari* of the autonomous Basque government in April 1980.

In 1982 the PNV secured eight seats in the Spanish Congress and nine in the Senate. In the February 1984 Basque elections it won 42% of the vote and 32 of the 75 seats. Garaikoetxea was forced to resign due to intra-party disputes in December 1984, and in February 1985 was succeeded as party leader by Xabier Arzalluz and as *lendakari* by José Antonio Ardanza Garro, a PNV member, who agreed a "pact of government" with the Basque Socialist Party (later the →Basque Socialist Party–Basque Left, PSE-EE). In June 1986 the

PNV's representation in the *Cortes* fell to six seats in the lower chamber and seven in the upper. The party split in September, with supporters of Garaikoetxea leaving to form →Basque Solidarity (EA). In the Basque elections of November 1986 the PNV held only 17 of its seats and was again obliged to govern in coalition with the PSE (which won fewer votes but more seats than the PNV).

In January and March 1989 the PNV organized huge demonstrations in Bilbao calling upon separatist militants to end their armed struggle. However, subsequent efforts to form an electoral alliance with the EA and the →Basque Left (EE) failed, with the result that in October 1989 the PNV's national representation fell to five Congress and four Senate seats, although it was confirmed as the largest party in the 1990 Basque parliament elections, with 22 seats. The PNV again won five lower house seats in the 1993 general elections, after which the PNV usually gave external support to the PSOE minority government. In the June 1994 European Parliament election the PNV headed a regional list which won 2.8% of the vote and two seats, one of which was taken by a PNV candidate. In regional elections in October 1994, the PNV won 22 of the 75 Basque parliament seats and formed a coalition with the Basque Socialist Party–Basque Left (PSE-EE).

In the March 1996 national elections the PNV retained five lower house seats and improved from three to four in the Senate. The following month it joined with the Catalan →Convergence and Union and the →Canarian Coalition in undertaking to give external parliamentary support to a minority PP government, in exchange for certain concessions to its regionalist agenda. Having withdrawn its backing for the government in September 1997, the PNV fell out with the PSE-EE in the regional government in June 1998. In the October 1998 Basque elections the PNV slipped to 21 seats but in December became the leading party in the region's first-ever wholly nationalist coalition. In the June 1999 European elections the PNV was part of the Nationalist Coalition/Europe of the Peoples (*Coalición Nacionalista/Europa de los Pueblos*) regional alliance, winning one seat.

The PNV is a member party of the Christian Democrat International, although its European Parliament representative sits in the Greens/European Free Alliance group.

Basque Socialist Party–Basque Left
Partido Socialista de Euskadi–Euskadiko Ezkerra (PSE-EE)
Address. Plaza de San José 3, Bilbao 9, Euzkadi
Telephone. (+34–94) 424–1606
Leadership. José María (Txiki) Benegas (president); Nicolás Redondo Terreros (secretary-general)
The PSE-EE was created in March 1993 when the PSE (the autonomous Basque federation of the →Spanish Socialist Workers' Party, PSOE) merged with the smaller and more radical EE. The merged party continued with the PSE's pro-autonomy line, whereas the Marxist EE had previously been committed to independence for the Basque provinces. That the latter was able to accept the PSE's stance for the merged party was in part because its militant pro-independence wing rejected the merger and broke away to maintain the →Basque Left (EuE) in being as an independent formation.

Founded in 1977, the PSE won seven seats in the Congress of Deputies in 1977, and five in 1979. It was in an autonomist pact until late 1979, when it parted company with the →Basque Nationalist Party (PNV) over the latter's insistence on the necessity of including Navarra in the Basque autonomy statute. However, having won eight lower house seats in the 1982 national elections, the PSE from early 1985 agreed to support a PNV administration. In June 1986, for the first time, the PSE-PSOE won more seats in the Congress than any other party in the region, with seven deputies to the PNV's six, although the Socialist vote in the three provinces of the Basque autonomous region was the lowest anywhere in Spain, at around 25%. In November 1986, after a split in the PNV, the PSE was confirmed as the largest single party, winning 19 of the 75 seats in elections to the Basque parliament. Early in 1987 the PSE joined a coalition administration with the PNV, with a PSE member Jesus Eguiguren, being elected president of the parliament. In the 1990 Basque elections the PSE slipped to 16 seats.

The EE had been launched in 1976 as a pro-independence electoral alliance which had as its main component the Basque Revolutionary Party (*Euskal Iraultzarako Alderdia*, EIA), which had been formed by supporters of Mario Onaindía Machiondo, then a political prisoner, as a non-violent Marxist offshoot of the *Politico-Militar* faction of the terrorist group, Basque Nation and Liberty (ETA). Onaindía was secretary-general of the EE for some ten years after its foundation. In June 1977 the EE secured one seat in each chamber of the Spanish parliament, both EE representatives subsequently voting against the 1978 constitution because of its limited provisions for Basque autonomy. The party lost its Senate seat in 1979, but in the 1980 elections to the Basque parliament the EE won 9.7% of the vote and six seats (out of 60). The EIA dissolved itself in mid-1981, and the EE was reorganized shortly afterwards, incorporating Roberto Lertxundi Baraffano's faction of the Basque Communist Party (EPK). It was relaunched in March 1982, as the Basque Left–Left for Socialism alliance (EE-IS), and retained its Congress seat in October. A radical nationalist faction, the New Left (*Nueva Izquierda*), led by José Ignacio Múgica Arregui, broke away from the EE later in 1982; *Ezkerra Marxista*, a similar tendency formed in October 1983, sought to remain within the EE, but the leadership declared its intention to purge any dissident groups. The EE held its six Basque parliament seats in 1984, following which Onaindía resigned as general secretary in January 1985. In 1986 the EE won a second seat in the Congress, and nine in the Basque parliament. In the 1990 Basque elections the EE tally was again six seats.

The merged PSE-EE did not aggregate the two parties' previous electoral support, winning only 12 seats in the 1994 Basque parliament elections, although it joined a regional coalition headed by the PNV. In the October 1998 Basque elections the PSE-EE advanced to 14 seats, thereafter becoming part of the regional opposition.

Basque Solidarity
Eusko Alkartasuna (EA)
Address. Camino de Portuetxe 23/1°, 20080 San Sebastián
Telephone. (+34–943) 311-377
Fax. (+34–943) 311-361
Leadership. Carlos Garaikoetxea (president); Inaxio Oliveri Albizu (secretary-general)
Email. gbe@euskoalkartasuna.es
Website. http://www.ea-euskadi.com
The EA is a radical nationalist (pro-independence), pacifist and social democratic movement, which rejects revolutionary nationalism. Its ideological determinants have included the anti-communist *Bultzagilleak* group from Guipúzcoa, the traditional nationalists known as *sabinianos* after early nationalist leader Sabino Arana and the *abertzales* or patriots. The party was founded in October 1986 as the Basque Patriots (*Eusko Abertzaleak*), as a result of a split in the →Basque Nationalist Party (PNV) which precipitated early elections to the Basque parliament the following month, when the EA won 14 seats against 17 for the parent party. Its first congress in April 1987 showed that it then had the support of several hundred mayors and local councillors. (Garaikoetxea, the then leader of the PNV, had become *lendakari*, or president of the Basque government, in April 1980, but had been forced to resign in December 1984.)

In January 1987 the EA agreed a joint programme for government with the →Basque Left (EE/EuE), this document later applying to the EA's relations with the radical EuE following the main EE's decision to create the →Basque Socialist Party–Basque Left. In June 1987 the EA contested European Parliament elections as part of the autonomist Europe of the People's Coalition (EPC), Garaikoetxea winning a seat. In November the EA declined to sign an inter-party Basque accord against terrorism paralleling that signed by parties in the Spanish parliament; the EA stated that the accord did not address the fundamental issues of self-determination and national reintegration. It slipped to nine seats in the 1990 Basque parliament elections and to eight in 1994, but retained its single national lower house seat in the March 1996 elections on a joint list with the EuE.

The EA won only six seats in the October 1998 Basque regional elections but joined a minority coalition with the PNV, the first to be formed entirely by nationalist parties. In the June 1999 European elections it was part of the Nationalist Coalition/Europe of the Peoples (*Coalición Nacionalista/Europa de los Pueblos*) alliance, winning one seat, whose holder joined Greens/European Free Alliance group.

We Basques
Euskal Herritarrok (EH)
Address. Astarioa 8/3°, 48001 Bilbao, Euzkadi
Telephone. (+34–943) 424–0799
Fax. (+34–943) 423–5932
Leadership. Arnaldo Otegi

The EH was launched in 1998 as successor to United People (*Herri Batasuna*, HB) following action against the latter by the Spanish authorities. A Marxist-oriented Basque nationalist formation, HB/EH has called for the withdrawal of "occupation forces", i.e. the Spanish military and police, and negotiations leading to the complete independence of Euzkadi. It is regarded as the closest of the main parties to the illegal terrorist group Basque Nation and Liberty (*Euzkadi ta Askatasuna*, ETA).

The HB was founded in 1978 as an alliance of two legal Basque nationalist groups, the social democratic Basque Nationalist Action (*Accion Nacionalista Vasca*, ANV), formed in 1930, and the Basque Socialist Party (*Euskal Socialista Biltzarrea*, ESB), formed in 1976, with two illegal groups, the People's Revolutionary Socialist Party (HASI) and the Patriotic Workers' Revolutionary Party (LAIA). HASI and LAIA had formed the *Koordinadora Abertzale Sozialista* (KAS), which functioned in effect as the political wing of the main ETA faction, ETA *Militar*, and the KAS manifesto was adopted more or less in full by HB.

HB has contested Basque and Spanish elections since 1979, when it won three seats (which it refused to occupy) in the Spanish Congress of Deputies, one in the Senate and a total of 48 seats (out of 248) in the provincial assemblies of Guipúzcoa, Vizcaya and Navarra. In October 1979 HB called for abstention in the referendum on the creation of an autonomous Basque region excluding Navarra; in a 59% turnout the draft statute was supported by some 90.3% of voters. In March 1980 HB won 16.3% of the vote and 11 of the 60 seats in elections to the new Basque parliament, but it has consistently refused to take up its seats in assemblies above the level of *ayuntamientos* (local councils). Although it lost one of its Congress seats in the elections of October 1982, albeit with an increased vote, it won 12 seats (out of 75) in the Basque parliamentary elections of February 1984. Also in 1984 it won a High Court ruling obliging the Interior Ministry to recognize it as a party despite its alleged links with ETA.

In 1986 HB secured five seats in the Spanish Congress, one in the Senate and 13 in the Basque parliament. In February 1987 HB nominated one of its leaders, Juan Carlos Yoldi (then in prison charged with ETA activities), as its candidate for *lendakari* (Basque premier). Also in early 1987 HB called for the formulation of a joint nationalist strategy with the →Basque Nationalist Party (PNV) and →Basque Solidarity. In June an HB candidate was elected to the European Parliament (with 1.7% of the national vote). In January 1988 HB was the only one of the seven parties represented in the Basque parliament which was not invited to sign a pact against terrorism.

In the 1989 national elections HB lost one lower house seat and surprised observers by announcing that it would occupy its four remaining seats, ending a decade-long boycott. However, on the eve of the opening of parliament, HB deputy-elect Josh Muguruza was killed and HB leader Iñaki Esnaola wounded in an attack apparently carried out by right-wing terrorists. Later the remaining HB deputies were expelled for refusing to pledge allegiance to the constitution. HB won two Congress seats and one in the Senate in the 1993 national elections, while the October 1994 Basque parliament balloting yielded 11 seats (two less than in 1990). Meanwhile, HB had lost its European Parliament seat in June 1994, its share of the national vote falling to 0.97%.

In December 1997 the entire 23-member HB leadership received seven-year prison terms for "collaborating with an armed band" (i.e. the ETA). A new leadership was elected in February 1998, following which the party opted in change its name to *Euskal Herritarrok* (EH). In the October 1998 Basque elections EH improved to 14 seats, whereupon the party backed the formation of minority regional government headed by the PNV. In the June 1999 European elections the EH obtained one Spanish seat with a 1.5% national vote share, its representative becoming one of the non-attached members. The following month the old HB leadership was released from prison.

CANARY ISLANDS

Regional assembly elections on June 13, 1999, resulted as follows: Canarian Coalition 25 seats, PSOE 19, PP 14, Hierro Independent Grouping 2.

Canarian Coalition
Coalición Canaria (CC)
Address. Galcerán 7-9, 38004 Santa Cruz de Tenerife
Leadership. Román Rodríquez (president)
The broadly centrist CC was created prior to the 1993 general elections by the following parties: (i) the Canarian Independent Groupings (*Agrupaciones Independientes de Canarias*, AIC) led by Manuel Hermoso Rojas and Paulino Rivero; (ii) the Canarian Independent Centre (*Centro Canario Independiente*, CCI) led by Lorenzo Olarte Cullén; (iii) the Canarian Initiative/Left (*Iniciativa/Izquierda Canaria*, ICAN) led by José Mendoza Cabrero and José Carlos Mauricio Rodríguez; and (iv) the Mazorca Assembly (*Asamblea Majorera*, AM) led by José Miguel Barragan Cabrera.

Of these components, the AIC was formed in 1985 as an alliance of Hermoso's *Agrupación Tinerfeña Independiente* (ATI) of Santa Cruz de Tenerife with the *Agrupación Palmera Independiente* (API) of Las Palmas and the *Agrupación Gomera Independiente* (AGI) of Tenerife. In the June 1986 general elections the AIC won about 60,000 votes, securing one seat in the Congress of Deputies and two in the Senate. The AIC retained one lower house seat in the 1989 general elections and was subsequently the only party to support Prime Minister González's re-election apart from his own →Spanish Socialist Workers' Party (PSOE). In the 1991 Canaries regional elections the AIC, with 16 seats, took second place behind the PSOE and the AIC candidate, Manuel Hermoso Rojas, was elected to the island presidency with support from the ICAN (five seats), the AM (two) and other parties.

In the 1993 national elections the CC returned four deputies and six senators, who subsequently gave qualified support to the minority PSOE government. In June 1994 the CC captured one seat in elections to the European Parliament. In September 1994 the CC-led regional government lost its narrow majority when the →Canarian Nationalist Party (PNC) left the alliance. In the May 1995 regional elections the CC obtained a plurality of 21 assembly seats out of 60 and continued to lead the islands' government. In the March 1996 national elections the CC retained four lower house seats but won only two of the directly elected Senate seats. It thereupon pledged qualified external support for a minority government of the centre-right →Popular Party.

The CC increased its regional representation to 25 seats in June 1999, thus retaining leadership of the islands' government. In simultaneous European elections the CC was part of the European Coalition (*Coalición Europea*) of moderate regional parties, winning one seat.

The CC's representative in the European Parliament sits in the European Liberal, Democratic and Reformist group.

Canarian Nationalist Party (*Partido Nacionalista Canario*, PNC), led by Pablo Betancor Betancor and José Luis Alamo Suárez, was original component of →Canarian Coalition, but withdrew in 1994, won four seats in 1995 Canaries regional elections. *Address.* Sagasta 92, 35008 Las Palmas de Gran Canaria; *Telephone/Fax.* (+34-928) 221-736

Hierro Independent Grouping (*Agrupación Herreña Independiente*, AHI), led by Tomás Padrón Hernández, won one regional assembly seat in 1995 and two in 1999. *Address.* La Constitución 4, 38900 Valverde, El Hierro, Santa Cruz de Tenerife; *Telephone.* (+34-922) 551-134; *Fax.* (+34-922) 551-224

National Congress of the Canaries (*Congreso Nacional de Canarias*, CNC), led by Antoni Cubillo Ferreira, pro-independence group founded in 1986, favours leaving the EU and joining the OAU. *Address.* Avda 3 de Mayo 81, 1° y 2°, Santa Cruz de Tenerife; *Telephone/Fax.* (+34-922) 283-353

CANTABRIA

Regional assembly elections on June 13, 1999, resulted as follows: PP 19 seats, PSOE 14, Regionalist Party of Cantabria 6.

Regionalist Party of Cantabria (*Partido Regionalista Cántabro*, PRC), led by Migel Angel Revilla, centre-right formation which obtained two of the 35 seats in the May 1983 elections to the regional parliament; by the June 1999 elections it had improved to six seats out of 39.

Union for the Progress of Cantabria (*Unión para el Progreso de Cantabria*, UPCA), led by Juan Hormaechea Cazón, conservative formation, contested the 1991 regional elections on the →Popular Party (PP) list, winning 15 of that list's 21 seats (out of 39). In June 1993, however, the UPCA president of the regional government, Juan Hormaechea Cázon, broke with the PP, with the result that his party was reduced to seven seats in the May 1995 regional elections and lost the government presidency.

CASTILLA Y LEON

Regional assembly elections on June 13, 1999, resulted as follows: PP 48 seats, PSOE 30, Union of the León People 3, IU 1, others 1.

Union of the León People (*Unión del Pueblo Leonés*, UPL), separatist formation that won two seats (out of 84) in the 1995 regional elections, rising to three in 1999.

CASTILLA–LA MANCHA

Regional assembly elections on June 13, 1999, resulted as follows: PSOE 26 seats, PP 21.

CATALONIA

Regional assembly elections on Oct. 17, 1999, resulted as follows: Convergence and Union 56 seats, Party of Socialists of Catalonia 52, PP 12, Republican Left of Catalonia 12, Initiative for Catalonia/Greens 3.

Convergence and Union
Convergència i Unió (CiU)
Address. Valencia 231, 08007 Barcelona, Catalunya
Telephone. (+34–93) 487–0111
Fax. (+34–93) 215–8428
Email.
Website.
Leadership. Jordí Pujol i Soley (secretary-general)
The pro-autonomy CiU was founded in 1979 as an alliance of the Democratic Convergence of Catalonia (*Convergència Democrática de Catalunya*, CDC) and the Democratic Union of Catalonia (*Unió Democrática de Catalunya*, UDC), and later absorbed the small Catalan Democratic Left Party (*Esquerra Democrática de Catalunya*, EDC). The CDC and UDC had contested the 1977 general elections as part of a Democratic Pact (*Pacte Democràtic*), which obtained 11 seats in the Congress of Deputies (and voted for the 1978 constitution). In the 1979 elections the CiU won eight seats in the Congress and one in the Senate. In elections to the new Catalan parliament in March 1980 the CiU displaced the →Party of Socialists of Catalonia (PSC) as the region's main political force, winning 28% of the vote and 43 of the 135 seats. Pujol was elected premier of the *Generalitat* (the Catalan administration) and formed a coalition with the local affiliate of the Union of the Democratic Centre, then the ruling party in Madrid, and a number of independents. In the October 1982 general elections the CiU increased its representation in the Spanish Congress to 12 members (and nine in the Senate). In the April 1984 Catalan elections the CiU won 46.8% of the vote and 72 seats, enabling it to form a majority administration.

In the 1986 national elections the CiU returned 18 deputies and eight senators, thus becoming the fourth-largest party in the Spanish parliament. It was allied with the new liberal Democratic Reformist Party (PRD), which failed to win any seats, their joint candidate for Prime Minister having been Miquel Roca Junyent, the CiU parliamentary leader who had formed the PRD and was regarded as the national leader of the reformist-liberal bloc. The CiU obtained three seats in the 1987 European Parliament elections. In March 1992 the CiU confirmed its regional dominance by winning 71 of the 135 seats in the Catalan assembly, while national elections in June 1993 yielded 17 lower house and 14 Senate seats, on a vote share of nearly 5%. The party thereafter gave qualified parliamentary support to the minority government of the →Spanish Socialist Workers' Party (PSOE). In June 1994 the CiU retained three seats in the European Parliament elections with 4.7% of the vote.

The travails of the PSOE government in 1994–95 encouraged the CiU to attach more autonomist conditions to its continued support, beyond the original demand for greater transfer of tax receipts to the Catalan government. After much confusion, the CESID phone-tapping scandal of mid-1995 finally impelled the CiU into formal opposition and support for new general elections. This switch enabled the party to maintain its ascendancy in regional elections in Catalonia in November 1995, although it fell back to 60 seats (out of

187

135). Held in March 1996, early national elections resulted in the CiU slipping to 16 lower house and eight Senate seats, with 4.6% of the overall vote. After protracted negotiations, the CiU agreed to give external support to a minority government of the anti-regionalization →Popular Party (PP), which in return was obliged to swallow a dose of further devolution and to express admiration for Catalan culture. Featuring a doubling (to 30%) of tax receipt transfers from Madrid to Barcelona (and to the other autonomous regions), the deal with the PP was approved by the CiU executive in late April 1996 by 188 votes to 20 with 21 abstentions.

The CiU retained three seats in the June 1999 European elections (two for the CDC and one for the UDC), with 4.4% of the vote. In regional elections in October 1999 the CiU's long dominance came under serious challenge from the PSC, but the party just managed to remain the largest party with 56 seats (though with only 37.7% of the vote against 37.9% for the PSC). Pujol was therefore able to form a further minority administration.

Of the CiU components, the UDC is affiliated to the Christian Democrat International and its representative in the European Parliament sits in the European People's Party/European Democrats group. The two CDC representatives sit in the European Liberal, Democratic and Reformist group.

Initiative for Catalonia
Iniciativa per Catalunya (IC)
Address. Ciutat 7, 08002 Barcelona, Catalunya
Telephone. (+34–93) 301-0612
Fax. (+34–93) 412-4252
Leadership. Rafael Ribó Massó (president)
The IC was launched in 1986 as an alliance of Communist and other left-wing formations in Catalonia, headed by the Unified Socialist Party of Catalonia (*Partit Socialista Unificat de Catalunya*, PSUC) led by Ribó Massó and also including the Party of Communists of Catalonia (*Partit dels Comunistes de Catalunya*, PCC) and the Union of Left Nationalists (*Entesa des Nacionalistas d'Esquerra*, ENE).

Founded in 1936 by the merger of four left-wing groups, the PSUC took part in the government of Catalonia until 1939, when it was forced underground by the Francoist victory. Legalized again in 1976, it became a member of the provisional government of Catalonia. In the 1980 elections to the new Catalan parliament the PSUC obtained 19% of the vote and 25 of the 135 seats; but in the 1984 elections it was reduced to six seats and 5.8% of the vote. In the June 1986 national elections the PSUC retained the single seat in the Congress of Deputies which it had won in 1982 (as against eight won in 1979 and 1977).

Contesting the 1992 regional and 1993 national elections as effectively the Catalan version of the national →United Left, the IC made little impact. For the November 1995 regional elections it formed an alliance with the Catalan →Greens (*Els Verds*), their joint list obtaining 11 of the 135 seats. It maintained the alliance in the October 1999 regional elections but also gave tactical support to the →Party of Socialists of Catalonia and confined its own effort to Barcelona, with the result that its representation fell to three seats.

Party of Socialists of Catalonia
Partit dels Socialistes de Catalunya (PSC)
Address. Calle Nicaragua 75-77, 08029 Barcelona, Catalunya
Telephone. (+34–93) 495-5400
Fax. (+34–3) 495-5435
Email. psc@psc.es
Website. http://www.psc.es

Leadership. Pasqual Maragall (president); Narcís Serra (first secretary)
The PSC is affiliated to, but not formally part of, the →Spanish Socialist Workers' Party
(PSOE), pursuing similar economic and social policies but seeking the transformation of the
current autonomist constitution into a federal one. The present party was founded in July 1978
as a merger of three pre-existing socialist formations, including the Catalan branch of the
PSOE. After winning 15 lower house seats in the 1977 national elections, the following year
the PSC affiliated to the PSOE, contesting subsequent national elections as a federation of the
Spanish party.

In the 1979 general elections the PSC returned 17 lower house deputies, but was
defeated by the centrist →Convergence and Union (CiU) alliance in the 1980 elections to the
Catalan parliament, obtaining 33 of the 135 seats. In the 1982 national elections the PSC won
an absolute majority (25) of the Catalan seats in the lower house. In the 1984 Catalan
elections it obtained 30% of the vote and 41 seats, while in the 1986 national elections it fell
back to 21 seats but remained ahead of other Catalan parties. The same pattern of ascendancy
in national contests and inferiority at regional level was apparent in subsequent elections. In
the November 1995 Catalan elections the PSC won 34 seats (against 39 in 1992), again
coming a distant second to the CiU.

In June 1999 three PSC members were elected to the European Parliament on the PSOE
list. In the October 1999 regional elections the PSC mounted a strong challenge against the
CiU, on a platform of less strident Catalan nationalism and greater accommodation with the
rest of Spain. It outpolled the CiU in popular vote terms (37.9% to 37.7%) and increased its
representation to 52 seats, but narrowly failed to become the leading party and so remained in
opposition.

Republican Left of Catalonia
Esquerra Republicana de Catalunya (ERC)
Address. Carrer Villarroel 45 ent., 08011 Barcelona, Catalonia
Telephone. (+34–93) 453–6005
Fax. (+34–93) 323–7122
Email. international@esquerra.org
Website. http://www.esquerra.org
Leadership. Josep Lluís Carod-Rovira (secretary-general); Jordí Carbonell (president)
Dating from 1931, the ERC was the majority party in the Catalan parliament of 1932 but was
forced underground during the Franco era. Re-legalized in 1977, it adopted a moderate
left-wing economic programme, also advocating Catalan self-determination and defining
languages other than Catalan as foreign. It contested the June 1977 national elections along
with the *Partido del Trabajo de España*, other groups and independent candidates in an
alliance, the *Esquerra de Catalunya–Front Electoral Democràtic*, and elected one deputy. In
1979 the ERC allied with the *Front Nacional de Catalunya*, and won one seat each in the
Spanish Congress of Deputies and the Senate. In elections for the new Catalan parliament in
March 1980 the ERC gained 9% of the vote and 14 of the 135 seats. In the October 1982
Spanish elections it held its single seat in the Congress, and in the Catalan elections in April
1984 it won 4.4% and its strength was reduced to five members.

The ERC divided during the 1980s between a liberal wing, which favoured participation
in the Catalan *Generalitat* (government), and the left, which favoured an independent line.
The 15th (1985) ERC congress elected the liberal Joan Hortalà i Arau (the Catalan industry
minister) as the party's leader, succeeding the more nationalistic Heribert Barrera i Costa. The
1986 elections deprived the ERC of its representation in the Madrid parliament, but in 1987
the party was part of the Europe of the Peoples Coalition (CEP) that secured a seat in the
European Parliament (this being retained in 1989 but lost in 1994).

In 1991 the ERC absorbed the radical separatist Free Land (*Terre Lliure*) movement, the consequences being a switch from a pro-federalism line to advocacy of outright independence for Catalonia. The ERC retained its single seat in the national lower house in the 1993 and 1996 elections. In Catalonia it won 11 of 135 regional parliament seats in 1992, rising to 13 in November 1995. The ERC was part of the Nationalist Coalition/Europe of the Peoples (*Coalición Nacionalista/Europa de los Pueblos*) of regional parties in the June 1999 European elections, though it failed to win one of the Coalition's two seats. In the October 1999 regional elections the ERC slipped to 12 seats on a vote share of 8.7%.

EXTREMADURA

Regional elections on June 13, 1999, resulted as follows: PSOE 34 seats, PP 28, IU 3.

GALICIA

Regional elections on Oct. 19, 1997, resulted as follows: PP 42, Galician Nationalist Bloc 18, Party of Galician Socialists 15.

Galician Nationalist Bloc
Bloque Nacionalista Galego (BNG)
Address. Avda Rodríquez de Viguri, Bloque 3 Baixo, 15703 Santiago de Compostela, Galicia
Telephone. (+34-981) 555-850
Fax. (+34-981) 555-851
Email. sedenacional1@bng-web.org
Website. http://www.arrakis.es/~bng
Leadership. Xosé Manuel Beiras (secretary-general)
Founded in 1983, the BNG advocates greater autonomy for Galicia and traditional left-wing economic policies. Its regional electoral support had risen steadily, from five seats in 1989 to 13 (out of 75) in 1993. In 1991 it absorbed the more centrist Galician National Party (*Partido Nacionalista Galego*, PNG) led by Pablo González Mariñas, which had been formed in 1986 by a progressive faction of the Galician Coalition. The BNG advanced to 18 seats in the October 1997 regional elections and won one seat in the June 1999 European elections with 1.7% of the national. Its representative in the European Parliament joined the Greens/European Free Alliance group.

Party of Galician Socialists
Partido dos Socialistas de Galicia (PSdG)
Address. Pino 1-9, 15704 Santiago de Compostela
Telephone. (+34–981) 589-622
Leadership. Emilio Pérez Touriño (secretary-general)
The PSdG is the autonomous regional federation of the →Spanish Socialist Workers' Party (PSOE). It is the largest party in the region as regards national, but not regional, elections, having won 18 seats in the Congress of Deputies in 1982 and 15 in 1986. In 1981 it secured 17, and in 1985 22, of the 71 seats in the Galician parliament, control of the Xunta passing in 1985 to what became the →Popular Party (PP), although in 1987 the PSdG-PSOE again established control briefly. Despite advancing to 28 seats in 1989, the party went into opposition to the PP. It slumped to 19 seats in the 1993 regional elections and continued in opposition, falling further to 15 seats in October 1997, when it was allied with the regional United Left–Galiciian Left (*Esquerda Unida–Esquerda Galega*, EU-EG) and the →Greens.

MADRID

Regional elections on June 13, 1999, resulted as follows: PP 55 seats, PSOE 39, IU 8.

MURCIA

Regional elections on June 13, 1999, resulted as follows: PP 27 seats, PSOE 17, IU 1.

NAVARRA

Regional elections on June 13, 1999, resulted as follows: Union of the Navarrese People 22 seats, Socialist Party of Navarra 11, We Basques (EH) 8, Basque Solidarity (EA) 3, Convergence of Navarran Democrats 3, IU 3. (The EH and EA are covered above under Basque Country.)

Socialist Party of Navarra
Partido Socialista de Navarra (PSN)
Address. c/o Regional Assembly, Pamplona, Navarra
Leadership. Víctor Manuel Arbeloa (president); Juan José Lizarbe (secretary-general)
The PSN is the regional federation of the →Spanish Socialist Workers' Party (PSOE). Formed in 1975 as the *Federación Socialista de Navarra*, it was integrated into the PSOE in 1982, although it retained its own identity and structure. Having won 19 of the 50 regional seats in 1991, the PSN was in opposition to the →Union of the Navarrese People until the 1995 elections, in which it fell back to 11 seats but nevertheless secured the election of Javier Otano as regional premier by virtue of support from other parties. It again won 11 seats in the June 1999 regional elections.

Union of the Navarrese People
Union del Pueblo Navarro (UPN)
Address. Plaza Príncipe de Viana 1/4°, 31002 Pamplona, Navarra
Telephone. (+34–948) 227-211
Fax. (+34–948) 210-810
Leadership. Miguel Sanz Sesma (president); Rafael Gurrea Induraín (secretary)
Founded in 1979, the conservative and Christian democratic UPN won a single seat in the Congress of Deputies in 1979 but lost it in 1982. In the 1982 and 1986 national elections the UPN allied with the right-wing Popular Alliance, precursor of the →Popular Party (PP); it also co-operated with the Popular Democratic Party (PDP) and the Liberal Union (UL), now the →Liberal Party. In the 1983 Navarra regional elections the UPN (then led by Javier Gomara) won 13 of the 50 seats, increasing to 14 in 1987 and to a plurality of 20 in 1991, when its candidate Juan Cruz Alli Aranguren was elected president of the regional government. It slipped to 17 seats in 1995 and went into opposition to a coalition headed by the →Socialist Party of Navarre.

LA RIOJA

Regional assembly elections on June 13, 1999, resulted as follows: PP 18 seats, PSOE 13, Rioja Party 2.

Rioja Party
Partido Riojano (PR)
Address. Portales 17/1°, 26001 Logroño, La Rioja

Telephone. (+34–941) 238-199
Fax. (+34–941) 254-396
Leadership. Miguel González de Legarra (president); Jesús María Resa Fernández de Manzanos (secretary-general)
This small regionalist grouping has attempted, with little success, to challenge the dominance in the Rioja region of the national parties (mainly the PP and the PSOE, the latter organized locally as the *Partido Socialista de La Rioja*). It has usually returned two successful candidates in regional elections, most recently in June 1999.

VALENCIA

Regional elections on June 13, 1999, resulted as follows: PP 49 seats, Socialist Party of Valencia 35, Unity of the Valencian People 5.

Socialist Party of Valencia
Partido Socialista del País Valenciano (PSPV)
Address. Almirante 3, 46003 Valencia
Leadership. Antonio García Miralles (president); Antoni Asunción (secretary-general)
The PSPV is a regional wing of the →Spanish Socialist Workers' Party (PSOE) and was the dominant Valencian party in regional and national elections of the 1980s and early 1990s. In both the May 1995 and June 1999 regional elections, however, it came a poor second to the →Popular Party, winning only 32 and 35 of the 89 seats respectively.

Unity of the Valencian People (*Unitat del Poble Valencià*, UPV), led by Pere Mayor Penadés, founded in 1982 by two regionalist parties as a "democratic, left nationalist, egalitarian, ecologist and pacifist" formation; in alliance with the →United Left, it won two regional seats in 1987, failed to win representation in 1995 and advanced to five seats in June 1999.

Valencian Nationalist Party (*Partido Valenciano Nacionalista/Partit Valencià Nacionalista*, PVN), seeking the restoration of the ancient Valencian kingdom. *Address.* Passeig de Russafa 10/3r/4, 46002 Ciutat de Valencia. *Telephone/Fax.* (+34-96) 394-2615; *Email.* pvn@arrakis.es

Valencian Union
Unió Valenciana (UV)
Address. Avda de César Giorgeta 16/1°, 46007 Valencia
Telephone. (+34-96) 380-6267
Fax. (+34-96) 380-2308
Leadership. Héctor Villalba Chirivella (president)
The centre-right regionalist UV was founded in 1982, describing itself as "progressive and independent, inter-classist and democratic". At first allied with national conservative parties, it stood on its own in the 1986 national elections and won one lower house seat, which it has retained in subsequent elections. At regional level it maintained a small but significant presence, winning five seats in May 1995 and securing the election of its leader as president of the regional parliament. It failed to win representation in June 1999.

CEUTA AND MELILLA

Under legislation approved in September 1994 the North African enclaves of Ceuta and Melilla acquired full autonomous status as regions of Spain. Political life in both possessions was dominated until recently by local branches of metropolitan formations, notably the →Popular Party (PP) and the →Spanish Socialist Workers' Party (PSOE). However, elections on June 13, 1999, in Ceuta resulted in the newly-founded Independent Liberal Group (GIL) winning 12 seats, against eight for the PP, two for the PSOE and three for others, while in Melilla the GIL won seven seats, the Coalition for Melilla five, the PP five, the PSOE two and others six.

Independent Liberal Group (*Grupo Independiente Liberal*, GIL), led by Jesús Gil (mayor of the mainland city of Marbella), won pluralities in both Cenuta and Melilla in June 1999, on a platform of closer integration of the enclaves with mainland Spain.

Initiative for Ceuta (*Iniciativa por Ceuta*, IC), led by Ahmed Subair, leftist grouping formed in December 1990, based in the Muslim community and named after the →Initiative for Catalonia.

Progress and Future of Ceuta (*Progreso y Futuro de Ceuta*, PFC), led by Francisco Fraiz Armada, supports continued Spanish status, won six Ceuta assembly seats in 1995, its leader being elected government president with support from other parties.

Coalition for Melilla (*Coalición por Melilla*, CpM), led by Mustafa Aberchan Hamed, won five seats in June 1999 elections.

Union of the Melilla People (*Unión del Pueblo Melillense*, UPM), led by Juan José Imbroda Ortíz, right-wing formation founded in 1985.

Sweden

Capital: Stockholm   **Population:** 8,900,000

The Kingdom of Sweden is a parliamentary democracy in which the monarch has purely ceremonial functions as head of state. There is a Cabinet headed by a Prime Minister and responsible to a unicameral Parliament (*Riksdag*) of 349 members

Parliamentary elections on Sept. 22, 1998, resulted as follows:		
	Seats	Percentage
	1998 (1994)	*1998 (1994)*
Social Democratic Labour Party	131 (161)	36.4 (45.3)
Moderate Alliance Party	82 (80)	22.9 (22.4)
Left Party	43 (22)	11.9 (6.2)
Christian Democratic Community Party ...	42 (15)	11.8 (4.1)
Centre Party	18 (27)	5.1 (7.7)
Liberal People's Party	17 (26)	4.7 (7.2)
Green Ecology Party	16 (18)	4.5 (5.0)

elected for a four-year term by universal adult suffrage of citizens above the age of 18 years under a system of proportional representation, with 310 seats being filled in 28 multi-member constituencies and the remaining 39 allocated to parties according to a complex formula. A party must obtain 4% of the national vote to qualify for a seat. Sweden joined what became the European Union on Jan. 1, 1995, and elects 22 members of the European Parliament.

Since 1966 state subsidies have been paid to political parties which have at least one representative in the *Riksdag* or have obtained at least 2.5% of the national vote in either of the two most recent elections, with an additional "secretariat subsidy" being available for parties achieving 4% or more of the vote. The amount of the subsidies is related to party representation or voting strength, but "secretariat subsidies" are higher for opposition parties than for those in the government. Similar arrangements apply at the level of regional and local government. In 1999 the total amount allocated for party subsidies in the state budget was Skr221.2 million (about $26 million), of which the Social Democratic Labour Party, for example, was eligible for Skr74 million (about $8.7 million).

Centre Party
Centerpartiet (CP)
Address. Bergsgatan 7B, PO Box 22087, 104 22 Stockholm
Telephone. (+46–8) 617–3800
Fax. (+46–8) 652–6440
Email. centerpartiet@centerpartiet.se
Website. http://www.centerpartiet.se
Leadership. Lennart Daléus (chair); Agne Hansson (parliamentary chair); Ola Alterå (secretary-general)

The Centre Party works for a decentralized society with a social market economy, with all parts of the country having an equal chance to develop; for the protection of the environment; and for the use of technology not only for man's material welfare but also for his mental well-being. The party is strongly opposed to the development of nuclear energy capacity.

The party was founded in 1910 as the Farmers' Union Party for the purpose of representing the population in country's rural areas; it has developed into one of the centre with supporters in both rural and urban districts. It first gained parliamentary representation in 1917 and formed its first government in June 1936. From October 1936 it co-operated in government with the →Social Democratic Labour Party (SAP), and in 1939–45 in a national coalition government. In 1951–57 the party was again a partner with the SAP in a coalition government, at the end of which it changed its name to Centre Party–Farmers' Union Party (1957), shortening this to Centre Party a year later.

In 1976–78 the CP headed a three-party non-socialist government including also the →Liberal People's (FP) and →Moderate Alliance (MSP) parties, this coalition, led by Thorbjörn Fälldin, being re-established after the September 1979 elections. In elections to the *Riksdag* in September 1982 the CP obtained 15.5% of the valid votes and 56 (out of 349) seats and went into opposition. In the September 1985 elections, which it contested jointly with the →Christian Democratic Community Party (KdS), the CP slipped to 12.4% and 44 seats (including one Christian Democrat) and continued in opposition. In view of this setback Fälldin resigned the party leadership in December 1985, having come under sharp criticism for his opposition to a rapprochement with the SAP, the party's traditional allies. He was replaced by Karin Söder (who became Sweden's first female party leader), but she resigned in January 1987 for health reasons and was succeeded by Olof Johansson.

The CP's decline continued in the 1988 and 1991 elections, to 42 and 31 seats respectively, but after the latter contest the party entered a centre-right coalition headed by the MSP. In June 1994 its participation was shaken by the resignation of party chairman Johansson as Environment Minister, in opposition to the controversial Öresund Sound bridge project. In the September 1994 parliamentary elections the CP was further reduced to 27 seats (on a vote share of 7.7%) and again went into opposition. The CP supported Swedish accession to the European Union (EU), while advocating non-participation in a single European currency or in any EU defence co-operation. In Sweden's first direct elections to the European Parliament in September 1995, the CP won two of the 22 seats on a 7.2% vote share.

In April 1998 Olof Johansson was succeeded as CP leader by Lennart Daléus, who led the party to a further defeat in the September 1988 general elections, when its vote fell to 5.1% and its representation to only 18 seats. In the June 1999 European elections the CP vote slipped to 6.0%, giving the party only one seat.

The CP's representative in the European Parliament sits in the European Liberal, Democratic and Reformist group.

Christian Democratic Community Party
Kristdemokratiska Samhällspartiet (KdS)
Address. Malargatan 7, PO Box 451, 101 26 Stockholm
Telephone. (+46–8) 723-2550
Fax. (+46–8) 723-2510
Email. brev.till@kristdemokrat.se
Website. http://www.kristdemokrat.se
Leadership. Alf Svensson (chair); Göran Hägglund (parliamentary chair); Sven Gunnar Persson (secretary-general)

The KdS has described itself as "the third alternative in Sweden, where all [other] parties are socialistic or non-socialistic". It propagates "a new way of life" and concentrates on social problems, calling for a review of the abortion law among other things. It also calls for a halt to the building of nuclear power stations. The party was founded in 1964 and obtained some 78,000 votes in its first general election in 1964. By 1982 this total had increased to 103,820 (1.9%). Having thus failed to pass the 4% barrier to representation in the *Riksdag*, in September 1985 it entered into an electoral pact with the →Centre Party, winning some 2.6% of the vote in its own right and being allocated one of the Centre Party's 44 seats (Alf Svensson becoming the party's first representative in the *Riksdag*). Meanwhile, the party had established a significant local government presence, with almost 300 elected councillors by the mid-1980s.

Originally called the Christian Democratic Assembly (*Kristen Demokratisk Samling*), the party assumed its present name in 1987, when it also adopted a new programme. The KdS failed to secure representation in the 1988 parliamentary elections, but again came back strongly three years later, winning 26 *Riksdag* seats in 1991 (with 7.1% of the vote) and becoming a member of a centre-right coalition government. It slipped back in the 1994 contest, only just clearing the 4% barrier and winning 15 seats. It thereupon went into opposition to a minority government of the →Social Democratic Labour Party. The KdS was strongly in favour of Swedish accession to the EU in 1995.

Campaigning on a platform of family values and opposition to sleaze, the KdS registered a record advance in the September 1998 general elections, winning 42 seats on a vote share of

11.8%. It remained in opposition and lost impetus by the time of the June 1999 European elections, in which it won two seats and 7.6% of the vote.

The KdS is affiliated to the Christian Democrat International. Its representatives in the European Parliament sit in the European People's Party/European Democrats group.

Green Ecology Party
Miljöpartiet de Gröna
Address. PO Box 12660, 112 93, Stockholm
Telephone. (+46–8) 208-050
Fax. (+46–8) 201-577
Email. ursula@mp.se
Website. http://www.mp.se
Leadership. Lotta Nilsson Hedström and Birger Schlaug (spokespersons); Gunnar Goude and Marianne Samuelsson (parliamentary chairs); Håkan Wåhlstedt (secretary)
Founded in September 1981, the party stands for nature conservation, anti-pollution taxation and other measures, agricultural production to achieve national self-sufficiency in basic foodstuffs, the phasing-out of nuclear energy, support for the peace movement, the creation of nuclear-weapons-free zones in Scandinavia and Europe, a flexible retirement age and the ending of discrimination against immigrants. It has also called for a six-hour day, lower interest rates and reduced economic growth (this last goal being achieved in the early 1990s, although not quite in the way envisaged by the party).

In the 1982 and 1985 general elections the party fell well short of the 4% vote minimum required for representation in the *Riksdag*, not least because the major parties, particularly the →Social Democratic Labour Party (SAP) and the →Centre Party, have incorporated a strong environmentalist strand in their platforms. On the other hand, it succeeded in obtaining representation in over 30% of local councils by 1988, in which year it became the first new party to enter the *Riksdag* for 70 years, winning 20 seats on a 5.5% vote share. It slumped to 3.4% in 1991 and so failed to gain representation; but in 1994 it recovered strongly to 5.0% and 18 *Riksdag* seats, thereafter giving qualified external support to the minority government of the SAP.

Opposed to Sweden's accession to the EU, the Greens were prominent in the "no" campaign for the November 1994 referendum on EU membership, finishing on the losing side. The party nevertheless polled strongly in Sweden's first direct elections to the European Parliament in September 1995 winning four seats on a vote share of 17.2%. In the September 1998 general elections, however, the party slipped to 4.5% and 16 seats, thereafter giving external support to a further minority SAP government. In the June 1999 European elections the Greens were reduced to two seats, with a 9.5% vote share.

The Greens are affiliated to the European Federation of Green Parties. Its representatives in the European Parliament are members of the Greens/European Free Alliance group.

Left Party
Vänsterpartiet (VP)
Address. Kungsgatan 84, PO Box 12660, 112 93 Stockholm
Telephone. (+46–8) 654–0820
Fax. (+46–8) 653–2385
Email. orjan.svedberg@vansterpartiet.se
Website. http://www.vansterpartiet.se
Leadership. Gudrun Schyman (chair); Lars Bäckström (parliamentary chair); Lars Ohly (secretary)

The VP is the latter-day successor to the historic Swedish Communist Party, which was founded as early as May 1917 under the name Left Social Democratic Party by the revolutionary wing of the →Social Democratic Labour Party (SAP). It changed its name to Communist Party in 1921, having joined the Communist International (Comintern), to which it belonged until that organization's dissolution in 1943. In the post-1945 era, the party at first displayed pro-Soviet orthodoxy but in the 1960s embarked upon a revisionist course in line with "Euro-communist" prescriptions. To signify the party's aim of becoming "a forum for the whole socialist left", the new designation Left Party-Communists (*Vänsterpartiet-Kommunisterna*, VPK) was adopted in 1967. This decision, combined with attendant policy evolution, generated much dissension within the party prior to the withdrawal of an orthodox faction in early 1977 to form the →Communist Workers' Party. The suffix "Communists" was dropped from the party's title by a congress decision of May 1990.

The party has been represented in the *Riksdag* since its foundation, and for long periods minority SAP governments have relied on its support. In both the 1979 and 1982 general elections what was then the VPK obtained 20 seats and 5.6% of the valid votes, while in September 1985 it slipped to 5.4% and 19 seats (out of 349); but a concurrent SAP decline meant that VPK voting strength became crucial to the SAP government's survival in the late 1980s. The renamed VP won 16 seats in the 1991 general elections (on a vote share of 4.5%), thereafter going into full opposition to a centre-right coalition government. In a general swing to the left in September 1994, the VP achieved the party's best result since 1948, winning 6.2% of the vote and 22 seats.

The VP campaigned vigorously against Sweden's accession to the European Union (the only parliamentary party to do so), but was on the losing side in the November 1994 referendum. In Sweden's first direct elections to the European Parliament in September 1995 the VP won three seats on a 12.9% vote share. In September 1997 party leader Gudrun Schyman announced that she was taking leave of absence for the latest round in her long public struggle against alcoholism. She returned to lead the party to a record result in the September 1998 general elections, in which the VP vote, boosted by disaffected SAP supporters, climbed to 11.9% and its representation to 43 seats. It thereafter gave external support to a further SAP minority government and maintained its forward impetus in the Juhe 1999 European elections, in which it again won three seats but with an increased vote share of 15.8%

The party's representatives in the European Parliament sit in the European United Left/Nordic Green Left group.

Liberal People's Party
Folkpartiet Liberalerna (FPL)
Address. Drottninggatan 97/1tr, PO Box 6508, 113 83 Stockholm
Telephone. (+46–8) 5091-1600
Fax. (+46–8) 5091-1660
Email. info@liberal.se
Website. http://www.folkpartiet.se
Leadership. Lars Leijonborg (chair); Bo Könberg (parliamentary chair); Torbjörn Pettersson (secretary-general)
Although the present party dates from 1934, organized liberalism began in Sweden at the end of the 19th century with the objectives of social justice, universal suffrage and equality. After World War I a coalition government with the →Social Democratic Labour Party (SAP), led by a Liberal Prime Minister, completed the process of democratization. At the same time, the introduction of universal suffrage reduced the party's influence, while between 1923 and 1934 the party was split over the issue of alcohol prohibition. Nevertheless, it formed governments in 1926–28 and 1930–32, and it took part in the national government during World War II.

In 1948 the party became the second strongest in the then lower chamber of the *Riksdag*, with 57 seats, but by 1968 its representation had declined to 34. In the unicameral *Riksdag* established in January 1971 the party won 58 seats in 1970, but only 34 in 1973 and 39 in 1976. It then took part in the first non-socialist government to be formed in Sweden for 44 years in coalition with the →Centre and →Moderate Alliance (Conservative) parties. The collapse of this coalition in October 1978 over the nuclear issue was followed by a year of minority Liberal rule under Ola Ullsten; but as a result of the September 1979 elections the three-party non-socialist coalition was re-established. However, the Conservatives left this government in 1981 after disagreements on taxation, and the Liberal and Centre parties formed a minority government until the September 1982 elections brought the Social Democrats back to power. In those elections the Liberal vote dropped to 5.9% and its representation to 21 seats.

The FPL staged a significant recovery in the September 1985 elections, winning 14.2% of the vote and 51 seats, but remaining in opposition. It fell back to 44 seats to 1988 (12.2%) and to 33 in 1991 (9.1%), when it joined a four-party centre-right coalition. Another setback followed in the September 1994 elections, which yielded only 7.2% and 26 seats, after which the party reverted to opposition status and party leader Bengt Westerberg gave way to Maria Leissner. The FPL was strongly in favour of Swedish accession to the EU in January 1995, but in Sweden's first direct elections to the European Parliament in September 1995 it managed only 4.8% of the vote and one seat.

Elected party leader in March 1997, Lars Leijonborg led the FPL to a further defeat in the September 1998 general elections, in which the party fell back to 4.7% of the vote and 17 seats. In the June 1999 European elections, however, the FPL recovered strongly to 13.9% of the vote, which gave it three seats.

With an official membership of 23,000, the FPL is a member of the Liberal International. Its representatives in the European Parliament sit in the European Liberal, Democratic and Reformist group.

Moderate Alliance Party
Moderata Samlingspartiet (MSP)
Address. PO Box 1243, 111 82 Stockholm
Telephone. (+46–8) 676–8000
Fax. (+46–8) 216-123
Email. info@moderat.se
Website. http://www.moderat.se
Leadership. Bo Lundgren (chair); Chris Heister (first vice-chair); Gunilla Carlsson (second vice-chair); Per Unckel (parliamentary chair); Johnny Magnusson (secretary-general)
The MSP combines a conservative heritage with liberal ideas to advocate a moderate, anti-socialist policy in favour of a free-market economy and individual freedom of choice. The party was originally founded in 1904 as the political expression of better-off peasants and the emerging industrial bourgeoisie, the party participated in coalitions or formed minority governments several times hefore 1932. after which the →Social Democratic Labour Party (SAP) was in almost uninterrupted power for 44 years (though during World War II all democratic parties took part in the government). The party increased its support during the 1950s, winning more than 20% of the vote in the 1958 general elections, but declined in subsequent contests, obtaining only 11.6% in the 1970 elections, prior to which it changed its name from Conservative to Moderate Alliance Party.

Later the party advanced again, gaining 15.6% of the vote in the 1976 elections whereupon it entered the first non-socialist coalition for 40 years (with the Centre and Liberal parties). This was dissolved in October 1978 but re-established after the September 1979 elections, in which the party made a significant advance, to 20.3% and 73 seats. It withdrew from the coalition in May 1981 amid disagreements over fiscal policy, although it generally gave external support to the government thereafter. In the elections of September 1982 the party gained further support (23.6% of the vote and 86 seats) and thus became the dominant non-socialist party in Sweden, although the Social Democrats were returned to power as a minority government. In the September 1985 elections the MSP slipped to 21.3% and 76 seats (out of 349) and continued in opposition. In light of this setback, Ulf Adelsohn resigned as party chairman in June 1986 and was succeeded by Carl Bildt (son-in-law of Adelsohn's immediate predecessor, Gösta Bohman).

A further decline in 1988 (to 18.3% and 66 seats) was followed by recovery in 1991 to 21.9% and 80 seats, enabling Bildt to form a four-party centre-right coalition with the →Centre, →Christian Democratic Community and →Liberal People's parties. In the September 1994 elections the MSP again won 80 seats (and a slightly higher 22.4% vote share), but a general swing to the left resulted in a minority SAP government. Two months later the MSP warmly welcomed the referendum decision in favour of EU membership. Released of the burdens of government, Bildt accepted appointment as the EU's chief mediator in former Yugoslavia, while retaining the less taxing post of MSP chair. In Sweden's first direct elections to the European Parliament in September 1995 the MSP took five of the 22 seats with a vote share of 23.2%.

Despite the unpopularity of the SAP government, the MSP failed to make major inroads in the September 1998 general elections, winning 82 seats on a slightly higher vote of 22.9%. Remaining in opposition, the party also registered a lacklustre performance in the June 1999 European elections, retaining five seats but on a rediced vote share of 20.7%. In August 1999 Bildt was succeeded as party leader by Bo Lundgren, a former MSP Finance Minister.

With an official membership of 97,000, the MSP is affiliated to the Christian Democrat International, the International Democrat Union and the European Democrat Union. Its members of the European Parliament sit in the European People's Party/European Democrats group.

Swedish Social Democratic Labour Party
Sveriges Socialdemokratiska Arbetareparti (SAP)
Address. Socialdemokraterna, Sveavägen 68, 105 60 Stockholm
Telephone. (+46–8) 700–2600
Fax. (+46–8) 219-331
Email. sap.international@sap.se
Website. http://www.sap.se
Leadership. Göran Persson (chair); Sven Hulterström (parliamentary chair); Lars Stjernkvist (general secretary)
The SAP seeks "to transform society in such a way that the right of decision over production and its distribution is placed in the hands of the entire nation"; to replace "a social order based on classes" by "a community of people in partnership on a basis of liberty and equality"; and to work for "Sweden's non-alignment and neutrality in war" and for "world peace on the basis of self-determination for every nation, of social and economic justice, of détente and disarmament and of international co-operation". The party has shown majority support for Sweden's participation in the European Union (EU), though a significant SAP minority is opposed to further EU integration.

Founded in April 1889, the party sent its first member to the *Riksdag* in 1896, namely Hjalmar Branting, who, after serving as Minister of Finance in 1917–18, became Prime Minister in Sweden's first Social Democratic government in 1920; he was Prime Minister again in 1921–23 and in 1924–25. The share of national vote gained by the party in elections rose from 28.5% in 1911 to 53.8% in 1940, whereafter it declined to 46.7% in 1944 and remained more or less stable until 1968, when it rose to 50.1%. In the four succeeding elections the SAP share fell to 42.9% in 1976, rose slightly to 43.3% in 1979 and to 45.6% in 1982, but slipped to 45.1% in September 1985, when it won 159 seats in the *Riksdag* (out of 349).

Except for a short interval in 1936, the party was in office from 1932 to 1976, in coalition with the →Centre Party between 1936 and 1939 and between 1951 and 1957, in a four-party coalition during World War II, and at other times as a minority party requiring the support of one or more other parties on important issues. The party's 44 years of virtually uninterrupted power established the record for continuous governmental power by a social democratic party, and also resulted in Sweden becoming what was widely regarded as a model social democracy. In over 100 years of existence, the SAP has had only six leaders, namely Hjalmar Branting, Per-Albin Hansson, Tage Erlander, Olof Palme, Ingvar Carlsson and Göran Persson (since March 1996). Carlsson succeeded to the party leadership and premiership following the assassination of Palme on a Stockholm street on Feb. 28, 1986 (the responsibility and motives for which remained uncertain at the end of the century).

Having formed a minority government since 1982, the SAP went into opposition after the September 1991 elections, when its share of the vote fell from 43.2% in 1988 to 37.6% and its representation from 156 seats to 138. It recovered in a general swing to the left in the September 1994 elections, bringing it 45.3% of the vote and 161 seats and enabling it to form another minority government under Carlsson. For the November 1994 referendum on EU membership, the official government and party line was to favour a "yes" vote; but the extent of anti-EU opinion within SAP ranks compelled the leadership to allow the contrary case to be made within the party. In both the 1994 general elections and the September 1995 European Parliament polling anti-EU candidates were included on the SAP lists. The result on the latter occasion was that three of the seven Social Democrats elected (on a vote share of only 28%) were "Eurosceptic" to a greater or lesser extent.

Meanwhile, Carlsson had surprised the political world by announcing in August 1995 that he intended to stand down as party leader and Prime Minister the following March, marking the 10th anniversary of his elevation. The initial favourite to succeed him was Deputy Prime Minister Mona Sahlin; but disclosures about irregularities in her financial affairs forced her not only to withdraw from the leadership race but also to resign from the government. Instead, the succession went to the current Finance Minister, Göran Persson, who was elected SAP chair unopposed at a special party congress on March 15, 1996, and appointed Prime Minister two days later.

The Persson government came under pressure in 1997-98 for sticking to unpopular economic retrenchment policies. In the September 1998 general elections the SAP recorded its worst result for 70 years, winning only 36.4% of the vote and 131 seats. It nevertheless continued as a minority government, with the external support of the →Left Party and the →Green Ecology Party. In the June 1999 European elections the SAP slipped to 26.0% of the vote, winning only six seats.

Having an official membership of 177,300, the SAP is a member party of the Socialist International. Its European Parliament representatives are members of the Party of European Socialists group.

Other Parties

Alliance Party (*Allianspartiet*, AP), led by Jerry Larsson, centrist formation; won 175 votes in 1998 general election. *Address*. Wemmenhögsgatan 23, 231 45 Trelleborg; *Telephone/Fax*. (+46-410) 40904; *Email*. jlm-trbg@algonet.se; *Website*. http://www.allianspartiet.se

Centre Democrats (*Centrum-Demokraterna*, CD), led by Harry Franzén, right-wing party advocating traditional values; won 377 votes in 1998 general election. *Address*. Marieholmsvägen 10, 260 24 Röstånga; *Telephone*. (+46-435) 91054; *Fax*. (+46-435) 91092

Communist Party of Marxist-Leninist Revolutionaries (*Kommunistiska Partiet Marxist-Leninisterna Revolutionärerna*, KPMLr), led by Anders Carlsson, founded in 1970 as a pro-Albanian party, broke away from the Communist League of Marxist-Leninists (now the Communist Party of Sweden) and was originally known as the Communist League of Marxist-Leninist Revolutionaries; has contested elections, although with minimal support. *Address*. PO Box 31187, 400 32 Göteborg ; *Telephone*. (+46-31) 122-631; *Fax*. (+46-31) 244-464; *Email*. kpmlr@proletaren.se; *Website*. http://www.proletaren.se/kpmlr

Communist Party of Sweden (*Sveriges Kommunistiska Parti*, SKP), led by Roland Pettersson (chair) and Jan-Olof Norell (secretary), an independent communist party founded in 1967 by pro-Chinese elements of the old Communist Party, notably the Clarte League (named after the Clarte movement of Henri Barbusse in 1916); bases itself on the Swedish people's "tradition of rebellion", the European democratic tradition and the international Marxist/Maoist tradition; emphasizes that national independence and democratic freedom are essential for the working people to prevent decline into "a new brutal system of exploitation and oppression"; claimed to have influenced Sweden's foreign policy to shift from "informally US-allied to heavily pro-Vietnamese" during the Vietnam War; from 1974 the SKP campaigned strongly against the Soviet Union and what it regarded as the latter's growing influence on Sweden's public opinion; in its last electoral contest (1979) the party obtained 10,862 votes (0.2%). *Address*. PO Box 1566, 171 29 Solna; *Telephone*. (+46-8) 735-8640; *Fax*. (+46-8) 735-7902; *Email*. skp@skp.se; *Website*. http://www.skp.se

Conservative Party (*Konservativa Partiet*, KP), standing for traditional Swedish family values, critical of the main →Moderate Alliance Party. *Address*. PO Box 1700, 114 79 Stockholm; *Telephone*. (+46-8) 600-3345; *Email*. kp@altmedia.se; *Website*. http://www.flashback.net/~grinden

European Labour Party (*Europeiska Arbertarpartiet*, EAP), led by Tore Fredin, won 117 votes in 1998 general election. *Address*. PO Box 11918, 161 11 Bromma

Freedom Front (*Frihetsfronten*), led by Henrik Bejke, radical free market formation. *Address*. PO Pox 620, 114 79 Stockholm; *Telephone*. (+46-8) 345-647; *Fax*. (+46-8) 328-664; *Email*. frihetsfronten@bahnhof.se; *Website*. http://www.frihetsfronten .pp.se

Humanist Party (*Humanistiska Partiet*, HP), led by Bo Höglund, contested 1994 elections. *Address*. 46 Södermannagatan, 116 40 Stockholm

Natural Law Party (*Partiet för Naturens Lag*, PNL), Swedish branch of worldwide network of such parties. *Address*. Abbotvägen 1, 746 95 Skokloster; *Telephone*. (+46-18) 386-933; *Fax*. (+46-18) 386-813; *Email*. info@naturens-lag.org; *Website*. http://www.naturens-lag .lafdata.se

New Democracy (*NyDemokrati*, NyD), led by Ulf Eriksson, founded in February 1990 on a populist platform of massive tax cuts, abolition of the welfare state, stringent curbs on immigration, opposition to EU membership and cheaper alcohol. It caused a sensation in the 1991 general elections, winning 24 *Riksdag* seats with a vote share of 6.7%. For most of the subsequent parliamentary term it gave often vital external voting support to the centre-right minority government. In March 1994, however, the resignation of its controversial leader, Count Ian Wachmeister (known as "the crazy count"), assisted a reorientation which resulted in the party joining the opposition. Having lost its early momentum, New Democracy fell well short of the 4% barrier to representation in the 1994 elections, taking only 1.2% of the vote; failed again in 1998, winning only 8,297 votes. *Address.* PO Box 1255, 111 82 Stockholm; *Telephone/Fax.* (+46–31) 262-543; *Email.* info@nydemokrati.org; *Website.* http://www.nydemokrati.org

New Progress (*Ny Framtid*), led by Sune Lyxell, won 9,171 votes in 1998 general election. *Address.* PO Box 84, 565 22 Mullsjö; *Telephone.* (+46-392) 31500; *Fax.* (+46-392) 12610; *Email.* feedback@nyframtid.com

Socialist Party (*Socialistiska Partiet*, SP), a Trotskyist grouping founded in 1953 as the Communist Workers' League by dissidents of the main Communist Party (later the →Left Party); took its present name in 1982; has contested elections but with minimal support (winning only 1,466 votes in 1998). *Address.* PO Box 6087, 102 32 Stockholm; *Telephone.* (+46-8) 310-850; *Fax.* (+46-8) 441-4576; *Email.* intis@internationalen.se; *Website.* http://www.internationalen.se/sp

Socialist Justice Party (*Rättvisepartiet Socialisterna*, RS), Trotskyist formation founded in 1997, claims to be biggest Trotskyist party in Scandinavia, affiliated to Committee for a Workers' International; won 3,044 votes in 1998 general election. *Website.* http://www.socialisterna.org/rs

Stockholm Party (*Stockholmspartiet*), aiming to promote the interests of the capital city. *Address.* Kungsgatan 37/2tr, 111 56 Stockholm. *Telephone.* (+46-8) 219-959; *Fax.* (+46-8) 219-279; *Email.* kontakt@stockholmspartiet.se. *Website.* http://www.stockholmspartiet.se

Swedish Democrats (*Sverigedemokraterna*, SD), led by Mikael Jansson, radical right-wing formation opposed to immigration and multiculturalism; received 19,624 votes in 1998 general election. *Address.* PO Box 20850, 104 60 Stockholm; *Telephone.* (+46-8) 641-2011; *Fax.* (+46-8) 643-9260; *Email.* kansli@sverigedemokraterna.se; *Website.* http://www.sverigedemokraterna.se

Swedish Pensioners' Interests Party (*Sveriges Pensionärers Intresseparti*, SPI), led by Nils-Olof Persson, won 52,869 votes in 1998 general election. *Address.* PO Box 5187, 200 72 Malmö

Viking Party (*Vikingapartiet*, VP), led by Bosse Persson, advocating principles and policies drawn from a former age; won a total of 28 votes in 1998 general election. *Address.* PO Box 4403, 203 15 Malmö; *Telephone.* (+46-40) 943-031; *Email.* m-2829@mailbox.swipnet.se; *Website.* http://home1.swipnet.se/~w-18297/vikingapartiet

United Kingdom

Capital: London   **Population** (including N. Ireland): 59,000,000

The United Kingdom of Great Britain and Northern Ireland is a hereditary constitutional monarchy in which the monarch, as head of state, has numerous specific responsibilities. The supreme legislative authority is Parliament, consisting of (i) a 659–member House of Commons, with a life of not more than five years, directly elected under a simple-majority system in single-member constituencies, the right to vote being held by British subjects (and citizens of any Commonwealth member country or the Republic of Ireland resident in the United Kingdom) above the age of 18 years, and (ii) a House of Lords. Under a reform enacted in November 1999 the majority hereditary component of the House of Lords was abolished and a 670-member "interim chamber" (of 578 life peers, bishops and law lords plus 92 ex-hereditaries elected by their peers) was set up pending definitive reform of the upper chamber. The government is headed by a Prime Minister who is leader of the party which commands a majority in the House of Commons. Each candidate standing for election to the House of Commons has to pay a deposit of £500, which is forfeited if he or she obtains less than 5 per cent of the valid votes in his constituency. Any vacancies arising are filled through by-elections. The UK joined what became the European Union on Jan. 1, 1973, and elects 87 members of the European Parliament, including three from Northern Ireland. Under devolution legislation enacted in 1998, a 129-member Scottish Parliament and a 60-member Welsh Assembly were elected for five-year terms on May 6, 1999 (by forms of proportional representation), while a revived 108-member Northern Ireland Assembly was elected on June 25, 1998 (see separate section on Northern Ireland below).

General elections to the House of Commons held on May 1, 1997, resulted as follows:

	Seats		Percentage	
	1997	*(1992)*	*1997*	*(1992)*
Labour Party...	418	(271)	43.2	(34.4)
Conservative and Unionist Party	165	(336)	30.7	(41.9)
Liberal Democrats	46	(20)	16.8	(17.9)
Ulster Unionist Party*...	10	(9)	0.8	(0.8)
Scottish National Party	6	(3)	2.0	(1.9)
Plaid Cymru (Party of Wales)	4	(4)	0.5	(0.5)
Social Democratic and Labour Party*	3	(4)	0.6	(0.6)
Sinn Féin*	2	(–)	0.4	(–)
Democratic Unionist Party*	2	(3)	0.3	(0.3)
United Kingdom Unionist Party*	1	(0)	n/a	(–)
Others...	2	(0)	4.7	(n/a)

*Northern Ireland party: see separate section below

Opposition parties in the House of Commons are entitled to receive financial assistance from state funds to assist them in fulfilling their essential parliamentary duties, the subsidy being known as "Short Money", after the minister (Edward Short) who first introduced the arrangement in 1975. As announced in May 1999, the latest revision of the "Short Money" rules set the assistance available at an annual rate of £10,732.60p per seat and £21.44p per 200 votes won in the most recent general election. To qualify for the subsidy, a party was required to have at least two MPs, or one MP plus at least 150,000 votes in aggregate. In addition, the travel fund for opposition spokesmen was increased in line with inflation and the specific allocation for the Leader of the Opposition's Office was increased to £500,000 a year. Under this formula, the Conservative and Unionist Party became eligible for £3,377,973 in state subsidies in the 1999-2000 financial year, the Liberal Democrats £1,085,010, the Ulster Unionist Party £138,750, the Scottish National Party £134,643, *Plaid Cymru* £61,859, the Social Democratic and Labour Party £54,112 and the Democratic Unionist Party £33,871.

Conservative and Unionist Party

Address. Conservative Central Office, 32 Smith Square, London, SWIP 3HH
Telephone. (+44–20) 7222–9000
Fax. (+44–20) 7222–1135
Email. ccoffice@conservative-party.org.uk
Website. http://www.tory.org
Leadership. William Hague (leader); Michael Ancram (chair)
Founded in the 1830s, the Conservative Party regards freedom of the individual under the rule of law as its guiding principle. It believes that political arrangements should be so designed as to give people "the maximum degree of control over their own lives, whilst restricting the role of government so that the state exists for the benefit of the individual and not vice versa". The party stands for wider ownership of property and wealth and for lower taxes on earnings, and is strongly committed to the free enterprise system. Believing in the maintenance of the United Kingdom, it is opposed to devolution of power to Scotland and Wales; it is also opposed to proportional representation and supportive of retention of the hereditary principle in the House of Lords. The party is pledged to the maintenance of strong defences and regards the concept of deterrence as central to the nation's nuclear and conventional defence capability.

The Conservatives trace their history back to the 17th and 18th century, but the modern party was formed by Sir Robert Peel, who established the first Conservative government in 1834, shortly before which the term "Conservative" was first used as opposed to "Tory" (a term of Irish origins applied to members of the political grouping which from 1679 opposed Whig attempts to exclude the future James II from the succession to the throne). The party assumed its present official name in 1912 when it was formally joined by the Liberal Unionists (former Liberals who opposed home rule for Ireland and had supported the Conservative Party since 1886). During World War I the party took part in a coalition government. It was returned to power in 1922 and remained in government for most of the inter-war years (from 1931 as the dominant party in a National government) and in the World War II all-party coalition (under Winston Churchill from May 1940 to July 1945).

In the post-war era the Conservative Party has been led by Churchill (1940–55), Anthony Eden (1955–57), Harold Macmillan (1957–63), Sir Alec Douglas-Home (1963–65),

Edward Heath, the first leader elected by the Parliamentary Conservative Party (1965–75), Margaret Thatcher (1975–90), John Major (1990-97) and William Hague (since June 1997). After heavily losing the 1945 elections, the Conservatives were in opposition until 1951 and thereafter in power until 1964. The next Conservative government, under Heath in 1970–74, successfully negotiated Britain's entry into the European Community. After being in opposition from 1974, the party was returned to power in May 1979 under the premiership of Margaret Thatcher (the first woman leader of a major British political party). The party was confirmed in power with large majorities in June 1983 (benefiting from the successful British military action in 1982 to reverse Argentina's occupation of the Falkland Islands) and again in June 1987, although its percentage share of the vote slipped from 43.9% in 1979 to 42.4% in 1983 and to 42.3% in 1987. Thatcher's 1987 victory, with a Commons majority of 102 seats, made her the first British Prime Minister in modern history to win three consecutive terms in office.

Under the Thatcher premiership the Conservatives pursued radical right-wing social and economic policies, with the party's moderate "one nation" wing being increasingly marginalized (and referred to dismissively by the Thatcherites as "wets"). Major reforms included stringent curbs on the powers of trade unions, the promotion of individual choice and market mechanisms within the welfare state structure, the sale of council houses and the privatization of many industries and companies previously under public ownership. Her government also cut income tax rates to pre-war levels (although without appreciably reducing the proportion of GDP spent by the state) and presided over an economic boom in the late 1980s, when for a while there was an actual surplus in government finances. During her third term, however, an attempt to reform the financing of local government so that all residents paid a "community charge", not just house-owners, provoked large-scale opposition to what was dubbed a "poll tax". There were also deepening divisions within Conservative ranks over British membership of the European Community (later Union), which many Conservatives saw as being intent on eroding the national sovereignty of member states.

Thatcher positioned herself on the "Euro-sceptic" wing of the party, delivering a celebrated speech in Bruges (Belgium) in September 1988 in which she categorically rejected schemes for a federal European state. However, a series of by-election defeats in 1989–90 weakened her position, which was fatally undermined by the pro-European Sir Geoffrey Howe, who delivered a blistering critique of her stewardship following his exit from the government in November 1990. The speech precipitated an immediate leadership challenge by the pro-European former Defence Minister, Michael Heseltine, who obtained enough first-round votes to force a second round, whereupon Thatcher resigned in the face of almost certain defeat. Two other contenders then entered the lists, including the Chancellor of the Exchequer, John Major, who was regarded as the Thatcherite candidate and for that reason was elected in the second-round ballot by a comfortable margin.

At 47 Britain's youngest 20th-century Prime Minister so far, Major quickly jettisoned his predecessor's more controversial policies (which he had staunchly supported), including the "poll tax". The Conservatives fought the April 1992 election on a somewhat more centrist platform of further privatization (including British Rail and the coal mines), financial accountability in the National Health Service and freedom of choice in the state education sector. In the sphere of economic policy, they contended that the recession into which Britain had descended in the early 1990s would be much worse under a Labour government. Assisted by public doubts as to the prime ministerial calibre of →Labour Party leader Neil Kinnock, the Conservatives won an almost unprecedented fourth term, although by the much narrower margin of 336 seats out of 651 (from an aggregate vote of 14.1 million, representing a 41.9% share). Also almost unprecedented was the massive post-election slump in the Conservative government's public standing, as evidenced by disastrous local election results in 1993 and

1994 and the more threatening loss of several hitherto safe Conservative parliamentary seats to the →Liberal Democrats. Contributing factors included Britain's humiliating enforced exit from the European exchange rate mechanism in September 1992, representing a traumatic collapse of government economic policy (but not generating any immediate ministerial resignations) and leading to a ramp of additional taxation in direct breach of the party's election pledge to reduce taxes. Also damaging were related internal Conservative divisions over Europe, evidenced in protracted resistance to ratification of the 1991 Maastricht Treaty creating a European Union (despite the much-trumpeted opt-outs negotiated for Britain by Major), and a never-ending series of "sex and sleaze" scandals featuring prominent Conservatives.

In June 1994 the Conservatives fared badly in elections for the European Parliament, falling from 34 to 18 seats (out of 87) with only 26.8% of the vote and losing several seats in the Conservative heartland of southern England. Further by-election and local election disasters in late 1994 and early 1995, with Labour now the main beneficiary, fuelled increasing Conservative criticism of Major's leadership, which the Prime Minister unexpectedly decided to confront in June 1995, when he announced his resignation as party leader (although not as Prime Minister) to force a leadership election in which he requested his critics to "put up or shut up". Only one Conservative dared to "put up", namely Welsh Secretary John Redwood, representing the Euro-sceptic and anti-centrist wing of the party. Major was duly re-elected in July 1995 with the support of 218 of the 329 Conservative MPs and therefore continued as Prime Minister, immediately elevating Heseltine to "number two" in the government as reward for his crucial support during the leadership contest.

Major's leadership election victory had no impact on the historically low opinion poll ratings being accorded to the Conservative Party, which kept losing by-elections no matter how "safe" the seat. It also, unusually, suffered defections from the parliamentary party, one to Labour in September 1995, another to the Liberal Democrats at the end of the year and a third who became an independent in February 1996, before opting for the Liberal Democrats in October. Yet another by-election defeat in April 1996 reduced the government's overall theoretical majority in the Commons to one and another local election disaster in May all but eliminated the Conservative Party from local government. The following month internal party dissension over Europe intensified when 74 Conservative back-benchers voted in favour of an early referendum on whether Britain should surrender further sovereignty to the EU. An important factor in the latest manoeuvrings was the perceived threat to Conservative re-election prospects posed by the new Referendum Party (→Referendum Movement).

The Conservatives were decimated in the May 1997 general elections, retaining only 165 seats on a vote share of 30.7%, its worst result of the 20th century, which left it without representation in Scotland and Wales. Major immediately resigned as leader and was succeeded by William Hague, who at 36 became the party's youngest leader for over 200 years. Inheritor of the "Thatcherite" mantle, Hague quickly came into conflict with the party's pro-European wing, as he moved to a stance of opposition to UK participation in the single European currency (euro). On the eve of the Conservative conference of October 1998 Hague secured 84% endorsement from party members for the proposition that a Conservative government would not join the euro during the lifetime of the next parliament. Nevertheless, infighting on the issue continued, with Heseltine and former Chancellor Kenneth Clarke to the fore in insisting that the party should not rule out participation in the single currency.

The Conservatives began to recover in the May 1999 local elections, displacing the Liberal Democrats as the second strongest party in local government. The party also secured representation in the new legislatures of Scotland and Wales, though they were in opposition in both. In June 1999 the Conservatives were the main victors in European Parliament elections, winning 36 of the 87 UK seats on a vote share of 35.8% despite a powerful performance by the anti-EU →UK Independence Party. However, the party continued to be dogged by internal division and controversy, notably when its candidate for the new post of mayor of London, Lord (Jeffrey) Archer of Weston-super-Mare, was forced to withdraw in November 1999 over disclosures that he had suborned a potential witness in a 1987 libel trial. In the same month the return to the Commons of former Defence Secretary Michael Portillo in a London by-election served to increase the pressure on Hague, though Portillo pledged that he would be loyal. In December 1999 Hague suffered another major blow when former front-bench spokesman Shaun Woodward defected to the Labour Party, claiming that the Conservatives had moved too far to the right.

The Conservative Party is a founder member of the International Democrat Union. Its representatives in the European Parliament sit in the European People's Party/European Democrats group (consisting mainly of Christian Democrats).

Green Party of England and Wales (GPEW)
Address. 1A Waterlow Road, Archway, London, N19 5NJ
Telephone. (+44–20) 7272–4474
Fax. (+44–20) 7272–6653
Email. office@greenparty.org.uk
Website. http://www.greenparty.org.uk
Leadership. Alan Francis (chair); Mike Woodin (male spokesperson); Margaret Wright (female spokesperson)

The Green Party propagates policies which are based on the principle that people must live in harmony with nature within the limitations of the earth's finite supply of resources. Its aims include unilateral disarmament, a ban on all nuclear as well as chemical and biological weapons, an end to Britain's involvement in NATO, an end to nuclear power generation, material security through a Basic National Income scheme, land reform, decentralization, proportional representation and increased aid for third-world countries in the form of grants not loans. The Scottish Green Party is organizationally separate from the GPEW.

The party was founded in 1973 as the Ecology Party, which nominated 54 candidates for the 1979 general elections, All of them lost their deposits and gained an average of only 1.2% of the vote in the contested constituencies, the party's best results being 2.8% in two. In the 1983 general elections Ecologists contested 109 seats, the highest vote for any candidate being 2.9%. In September 1985 the party changed its name to Green Party, which in the 1987 general elections fielded 133 candidates, the highest vote obtained by any of them being 3.7%. Meanwhile, the party had elected its first two local councillors in the district elections of May 1986, when its candidates averaged 6% in the wards which it contested.

The Greens seemed to make a breakthrough when they obtained 2.3 million votes (15% of the total) in the June 1989 European Parliament elections in Britain (but no seats). However, internal divisions between the moderates and a radical wing weakened the party in the early 1990s. It was also damaged when well-known television sports commentator David Icke, a party member, announced in 1991 that he was the new messiah sent to save mankind (and also left himself open to charges of antisemitism in a new book). The party obtained only 171,927 votes (0.5%) in the April 1992 general elections, when all 253 Green candidates lost their deposits. Four months later Sara Parkin resigned as leader, stating that because of perpetual infighting "the Green Party has become a liability to green politics". Britain's other best-known environmentalist, Jonathon Porritt, also distanced himself from the party. Nevertheless, the Greens staged a minor recovery in the June 1994 European Parliament elections, winning 3.1% of the vote (but no seats).

The Greens put up 95 candidates in the May 1997 general elections, all of whom lost their deposits in amassing an aggregate vote of 63,991 (0.2%). In the Scottish Parliament elections in May 1999, however, the Greens won 3.6% of the vote and returned one candidate, who became the first Green ever to be elected in a major UK poll. In the June 1999 European elections, moreover, the Greens won two seats on the basis of a national vote share of 6.3% , while in November 1999 the party obtained formal national representation for the first time when Lord Beaumont of Whitley, hitherto a Liberal Democrat life peer, crossed the floor in the House of Lords.

With an official membership of 4,500, the GPEW is affiliated to the European Federation of Green Parties. Its representatives in the European Parliament sit in the Greens/European Free Alliance group.

Labour Party

Address. Millbank Tower, Millbank, London, SW1P 4GT
Telephone. (+44–20) 7802-1000
Fax. (+44–20) 7272-6653
Email. labour-party@geo2.poptel.org.uk
Website. http://www.labour.org.uk
Leadership. Tony Blair (leader); John Prescott (deputy leader); Margaret McDonagh (general secretary)

The party was founded in 1900 as the Labour Representation Committee at a conference held in London attended by representatives of the trade unions, the Independent Labour Party, the Fabian Society and other socialist societies, having been convened as a result of a decision by the Trades Union Congress to seek improved representation of the labour movement in parliament. Later in 1900 two Labour members were elected to parliament. The name of the Committee was changed to the Labour Party in 1906, when there were 29 Labour members in the House of Commons. The first Labour government was in office from January to November 1924 and the second from June 1929 to August 1931, both under the premiership of Ramsay MacDonald, although the latter then headed a National government from which the bulk of the Labour Party dissociated itself.

Labour joined an all-party coalition during World War II and won an overwhelming victory in the 1945 general elections under the leadership of Clement Attlee (party leader from 1933 to 1955). His government carried out many social and economic reforms, among them the National Insurance and National Health Acts, remaining in office until 1951. After 13 years in opposition (for part of which the party was led by Hugh Gaitskell), Labour was narrowly returned to power in 1964 and consolidated its majority in the 1966 elections, on both occasions under the leadership of Harold Wilson, who remained in office until losing the 1970 elections to the Conservatives.

Labour returned to office as a minority administration in March 1974 after becoming the largest single parliamentary party in the elections of the previous month, and subsequently achieved a narrow overall majority in the October 1974 elections. Wilson vacated the leadership in 1976 to be replaced by James Callaghan, who was obliged to enter into a parliamentary pact with the small Liberal Party (later the →Liberal Democrats) after Labour's majority had been eroded by by-election losses. In the May 1979 general elections the Labour Party suffered a decisive defeat at the hands of Margaret Thatcher's →Conservative Party and was in opposition through the 1980s and into the 1990s.

After the 1979 election defeat Labour's left wing gained the ascendancy within the party, this development contributing to the defection of some right-wing elements and the formation in March 1981 of the breakaway Social Democratic Party (later mostly subsumed into what became the Liberal Democrats). Personifying Labour's "old left", Michael Foot (who succeeded Callaghan in 1980) sought to unify the party on the basis of radical policy commitments, while at the same time moving to expel Trotskyist infiltrators of the Militant

Tendency". Nevertheless, in the June 1983 elections Labour went down to a further heavy defeat, its 27.6% share of the votes being the party's lowest since 1918. In an attempt to repair Labour's public image, the party conference in October 1983 elected Neil Kinnock (then 41) as the party's youngest-ever leader. However, in June 1987 Labour suffered its third general election defeat in a row, albeit with the consolation of having reversed its electoral decline by increasing its share of the vote to 31.6% and its seat total to 229 (out of 650).

Subsequent to its 1987 defeat, Labour revised its policies in key areas, notably by abandoning its commitment to unilateral nuclear disarmament and its opposition the UK membership of the European Community (later Union, EC/EU), for which the party quickly became a great enthusiast. It also moved towards acceptance of the market economy (subject to "regulation" in the general interest), while remaining opposed to privatization. Nevertheless, Labour was again defeated by the Conservatives in the April 1992 elections, although its seat total of 271 and 11.6 million votes (34.4%) represented a significant improvement. Kinnock resigned immediately after the contest and was succeeded by John Smith, a pro-European Scottish lawyer on Labour's moderate wing. Smith continued with the modernization programme, securing the adoption of "one member one vote" (OMOV) arrangements for the selection of Labour candidates and leadership elections, and led Labour to major advances in the 1993 and 1994 local elections.

Smith died of a heart attack in May 1994 and was succeeded in July, under the new voting arrangements, by another "modernizing" and pro-European lawyer, Tony Blair (41). Meanwhile, under the interim leadership of Margaret Beckett, Labour had won a decisive victory in the June 1994 European Parliament elections, taking 62 of the 87 UK seats with 42.7% of the vote and for the first time in recent memory breaking through in hitherto "safe" Conservative areas in southern and central England. Moreover, the so-called "Blair factor" accelerated Labour's electoral resurgence not only in the 1995 and 1996 local elections but also in parliamentary by-elections. Labour was also boosted in September 1995 by the almost unprecedented defection to its ranks of a sitting Conservative MP.

In a symbolic revision of clause 4 of Labour's constitution, a special party conference in April 1995 approved the abandonment of the party's 77–year-old commitment to "the common ownership of the means of production, distribution and exchange". It was replaced by a general statement of democratic socialist aims and values asserting that the party seeks "a dynamic economy, serving the public interest, in which the enterprise of the market and the rigour of competition are joined with the forces of partnership and co-operation to produce the wealth the nation needs and the opportunity for all to work and prosper". In another significant policy shift, the Labour leadership in June 1996 announced that plans for the creation of directly-elected assemblies in Scotland and Wales would be submitted to referendums in each country before the necessary legislation was introduced by a Labour government at Westminster.

Blair led the Labour Party to a landslide victory in the May 1997 general elections, achieving a national swing from Conservative to Labour of 10.6%. The party won 418 of the 659 seats (with a vote share of 43.2%), giving it the largest parliamentary majority since 1945. The new Labour cabinet included John Prescott as Deputy Prime Minister and Secretary of State for Environment, Transport and the Regions, as well as Gordon Brown as Chancellor of the Exchequer, Jack Straw as Home Secretary and Robin Cook as Foreign and Commonweath Secretary. Scottish and Welsh devolution bills were introduced and enacted in 1998, elections to the new legislatures in May 1999 producing Labour pluralities of 56 seats out of 129 in Scotland and 28 out of 60 in Wales. Accordingly, Labour formed a coalition with the Liberal Democrats in Scotland under Donald Dewar as first minister and a minority government in Wales under Alun Michael.

The Blair government was buffeted in 1998 by a series of disclosures involving claims that power and influence under Labour were concentrated in a small group of "Tony's cronies"; it was also accused of "control freakery" and of excessive "spin-doctoring" of the news. In December 1998 close Blair aide Peter Mandelson was forced to resign as Trade and Industry Secretary over a controversial private loan at a preferential rate received from another government minister. In the June 1999 European elections, held for the first time by proportional representation based on regional lists, Labour was outpolled by the Conservatives, winning only 28.0% of the vote and dropping from 62 to 29 seats. Nevertheless, Labour held its own in parliamentary by-elections and remained well ahead of the Conservatives in opinion polls, assisted by a generally buoyant economy and falling unemployment, so that Blair felt able to restore Mandelson to the cabinet in October 1999 as Northern Ireland Secretary. In December 1999, moreover, Labour pulled off a major publicity coup when it persuaded former Conservative front-bench spokesman Shaun Woodward to defect to the Labour Party, citing as his reason that the Conservatives under William Hague had moved too far to the right.

The Labour Party is a founder member of the Socialist International. Its representatives in the European Parliament sit in the Party of European Socialists group.

Liberal Democrats
Address. 4 Cowley Street, London, SWIP 3NB
Telephone. (+44–20) 7222–7999
Fax. (+44–20) 7799–2170
Email. libdems@cix.co.uk
Website. http://www.libdems.org.uk
Leadership. Charles Kennedy (leader); Alan Beith (deputy leader); Baroness (Diana) Maddock (president)
The Liberal Democrats are directly descended from the historic Liberal Party, by way of an alliance and then merger between the latter and the bulk of the new Social Democratic Party, initially under the title Social and Liberal Democrats, which was shortened in late 1989 to Liberal Democrats. The party's federal constitution states that the party "exists to build and defend a fair, free and more equal society, shaped by the values of liberty, justice and community, in which no-one shall be enslaved by poverty, ignorance or conformity". The party is committed to continued British membership of the European Union (EU) and of the North Atlantic Treaty Organization (NATO), while advocating the freezing of Britain's nuclear deterrent capacity at the existing level. It also advocates devolution of power to Scotland, Wales and the English regions, an elected second chamber at Westminster and the introduction of a form of proportional representation.

Of the two components of the Liberal Democrats, the Liberal Party traced its earliest origins to the 17th-century struggle by English Whigs in favour of freedom of conscience and civil rights which led ultimately to parliament rather than the monarch being accepted as the country's supreme authority. (The Scottish term Whig was applied to those who opposed the succession of James II in 1685 on account of his Catholic sympathies.) The term Liberal Party was first formally used by Lord John Russell in 1839 in letters to Queen Victoria, Liberal governments holding office for over 50 of the 83 years up to 1914. The National Liberal Federation, set up in 1877, was the national political organization and Liberals were the first to produce party manifestos; they also introduced a national system of education, the secret ballot, the foundations of the welfare state and a reform of the House of Lords. During World War I, when the party led a coalition government under David Lloyd-George, it became divided and began to decline, a process accelerated by the rise of the →Labour Party on the strength of universal adult suffrage and its trade union base.

210

Liberals held office in the World War II coalition government, and Sir William Beveridge, a Liberal MP in 1944–45, was the architect of the post-war National Health Service and other welfare state structures created by the Labour government. By now the Liberals' representation in the Commons was tiny, remaining at six seats in the three elections of the 1950s, rising to nine in 1964 and 12 in 1966, and then falling back to six in 1970. In this period the party was led by Clement Davies (1945–56), Jo Grimond (1956–67) and Jeremy Thorpe (1967–76). Under Thorpe's leadership the party obtained over 6 million votes (19.3% of the total) and 14 seats in the February 1994 elections, although in October 1974 it fell back to 5.3 million votes (18.3%) and 13 seats. Undone by scandal, Thorpe was succeeded in July 1976 by David Steel, who became the first Liberal leader to be elected directly by party members. Steel took the party into the 1977–78 "Lib-Lab pact", under which the Liberals supported the minority Labour government in its pursuit of economic recovery between March 1977 and July 1978. But his hope that the Liberals would thereby acquire a beneficial "governmental" aura was disappointed in the May 1979 elections, in which the party won only 11 seats on a 13.8% vote share.

With the →Conservative Party now in power under the radical right-wing leadership of Margaret Thatcher and the Labour Party having moved sharply to the left following its election defeat, the Liberal Party's hopes of presenting a viable centrist alternative appeared to be strengthened in early 1981 when a right-wing Labour faction broke away to form the Social Democratic Party (SDP). In June 1981 the Alliance of the Liberals and the SDP was launched in a joint statement entitled *A Fresh Start for Britain*, in which the two parties agreed not to oppose each other in elections. After winning a number of Commons by-elections on the basis of this agreement, the Alliance contested the June 1983 general elections with an agreed distribution of candidates between the two parties. However, although it garnered 7.8 million votes (25.4% of the total), the yield in seats was only 23, of which the Liberals took 17. The Alliance was nevertheless maintained and contested the June 1987 elections under the uneasy joint leadership of Steel and former Labour Foreign Secretary Dr David Owen (who had become leader of the SDP immediately after the 1983 elections). However, a further decisive Conservative victory and a partial Labour recovery denied the Alliance its minimum target of securing the balance of power between the two major parties: its aggregate support fell to 22.6%, with the Liberals winning 4.2 million votes (12.8%) and 17 seats and the SDP 3.2 million (9.8%) and five seats.

Three days after the June 1987 elections Steel unexpectedly proposed a "democratic fusion" of the two Alliance parties, a proposal supported with some reservations within his own party but which divided the SDP into pro-merger and anti-merger factions, the latter including Dr Owen and, at that stage, three of the other four SDP MPs. A subsequent ballot of the SDP membership showed a 57.4% majority of those voting in favour of merger negotiations, whereupon Dr Owen resigned as SDP leader (on Aug. 6, 1987) and launched an anti-merger Campaign for Social Democracy. His successor, elected unopposed by the SDP MPs, was Robert Maclennan, a former Labour MP who had joined the SDP on its formation, had initially opposed merger with the Liberals but was now prepared to negotiate in good faith in accordance with the membership ballot verdict. After both the SDP and Liberal 1987 annual conferences had given overwhelming approval to the concept of a merger, detailed negotiations on the constitution and platform of a unified party took place between the two sides. After one false start, these resulted in a modified policy document (published in January 1988) and agreement that the new party should be called the Social and Liberal Democrats (and Democrats for short). Whereas a first policy document had pledged firm support for British acquisition of the Trident nuclear missile system (notwithstanding the Liberal Party's official commitment to nuclear disarmament), the revised version called for the freezing of Britain's nuclear deterrent at a level no greater than the existing Polaris force, adding that the

Alliance's 1987 election commitment to cancel Trident would be considered in the light of realities applying when the new party came to power.

Later in January 1988 special conferences of the two parties each voted heavily in favour of proceeding to a further ballot of their memberships to secure final approval of the merger plan. Both of these ballots showed large majorities in favour of a merger, enabling the new SLD to be formally launched on March 6, 1988, under the joint interim leadership of Steel and Maclennan pending an election for a single leader later in the year. On the declaration of the SDP's final ballot decision in favour of merger, Dr Owen announced the relaunching of the Social Democratic Party as an independent formation. It did not prosper and was dissolved in June 1990.

Meanwhile, in July 1988, the merged party had elected Paddy Ashdown as its leader in succesion to Steel. He led what had become the Liberal Democrats to some improvement in the April 1992 general elections, when the party won 20 seats and almost 6 million votes (17.9% of those cast) on a platform which included a commitment to a general increase in the basic income tax. By June 1994 its Commons representation had risen to 23 seats on the strength of a series of stunning by-election victories in hitherto "safe" Conservative seats. In the same month the party at last achieved European Parliament representation, winning two of the 87 UK seats, although its share of the national vote fell back to 16.1%. Thereafter the Liberal Democrats were somewhat eclipsed by Tony Blair's "new" Labour Party, which gained ascendancy as the main opposition party, although the Liberal Democrats were boosted to 26 Commons seats by two Conservative defectors, one at the end of 1995 and a second in October 1996. The response of Ashdown and other Liberal Democrat leaders to the resurgence of Labour was to make increasingly explicit offers of support for a future Labour government in the event that the Liberal Democrats held the balance of power.

In the event, the Liberal Democrats did not hold the balance of power after the May 1997 general elections, although thanks to anti-Conservative tactical voting their seat tally rose sharply to 46 (the highest since 1929) on the basis of a reduced vote share of 16.8% (5,242,947 votes). Liberal Democrats thereafter accepted appointment to a special cabinet committee of the new Labour government concerned with constitutional and electoral reform (later extended to cover other issues); but the party's influence was limited in the face of Labour's large majority and it made no progress on its aim of bringing in proportional representation for general elections. A form of PR was introduced for elections to the new devolved legislatures of Scotland and Wales in May 1999, the Liberal Democrats winning 17 Scottish seats (and joining a formal coalition with Labour) and six Welsh seats. Regional PR also operated in the European elections in June 1999, when the Liberal Democrats lifted their seat tally to 10, though on a reduced vote share of 12.7%.

Meanwhile, Ashdown had in January 1999 announced his imminent departure as Liberal Democrat leader after 11 years in the post. His successor, elected in August, was Scottish MP and former SDP member Charles Kennedy (39), whose nearest challenger was London MP Simon Hughes. Kennedy pledged that he would seek to build a "strong, independent, progressive" party, while backing the continuation of political co-operation with the Labour government.

With an official membership of 90,000, the Liberal Democrats are affiliated to the Liberal International. Their representatives in the European Parliament sit in the European Liberal, Democratic and Reformist group.

Plaid Cymru–The Party of Wales

Address. Ty Gwynfor, 18 Park Grove, Caerdydd/Cardiff, CF10 3BN, Wales
Telephone. (+44–29) 2064-6000
Fax. (+44-29) 2064-6001

Email. post@plaidcymru.org
Website. http://www.plaidcymru.org
Leadership. Dafydd Wigley (president); Marc Phillips (chair); Karl Davies (general secretary)
Founded in August 1925, *Plaid Cymru* seeks full self-government for Wales based on socialist principles, representation at the United Nations and restoration of the Welsh language and culture. It has contested all elections to the Westminster parliament since 1945 but remained unrepresented until July 1966, when its then president, Dafydd Elis Thomas, won a by-election at Carmarthen. Although the party lost that seat in 1970, it won two others in the February 1974 elections (Carnarvon and Merioneth) and added the Carmarthen seat in October of that year, for a tally of three. The party also built up significant representation in local government. In light of this performance, the then Labour government tabled proposals for an elected Welsh assembly, but the idea was rejected by Welsh voters in a referendum of March 1979.

In the May 1979 general elections *Plaid Cymru* obtained 132,544 votes, holding the Carnarvon and Merioneth seats but losing Carmarthen to Labour. It retained its two seats in the 1983 elections, winning a total of 125,309 votes. In the June 1987 elections the party again moved up to three Commons seats by winning Ynys Môn, although its total vote slipped to 123,595 (7.3% of the Welsh total). A month before that contest *Plaid Cymru* had signed an agreement with the →Scottish National Party under which they were to form a single parliamentary group. The April 1992 general elections yielded the party's best-ever result, four of the 32 seats contested (out of 38 in Wales) being won, including Pembroke North, with an aggregate vote of 148,232 (about 8.5% of the Welsh total). In the June 1994 European Parliament elections, moreover, *Plaid Cymru* advanced to over 17% of the Welsh vote, although without winning any seats.

In the May 1997 general elections *Plaid Cymru* presented 40 candidates, winning four seats with an aggregate vote of 161,030 (9.9% in Wales). It thereafter backed the new Labour government's introduction of a devolved legislature for Wales, while regretting its lack of tax-raising powers. In the Welsh assembly elections in May 1999 *Plaid Cymru* made inroads in Labour strongholds in south Wales, taking second place with 17 of the 60 seats on a vote share of 30.5%. In the June 1999 European elections the *Plaid Cymru* share of the vote in Wales leapt forward to 29.6%, giving it representation (two seats) for the first time.

Plaid Cymru is a member of the Democratic Party of the Peoples of Europe–European Free Alliance. Its representatives in the European Parliament sit in the Greens/European Free Alliance group.

Scottish National Party (SNP)
Address. 6 North Charlotte Street, Edinburgh, EH2 4JH, Scotland
Telephone. (+44–131) 226–3661
Fax. (+44–131) 226–9597
Email. snp.hq@snp.org.uk
Website. http://www.snp.org.uk
Leadership. Alex Salmond (leader/national convenor); Winifred Ewing (president); Stewart Hosie (national secretary)
The SNP identifies itself as "moderate, left-of-centre" on economic and social questions; its basic aim is Scottish independence within the European Union (EU) and the Commonwealth, with a democratic Scottish parliament elected by proportional representation. The party was founded in 1934 as a merger of the National Party of Scotland and the Scottish Party. It won a by-election at Motherwell in April 1945 but lost this Commons seat in the general elections three months later. Thereafter the SNP held only single seats in the House of Commons: Hamilton from 1967 to 1970, Western Isles from 1970 to 1974 and Govan from 1973 to

February 1974. In the February 1974 elections, however, the party won seven seats with 21.9% of the vote in Scotland, boosted by the discovery of oil in the North Sea and the prospect that an independent Scotland would be financially viable on the basis of oil revenues.

In the October 1974 elections the SNP advanced further to 11 seats with 30.4% of the Scottish vote, whereupon the then →Labour Party government tabled proposals for the creation of a devolved Scottish assembly. But the tide of pro-independence feeling had ebbed somewhat by the time of the March 1979 referendum on the plans, the outcome being that the 52% vote in favour represented only 32.8% of those entitled to vote (the turnout having been only 63.7%). Basing itself on an earlier decision that a higher real vote in favour would be required, the UK parliament thereupon refused to set up the assembly. In the May 1979 general elections the SNP lost all but two of its seats, although it still polled 17.2% of the Scottish vote. Both of these seats were retained in the 1983 elections, but the SNP's share of the Scottish vote contracted to 11.8% (331,975 votes), which was only slightly more than in 1970. In the June 1987 elections the SNP polled 416,873 votes (14% of the Scottish total) and won three parliamentary seats. Immediately prior to the 1987 general elections, the SNP signed an agreement with →*Plaid Cymru* (Welsh Nationalists) pledging mutual support in parliament.

By-election successes increased the SNP's Commons representation to five seats in the course of the 1987–92 parliament, but the party fell back to three in the April 1992 general elections despite increasing its share of the Scottish vote to 21.5% (629,564 votes), just behind the →Conservative Party. The SNP recovered the status of Scotland's second party (after Labour) in the June 1994 European Parliament elections, obtaining nearly a third of the Scottish vote and winning two Euro-seats (compared with one in 1979). In May 1995, moreover, the party increased in Commons representation to four seats as a result of a by-election victory over the Conservatives in which it took 40% of the vote.

In the May 1997 general elections the SNP increased its representation in the Commons to six seats, although it vote aggregate fell to 621,550. It thereafter opted to work with the incoming Labour government's devolution plan for Scotland, although it fell far short of core SNP aims. In elections to the new Scottish parliament in May 1999 the SNP came second behind Labour, winning 35 of the 129 seats with a 27.3% share of the list vote and becoming the principal opposition to a Labour–Liberal Democrat coalition in Scotland. In the June 1999 European elections the SNP again won two seats on a national vote share of 2.7%. At the SNPannual conference in Inverness in September 1999 SNP leader Alex Salmond told delegates that he expected Scotland to be fully independent within eight years.

The SNP is a member of the Democratic Party of the Peoples of Europe–European Free Alliance. Its representatives in the European Parliament sit in the Greens/European Free Alliance group.

UK Independence Party (UKIP)
Address. Triumph House, 93 Regent Street, London, W1R 7TD
Telephone. (+44-20) 7434-4559
Fax. (+44-20) 7439-4659
Leadership. Michael Holmes (leader); Nigel Farage (chair)
The UKIP was founded by Alan Sked to oppose what it regards as the unacceptable surrender of British sovereignty to the European Union (EU). Having contested the 1992 general elections as the Anti-Federalist League (its 16 candidates all losing their deposits), the UKIP fought most UK seats in the 1994 European Parliament elections, winning an overall vote share of 1%. In the May 1997 general elections 193 UKIP candidates took only 0.3% of the vote, all but one losing their deposits. However, the party broke through in the June 1999

European elections, winning 7.0% of the national vote and returning three MEPs. The latter joined the Europe of Democracies and Diversities group in the European Parliament.

Other Parties

The proliferation of small right-wing, left-wing and other parties and groups which have been active in Great Britain in recent years includes the following:

British National Party (BNP), led by Nick Griffin, an extreme right-wing formation founded in 1960 as an alliance of the League of Empire Loyalists, the White Defence League and the National Labour Party. A split in the BNP was caused by the formation of a paramilitary elite corps (named "Spearhead") under the leadership of Colin Jordan and John Tyndall, the rump BNP being one of the founder members of the →National Front in 1967. In 1982 the BNP re-emerged as an independent party under Tyndall's leadership, contesting 53 seats in the 1983 general elections (losing 53 deposits) and a smaller number in 1987 (with the same result). Although Tyndall had been sentenced to 12 months' in prison in 1986 for incitement to racial hatred, the party subsequently sought to give a "respectable" face to extreme right-wing politics and to develop contacts with like-minded movements in continental Europe. Standing for "rights for whites" and the repatriation or exclusion of coloured immigrants, the BNP attracted some support in inner city areas of high minority population in the early 1990s. Although its 13 candidates all lost their deposits in the 1992 general elections (achieving an aggregate vote of 7,005), in September 1993 it won its first local council seat in the east London borough of Tower Hamlets, an area of high Bangladeshi settlement. It lost the seat in the May 1994 local elections, although its overall vote in the borough increased. In the 1997 general elections 57 BNP candidates won a total of 35,832 votes (0.1%), all but three losing their deposits. *Address.* PO Box 1032, Ilford, Essex, IG1 1DY; *Telephone/Fax.* (+44-374) 454-893; *Email.* letters@bnp.net; *Website.* http://www.bnp.net

Christian People's Alliance (CPA), founded in 1999 as an attempt to create a continental-style Christian democratic party in Britain, presented Kenyan Asian businessman Ram Gidoomal as its candidate for May 2000 London mayoral election.

Communist Party of Britain–Marxist-Leninist (CPB-ML), founded in 1968 by Reg Birch (a trade union official) after his expulsion from the Communist Party of Great Britain (later the →Democratic Left); once regarded as the largest British Maoist party, the CPB-ML publishes *The Worker.*

Communist Party of Britain (CPB), led by Robert Griffiths, derived from a 1988 breakaway by a hard-line minority faction of the CPGB opposed to the latter's espousal of "Euro-communism", leading to its conversion into the →Democratic Left in 1991, whereupon the hard-line group took over the historic party name and rejected any theoretical accommodation with the collapse of communism in Eastern Europe. The new CPGB is closely aligned with the hard-line co-operative that has retained control of *The Morning Star* (once the official daily newspaper of the old CPGB). *Address.* 1–3 Ardleigh Road, London, N1 4HS; *Telephone.* (+44-20) 7275-8162; *Fax.* (+44-20) 7249-9188; *Email.* cpb@postweb.net; *Website.* http://members.xoom.com/_xmcm/cpgb

Co-operative Party, led by J. Lee (chair) and Peter Hunt (secretary), founded in 1917 by the British Co-operative Union (the central body representing British consumer and other co-operatives) in order to secure for the co-operative movement direct representation. The party has been represented in parliament ever since, in alliance with the →Labour Party whereby its representatives stand as "Labour and Co-op" candidates. There have been Cooperative members in all Labour governments since 1924. *Address*. Victory House, 10–14 Leicester Square, London, WC2H 7QH; *Telephone*. (+44-20) 7439-0123; *Fax*. (+44-20) 7439-3434; *Email*. p.hunt@co-op-party.org.uk

Democracy Movement (DM), led by Paul Sykes, launched in January 1999 as a merger of the Referendum Movement (RM), founded by Sir James Goldsmith in 1994 as the Referendum Party (RP), and the Euro-Information Campaign. The RP had been created to campaign on the single issue of its demand for a referendum on British participation in European economic, monetary and political union as envisaged under the 1991 Maastricht Treaty of the European Union (EU). A multi-millionaire businessman with dual French and British nationality, Goldsmith had been elected to the European Parliament in 1994 in France for what became the ⇒Rally for France and the Independence of Europe and had announced his willingness to put up £20 million to finance an election campaign by the RP in Britain, targeted at constituencies where the sitting →Conservative Party MP would not declare support for a referendum. His initiative alarmed many Conservative MPs concerned about their majorities in the next elections. A furore erupted in June 1996 over the disclosure that an anti-EU think tank run by "Euro-sceptic" Conservative MP Bill Cash had accepted financial donations from Goldsmith. Cash was obliged to end his indirect connection with the RP, but received recompense when former Conservative leader Baroness (Margaret) Thatcher made a "substantial" donation to his think tank. In early October 1996 the former Conservative treasurer Lord McAlpine caused a stir by declaring his support for the Referendum Party. Goldsmith died soon after the 1997 general elections, in which 547 RP candidates won a total of 811,849 votes (2.6%), mainly at the expense of the Conservatives. The new DM has renounced electoral participation in favour of operating as an anti-euro pressure group. *Address*. 2 Beaufort Mews, London, SW6 1PF; *Telephone*. (+44-20) 7610-0865; *Fax*. (+44-20) 7381-2062; *Email*. mail@democracymovement.org.uk; *Website*. http://www.democracy-movement.org.uk

Democratic Left (DL), led by Nina Temple (secretary) and Mhairi Stewart (chair), founded in 1991 in succession to the →Communist Party of Great Britain (CPGB), itself founded in 1920 and for 70 years Britain's main Communist formation with the considerable influence in the labour movement in the post-war decades, although its attempts to establish formal co-ooperation with the →Labour Party were consistently rebuffed. For long an orthodox pro-Soviet party, the CPGB had moved to a "Euro-communist" line in 1985, backing the return of a Labour government, despite fierce resistance from a hard-line minority. Having fielded 19 deposit-losing candidates in the 1987 elections, the bulk of the CPGB reacted to the collapse of communism in Eastern Europe in 1989–90 by abandoning Marxist-Leninist theory and launching the DL, whose programme stresses environmentalist concerns and the need for left-wing unity, including co-operation with the Labour Party. The DL did not contest the 1992 or 1997 elections. *Address*. 6 Cynthia Street, London, N1 9JF; *Telephone*. (+44-20) 7278-4443; *Fax*. (+44-20) 7278-4425

Fellowship Party (FP), led by R.S. Mallone, founded in 1955 on a pacifist, socialist and environmentalist platform, claims to have been instrumental in the establishment of the Campaign for Nuclear Disarmament (CND). It has contested numerous elections without any real success, its single candidate in 1992 winning only 147 votes. *Address*. Woolacombe House, 141 Woolacombe Road, Blackheath, London, SE3 8QP

Islamic Party of Britain (IPB), led by David Musa Pidcock, founded in 1989 in part to campaign for the banning of Salman Rushdie's *Satanic Verses* but also for other religions to be brought under the protection of the blasphemy laws currently only giving (notional) protection to the established Protestant Christian faith. Advocating state funding for Muslim schools (achieved under the post-1997 Labour government), the IPB fielded four candidates in the 1992 elections, obtaining a total of 1,085 votes and losing all four deposits; party has official membership of 1,000. *Address.* PO Box 844, Oldbrook, Milton Keynes, MK6 2YT; *Telephone.* (+44-1908) 671-756; *Fax.* (+44-1908) 694-035; *Email.* islamparty@breathemail.net; *Website.* http://www.muslims.net/islamparty

Legalize Cannabis Alliance (LCA), led by Howard Marks, presented first parliamentary candidate in Kensington and Chelsea by-election in November 1999. *Address.* PO Box 198, Norwich, Norfolk, NR2 2DE; *Telephone.* (+44-1603) 442-215; *Email.* howard@mrnice.co.uk; *Website.* http://www.lca-uk.org

Liberal Party (LP), led by Michael Meadowcroft (a former Liberal MP), founded as an attempt to keep the historic LP in existence following the formation of what became the →Liberal Democrats in 1989. The LP obtained 64,744 votes in the 1992 general elections, although only one of its 73 candidate saved his/her deposit. In 1997 its 55 candidates obtained a total of 45,166 votes (0.1%), all but two losing their deposits. *Address.* 1A Pine Grove, Southport, Lancashire, PR9 9AQ; *Telephone.* (+44-1704) 500-115; *Fax.* (+44-1704) 539-315; *Email.* libparty@libparty.demon.co.uk; *Website.* http://www.libparty.demon.co.uk

Mebyon Kernow (Cornish National Movement), led by Dick Cole, founded in 1951 to campaign for the self-government of Cornwall. By 1960 it claimed to have the active support of three Cornish MPs of other parties, although such became ineligible for membership following the movement's 1974 decision to contest parliamentary elections itself. It has gained representation in Cornish local government, often under the "independent" label, but has failed at national level. *Address.* Shell Cottage, Moorland Road, Indian Queens, St Columb, Cornwall; *Telephone.* (+44-1726) 861-454; *Email.* martyn@caradonflm.freeserve.co.uk; *Website.* http://www.caradonflm.freeserve.co.uk/mk

Militant Labour Party (MLP), led by Peter Taafe, founded in 1993 by the Trotskyist faction grouped around the *Militant* newspaper which had sought to act as a radical pressure group within the →Labour Party in the 1980s, until the Labour leadership had resolved to expel such activists. *Address.* 3–13 Hepscott Road, London, E9 5HB

Monster Raving Loony Party (MRLP), led by Alan ("Howling Lord") Hope and his ginger tomcat Mandu, Britain's premier "alternative" party, founded in the early 1960s by David ("Screaming Lord") Sutch, deserving of a listing in a serious reference work because Sutch (a former rock musician) contested over 40 by-elections before he committed suicide in June 1999, never saving a deposit but sometimes registering a not insignificant vote, as when he obtained 4.8% in a 1994 contest. Known by many variants of its historic title (and sometimes suffering from the intervention of similarly-named but unrelated parties), the MRLP has significant support in the West Country (Hope being mayor of Ashburton in Devon when he became leader). It fielded 18 candidates in the 1997 general elections, all of whom lost their deposits.

National Democrats (NDs), led by Ian Anderson, right-wing anti-European formation which presented 21 candidates in 1997 general elections, all but one losing their deposits and winning an aggregate vote of 10,829. Address. BCM Natdems, London, WC1N 3XX; *Telephone.* (+44-7071) 226-074; Website. http://www.natdems.org.uk

National Front (NF), led by Ian Anderson, far-right formation founded in 1967, seeking the restoration of Britain as an ethnically homogeneous state by means of the "repatriation" of coloured immigrants and their descendants. It also seeks to liberate Britain from international ties such as the United Nations, NATO and the European Union, and opposes the international financial system and "big business capitalism", favouring instead small privately-owned enterprises and workers' co-operatives. The NF was founded as a merger of the →British National Party (BNP), the League of Empire Loyalists and the Racial Preservation Society. It has nominated candidates in all general elections since its formation, rising to 303 in 1979, but has received only negligible support, although a 1973 by-election in West Bromwich yielded 16.02% of the vote. In the 1970s NF meetings frequently led to serious violence, as opponents mounted counter-demonstrations. The right of NF candidates to hire halls for election meetings was upheld by the High Court in November 1982, but NF marches have been banned under a Public Order Act; moreover, NF leaders have been sentenced for "incitement to racial hatred" under the Race Relations Act. In 1984–85 the NF gained publicity when one of its activists, Patrick Harrington, registered at a North London college, provoking a long confrontation with anti-fascist students. Subsequently, the Front sought to improve its image by electing a new generation of university-educated leaders who developed a new intellectual basis for the movement (described as "new positivism") and publicly distanced themselves from the violent street activism previously associated with Martin Webster (the controversial NF organizer ousted from the party in 1983–84). Nevertheless, internal divisions continued, leading to a split in 1986–87 between a "revolutionary nationalist" group and a "radical nationalist" group in 1986–87, by which time the NF had largely been eclipsed on the far right by the revived BNP. The NF's 14 candidates in the 1992 elections all lost their deposits, obtaining a total of 4,816 votes. In 1997 six NF candidates won 2,716 votes, all losing their deposits. *Address.* PO Box 760, London, N17 7SB

Natural Law Party (NLP), led by Geoffrey Clements, launched in Britain and other developed countries in a well-funded attempt to secure electoral support for the mystic Indian religious concepts of the Maharishi once espoused by the Beatles pop group. The supposed bliss of "yogic flying" made little impact on British voters in the 1992 elections, when the NLP's 310 candidates all lost their deposits. Similarly, in the 1997 contest none of the 197 NLP candidates retained their deposits, winning a total of 30,604 votes (0.1%).

New Communist Party (NCP), Marxist-Leninist grouping, standing for peace and nuclear disarmament, publisher of the weekly *New Worker. Address.* PO Box 73, London, SW11 2PQ; *Telephone.* (+44-20) 7223-4050; *Fax.* (+44-20) 7223-4057; *Website.* http://www.geocities.com/capitolhill/2853

Pro-Life Alliance, anti-abortion movement, fielded 56 candidates in May 1997 elections, all losing their deposits in winning an aggregate vote of 19,332 (0.1%). *Address.* PO Box 13395, London, SW3 6XE; *Telephone.* (+44-20) 7351-9955; *Fax.* (+44-20) 7349-0450; *Email.* info@prolifealliance.org.uk; *Website.* http://www.prolifealliance.org.uk

Revolutionary Communist Group (RCG), leftist grouping founded in 1981. Its eight candidates all lost their deposits in the 1992 general elections, obtaining an aggregate vote of 745 electors; party did not contest 1997 elections. *Address.*BCM Box 5909, London,

WC1N 3XX; *Telephone*. (+44-20) 7837-1688; *Email*. rcgfrfi@easynet.co.uk; *Website*. http://www.rcgfrfi.easynet.co.uk

Scottish Socialist Alliance (SSA), left-wing formation in Scotland opposed to the "revisionism" of Blair's →Labour Party, failed to make an impact in 1997 general elections, but won one seat in Scottish Parliament elections in May 1999.

Socialist Equality Party (SEP), Trotskyist formation. *Address*. PO Box 1306, Sheffield, S9 3UW; *Telephone*. (+44-114) 244-3545; *Fax*. (+44-114) 244-0224; *Email*. sep@socialequality.org. uk; *Website*. http://www.socialequality.org.uk

Socialist Labour Party (SLP), launched in 1996 by Arthur Scargill to provide a radical left-wing alternative to the "new" →Labour Party of Tony Blair. As president of the National Union of Mineworkers, Scargill had led abortive trade union opposition to the policies of the Thatcher government in the 1980s, becoming increasingly disenchanted with the line of the Labour leadership. In the new party's first electoral contest, at the Hemsworth by-election in February 1996, the SLP candidate won 5.4% of the vote. In the 1997 general elections 61 of 64 SLP candidates lost their deposits, the party's aggregate vote being 52,109 (0.2%). *Address*. 9 Victoria Road, Barnsley, S. Yorks, S70 2BB; *Telephone/Fax*. (+44) 1226) 770-957

Socialist Party (SP), Trotskyist formation. *Address*. PO Box 24697, London, E9 5FP; *Telephone*. (+44-20) 8533-3311; *Fax*. (+44-20) 8985-2932; *Email*. enquiries@socialistparty.org.uk; *Website*. http://www.socialistparty.org.uk

Socialist Party of Great Britain (SPGB), led by Adam Buick, a Marxist formation founded in 1904 in quest of "a world-wide community based on the common ownership and democratic control of the means of wealth distribution and production". In the course of its long history the SPGB opposed both world wars, without success. Its parliamentary and local election forays have also met with regular lack of success. The SPGB has links with similarly named and orientated parties in a number of other developed countries, together constituting the World Socialist Movement. *Address*. 52 Clapham High Street, London SW4 7UN; *Telephone*. (+44-20) 7622-3811; *Fax*. (+44-20) 7720-3665; *Email*. spgb@worldsocialism.org; *Website*. http://www.worldsocialism.org/spgb

Socialist Workers' Party (SWP), led by Duncan Hallas, a Trotskyist grouping founded in 1950 as the International Socialists and known under that name until 1977. The SWP has worked towards "the building of a nucleus of a serious revolutionary party", not by infiltrating the labour movement but in influencing it in a leftward direction from outside. It does not rule out the use of force in support of socialist legislation opposed by forces of the right. It has not taken part in recent general elections, but it has led militant campaigns through the Anti-Nazi League and the Right to Work movement. It has also worked to oppose what it regards as the rightward drift in the "new" →Labour Party. *Address*. PO Box 82, London E3 3LH; *Telephone*. (+44-20) 7538-5821; *Fax*. (+44-20) 7538-0018; *Email*. enquiries@swp.org.uk; *Website*. http://www.swp.org.uk

Workers' Revolutionary Party (WRP), led by Mike Banda, leftist formation which rejects "the parliamentary road to socialism" but has contested general elections. A WRP government would nationalize banks, insurance companies, the media and all major industries, repeal all immigration and anti-union laws, end private education, close down the nuclear power industry, establish workers' militias in place of the army, withdraw British troops from

Northern Ireland, leave NATO and seek to replace the European Union by a socialist United States of Europe. Descended from the pre-war Militant Group, by way of the Workers' International League and the Revolutionary Communist Party (among other earlier formations), the WRP succeeded the Socialist Labour League (founded in 1959) and at first worked inside the Labour Party. Since 1974 it has unsuccessiully contested general elections. In 1979 it nominated 60 parliamentary candidates who gained a total of 12,631 votes (and no seats). In the 1983 and 1987 general elections it unsuccessfully contested 22 and 10 seats respectively. In October 1985 the WRP's founder and former leader, Gerry Healy, was expelled from the party after an internal inquiry had found him guilty of gross sexual misconduct against young female party members. This action was opposed by a minority faction that included the party's best-known members, actress Vanessa Redgrave and her brother Corin Redgrave, and led to a split which also reflected internal opposition to moves by the leadership to initiate co-operation with other left-wing groups (including the →Labour Party). A more immediate cause of the split was a dispute over the ownership of the party's assets of some £1.5 million. The WRP's two candidates in the 1992 general elections won 330 votes between them.

Northern Ireland

Capital: Belfast   **Population:** 1,660,000

Northern Ireland was created in 1921 as an autonomous component of the United Kingdom of Great Britain and Northern Ireland, its territory comprising six counties (four with a Protestant majority) of the historic nine-county Irish province of Ulster. Amid a descent into sectarian violence between Protestants and the Catholic minority and the launching by the Irish Republican Army (IRA) of an armed campaign against British rule, the Northern Ireland parliament was suspended in 1972. For the next 27 years (apart from a brief period in 1974) Northern Ireland was ruled directly from Westminster, the responsible member of the UK Cabinet being the Secretary of State for Northern Ireland. However, the multi-party Good Friday Agreement signed in Belfast on April 10, 1998, provided for the restoration of a

Elections to the 108-member Northern Ireland Assembly on June 25, 1998, resulted as follows (comparative percentages being shown for elections to the 110-seat Northern Ireland Forum on May 30, 1996):

	Seats 1998	Percentage 1998 (1996)
Ulster Unionist Party	28	21.3 (24.7)
Social Democratic and Labour Party	24	22.0 (21.4)
Democratic Unionist Party	20	18.1 (18.8)
Sinn Féin	18	17.6 (15.5)
Alliance Party of Northern Ireland	6	6.5 (6.5)
United Kingdom Unionist Party...	5	4.5 (3.7)
Independent Unionists...	3	3.0 (n/a)
Progressive Unionist Party	2	2.5 (3.5)
Northern Ireland Women's Coalition	2	1.6 (1.0)

Northern Ireland legislature and government (executive) with substantial economic and social powers, the executive to be constituted under power-sharing arrangements giving all major parties representation. Elections to a new Northern Ireland Assembly were held on June 25, 1998, the 108 seats being filled by the single transferable vote method in 18 six-member constituencies. A year and a half later, on Dec. 2, 1999, the new power-sharing executive was formally established, whereupon the Irish government promulgated amendments to the Republic's 1937 constitution (approved by referendum on May 22, 1998) formally enshrining the principle of popular consent to any change in the status of the North (see introduction to Ireland chapter). Also inaugurated on Dec. 2, 1999, were a consultative North-South Ministerial Council, a relaunched UK-Irish Intergovernmental Council and a "Council of the Isles" (representing the parliaments of the UK, the Irish Republic, Northern Ireland, Scotland, Wales, the Channel Islands and the Isle of Man).

In the UK general elections of May 1, 1997, the 18 Northern Ireland seats (filled by simple majority in single-member constituencies) were distributed as follows: Ulster Unionist Party 10 seats (with 32.7% of the Northern Ireland vote), Social Democratic and Labour Party 3 (24.1%), *Sinn Féin* 2 (16.1%), Democratic Unionist Party 2 (12.3%), United Kingdom Unionist Party 1 (1.6%).

Alliance Party of Northern Ireland (Alliance/APNI)

Address. 88 University Street, Belfast, BT7 1HE
Telephone. (+44-28) 9032-4274
Fax. (+44-28) 9033-3147
Email. alliance@allianceparty.org
Website. http:// www.allianceparty.org/
Leadership. (Sean) Neeson (leader); Seamus Close (deputy leader); Richard Good (general secretary)

Alliance, as the party is usually known, was founded in April 1970 as a centrist, non-sectarian unionist party, drawing support from the moribund Ulster Liberal Party and the moderate (Faulknerite) Unionist Party of Northern Ireland. It advocates the restoration of a devolved government with the sharing of power between the Catholic and Protestant sections of the community. The party, which has tended to have a mainly Protestant following, but Catholic leaders, is generally regarded as a liberal middle-class formation, and is strongly opposed to political violence. It was the only unionist party to support the Anglo-Irish Agreement of November 1985.

It first contested elections in 1973, winning 9.2% of the vote for the Northern Ireland Assembly. In January 1974 it joined a power-sharing executive (provincial government) with Brian Faulkner's faction of the →Ulster Unionist Party and with the →Social Democratic and Labour Party (SDLP). (That executive collapsed in May 1974.) In the May 1975 Constitutional Convention elections Alliance obtained 9.8% of the vote, and its support peaked in the 1977 local government elections, when it came third with 14.3%. In the Assembly elections of October 1982 it won 10 of the 78 seats, with 9.3%. In the June 1983 UK general elections it polled 8% of the vote, and in those of June 1987 9.9%.

John Cushnahan, who had succeeded Oliver Napier as party leader in 1984, resigned in October 1987 and was succeeded by John T. Alderdice (who was ennobled in 1996). In the 1989 local, 1992 general and 1993 local elections the party secured 6%, 8.7% and 7.7% of the vote respectively, fell to 4.1% in the 1994 European polls but recovered to 6.5% in the 1996 Forum elections. Strongly supportive of the April 1998 Good Friday Agreement, the party again won 6.5% of the vote in the June 1998 Assembly, which gave it six seats (not enough for representation on the new power-sharing executive). Sean Neeson was elected party leader in September 1998 after Alderdice resigned on his appointment as initial presiding officer (speaker) of the new Assembly.

Alliance is a full member of the Liberal International, which it joined in 1991, and of the European Liberal Democratic and Reformist Party (ELDR). It has had close relations, but no organic link, with the Liberal Party in Great Britain, and subsequently with the ⇒Liberal Democrats.

Democratic Unionist Party (DUP)
Address. 91 Dundela Avenue, Belfast, BT4 3BU
Telephone. (+44-28) 9047-1155
Fax. (+44-28) 9047-1797
Email. info@dup.org.uk
Website. http://www.dup.org.uk
Leadership. Rev. Ian Richard Kyle Paisley (leader); Peter Robinson (deputy leader); Jim McClure (chairman); Nigel Dodds (secretary)

The DUP is a loyalist party closely identified with its leader's brand of fundamentalist Protestantism and drawing its main support from the urban working class and small farmers. The DUP is more populist than the →Ulster Unionist Party (UUP, formerly OUP). It is vehemently opposed to any involvement of the Dublin government, which it regards as alien and Catholic-controlled, in the administration of the North. It also opposes the European Union, which it has denounced as a Catholic conspiracy, although the party has accepted representation in the European Parliament.

The holder of an honorary doctorate from the Bob Jones University of South Carolina (USA), Paisley founded and leads the Free Presbyterian Church, a fiery sect which provides much of the DUP's support. He was also founder and leader of the DUP's predecessor, the Protestant Unionist Party (PUP), which was formed in 1969 (by the amalgamation of the Ulster Constitution Defence Committee with Ulster Protestant Action) and which in 1970 won two seats in the Northern Ireland parliament and one in the UK parliament. The DUP was founded in 1971 (formally known as the Ulster Democratic Unionist Party, UDUP) and won eight of the 78 seats in the Northern Ireland Assembly in 1973. Paisley was re-elected to the UK House of Commons in February and October 1974, when the DUP and other groups combined as the United Ulster Unionist Council (UUUC). He was re-elected in 1979, when the DUP gained two other seats, and in the same year Paisley was elected to the European Parliament. In 1975–76 the party held 12 of the 46 UUUC seats in the inconclusive Northern Ireland Constitutional Convention.

In the October 1982 elections to a Northern Ireland Assembly the DUP secured 21 of the 78 seats (with 23% of the vote). The DUP's Westminster MPs, re-elected in 1983 (when the party secured 20% of the vote), resigned their seats along with their OUP colleagues in January 1986, forcing by-elections as a form of referendum on the 1985 Anglo-Irish Agreement: all three held their seats, as they did in the June 1987 UK general elections, when the DUP declined to 11.7% (having agreed not to contest any OUP-held seats). Peter Robinson, who had lost prestige in unionist circles by paying a fine imposed for participating in a riot in the Republic of Ireland, resigned after seven years as deputy leader in October 1987, but was reappointed in early 1988.

In the 1992 UK general elections the DUP increased its vote to 13.1%, retaining its three MPs, and in 1993 it won 17.2% in local elections (down from 17.7% in 1989). After the IRA ceasefire first declared in 1994 and reinstated in 1996, the DUP resolutely opposed any negotiations by political parties or government representatives with →*Sinn Féin*. In the 1996 Forum elections it increased its vote to 18.8%, winning 24 of the 110 seats.

The DUP slipped to two seats and a 12.3% vote share in the UK general elections in May 1997. It refused to participate in the negotiations that produced the Good Friday Agreement of April 1998 and claimed that only a minority of Protestants had endorsed it in the referendum held in May 1998. In the June 1998 Assembly elections the DUP won 18.0% of the vote and 20 of the 108 seats, therefore becoming entitled to two posts in the new power-sharing executive. In the June 1999 European elections the DUP again won one seat (heading the Northern Ireland poll with 28.0% of the vote). Having called unsuccessfully for the expulsion of *Sinn Féin* from the peace process, the two DUP ministers (Peter Robinson and Nigel Dodds) took their seats when the executive was eventually inaugurated in December 1999, although they refused to sit in meetings with *Sinn Féin* representatives.

The DUP representative in the European Parliament is one of the non-attached members.

Northern Ireland Women's Coalition (NIWC)

Address. 52 Elmwood Avenue, Belfast, BT9 6AZ
Telephone. (+44-28) 9068-1118
Fax. (+44-28) 9068-1118
Email. niwc@iol.ie
Website. http://www.pitt.edu/~novosel/northern.html
Leadership. Monica McWilliams, Pearl Sagar and Jane Morrice
The NIWC began as an ad hoc grouping formed to raise the profile of women's issues in the May 1996 Forum elections and the subsequent discussions. It obtained just over 1% of the vote and its regional-list nominees, Monica McWilliams and Pearl Sagar, were among only 14 women elected to the 110–seat body, in which they frequently protested that their interventions were not taken seriously. Strongly supportive of the April 1998 Good Friday Agreement, the NIWC won two seats and a 1.6% vote share in the June 1998 Assembly elections.

Progressive Unionist Party (PUP)

Address. 182 Shankill Road, Belfast, BT13 2BL
Telephone. (+44-28) 9032-6233
Fax. (+44-28) 9024-9602
Website. http://www.pup.org
Leadership. Hugh Smyth (leader); David Ervine (spokesperson); Billy Hutchinson (press officer)
Formed in 1977 (succeeding the Volunteer Political Party, VPP), the PUP is the political wing of one of the two largest "loyalist" paramilitary groupings, namely the Ulster Volunteer Force (UVF), and also speaks for the Red Hand Commando (RHC). Although the UVF has been illegal almost since its formation, the existence of the PUP permitted the British government to engage openly in ministerial-level negotiations with it from late 1994, the declared aim of the government being to secure the disarmament of the loyalist groups. It was widely accepted that the electoral system for the 1996 Forum elections, in which the PUP secured 3.5% of the vote and two seats, was designed to ensure representation for the two parties euphemistically described as "close to the thinking of" the loyalist paramilitaries.

The PUP has been strongly supportive of the peace process which resulted in the April 1998 Good Friday Agreement, being regarded as the most left-wing of the unionist parties. In the June 1998 elections to a new Northern Ireland Assembly it won two seats on a vote share of 2.5%.

Sinn Féin (SF)
Address. 51–55 Falls Road, Belfast, BT12 4PD
Telephone. (+44-28) 9062-4421
Fax. (+44-28) 9062-2112
Email. sinnfein@iol.ie
Website. http://www.sinnfein.ie
Leadership. Gerry Adams (president); Mitchel McLaughlin (chair); Martin McGuinness (vice-president)

Sinn Féin (the name, which means "ourselves" in Irish, is not translated) is one of a small number of parties active in both jurisdictions on the island of Ireland (see also entry in Ireland chapter). The Northern membership, which forms a majority within the party, is formally integrated in the all-Ireland structure, although a Northern executive deals with matters specific to what it would term "the occupied area" or "the six counties".

Founded in 1905 as a nationalist pressure group, *Sinn Féin* became associated with militant republicanism. After the partition of Ireland in 1922 it was the political wing of the republican movement, supporting the periodic guerrilla campaigns of the Irish Republican Army (IRA) against British rule. The main party of the Catholic electorate in the North after 1922 was the Nationalist Party, as *Sinn Féin* candidates stood on a policy of refusing to recognize or participate in any of the three parliaments claiming jurisdiction on the island. In the 1955 Northern Ireland parliamentary elections, however, SF won 150,000 votes (some 56% of the Catholic total). The party was banned in Northern Ireland in 1956 (and remained so until 1973).

A period of left-wing activity from 1967 moved *Sinn Féin* to an overtly socialist position, but communal violence in 1969 led to a resurgence of the traditional nationalist tendency. A split in 1970 led to the creation of a "Provisional" Army Council, which rebuilt the IRA to pursue a military campaign against British rule; the political wing of this more militant faction became known as Provisional or (after its Dublin headquarters) Kevin Street *Sinn Féin*, to distinguish it from "Official" (Gardiner Place) *Sinn Féin*. The latter group evolved into the Workers' Party, leaving only one *Sinn Féin* and making redundant the Provisional prefix (which was never formally adopted but is still widely used in the abbreviated "Provos" form).

The Provisional tendency portrayed itself through the 1970s as a classic national liberation movement, adopting Marxist rhetoric for non-American audiences, but in fact having almost no party political activity because of its principle of abstention from the institutions of the "partitionist" states. In the early 1980s, however, the movement was transformed by the emotional reaction and mass demonstrations generated by the hunger strikes of IRA (and other) prisoners, and by the election of abstentionist republican (not, formally, *Sinn Féin*) candidates to the Westminster and Dublin parliaments. *Sinn Féin* capitalized on the hunger strike issue to involve a new generation in its political activities, which broadened to include participation in community issues and contesting local and parliamentary elections. It continued to demand British disengagement from the North and the negotiation of a new all-Ireland framework. In 1981 it won the UK Commons seat which had been held by an IRA volunteer (Bobby Sands) who had died on hunger strike.

In the 1982 elections to the Northern Ireland Assembly SF candidates secured 10.1% of the vote. In the 1983 UK general elections SF won 13.1% in Northern Ireland (43% of the Catholic vote), with Gerry Adams (who had become national leader of SF in 1983) being the only SF candidate elected (and holding to the abstentionist policy). By late 1987 SF had some 60 seats on local councils in the North, having won its first in 1983. In the UK general elections of June 1987 SF received 11.2% of the vote; Adams held his seat in West Belfast but lost it to the →Social Democratic and Labour Party (SDLP) in 1992, when the SF vote slipped to 10%. In the 1993 local polls the SF vote rose to 12.5%.

From January 1988 *Sinn Féin* had a series of discreet meetings with the SDLP, much to the consternation of the unionist camp, which spoke of a "pan-nationalist pact". The contacts were, however, instrumental in bringing about secret negotiations with the British government in 1991–93, and the announcement of an IRA ceasefire in August 1994. During the ceasefire the party sought to become involved in ministerial-level negotiations with Britain and in all-party talks on a new constitutional framework, but the British government and most unionist parties insisted that substantive talks had to be preceded by the partial or complete disarmament of the IRA. The IRA resumed its bombings in February 1996, and SF continued to press for its unconditional inclusion in negotiations, bolstered by its increased share of the vote (15.5%) in the June 1996 elections to the Forum (the proceedings of which SF boycotted because of its continued exclusion from constitutional talks).

Sinn Féin scored a major success in the May 1997 UK elections, returning two candidates (Adams and McGuinness) and securing 16.1% of the vote. Both declined to swear the oath of allegiance and so were barred from taking up their seats (their attempt to obtain members' facilities at Westminster also being rebuffed by decision of Speaker Betty Boothroyd). The reinstatement of the IRA ceasefire in July 1997 and the referral of the arms decommissioning issue to an international commission facilitated the inclusion of *Sinn Féin* in peace talks which yielded the Good Friday Agreement of April 1998. In elections to the new Assembly in June 1998 SF candidates took 17.6% of the vote, winning 18 of the 108 seats, which entitled the party to two seats on the new power-sharing executive. In the June 1999 European elections the SF vote held up at 17.1%, but the party did not gain representation. On the eventual implementation of the April 1998 accord in December 1999, McGuinness and Bairbre de Brun became the two SF ministers in the new Northern Ireland executive.

The party has no formal international affiliations, although it corresponds with many overseas socialist parties and nationalist movements. It has a particular affinity with the ⇒We Basques (*Eukal Herritarrok*) separatist party in Spain.

Social Democratic and Labour Party (SDLP)
Address. 121 Ormeau Road, Belfast, BT7 1SH
Telephone. (+44-28) 9024-7700
Fax. (+44-28) 9023-6699
Email. sdlp@indigo.ie
Website. http://www.sdlp.ie
Leadership. John Hume (leader); Séamus Mallon (deputy leader); Jonathan Stephenson (chair); Gerry Cosgrove (general secretary)
The nationalist, centre-left SDLP is the main party of the Catholic minority, and has as its long-term objective the reunification of Ireland by consent; it rejects political violence and seeks co-operation with the Protestant majority. It was the only major party in Northern Ireland committed to the maintenance of the 1985 Anglo-Irish Agreement, and to the institutionalization of the Dublin government's advisory role in respect of Northern affairs; subsequently it became a driving-force in the peace process which led to the Good Friday Agreement of April 1998. There are within the SDLP various currents of opinion committed to greater or lesser degrees to traditional nationalism; the social democratic aspect of its ideology has tended to be understated.

The SDLP grew out of the civil rights agitation of the late 1960s; it was formed in August 1970 by members of the then Northern Ireland Parliament. Two of its founders sat for the Republican Labour Party (including Gerry Fitt, also a Westminster MP, who became leader), one for the Northern Ireland Labour Party, one for the Nationalist Party and three as independents. The new party rapidly overtook the Nationalist Party as the main party of the Catholic community, and it continues to exercise that role while rejecting sectarianism.

The SDLP participated with moderate unionist members of the Northern Ireland Assembly in the short-lived power-sharing executive formed in 1974. John Hume was elected to the European Parliament in 1979, in which year he won the party leadership from Fitt (who left the party, lost his Westminster seat and was later appointed to the UK House of Lords). In the 1982 Assembly elections the SDLP won 14 seats, with 18.8% of the vote, but did not take them up because of the opposition of the unionist parties to power-sharing. Hume entered the UK Parliament in 1983; the SDLP advantage over →Sinn Féin (SF) fell to 4.5 percentage points (17.9 to 13.4%), but it recovered ground thereafter. The party won an additional Westminster seat in the 15 by-elections held in Northern Ireland in early 1987, and a third seat in the 1987 UK general elections, with 21.6% of the vote.

In the 1992 UK general elections the SDLP won 23.5% of the Northern Ireland vote and captured a fourth seat, in West Belfast, from SF. Hume's central role in bringing about the IRA ceasefire of 1994–96 and its reinstatement in July 1997, and in persuading SF to commit itself publicly to a negotiated settlement, proved of more electoral benefit to SF than to the SDLP; in the 1996 Forum elections the decline in the SDLP vote (to 21.4%) contributed significantly to the dramatic increase in the SF vote. In the May 1997 UK general elections the SDLP fell back to three seats, although its share of the Northern Ireland vote improved to 24.1%, eight points ahead of *Sinn Féin*.

Strongly supportive of the April 1998 Good Friday Agreement, the SDLP won 24 of the 108 seats in the new Northern Ireland Assembly elected in June 1998, taking a 22.0% vote share. Hume was again elected in the June 1999 European elections, the SDLP winning 27.7% of the Northern Ireland vote, well ahead of the →Ulster Unionist Party. In the new power-sharing executive inaugurated in December 1999, Séamus Mallon became Deputy First Minister and three SDLP ministers were appointed (Mark Durkan, Seán Farren and Brid Rodgers).

The SDLP is a full member of the Socialist International. Its representative in the European Parliament sits in the Party of European Socialists group.

Ulster Unionist Party (UUP)

Address. 3 Glengall Street, Belfast, BT12 5AE
Telephone. (+44-28) 9032-4601
Fax. (+44-28) 9024-6738
Email. uup@uup.org
Website. http://www.uup.org
Leadership. David Trimble (leader); John Taylor (deputy leader); Sir Josias Cunningham (president); Rev. Martin Smyth (chief whip); Ken Maginnis (security spokesman)
Dating from 1905, the UUP is the largest party of the (mainly Protestant) unionist majority in Northern Ireland and stands for the maintenance of the union with Great Britain, while also accepting in recent years the need for power-sharing with the Catholic minority and a consultative all-Ireland dimension in the governance of the province. Generally conservative on social and economic issues, the party was closely linked for most of its existence with the British ⇒Conservative Party, but those ties were considerably weakened during the early 1970s and were terminated as a result of the Conservative Party's commitment to the 1985 Anglo-Irish Agreement.

The original Unionist Party, which with the semi-secret Orange Order (still linked organically with the UUP) mobilized the Protestant majority in north-eastern Ireland in defence of the union with Britain, was founded in 1905. It was the monolithic ruling party from the creation of Northern Ireland in 1921 (by the partition treaty which gave the rest of the country autonomy within the British Empire) until the prorogation of the regional parliament and the introduction of direct rule from London in 1972. During this period of Protestant unionist hegemony, which was challenged from time to time by upsurges of republican violence, the region was ruled by a parliament and government based at Stormont, although it continued to be represented in the UK legislature at Westminster.

The party fragmented in 1970–73 under pressures arising from the agitation of the Catholic minority for civil rights. The faction informally known as the Official Unionist Party (OUP) was the largest and the most successful in claiming historical continuity with the old Unionist Party, whereas the →Democratic Unionist Party (DUP) was the only breakaway party to achieve and retain a significant electoral following. James Molyneaux succeeded Harry West as OUP leader in 1974, and was himself succeeded in September 1995 by David Trimble.

The OUP, which during the 1980s gradually reasserted the original title of Ulster Unionist Party (although legally constituted as the Ulster Unionist Council, UUC), has consistently won a large proportion of parliamentary and local council seats, sometimes in coalition with other unionist parties. In 1982 it secured 26 of the 78 seats in the Northern Ireland Assembly, with 29.7% of the vote; in 1983 it won 34% and 11 of the 17 Northern Ireland seats in the Westminster parliament (losing one in a subsequent by-election). In June 1987 it won nine Westminster seats, with 37.7% of the vote, holding them in 1992 with a 34.5% vote share). In 1994 it held its European Parliament seat with 23.8% of first-preference votes. In the June 1996 Forum elections it headed the list of successful parties, winning 30 of the 110 seats on a 24.7% vote share.

In the May 1997 UK general elections the UUP advanced to 10 out of 18 seats, although its share of the Northern Ireland vote slipped to 32.7%. The party was a leading participant in the subsequent multi-party peace negotiations which yielded the Good Friday Agreement of April 1998, although a substantial section of the party persistently opposed accommodation with the nationalist minority on the terms proposed and in particular any dealings with →*Sinn Féin*. In the June 1998 elections for a new Northern Ireland Assembly, the UUP headed the poll by winning 28 of the 108 seats, but its share of the vote fell to 21.3% because of defections by anti-agreement unionists. In the June 1999 European elections the UUP slipped further to 17.4% of the Northern Ireland vote, although it retained its single seat.

Seeking to preserve unionist support for the April 1998 agreement, Trimble subsequently demanded that arms decommissioning by the IRA must precede the creation of a power-sharing executive on which *Sinn Féin* would be represented. His eventual acceptance in November 1999 that decommissioning would follow the establishment of the executive was endorsed by the UUP party council, although with significant minority dissent. Trimble became First Minister of the new executive inaugurated in early December 1999, the other UUP ministers being Sir Reg Empey, Sam Foster and Michael McGimpsey.

The UUP representative in the European Parliament is a member of the European People's Party–European Democrats group.

United Kingdom Unionist Party (UKUP)

Address. 10 Hamilton Road, Bangor, BT20 4LE
Telephone. (+44-28) 9147-9538
Fax. (+44-28) 9146-5037
Email. webmaster@ukup.org
Website. http://www.ukup.org
Leadership. Robert McCartney (chair); Anne Moore (secretary)
Not so much a party as the personal vehicle of McCartney, a leading barrister, the UKUP arose to support his successful bid to succeed the similarly independent-minded unionist Sir

James Kilfedder as MP for the affluent constituency of North Down after the latter's death in 1995. McCartney, formerly a leading member of the Campaign for Equal Citizenship, fought the by-election in June 1995 as an independent "United Kingdom Unionist" candidate on a platform of resolute opposition to the involvement of the Republic in what he saw as the internal affairs of Northern Ireland. Thus he opposed the Anglo-Irish Agreement of 1985, the Downing Street Declaration issued by the UK and Irish governments in 1993 and the post-1997 peace process which yielded the April 1998 Good Friday Agreement. He is identified with hard-line unionism, although vigorously rejecting the religious sectarianism associated with others of that tendency.

In the June 1996 Forum elections McCartney headed a list which became known as the UKUP, although it was not formally constituted as a party. McCartney was the only UKUP candidate elected to a constituency seat, but two regional-list seats went to the curious pairing of Conor Cruise O'Brien (a former Foreign Minister in the Dublin government representing the Irish ⇒Labour Party, latterly a journalist sympathetic to the Northern unionists) and Cedric Wilson (an inveterate protester against "Dublin interference", formerly a member of the →Democratic Unionist Party and subsequently founder of the →Northern Ireland Unionist Party). McCartney retained his Westminster seat in the May 1997 UK general elections. Opposed to the Good Friday Agreement, the UKUP won five seats and 4.5% of the vote in the Northern Ireland Assembly elections in June 1998.

The UKUP describes itself as a sister party of the London-based anti-European ⇒United Kingdom Independence Party.

Other Parties

Communist Party of Ireland (*Páirtí Cummanach na hÉireann*, CPI), based in Dublin (see Ireland section), but its Northern area, based in Belfast and organized by Margaret Bruton, has a degree of autonomy. The CPI has contested many elections without success, most recently the 1996 Forum elections, in which it won 66 votes. *Address.* PO Box 85, Belfast, BT1 1SR; *Telephone/Fax.* (+44-28) 9023-0669

Conservative Party, an attempt to extend the British ⇒Conservative and Unionist Party to Northern Ireland in the late 1980s, following the breakdown of the Conservatives' long relationship with the →Ulster Unionist Party. The party in Northern Ireland has failed to achieve a significant following in terms of membership or electoral support. It has constituency associations in several parts of the region, but has local council representation only in the commuter belt of North Down. Despite securing 5.7% in the 1992 general election, and several council seats in 1993, it won less than 0.5% in the 1996 Forum elections. *Address.* North Down Conservative Association, 2 May Avenue, Bangor, Co. Down; *Telephone.* (+44-28) 9146-9210

Democratic Left (DL), an anti-sectarian socialist movement formed in 1992 (when it was known briefly as New Agenda). The product of a split in the →Workers' Party (WP), it operated in both parts of Ireland, and won parliamentary representation in the Republic, where its more moderate socialist policies quickly won over most of the WP support. In the North, where more members remained with the hardline WP, DL failed to achieve a significant following, its local council representation falling in 1993 to one seat. The southern membership of DL merged in 1998 with the Irish ⇒Labour Party. The Northern members, led by Paddy Joe McClean (regional chair), are currently involved in merger discussions with other groupings in →Northern Ireland Labour. The party has no office. *Telephone.* (+44-28) 8075-8343

Green Party, whose leading member is Peter Emerson, an ecologist group present in elections since 1981, receiving 0.5% of the vote in the 1996 Forum elections; has close links with other Green parties, especially in Britain and the Irish Republic. *Address.* 537 Antrim Road, Belfast, BT7 1JR; *Telephone.* (+44-28) 9077-6731; *Email.* nigreens@belfast.co.uk; *Website.* http://www.belfast.co.uk/nigreens

Irish Republican Socialist Party (IRSP), a small revolutionary formation founded in 1974 by dissident members of the "Official" republican movement (later the →Workers' Party). Damaged by allegations of gangsterism and drug dealing, and by frequent and bloody feuding among members of its armed wing (the Irish National Liberation Army, INLA) and between the INLA and other republican groups, the IRSP has never been numerically significant and by 1999 had only a few dozen active members in Northern Ireland (and others in the Republic, being established, like other republican organizations, on an all-Ireland basis). The IRSP currently calls for a broad front of republican and socialist groupings to oppose what it regards as the unduly moderate position of →*Sinn Féin* and to speak for "the subject people of the six counties and the oppressed working class of Ireland". *Address.* 392 Falls Road, Belfast, BT12; *Email.* irsp-web@irsm.org; *Website.* http://www.irsm.org/irsp

Natural Law Party (NLP), one of a worldwide network of such parties, contests elections to advertise the beliefs and practices of the Maharishi cult. In the Northern Ireland context it proposes that the civil conflict, in which 3,100 people have been killed since 1969, can usefully be addressed by a small proportion of the population engaging in meditation and "yogic flying". The party has contested several elections in the region with discouraging results, securing 0.3% in the 1992 general election, 0.4% in the 1994 European polls and 0.05% in the 1996 Forum contest (from which it announced its withdrawal too late to be removed from the ballot papers). *Address.* 103 University Street, Belfast BT7; *Telephone/Fax.* (+44-28) 9031-1466; *Website.* http://nlp.nmtl.com

Northern Ireland Labour. Although a single Labour list was put forward in the 1996 Forum elections, securing 0.8% of the vote and two regional-list seats, its subsequent internal wrangles illustrated the difficulties which have frustrated all efforts to organize a region-wide socialist party across the sectarian divide. The Labour Coalition brought together supporters of a wide range of extinct or obscure, ephemeral and often ideologically incompatible labour formations, including (i) the defunct Northern Ireland Labour Party (NILP), a former affiliate of the Socialist International which had had no significant electoral support since 1975, when it secured 1.4% of the vote in constituent elections; (ii) the Labour and Trade Union Groups (L&TU), a network of local democratic socialist formations which contested elections in Belfast, Derry and other centres without success, from 1975 onwards (securing 0.2% in the 1992 general election); (iii) the Newtownabbey Labour Party, which won a single council seat in 1993 for Mark Langhammer (then the only public representative elected on any Labour ticket); (iv) the Labour Party '87, which also contested the 1993 local elections; (v) the Labour Co-ordinating Committee, chaired by Langhammer, which joined and then broke away from the Coalition; (vi) the Labour Movement in Local Government, formed by Paddy Devlin and Robert Clarke in May 1984 as an anti-sectarian socialist group which sought to unite the working class on economic and social issues; (vii) the Labour Representation Committee (LRC), formed in 1984 (succeeding the Campaign for Labour Representation in Northern Ireland) to seek the extension of the British ⇒Labour Party to Northern Ireland, to provide an alternative to the nationalist-unionist or Catholic-Protestant divisions; and (viii) Militant Labour, which fought the 1993 council elections without success and is allied with the British and Irish Militant movements. There have also been a number of independent

Socialist, Labour or Independent Worker candidates in local, parliamentary and European elections since 1992, but only one (Davey Kettyles), a →Workers' Party defector running as a Progressive Socialist, secured a council seat in 1993 (having won 0.1% of the Northern Ireland vote in the 1992 parliamentary polls). Following the disintegration of the Labour Coalition, several activists established a grouping known as Labour Northern Ireland (LNI), which in 1998 entered into discussions with member of the →Democratic Left (DL). The latest attempt to unite the various socialist groupings led to the launch of Northern Ireland Labour in May 1999, when a conference elected a steering group including Oliver Frawley (chair and a prominent DL member) and Alan Evans (secretary). *Address.* 16 Garland Heights, Lurgan, BT66 6BZ; *Telephone/Fax.* (+44-28) 3832-4303; *Email.* secretary@labourni.org; *Website.* http://www.labourni.org

People's Democracy (PD), led by Eamonn McCann and former Westminster MP Bernadette McAliskey; formed in 1968 as a civil rights group, the PD (also active in the Republic of Ireland) is a Trotskyist group (affiliated to the Fourth International, United Secretariat). It has offered conditional but often critical, support to the IRA. It has not recently contested elections and has no party office.

Republican Sinn Féin (RSF), a small splinter group of →*Sinn Féin* with negligible support, which does not contest elections to institutions of the two "partitionist" states as a matter of principle; led by Ruairí Ó Brádaigh and based in Dublin, it is allegedly linked with an IRA splinter group under a Continuity Army Council. *Address.* 229 Falls Road, Belfast, BT12; *Email.* saoirse@iol.ie; *Website.* http://come.to/Republicansf

Socialist Party (SP), a Dublin-based Trotskyist party affiliated to the Com m ittee for a W orkers' International and led in Northern Ireland by Peter Hadden (regional secretary); it calls for a "secular, democratic and socialist society" and opposes "the dictatorship of the bosses and the capitalist market".

Socialist Workers' Party (SWP), a Trotskyist formation with minimal membership in Northern Ireland. *Address.* PO Box 354, Tomb Street, Belfast; *Website.* http://www.clubi.ie/swp

Ulster Democratic Party (UDP), founded in the 1970s (as the Ulster Loyalist Democratic Party, ULDP, dropping the second word in 1992) as a political front for the Ulster Defence Association (UDA). The UDA, a loyalist paramilitary group responsible for many hundreds of murders, mainly of Catholic non-combatants, was eventually declared illegal in 1992; by that time the party had established some distance between itself and the parent organization, presenting itself as quite independent. The UDP, led by Gary McMichael and David Adams, has contested local government elections, securing a handful of council seats by election or defection, but its main role is as a channel of communication with the UDA and the Protestant underclass which supports it. In that capacity it participated in talks with the British government, some at ministerial level, following the loyalist ceasefire declared in October 1994, four months after that of the IRA. It secured only 2.2% of the poll in the 1996 Forum elections, winning no constituency seats, but was accorded two at-large seats under the formula designed to bring the UDP and its associated party, the PUP, into negotiations. McMichael is the son of a UDA commander who founded the ULDP, and who was assassinated in 1987. *Address.* 36 Castle Street, Lisburn, BT27 4XE; *Telephone.* (+44-28) 9266-7056. *Fax.* (+44-28) 9260-5159. *E-mail.* info@udp.org. *Website.* http://www.udp.org

Ulster Independence Movement (UIM), a pressure group led by Rev. Hugh Ross and Robert McGrath, which draws very limited support, mainly from the rural Protestant community, for its goal of independence for Ulster (meaning some or all of the six counties of Northern Ireland, rather than the nine counties of the historic province of Ulster). The Movement came sixth in the 1994 European Parliament election, with 1.4% of the vote (two other pro-independence candidates securing a total of 0.2%), and it has since lobbied unsuccessfully for admission to the discussions which have taken place between the British government and other parties. In the 1996 Forum elections its vote fell to 0.3%, placing it 14th. *Address*. 316 Shankill Road, Belfast, BT13; *Telephone*. (+44-28) 9023-6815

United Unionist Assembly Party (UUAP), launched in September 1998 by Denis Watson, who had been elected to the new Northern Ireland Assembly in June 1998 as an independent unionist candidate.

The Workers' Party (WP), a semi-autonomous Northern section of the Dublin-based WP, a Marxist republican party which arose from the "Official" majority faction which remained loyal to the then leadership of →*Sinn Féin* in the 1969–70 split, at which time the Northern section of *Sinn Féin* operated under the name Republican Clubs. The associated armed faction known as the Official IRA wound down its activities during the 1970s and was said to have disbanded in the 1980s. The movement's attempts to develop radical anti-sectarian socialist politics in the North, reflected in its change of name to The Workers' Party–Republican Clubs and its subsequent abandonment of the suffix, were hampered not only by the climate of violence in the 1970s and 1980s but by allegations of gangsterism associated with the Official IRA and by factionalism within the political wing, leading to the breakaway of what became the →Democratic Left. The WP, which campaigns for peace, full employment and class politics, has been represented on local councils, with one remaining councillor in 1996, but has rarely secured more than 2% of the parliamentary poll, and only 0.6% in 1992; in the 1996 Forum elections its share fell to 0.5%. Organized in both Irish jurisdictions, it is led nationally by a Northerner, Tom French (president); its Northern secretary is Tommy Owens. *Address*. 6 Springfield Road, Belfast, BT12 7AG; *Telephone*. (+44-28) 9032-8663; *Fax*. (+44-28) 9033-3475; *Email*. info@workers-party.org; *Website: http://www.workers-party.org*

World Socialist Party of Ireland (WSPI), a sister party of the ⇒Socialist Party of Great Britain, with the same programme and a similarly miniscule following. *Address*. 151 Cavehill Road, Belfast, BT15 1BL

APPENDIX:
European Parliament
Party Groups

Listed below are the party groups established in the European Parliament as a result of the direct elections held in the 15 European Union (EU) member states in June 1999. For ease of cross-reference, the party titles shown in the tables correspond to the names used in the country sections of the present volume. It should be noted that in some cases the party name changed after the June 1999 European elections, while in others the list title used in the elections was not the same as the official party name.

European People's Party-European Democrats (EPP-ED)
Address. European Parliament, Rue Wiertz, B-1047 Brussels, Belgium
Telephone. (+32-2) 284-2111
Fax. (+32-2) 230-9793
Email. epp-ed@europarl.eu.int
Website. http://www.europarl.eu.int/ppe
Leadership. Hans-Gert Pöttering (chair); Klaus Welle (secretary-general)
The EPP/ED group dates from June 1953 and was called the Christian Democratic Group until 1979. The original Christian democratic core has been diluted in recent years by the sometimes controversial adhesion of other centre-right parties, notably the British and Scandinavian Conservatives and *Forza Italia*. The group has provided over half of the presidents of the Parliament, including the two most recent, José Maria Gil-Robles of Spain (1994-99) and the present incumbent, Nicole Fontaine of France. The 1999 elections resulted in the EPP/ED group becoming substantially the largest in the European Parliament (for the first time since 1975), with members from every EU country, representing a total of 33 political parties and movements (as shown below).

Austria	Austrian People's Party/*Österreichische Volkspartei* (ÖVP)	7
Belgium	Christian People's Party/*Christian Christelijke Volkspartij* (CVP) … … … … … … … … … … … … … … … … …	3
	Christian Social Party/*Parti Social Chrétien* (PSC) … … …	1
	Citizens' Movement for Change/*Mouvement des Citoyens pour le Changement* (MCC) … … … … … … … … … … …	1
	Christian Social Party/*Christlich-Soziale Partei* (CSP) … …	1
Denmark	Conservative People's Party/*Konservative Folkeparti* (KFP)	1
Finland	National Coalition/*Kansallinen Kokoomus* (KOK) … … … …	4
	Swedish People's Party/*Suomen Kristillinen Liitto* (SKL) …	1

France	New Union for French Democracy/*Nouvelle Union pour la Démocratie Française* (NUDF)	9
	Rally for the Republic/*Rassemblement pour la République* (RPR)	6
	Liberal Democracy/*Démocratie Liberale* (DL)...	4
	Civil Society/*Société Civile*	1
	Ecology Generation/*Génération Écologie*	1
Germany	Christian Democratic Union/*Christlich Demokratische Union* (CDU)...	43
	Christian Social Union/*Christlich Soziale Union* (CSU)	10
Greece	New Democracy/*Nea Dimokratia* (ND)	9
Ireland	*Fine Gael*	4
	independent (Rosemary Scallon/Dana)	1
Italy	*Forza Italia*	22
	Italian Popular Party/*Partito Popolare Italiano* (PPI)	4
	Christian Democratic Centre/*Centro Cristiano Democratico* (CCD)...	2
	United Christian Democrats/*Cristiani Democratici Uniti* (CDU)	2
	Democratic Union for the Republic/*Unione Democratica per la Repubblica* (UDR)	1
	Italian Renewal/*Rinnovamento Italiano* (RI)	1
	Pensioners' Party/Partito Pensionati (PP)	1
	South Tyrol People's Party/*Südtiroler Volkspartei* (SVP) ...	1
Luxembourg	Christian Social People's Party/*Christlich Soziale Volkspartei* (CSV)	2
Netherlands	Christian Democratic Appeal/*Christen Demokratisch Appel* (CDA)...	9
Portugal	Social Democratic Party/*Partido Social Democrata* (PSD) ...	9
Spain	Popular Party/*Partido Popular* (PP)	27
	Democratic Union of Catalonia/*Unió Demócrática de Catalunya* (UDC)...	1
Sweden	Moderate Alliance Party/*Moderata Samlingspartiet* (MSP)...	5
	Christian Democratic Community Party/*Kristdemokratiska Samhällspartiet* (KdS)...	2
United Kingdom	Conservative and Unionist Party	36
N. Ireland	Ulster Unionist Party (UUP)	1
	Total	233

Party of European Socialists (PES)
Address. European Parliament, Rue Wiertz, B-1047 Brussels, Belgium
Telephone. (+32-2) 284-2111
Fax. (+32-2) 230-6664
Email. pesnet@europarl.eu.int
Website. http://www.europarl.eu.int/pes
Leadership. Enrique Baron Crespo (chair); Christine Verger (secretary-general)
The PES group dates from June 1953 and was known as Socialist Group until the formation of the PES in 1993 as a supranational grouping of the European member parties of the Socialist International. The Socialists were the largest group in the European Parliament from the first direct elections in 1979 until 1999, when the collapse of the representation of the British Labour Party (from 62 to 29 members) was the main reason for its relegation to the status of second largest group.

Austria	Social Democratic Party of Austria/*Sozialdemokratische Partei Österreichs* (SPÖ)	7
Belgium	Socialist Party/*Parti Socialiste* (PS)	3
	Socialist Party/*Socialistische Partij* (SP)	2
Denmark	Social Democratic Party/*Socialdemokratiet* (SD)	3
Finland	Finnish Social Democratic Party/*Suomen Sosialidemokraattinen Puolue* (SSDP)	3
France	Socialist Party/*Parti Socialiste* (PS)	18
	Left Radical Party/*Parti Radical de Gauche* (PRG)	2
	Citizens' Movement/*Mouvement des Citoyens* (MDC)	2
Germany	Social Democratic Party of Germany/*Sozialdemokratische Partei Deutschlands* (SPD)	33
Greece	Pan-Hellenic Socialist Movement/*Panellino Sosialistiko Kinima* (PASOK)	9
Ireland	Labour Party	1
Italy	Democrats of the Left/*Democratici di Sinistra* (DS)	15
	Italian Democratic Socialists/*Socialisti Democratici Italiani* (SDI)	2
Luxembourg	Luxembourg Socialist Workers' Party/*Lëtzebuerger Sozialistesch Arbechterpartei* (LSAP)	2
Netherlands	Labour Party/*Partij van de Arbeid* (PvdA)	6
Portugal	Socialist Party/*Partido Socialista* (PS)	12
Spain	Spanish Socialist Workers' Party/*Partido Socialista Obrero Español* (PSOE)	22
	Democratic Party of the New Left/*Partido Democrático de la Nueva Izquierda* (PDNI)	2
Sweden	Social Democratic Labour Party/*Socialdemokratiska Arbetarepartiet* (SAP)	6
United Kingdom	Labour Party	29
N. Ireland	Social Democrat and Labour Party (SDLP)	1
	Total	180

European Liberal, Democratic and Reformist Group (ELDR)

Address. European Parliament, Rue Wiertz, B-1047 Brussels, Belgium
Telephone. (+32-2) 284-3169
Fax. (+32-2) 231-1907
Email. eldrparty@europarl.eu.int
Website. http://www.eurolib.org/eldrparty
Leadership. Pat Cox (chair); Bo Jensen (secretary-general)
The ELDR group dates from the foundation in June 1953 of the Liberal Group, which became the Liberal and Democratic Group in November 1976 and the ELDR group in 1986. Its size as the third largest European Parliament group has remained relatively stable in recent years, although in the 1999 elections the number of EU countries represented in it fell from 13 to 10.

Belgium	Liberal Reformist Party/*Parti Réformateur Liberale* (PRL) and Democratic Front of French-Speakers/*Front Démocratique des Francophones* (FDF)...	2
	Flemish Liberals and Democrats/*Vlaamse Liberalen en Demokraten* (VLD)	3
Denmark	Liberal Party/*Venstre*	5
	Radical Liberal Party/*Det Radikale Venstre* (RV)	1
Finland	Centre Party of Finland/*Suomen Keskusta* (KESK)	4
	Swedish People's Party/*Svenska Folkpartiet* (SFP)	1
Ireland	independent (Pat Cox)...	1
Italy	Italian Republican Party/*Partito Repubblicano Italiano* (PRI) ...	1
	Democrats for the New Olive Tree/*I Democratici per il Nuovo Ulivo*	6
	independent (Marco Formentini)	1
Luxembourg	Democratic Party/*Demokratesch Partei* (DP)	1
Netherlands	People's Party for Freedom and Democracy/*Volkspartij voor Vrijheid en Democratie* (VVD)...	6
	Democrats 66/*Democraten 66* (D66)	2
Spain	Democratic Convergence of Catalonia/*Convergència Democràtica de Catalunya* (CDC)...	2
	Canarian Coalition/*Coalición Canaria* (CC)	1
Sweden	Centre Party/*Centerpartiet* (CP)	1
	Liberal People's Party/*Folkpartiet Liberalerna* (FPL)	3
United Kingdom	Liberal Democrats	10
	Total...	51

Greens/European Free Alliance (G/EFA)

Address. European Parliament, LEO 2C, Rue Wiertz, B-1047 Brussels, Belgium
Telephone. (+32-2) 284-3045
Fax. (+32-2) 230-7837
Email. jkutten@europarl.eu.int
Website. http://www.europarl.eu.int/greens

Leadership. Heidi Hautala and Paul Lannoye (co-chairs); Hans Nikolaus (Juan) Behrend (secretary-general)

The Greens first founded a European Parliament group after the 1989 elections but remained relatively small until more than doubling its size in the 1999 elections, thanks in part to the adhesion of regionalist parties of the European Free Alliance (EFA). The combined Greens/EFA group includes representatives from 12 of the 15 EU countries.

Austria	The Greens/*Die Grünen*	2
Belgium	Live Differently/*Anders Gaan Leven* (AGALEV)	2
	Ecologist Party (ECOLO)	3
	People's Union/*Volksunie* and Complete Democracy for the 21st Century (*Integrale Democratie voor de 21ste Eeuw* (ID21)	2
Finland	Green Union/*Vihreä Liitto* (VL)	2
France	The Greens/*Les Verts*	9
Germany	Alliance 90-The Greens/*Bündnis 90-Die Grünen*	7
Ireland	Green Party/*Comhaontás Glas*	2
Italy	Green Federation/*Federazione dei Verdi*	2
Luxembourg	The Green Alternative/*Dei Gréng Alternativ* (GA)	1
Netherlands	Green Left/*Groen Links* (GL)	4
Spain	Andalusianist Party/*Partido Andalucista* (PA)	1
	Basque Solidarity/*Eusko Alkartasuna* (EA)	1
	Basque Nationalist Party/*Partido Nacionalista Vasco* (PNV)	1
	Galician Nationalist Bloc/*Bloque Nacionalista Gallego* (BNG)	1
Sweden	Green Ecology Party/*Miljöpartiet de Gröna*	2
United Kingdom	Green Party	2
	Scottish National Party (SNP)	2
	Plaid Cymru–The Party of Wales	2
	Total	48

European United Left/Nordic Green Left (GUE/NGL)

Address. European Parliament, Rue Wiertz 45, B-1047 Brussels, Belgium
Telephone. (+32-2) 284-2683
Fax. (+32-2) 230-5582
Email. guewebmaster@europarl.eu.int
Website. http://www.europarl.eu.int/grue
Leadership. Francis Wurtz (chair); Maria d'Alimonte (secretary-general)

The GUE/NGL group dates from the formation of the Communist and Allies Group in October 1973 and has gone through many complex changes, as ex-Communist parties embraced democratic socialism and in some cases joined the Party of European Socialists. The GUE title was adopted after the 1994 European elections, the suffix "Nordic Green Left" being added on the accession of leftist parties from Finland and Sweden following EU enlargement in 1995. The 1999 elections produced an overall advance for the group, which now has member parties from 10 EU countries.

Denmark	Socialist People's Party/*Socialistisk Folkeparti* (SFP	1
Finland	Left Alliance/*Vasemmistoliitto* (VAS)	1
France	French Communist Party/*Parti Communiste Français* (PCF)	6
	Workers' Struggle/*Lutte Ouvrière* and Revolutionary Communist League/*Ligue Communiste Révolutionnaire* (LCR)	5
Germany	Party of Democratic Socialism/*Partei des Demokratischen Sozialismus* (PDS)	6
Greece	Communist Party of Greece/*Kommounistiko Komma Elladas* (KKE)	2
	Coalition of the Left and Progress/*Synaspismos tis Aristeras kai tis Proodou*	2
	Democratic Social Movement/*Dimokratiko Kininiko Kinima* (DIKKI)	2
Italy	Communist Refoundation Party/*Partito della Rifondazione Comunista* (PRC)	4
	Party of Italian Communists/*Partito dei Comunisti Italiani* (PdCI)	2
Netherlands	Socialist Party/*Socialistische Partij* (SP)	1
Portugal	Portuguese Communist Party/*Partido Comunista Português* (PCP)	3
Spain	United Left/*Izquierda Unida* (IU)	4
Sweden	Left Party/*Vänsterpartiet* (VP)	3
	Total	42

Union for a Europe of Nations (UEN)
Address. European Parliament, Rue Wiertz, B-1047 Brussels, Belgium
Telephone. (+32-2) 284-2111
Fax. (+32-2) 230-9793
Email. fwurtz@europarl.eu.int
Website. http://www.europarl.eu.int/groups
Leadership. Charles Pasqua (chair); Frank Barrett (secretary-general)
The UEN group was formed after the June 1999 European elections as an expansion of earlier groupings with reservations about further European integration, although the French Gaullist Rally for the Republic switched to the →European People's Party/European Democrats and was replaced by the more electorally successful and Eurosceptic Rally for France and the Independence of Europe.

Denmark	Danish People's Party/*Dansk Folkeparti* (DF)	1
France	Rally for France and the Independence of Europe/*Rassemblement pour la France et l'Indépendance de l'Europe* (RPF-IE)	12
Ireland	*Fianna Fáil*	6
Ital	National Alliance/*Alleanza Nazionale* (AN) and Segni Pact/*Patto Segni* (PS)	9
Portugal	Popular Party/*Partido Popular* (PP)	2
	Total	30

Europe of Democracies and Diversities (EDD)
Address. European Parliament, Rue Wiertz, B-1047 Brussels, Belgium
Telephone. (+32-2) 284-2111
Fax. (+32-2) 230-9793
Email. jpbonde@europarl.eu.int
Website. http://www.europarl.eu.int/groups
Leadership. Jean-Peter Bonde, Jean Saint-Josse and Hans Blokland (co-chairs)
The EDD is a new group consisting of parties from four EU countries which are highly critical of the EU and further European integration. The 1999 European elections yielded notable gains for such parties in France and the UK.

Denmark	People's Movement against the European Union/*Folkesbevægelsen mod EF-Unionen*	1
	June Movement/*Junibevægelsen* (JB)	3
France	Hunting, Fishing, Nature, Traditions/*Chasse, Pêche, Nature, Traditions* (CPNT)	6
Netherlands	Reformational Political Federation/*Reformatorische Politieke Federatie* (RPF), Reformed Political Association/ *Gereformeerd Politiek Verbond* (GPV) and Reformed Political Party/*Staatkundig Gereformeerde Partij* (SGP)...	3
United Kingdom	UK Independence Party (UKIP)	3
	Total	16

Non-attached members

Listed below are the parties represented in the 1999-2004 European Parliament which are not members of any of the above groups, largely because they are regarded as being too extremist to qualify for such membership.

Austria	Freedom Movement/*Die Freiheitlichen* (DF)	5
Belgium	Flemish Bloc/*Vlaams Blok* (VB)	2
France	National Front/*Front National* (FN)	5
	independent (Marie-France Garaud)...	1
Italy	Radical Party (Bonino List)/*Partito Radicale (Lista Bonino)* ...	7
	Northern League/*Lega Nord* (LN)	3
	Tricolour Flame Social Movement/*Movimento Sociale Fiamma Tricolore* (MSFT)	1
Spain	We Basques/*Euskal Herritarrok* (EH)	1
United Kingdom N. Ireland	Democratic Unionist Party (DUP)	1
	Total...	26

Index

Humanist Party of Spain (Spain), 177
Humanistic Party (Denmark), 32
Humanistische Feministische Partij/Parti
  Féministe Humaniste, HFP/PFH
  (Belgium), 20
Humanistiska Partiet, HP (Sweden), 201
Humanistiske Parti, Det (Denmark), 32
Hume, John (UK Northern Ireland), 225, 226
Hunt, Peter (United Kingdom), 215
Hunting, Fishing, Nature, Traditions
  (France), 57
Hutchinson, Billy (UK Northern Ireland),
  223

I Democratici per il Nuovo Ulivo (Italy),
  132
Ia Mana Te Nunaa (French Polynesia), 89
Ibarretxe Markuartu, Juan Jóse (Spain), 181
Ibárruri Gómez, Dolores (Spain), 171, 172
Icke, David (United Kingdom), 207
Iglesias Argüelles, Gerardo (Spain), 171,
  176
Iglesias, Pablo (Spain), 174
Ilaskivi, Raimo (Finland), 49
Imbroda Ortíz, Juan José (Spain), 193
Incerti, Matteo (Italy), 147
Independent Ecological Movement
  (France), 79
Independent Fianna Fáil (Ireland), 128
Independent Liberal Group (Spain), 193
Independent Martinique Movement
  (Martinique), 85
Independents, The (Austria), 7
Iniciativa per Catalunya (IC) (Spain), 188
Iniciativa por Ceuta, IC (Spain), 193
Initiative for Catalonia (Spain), 188
Initiative for Ceuta (Spain), 193
Initiative Républicaine, IR (France), 80
Instead of a Party (Germany), 111
Integrale Democratie voor de 21ste Eeuw,
  ID21 (Belgium), 20
International Socialists (Denmark), 32
Internationale Socialister, IS (Denmark),
  32
Internationalist Communist Party
  (France), 79
Inuit Ataqatigiit (IA) (Greenland), 40
Ipsen, Martin (Denmark), 26
Irish Republican Socialist Party (IRSP)
  (Ireland), 128

Irish Republican Socialist Party (IRSP)
  (UK Northern Ireland), 229
Ísakson, Finnbogi (Faroe Islands), 36
Isänmaallinen Kansallis-Litto, IKL
  (Finland), 52
Islamic Party of Britain (IPB) (United
  Kingdom), 217
Italian Democratic Socialists (Italy), 136
Italian Monarchist Movement (Italy), 149
Italian Popular Party (Italy), 137
Italian Renewal (Italy), 140
Italian Republican Party (Italy), 139
Izquierda Republicana, IR (Spain), 178
Izquierda Unida (IU) (Spain), 176

Jaakonsaari, Liisa (Finland), 44
Jääskeläinen, Jouko (Finland), 44
Jacobsen, Kirsten (Denmark), 27
Jacobson, Óli (Faroe Islands), 38
Jacoby, Abbès (Luxembourg), 152
Jakobsen, Erhard (Denmark), 22
Jakobsen, Mimi Stilling (Denmark), 22
Janmaat, Hans (Netherlands), 161
Janssens, Patrick (Belgium), 18
Jansson, Mikael (Sweden), 202
Jaurès, Jean (France), 66, 73
Javnadarflokkurin (Jvfl) (Faroe Islands),
  36
Jean-Baptiste, Henri (Mayotte), 90
Jensen, Bo (European Parliament), 235
Jensen, Lene (Denmark), 29
Jensen, Lis (Denmark), 33
Jobert, Michel (France), 80
Johans, Emmanuel (France), 78
Johansen, Lars Emil (Greenland), 40, 41
Johansson, Olof (Sweden), 195
Johansson, Per W. (Denmark), 32
Jønsen, Edmund (Faroe Islands), 37, 38
Jordan, Colin (United Kingdom), 215
Jørgensen, Anker (Denmark), 30
Jospin, Lionel (France), 56, 59, 73, 75
Juncker, Jean-Claude (Luxembourg), 151
June Movement (Denmark), 32
Junibevægelsen, JB (Denmark), 32
Juppé, Alain (France), 68, 72, 79
Juquin, Pierre (France), 55, 80, 81
Justice Party of Denmark (Denmark),
  33

Kallio, Kyösti (Finland), 42